*f*P

Other Books by Alfred D. Chandler Jr.

A Nation Transformed by Information:
*How Information Has Shaped the United States
from Colonial Times to the Present*
Alfred D. Chandler Jr. and James W. Cortada, Editors

Big Business and the Wealth of Nations
Alfred D. Chandler Jr., Frances Anatori, and Takashi Hikino, Editors

The Dynamic Firm:
The Role of Technology, Strategy, Organization, and Regions
Alfred D. Chandler Jr., Peter Hagstrom, and Orjan Solvell, Editors

Scale and Scope: *The Dynamics of Industrial Capitalism*
Alfred D. Chandler Jr.

The Essential Alfred Chandler
Thomas K. McCraw, Editor

Managerial Hierarchies:
Comparative Perspectives on the Rise of the Modern Industrial Enterprise
Alfred D. Chandler Jr. and Herman Daems, Editors

The Visible Hand: *The Managerial Revolution in American Business*
Alfred D. Chandler Jr.

The Papers of Dwight David Eisenhower (the first five volumes)
Alfred D. Chandler Jr., Editor, and Stephen E. Ambrose, Associate Editor

Pierre S. du Pont and the Making of the Modern Corporation
Alfred D. Chandler Jr. and Stephen Salsbury

Strategy and Structure:
Chapters in the History of the Industrial Enterprise
Alfred D. Chandler Jr.

Inventing the Electronic Century

THE EPIC STORY OF THE CONSUMER ELECTRONICS AND COMPUTER INDUSTRIES

Alfred D. Chandler Jr.

with the assistance of
Takashi Hikino and Andrew von Nordenflycht

The Free Press
New York   London   Toronto   Sydney   Singapore

THE FREE PRESS
A Division of Simon & Schuster, Inc.
1230 Avenue of the Americas
New York, NY 10020

For information about special discounts for bulk purchases,
please contact Simon & Schuster Special Sales:
1-800-456-6798 or business@simonandschuster.com

Designed by Leslie Phillips
Manufactured in the United States of America

1   3   5   7   9   10   8   6   4   2

Library of Congress Cataloging-in-Publication Data

Chandler, Alfred Dupont.
    Inventing the electronic century : the epic story of the consumer
    electronics and computer industries / Alfred D. Chandler Jr. with the assistance of
    Takashi Hikino and Andrew von Nordenflycht.
        p. cm.
        Includes index.
        (alk. paper)
        1. Electronic industries. 2. Computer industry. 3. Competition, International. I. Title.
    HD9696.A2 C43 2001
        338.4'7621381—dc21   2001045120
    ISBN 0-7432-1567-2

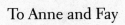

To Anne and Fay

Acknowledgments

Of the several persons who made possible the writing of this book, the most important were the two to whom I have dedicated it—Anne O'Connell and my wife, Fay Chandler. Anne, for the past decade, has been transcribing my garbled, dictated, handwritten copy into smooth readable typescript, at the same time keeping the numerous variations of the text and the endnotes in their proper place and order. As critical was Fay's constant encouragement and support, which becomes increasingly valuable as I begin life's ninth decade.

Nor would the book have been written without the assistance of Takashi Hikino and Andrew von Nordenflycht. Before Takashi had to return to his homeland, Japan, his assistance was essential in getting what has become two books underway as well as in the writing of the initial drafts of the chapters. Andrew played as critical a role in the completion of the book, for his computer skills and his knowledge of the computer industry helped to make up for my limited technical knowledge. His committed work on the final draft made possible the completion of Book One on schedule.

Nor could the book have been written without the support of the Harvard Business School. I am grateful to both Dean John H. McArthur and Dean Kim B. Clark for the continuing support of my work. I am particularly grateful to John McArthur for his establishment of the Senior Faculty Center, which provides facilities and personnel essential for emeritus professors to continue to write and publish. At the Center, Jan Simmons, Paula Alexander, and, most of all, Eileen Hankins provided essential secretarial and library services. At the School's Word Processing Center, Aimee Hamel, in assisting Anne O'Connell, became an expert in developing and updating the book's tables and appendices. At the front desk in my apartment building at 1010 Memorial Drive, Teresa Hardy faxed messages and correspondence and assisted in other ways.

I'm indebted to Alice Amsden, James Cortada, Michael Cusumano, Margaret Graham, Thomas McCraw, and Pasquale Scopelliti for reading and making essential comments on original drafts of chapters. Nathaniel Marshall, a former RCA manager, provided an inside picture of that enterprise. John Akers, of IBM, pointed me in the right direction as I started on the project. As in my earlier studies, I benefited greatly from Max Hall's essential copyediting, which he did for all but the last chapter, when the deadlines prevented rereading. I'm grateful, too, to Alexander Gourevitch, who helped me make a final reading of the completed text again under the pressure of the final deadline. Finally, I am grateful to Robert Wallace of the Free Press for his constant enthusiasm and support of the work and his arrangements that made it possible for the final completed typescript to be published on schedule.

Finally, I want to express my gratitude to the editors of *Datamation* for providing an unsurpassed source of information on the evolution of the computer industry in its annual review of the activities of the top 100 revenue producers in computers and then in the broader information technology industry. Particularly valuable were the reviews of the 1980s and early 1990s.

Many have contributed to this book but the final text is mine, and for it I take full responsibility.

—Alfred D. Chandler Jr.
Cambridge, Massachusetts
May 2001

Contents

Preface

This book had its beginnings as a study in comparative institutional history entitled "Paths of Learning: The Evolution of High Technology Industries." Part I was to have reviewed the evolution of consumer electronics and computers and Part II chemicals and pharmaceuticals in the United States, Europe, and Japan. As work progressed on that study, however, the differences between the evolution of the two sets of industries became apparent. They differed in terms of the success and failure of national industries and in the number of major players involved in competing for world markets. These basic differences, in turn, reflected different historical timings of the evolutionary process.

Chemicals and pharmaceuticals are representatives of the modern industries that appeared during what historians have termed the Second Industrial Revolution. These industries, created between the 1880s and the 1920s, laid the foundations for the twentieth century Industrial Age. The maturing of the consumer electronics and computer industries, on the other hand, came a half century later, after World War II.

Unlike the major industries of the Industrial Revolution, a much smaller number of firms shaped the evolution of the consumer electronics and computer industries. Furthermore, whereas chemicals and pharmaceuticals were among several of the major industries that shaped the Industrial Age, consumer electronics and computers were the primary reshapers of life and work during the second half of the twentieth century.

Because the evolution of the electronic-based industries was historically unique, because they have so changed the ways of life and work since World War II, and because their story remains almost unrecorded, I decided with Robert Wallace, Senior Editor of the Free Press, to publish two separate books, Book One on consumer electronics and computers, and Book Two on chemicals and pharmaceuticals.

Of the four major electronics industries, I chose to focus on consumer electronics and computers rather than on telecommunications and industrial electronics. Telecommunications had had a long history before the coming of electronics. Established in the 1880s, it was one of the major industries that laid the foundations of the Industrial Age. Moreover, the operations of telephone systems were, until the latter part of the twentieth century, government monopolies or, in the case of the United States, a government-regulated natural monopoly. The evolution of industrial electronics had a less unique pattern of evolutionary growth and less obvious impact on everyday life and work than consumer electronics and computers.

The decision to write a book on these two industries had risks. It meant that I had to accept the hazards of writing about current events rather than history, thus depriving myself as a historian of the advantage of knowing how the story came out. Indeed, a significant part of the epic told here occurred after I began recording this story in the early 1990s. Moreover, my understanding of the details of the technologies adopted was almost nonexistent. Nevertheless, to be the first to have the privilege of recording this epic story outweighed the risks.

This initial sketch of the evolution of these two industries world-wide will certainly be filled in, reshaped, and reinterpreted as historians, economists, and other researchers focus on the histories of the two. But the epic story remains. The basic infrastructure of these two increasingly technologically integrated industries was completed by the beginning of the twenty-first century, which I refer to as the Electronic Century. That infrastructure was the product of the successes and failures of a small number of players during the crucible of the competitive battles of the 1970s and 1980s. Those crucial battles—which resulted in Japan's conquest of world markets in consumer electronics, Japan's continuing challenge to the United States in information technology, and the collapse of both industries in Europe—have and will continue to shape the competitive landscape of the two industries in the Electronic Century.

1

INTRODUCTION:

CONCEPTS AND APPROACH

Consider the title. "The Electronic Century" is the twenty-first century. The "inventing" refers to the creation of the technological and institutional foundations—the "infrastructure"—during the latter decades of the twentieth century, which was the Industrial Century. Inventing the infrastructure for the Electronic Century became an epic story because some national industries died while others conquered. By the end of the twentieth century, no European-owned and -operated enterprise had the capabilities of commercializing—that is, bringing into widespread public use—major new products of either consumer electronics or computer hardware with their essential software technologies. In the United States, no enterprise had the capability to commercialize new consumer electronics technologies. On the other hand, in Japan, the four leading enterprises in consumer electronics had conquered world markets. And the five leading Japanese computer companies were seriously challenging the U.S. computer industry worldwide.

This epic story of the consumer electronics and computer industries has its tragic aspects. By the time the infrastructure of the Electronic Century was completed, Europe had lost both its computer and consumer electronics industries, and the United States no longer had its consumer electronics industry, with all that this meant in terms of employment and the growth of ancillary and supporting industries. In addition, RCA's Princeton Laboratories had been dismantled, and only remnants of Philips's once great electronics laboratories at Eindhoven remained. Of the three primary builders of the technological foundations of the consumer electronics industry, only Sony remained.

The epic story also has its heroic achievements. The worldwide triumph of the Japanese consumer electronics industry took place in a period of less than a decade, 1975 to 1985, largely on the basis of technologies developed by the Sony Corporation. In this same astonishingly brief period, Japan's computer makers had become Europe's dominant suppliers of large computer systems and had captured the U.S. market in memory chips.

International Business Machines (IBM) provides another epic in terms of defining the computer industry's products. In large computer systems its most successful competitors were those enterprises that produced and sold IBM-designed "plug-compatible" hardware and "unbundled" software. In personal computers they were those that made and sold IBM clones.

The concepts and approach I use to understand and explain the evolving historical story follow.

Basic Concepts

In market economies the competitive strengths of industrial firms rest on learned organizational capabilities. That is my basic premise—a premise that is based on the findings of this historical study. The capabilities are product-specific in terms of technologies used and markets served. These product-specific capabilities are learned and embodied in an organizational setting. Individuals come and go, but the organization remains. Thus, in modern industrial economies the large firm performs its critical role in the evolution of industries not merely as a unit carrying out transactions on the basis of information flows, but, more importantly, as a creator and repository of product-specific embedded organizational knowledge.

The process of organizational learning in industrial enterprises begins with the building of a viable profit-making enterprise, and this is done through the creation of organizational capabilities based on three types of knowledge—technical, functional, and managerial.

1. Technical capabilities are those learned by applying existing and new scientific and engineering knowledge. Such capabilities include those in well-defined scientific and engineering disciplines, professional organizations, and the like. Technical capabilities are knowledge related. They involve the knowledge used in basic and applied research to create new products and processes. They are the capabilities required for the R in R&D.

2. Functional knowledge, on the other hand, is product-specific. It results in organizational capabilities of the following kinds:

Development capabilities. These are created by learning the product-specific know-how required to transform an innovation into a commercial product to be sold in national and international markets. These capabilities are the D of R&D.

Production capabilities. These come from learning how to build and operate large-volume production facilities for the new product and to recruit and train the labor force essential to operating these facilities efficiently. A somewhat similar but less important set of capabilities is that of purchasing in volume the necessary materials for production.

Marketing capabilities. These are acquired in learning the nature of the product's markets and building extensive distribution systems to reach them.

The evolving relationship between technical and functional capabilities is a basic theme of this study. In addition to those two major types, there is one more:

3. Managerial capabilities. This third set of organizational capabilities, based on management knowledge and experience, is essential to the creation and continued existence of a viable profit-making enterprise. These capabilities are learned in order to administer the activities of the functional operating units, to integrate their activities, and to coordinate the flow of goods from the suppliers of raw materials through the processes of production and distribution to the retailers and final customers. Most essential to the successful maintenance of the long-term health and growth of the enterprise are the learned capabilities of *top* management. These managers make the critical decisions in allocating personnel and financial resources that determine the fate of an enterprise and often of the entire industry of the country in which it operates.

As important as managerial capabilities are, they are not a central focus of my two books that go under the blanket title *Paths of Learning*. One reason is the difficulty in generalizing about managerial capabilities. They are affected by different types of operating structures, national educational systems, and broader cultural patterns in which they have been learned and in which their enterprises have evolved. So capabilities differ from nation to nation, industry to industry, and often from company to company in the same industry. For example, the broader environment in which Japanese managers learn and work is quite unlike that in the United States and Europe.

The first enterprises whose managers learn to develop, produce, and sell in national and then world markets—that is to *commercialize*, to bring to market, a product of new technical learning—become the initial builders of the high-technology industries whose evolution is the subject of both volumes. I term such enterprises *first-movers*. They were not necessarily the first to produce and sell the new product. They were the first to develop an integrated set of functional capabilities essential to commercialize the new product in volume for worldwide markets.

Once the new enterprise's competitive power has been tested, its set of integrated organizational capabilities becomes a *learning base* for improving existing products and processes and for developing new ones in response to changes in technical knowledge and markets, and in response to macroeconomic developments, including wars and depressions.

Besides having the learning base, these firms as first-movers have available their retained earnings (one of the cheapest sources of long-term capital) for investment to expand and improve their facilities and personnel.

The creation of such an integrated learning base in a technologically new industry, together with the resulting continuing flow of funds, creates a powerful *barrier to entry*. Start-up firms have to begin to develop their basic set of capabilities while competing with first-movers who are enhancing their operations through continuing learning and through income from the sale of their initial products. Within each national economy only a small number of challengers succeed in building comparable learning bases. The first-movers and their successful challengers become what I term an industry's *core companies*.

Once these core companies establish a viable national industry, entrepreneurial start-ups are rarely able to enter. Instead, the core companies' competitors are either foreign core companies or domestic core companies in other industries—that is, industries with comparable technical knowledge and/or processes of production, distribution, or product development.

First-movers, of course, cannot create an industry by themselves. They have to develop close relationships with supporting enterprises—with suppliers both of capital equipment and materials to be processed, with research specialists, distributors, advertisers, and providers of financial, technical, and other services. Thus the needs of the core firms lead to the creation of a supporting *nexus*—interconnected and complementary (rather than competitive). The nexus may contain small, medium, and even large firms in supporting lines of products and services. It soon becomes a source for the creation of numerous "niche" firms, but only rarely do core companies emerge from the nexus.

In this way the competitive strength of national industries depends on the abilities of the core firms to function effectively and to maintain and enhance their integrated learning bases. If those bases begin to deteriorate, so too does the industry's supporting nexus and its competitive strength versus that of other countries.

Once an industry is established, however, learning continues with powerful momentum. The integrated learning bases of the first-movers become the primary engines for the continuing evolution of their industry through the commercializing of new technical knowledge. The integrated learning base embodies within the enterprise the procedures to integrate the enterprises' technical and functional organizational capabilities—to integrate and to coordinate those of applied research, product development, production, and marketing. The development of such integrating and coordinating procedures becomes a basic function of top management if the enterprise is to benefit from the internal economies of scale and scope and continuing advances in proprietary knowledge. Such integrated learning bases thus define an industry's continuing path of organizational learning. They set the direction in which an industry evolves.

The learning base not only sets the direction, but also, because of barriers to entry, defines the *boundaries* of the path. The concentrated power of technical and functional knowledge embedded in the first-movers' integrated learning bases is such that only a small number of enterprises defines the evolving paths of learning in which the products of new technical knowledge are commercialized for widespread public use.

The Approach–The Paths of Learning

My basic purpose in this volume is to carry out the fundamental task of the historian: to record where, when, how, and by whom technical knowledge was commercialized into the new products that laid the foundation for the Electronic Century and, in so doing, transformed life and work in the second half of the twentieth century. I chronicle the evolution of the new high-tech industries from their beginnings by the first-movers until the end of the twentieth century. I do this by focusing on the competitive success and failure of the national industries in Europe, the United States, and Japan. The continuing evolution of both consumer electronics and computers resulted from continuous learning in the commercializing of new technologies and enhancing of existing ones. To repeat: The initial first-movers who created their learning bases had competitive advantages by being first in developing their technical and functional capabilities that provided barriers to entry.

The Evolving Paths in Consumer Electronics

In consumer electronics, the commercializing of a new technology was based on the learning that created the previous innovation. The first-movers in radio were the Radio Corporation of America (RCA), a joint venture of the three leading United States producers of electrical and telecommunications equipment, and the German company Telefunken, a joint venture of the two foremost producers in Europe. They led the way in commercializing radio in the 1920s. The same two companies began the process of commercializing television in the 1930s. Telefunken, housed in Berlin, lost its learning base during World War II. So in the 1940s RCA took the lead in commercializing black-and-white television. In the 1950s it became solely responsible for the introduction of color television. Then in the late 1960s and early 1970s, the two Japanese first-movers, Matsushita and Sony, and the Dutch company Philips, all of which had created strong learning bases after World War II, began to move into global markets. Philips's home market was small, but its impressive learning base defined the evolution of consumer electronics in Europe.

In the late 1960s the remaining four of these first-movers (RCA, Matsushita, Sony, Philips) began a race to commercialize the videocassette recorder (VCR), a market that television had created. Matsushita's Video

Home System (VHS) captured the world market on the strength of that firm's functional capabilities. The failure of RCA's videodisk contributed to the company's collapse and with it the collapse of the U.S. national industry whose path it had defined. Although Sony and Philips had lost to Matsushita in the VCR battle, they, because of their technical capabilities, defined the evolving path of learning based on a disk technology. Together they commercialized the audio compact disk (CD) and the compact disk-read only memory (CD-ROM) and, again with Philips, the digital videodisk (DVD).

By the 1990s Philips's functional capabilities were unable to meet the Japanese competition. Its technical capabilities had been weakened by the failure of its attempt to commercialize a new video product on its own, the CD-interactive (CDi). So by the late 1990s Philips could no longer commercialize major new consumer electronics products. By then the Japanese first-movers and followers and their strong supporting nexus completely dominated markets worldwide. By then only Japanese companies had the integrated technical and functional capabilities required to commercialize products of new technologies.

The Evolving Paths of Learning in Computers

The evolution of the digital data-processing computer industry differed sharply from that of the consumer electronics industry. In consumer electronics, the managers of five enterprises—Telefunken, RCA, Philips, Matsushita, and Sony—determined the direction in which the industry's paths of learning evolved from its beginnings in the 1920s until the 1990s. But in computers, the managers of a single firm, IBM, played a determining role from the industry's beginning in the 1950s to the 1990s.

When the computer was invented, IBM was already the world's largest producer of punched-card tabulators, the most advanced data-processing device prior to computers. The company became the new electronic computer industry's first-mover in commercial markets when in 1954 it applied an electronic device to its previously electrically driven punched-card data processors. Within less than a decade, its long-established punched-card functional capabilities in product development, production, and marketing, learned over three decades, permitted its new product, the mainframe computer, to capture close to 80 percent of the world's markets.

On the basis of the continuing learning and high financial returns, IBM developed its System 360, which in terms of prices charged and performance expected was a full line of compatible mainframe computers, primarily for commercial and business markets. The commercializing of the System 360 required half a decade, at the cost of nearly $7 billion. That extraordinary learning experience immediately defined the computer industry worldwide. By the 1970s, with its System 360 and its successor, the System 370, IBM was competing at home and abroad with companies that primarily produced "plug-compatible" products based on IBM-licensed hardware and IBM-licensed software. By the end of the decade the European computer makers were buying their IBM imitations from Japan.

In the mid-1960s, when IBM was concentrating on developing the System 360, Kenneth Olsen's Digital Equipment Corporation created a second path of computer learning by commercializing an inexpensive, stripped-down "minicomputer" for more specialized and smaller engineering and scientific markets. Within a brief period a small number of followers entered the new path.

Then in the 1980s the microprocessor transformed the industry with the introduction of computers for use by individuals rather than corporations or other large institutions. Here again, IBM defined the recast industry by being the first to mass-produce and mass-market its personal computer (PC). By the end of the 1980s IBM's PC, its clones, and their two primary suppliers, Intel (microprocessors) and Microsoft (operating system software), had defined the computer industry as effectively as the IBM 360/370 and its plug-compatibles had done in the 1970s. Soon IBM was only one of a sizable number of personal computer makers. But because every IBM PC and its clones had to use an Intel processor and a Microsoft operating system, those two companies became the path definers in personal computers in the 1980s.

The inability of the British, French, Italian, and then German companies to compete with IBM's mainframes and the plug-compatibles in the 1970s and IBM and its PC clones in the 1980s brought the death of the European industries. On the other hand, the ability of the Japanese to produce and improve competitive IBM plug-compatible mainframes in the 1970s permitted them to take over their own domestic market and then that of Europe for large systems. Although the Japanese industry lost out in personal computers, their strength in large systems permitted them to meet the greatly increased demand for computing power called for in the 1990s. This demand for more power grew out of the coming of private networking systems for corporations and other institutions and the coming of the public Internet. Those developments enabled the Japanese to become and remain effective challengers to the U.S. industry.

Chart 1:1 indicates the evolutionary paths of learning within the consumer electronics and the computer industries. The chart's classifications are comparable (but not identical, because they are my classifications) to the Standard Industrial Classification (SIC) of the U.S. Office of Management and Budget, in which a product sector is defined by four numbers. The first two indicate the large industrial category in which it belongs. The third number indicates an industry within that category, and the fourth, the product sector within that industry.

In the consumer electronics industry, radio and television (including color television) were still the leading sectors in 1970. By then RCA and the two Japanese leaders had already entered the recording industry, the one long-existing preelectronic sector, based on the vinyl disk. By 1990 the VCR, the CD (and CD-ROM), and the DVD had become major product sectors.

In computers, the mainframe and minicomputer were the primary product sectors in 1970. By then the growing activities to which the new computer could be applied and the complexities of its operation led to the beginning of a third, nonmanufacturing sector, services.

In the early 1980s the coming of the microprocessor and IBM's mass production and mass marketing of the personal computer opened up a huge new market for commercial purposes as well as a new one for the home. The resulting massive expansion of the industry led to the formation of new product sectors—personal computers, peripherals, and operating system and application software. At the same time, the producers of minicomputers used the microprocessor to develop the workstation for its engineering and scientific customers. The new array of product sectors that existed in the 1990s is shown as the bottom row in the chart.

Within a sector, therefore, the learning base of a successful profit-making enterprise, either as a division within a multisector corporation or as an independent company, tied a specific technology to a broad national and international market. The enterprise had embedded within it the technical capabilities needed to commercialize products of new technology. Embedded, too, were the basic functional capabilities—product development, production, and distribution and marketing—that were needed in order to

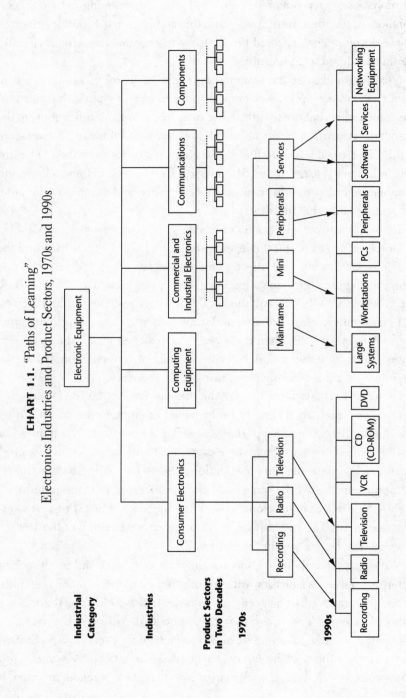

CHART 1.1. "Paths of Learning"
Electronics Industries and Product Sectors, 1970s and 1990s

continue to improve existing products and processes and to maintain the company's long-term share of its markets.

A Unique Epic in Industrial and Business History

The evolution of the consumer electronics and computer industries has been historically unique. It differs from the evolution of the capital-intensive and technologically advanced industries that during the last two decades of the nineteenth century and into the twentieth century had laid the foundations for the Industrial Century. Those earlier industries were based on a number of basic technological innovations: the electricity-producing dynamo, which brought the electric lighting that transformed urban life, and electric power, which so transformed industrial production techniques; the telephone, which brought the first voice transmission over distances; the internal combustion engine, which produced the automobile and the airplane; the new chemical technologies that permitted the production of man-made dyes and, of more significance, a wide range of man-made therapeutic drugs; and other man-made materials ranging from silicon and aluminum to a wide variety of plastics.

In these industries a small number of core companies—first-movers and their followers—created national industries that competed for worldwide markets. In electric light and power equipment, the U.S. and German first-movers led the way. Others soon followed in other European nations and Japan. In metals, the Aluminum Company of America built a monopoly in the United States; but it had effective competition from European counterparts. In motor vehicles, Ford was the initial path definer, but General Motors replaced it in the 1920s and was in turn replaced by the Japanese leaders in the 1970s. Nevertheless, the U.S. motor vehicle industry revived as a strong competitor and the European producers lived on. In electrical and telecommunications equipment, the U.S. and German first-movers continue to dominate, but followers appeared in other European nations, including Sweden and Switzerland, and continue to do so today. In chemicals and pharmaceuticals, the initial German and Swiss leaders were shortly challenged by American companies and those of other European nations.

In none of these industries did a single enterprise become the definer of its national industry's evolving paths of learning in the manner of RCA and IBM in consumer electronics and computers. Nor did a single national industry conquer the world as Japan did in consumer electronics through the elimination of the competing national industries. Nor did two national industries dominate world markets in the manner of the U.S. and Japanese computer industries. The point is that the national industries that invented the infrastructure for the Industrial Century did not compete, conquer, or die in the manner of the national industries that created the infrastructure of the Electronic Century.

The underlying reason for these differences is clear. The creation of the infrastructure for the Industrial Century rested on a broad variety of technological innovations. The unique epic story of the consumer electronics and computer industries was based on the invention of four small, closely related electronic devices—the vacuum tube, the transistor, the integrated circuit, and the microprocessor.

2

CONSUMER ELECTRONICS: THE UNITED STATES—THE CREATION AND DESTRUCTION OF A NATIONAL INDUSTRY

begin with consumer electronics because it came first, before computers. It began in the first and second decades of the twentieth century. I also begin with consumer electronics because it dramatically defines the causes of the success and/or failure of national industries. Indeed, it was the management decisions at the Radio Corporation of America in New York that led to the creation and then destruction of the U.S. industry. Those decisions made by the managers of Matsushita and Sony in Tokyo were responsible for Japan's global conquest.

Moreover, the evolutionary story illustrates in a straightforward manner the significance of cumulative learning, as the commercializing of one technology becomes based on the learning acquired in commercializing the previous one. The radio sector, appearing in the 1920s, evolved from the learning acquired in the initial commercializing of modern electrical and telephone equipment in the 1890s. The technical knowledge learned in commercializing the radio, in turn, laid the foundations for the commercializing of television in the 1940s and 1950s. That knowledge, in turn, provided the base for the innovative tape and disk technologies of the 1970s and

1980s. The one preelectronic sector in what became the consumer electronics industry was recordings, based on the phonograph. The phonograph, like so many electrical and telecommunications devices, evolved from the inventions of Thomas Edison.

The critical turning point in the evolution of the global consumer electronics industry came with the battle of the four first-movers—RCA, Europe's Philips Incandescent Lamp Works, and Japan's Matsushita Electric Industrial and Sony Corporation—to commercialize the videocassette recorder for world markets. RCA's defeat in this contest marked the demise of the U.S. consumer electronics industry and the dawn of Japan's hegemony. For that reason, chapter 2 takes the U.S. story up to the global VCR contest and then concludes with a brief consideration of the causes of the industry's death. Chapter 3 begins with a brief outline of the history of Matsushita and Sony before the VCR battle and then reviews the highlights of that battle and its broader impact on Japan's industry. The chapter concludes with a review of the ingredients of Japan's paths to global conquest.

Creating the American Learning Base

The initial radio technology was the two-way wireless telegraph invented by the Italian Guglielmo Marconi, first demonstrated in 1899 and based on a spark transmitter that could send only telegraph-type signals. Marconi then formed the Marconi Wireless Company with headquarters in London. In 1904 the two German leaders, Siemens & Halske AG (Siemens) and Allgemeine Elektricitäts-Gesellschaft (AEG), formed Telefunken to commercialize the new spark transmitter technology. Somewhat later, amateur hobbyists began to use the technology to communicate with each other on homemade "crystal sets," much as hobbyists in the late 1970s began to use the microprocessor to build their own computers.

It was, however, the continuous wave voice transmission technology, powered by the electronic vacuum tube that replaced the spark transmitter. It did so because it could transmit continuous voice and other sound, which brought into being the radio broadcasting and receiving industry. That technology began to evolve during the second decade of the twentieth century. In its evolution in Europe, Telefunken played the major role, Marconi only a minor one.

In the United States the technology emerged from the U.S. counterparts to the German pioneers, General Electric (GE), American Telephone and Telegraph (AT&T), and Westinghouse. General Electric contributions came before and during World War I, largely through the efforts of Irving Langmuir and his associates to improve the light bulb and the X-ray tube, both of which the company had been producing since the 1890s. At AT&T Lee DeForest's work on a line amplifier to improve long-distance telephony research led to commercializing the Audion tube. At Westinghouse technical capabilities came more from its World War I–related production of electronic tubes and voice transmittal equipment developed by GE, AT&T, and an independent inventor, Reginald Fessenden, than from its own inventions. In March 1921, Westinghouse and AT&T joined GE to use GE's newly formed Radio Corporation of America as a patent pool. One of RCA's initial purposes was to hold and allocate radio-related patents.[1]

RCA, which over time became independent from its sponsors, led the way under the guidance of David Sarnoff to the commercializing of the vacuum tube–based equipment for radio broadcasting and receiving, then to commercializing black-and-white television, and after World War II to the broadcasting and receiving of color television. So I begin the history of the U.S. consumer electronics industry with the coming of RCA.

RCA Created

RCA's formation was a complex affair. Its story begins in October 1919 when Owen D. Young, General Electric's general counsel and vice president, working with senior naval officers, acquired for $3.5 million the Marconi Wireless Company of America, a U.S. subsidiary of the British-owned and British-managed Marconi Wireless and Signal Company. Wireless spark technology for ship-to-ship and ship-to-shore transmissions had greatly increased in importance during World War I. The U.S. Navy wanted to assure that further research and production as well as operational learning would be in the hands of an American enterprise.[2]

Young next formed the Radio Corporation of America as a GE subsidiary, which then acquired American Marconi (the Marconi Wireless Company of America) and issued five million shares of RCA common stock and three million preferred. He then turned over GE's radio-related patents to the new subsidiary. The twenty-eight-year-old David Sarnoff, who had joined American Marconi in 1911, became its assistant chief engineer in 1913 and rose to commercial manager, a post he continued to hold in GE's new RCA subsidiary. During the war, patenting had been held in check in deference to wartime radio needs. But after war's end in November 1918, the advance of wireless technology and the rapid expansion of the continuous wave technologies brought forth a plethora of patents.

Westinghouse, for example, had begun to manufacture vacuum tubes and was beginning to make small-scale, low-powered radio transmitters and receivers. It made a major move into radio by acquiring the patents of Professor Edwin Armstrong of Columbia University, a leading noncorporate inventor in both the spark transmitting technology and the still-developing vacuum tube continuous wave voice transmitting technology. By that time, too, the company had developed four different types of radio receiving sets. On November 2, 1920, Westinghouse began to operate at its Pittsburgh plant the nation's first broadcasting station, KDKA. That venture resulted from work done earlier on spark technology by Frank Conrad, who headed much of the radio design and development work at Westinghouse during the war. In these same years United Fruit had pushed ahead on wireless technology, using it to link its banana boats with its Central American plantations.[3]

Owen Young believed that the growing number of legal battles over patents could only slow the continuing development of radio technologies. His solution was for RCA, which already held GE's patents and those of the navy, to obtain those of GE's competitors in exchange for obtaining shares of stock in RCA and having representatives on its board. Young delegated David Sarnoff to handle the negotiations. The final agreement was signed in March 1921. GE retained 30.1 percent of RCA's equity, Westinghouse received 20.6 percent, AT&T 10.3 percent, and United Fruit 4.1 percent. The remaining 34.9 percent went primarily to the stockholders of American Marconi, but also to individual patent holders. The U.S. government had no financial or managerial presence in this corporate venture.

According to the March 1921 agreement, AT&T was to concentrate on "radio-telephone" systems and on producing broadcasting transmission equipment. It would purchase other radio equipment from GE and Westinghouse. GE and Westinghouse were to concentrate on radio receivers, and RCA's Marconi unit would continue to focus on wireless spark technology. In addition, RCA would market the receivers produced by GE and Westinghouse under its own label. By this agreement, as pointed out by Hugh Aitken in his outstanding history of the beginnings of the United States radio industry, RCA "controlled continuous wave technology in the United States as it evolved up to that date. . . . And, beyond this, because it was backed by the formidable scientific and engineering resources of Western Electric, General Electric, and Westinghouse, not to mention the foreign firms such as Marconi, Philips, and Telefunken with which it had signed patent agreements, this group appeared likely to control developments in the future also." Aitken's statement makes clear why the industry remained dominated for the rest of the century by so very few firms.[4]

Young's timing was fortuitous. In March 1921 he and Sarnoff believed that RCA's immediate task was to build the American strength in wireless spark technology. They saw radio broadcasting and receiving based on continuous wave technology as a long-term potential only. Few persons anticipated the latent demand for radio broadcasting. But that demand came with dramatic and transforming speed. In October 1921, seven months after the signing of the agreement, the Department of Commerce licensed Westinghouse's KDKA broadcasting station. Twenty-six licenses were issued in 1922.

Amazing growth followed. By the end of 1923, 556 stations had been licensed. Then, as most of the available frequencies had been allotted, the number of new stations leveled off in 1925. During the next ten years the total number of stations remained between six hundred and seven hundred. These new broadcasting stations were established by a large number of enterprises — RCA, GE, Westinghouse, and other electric machinery makers; a variety of other manufacturers; newspapers; commercial enterprises; and individual entrepreneurs.[5]

With broadcasting facilities assured throughout the nation, hundreds of firms swarmed into this unexpected and swiftly growing market for radio receivers, much as they did in personal computers between 1982 and 1985. Like the personal computers of the early 1980s, radio receiving sets were easy to assemble. Receiver sales rose from $50.3 million in 1923 to $206.7 million in 1926, then dropped back to $181.5 million in 1927 and bounced up to $366.3 million in 1929.

When the radio receiver market leveled off around 1926, the death rate of their producers was even higher than that of personal computer makers when their market stabilized in 1985. According to Rupert Maclaurin, a historian of the radio industry before World War II, of the 648 radio manufacturing companies established during the four years of the boom (1923 to 1926), only 18 were still alive in 1934. Eleven of these had been started in 1923.

What is historically most significant in terms of learned organizational capabilities was that the most successful survivors were existing producers of electrical devices that had built their functional capabilities before the coming of the new radio technologies. Indeed, by the late 1920s the leaders were firms that had been established before 1920. They had been makers of auto batteries (Philco), auto ignition systems (Atwater Kent), telephone equipment (Stromberg Carlson), and light bulbs and electrical equipment (Sylvania and Magnavox). The only long-term survivors of that first boom that were start-ups, with no previous industrial experience, were Zenith and Raytheon in receivers and in tubes respectively. The others had already built their learning bases, integrating production and distribution, and had enjoyed a steady flow of income from their existing businesses that helped to finance a new one.

David Sarnoff's Challenges

For Sarnoff, who had been promoted to RCA's general manager in 1921 at the age of thirty, and to general manager and vice president in 1922, this unexpected explosive growth of radio receiving and broadcasting equipment brought daunting challenges. He remained responsible for maintaining the company's leadership in two-way radio wireless. At the same time, he had to create a marketing organization for the sale of radio receivers produced by Westinghouse and GE. A far more difficult task was to shape a response to the powerful outcry against the new "radio trust" by finding a licensing policy that satisfied the surge of new entrants into the radio broadcasting and receiving markets. Still another challenge was to work out the complex arrangements of the March 1921 agreement with its three major stockholders, AT&T, GE, and Westinghouse, so as to fulfill the unexpected profit potential of the new broadcasting and receiving markets. In meeting these challenges, David Sarnoff, working closely with chairman of the board Owen D. Young, more than any other person shaped RCA and the U.S. radio industry during the 1920s. RCA's president, General James G. Harbord, the retired chief of staff of the American Expeditionary Force in France during World War I, a public figure of high integrity, remained little more than a figurehead.[6]

Of his challenges, the creation of a marketing organization was relatively straightforward. In 1921 RCA had fourteen people in the sales organization. By the end of 1922 Sarnoff had built a nationwide network of more than two hundred distribution outlets. Sales grew from $11 million in 1922 to $50 million in 1924. By 1925 RCA had also built and operated four broadcasting stations.

At first Sarnoff hoped to enforce RCA's patents by allocating its receiving sets, tubes, and components only to distributors that agreed to handle RCA's entire product line, forbidding them to carry radio sets of unauthorized assemblers. The resulting protest immediately brought an investigation in 1922 by the Federal Trade Commission that made public all the details of the complex cross-licensing arrangements involved in RCA's formation. In 1924 the commission followed up its investigation by filing an antitrust suit against RCA.[7]

By then Sarnoff was coming to appreciate the difficulties and the resulting high cost of attempting to monitor patent violations in a swiftly growing industry. In 1927 Sarnoff defined RCA's new licensing policy. The company would liberally license its patents at 7½ percent on the wholesale value of a set. Through a system of "packaged licensing," royalties were paid on patents of all parts in a complete set even if only one was used. As a result, royalties became a major source of RCA's revenues, rising from $136,000 in 1926 to over $3.2 million in 1927, and to a peak of $7 million in 1929 and 1930, before the industry felt the full impact of the Great Depression. As important this all-or-nothing packaged licensing agreement assured continued dominance in the production of components manufactured by GE and Westinghouse, which required more complex and costly equipment than did the assembling of the final radio receiving sets.

Profiting on sales from components, rather than on completed receiving sets, became a standard RCA policy. In radio and then television, RCA's share of the receiving sets dropped quickly as the revenues from licensing fees and from components soared. The licensing revenues provided a major source of funding for RCA's continuing research and development. In addition to shaping RCA's market strategy, packaged licensing satisfied its major competitors. In 1928 the Federal Trade Commission, also satisfied, dropped its antitrust suit.

As Sarnoff and his managers were formulating a licensing policy—and so defining the industry's product standards—they had an even greater challenge in adjusting the March 1921 agreement to the sudden and unexpected transformation of the radio industry. As AT&T's executives had interpreted that agreement, its manufacturing unit, Western Electric, had exclusive rights to produce broadcasting equipment, and GE and Westinghouse had exclusive rights to produce broadcasting receivers and components. GE and Westinghouse, in turn, challenged AT&T's belief that "public telephony for toll" gave AT&T the right to operate broadcasting stations. The companies turned to arbitration in 1923, a process that dragged on until 1926. In the end, the parties agreed that AT&T would retain exclusive rights to public service telephony but "would withdraw from broadcasting; while GE, Westinghouse, and RCA would enjoy exclusive rights in the fields of wireless telegraph, entertainment broadcasting, and the manufacturing of tubes for public sale."[8]

As part of this 1926 agreement, RCA acquired AT&T's broadcasting stations, including its flagship in New York. It then formed the National Broadcasting Company (NBC), into which came the stations of GE and Westinghouse as well. RCA held 50 percent of the equity of the new broadcasting system, General Electric 30 percent, and Westinghouse 20 percent. That network grew from 19 stations in 1926 to 69 in 1929 and to 103 in 1936. From the start Sarnoff divided NBC into two networks, the Red concentrating more on commercial broadcasting and the Blue leaning more toward public service in terms of educational and cultural broadcasting. In 1942 RCA, under pressure from the Federal Communications Commission (FCC), sold the Blue system, which became the independent American Broadcasting Company (ABC).

NBC's major competitor, however, appeared in 1927 less than a year later when the twenty-seven-year-old William S. Paley put together a somewhat smaller network of stations in his Columbia Broadcasting System (CBS). There he followed what had become the RCA strategy of providing programs to local affiliates as a way of assuring advertisers with national audiences. NBC became and remained a major source of income for RCA. As the first-movers in national broadcasting systems, NBC, its spin-off ABC, and CBS long remained the nation's three leading broadcasting networks.

In this manner Sarnoff solidified the position that he and Young had established in 1921. In the words of Rupert Maclaurin, RCA by 1928 "had thus established a strong position in all major branches of the radio industry, and an RCA license was considered essential for the manufacturing of any up-to-date set or modern vacuum tube. No one challenged this for many years to come."[9] Retained earnings from sales of products still manufactured by GE and Westinghouse, royalties, and radio broadcasting from NBC made RCA the dominant enterprise in the U.S. radio industry. But as yet it did not have its own integrated learning base.

Sarnoff's Drive for Integration and Independence

After 1926 Sarnoff focused on freeing RCA from the control of GE and Westinghouse so that RCA could become a fully integrated industrial enterprise. During the 1920s RCA remained severely handicapped by its dependence on GE and Westinghouse for the design and production of the receiving sets it sold. Indeed, its performance provides a valuable example of the importance of the integration of production and distribution in modern industrial enterprises. Even though its smaller competitors had to pay RCA royalties and, with some exceptions, rely on it for components, they moved more quickly than RCA to meet changing market demands through innovative design and production engineering. Moreover, their smaller size and their smaller investment needs enabled a quicker response. Thus handicapped, RCA saw its share of the U.S. market for receiving sets drop even more than anticipated down to between 18 and 20 percent in the late 1920s. Of much more long-term significance was that it marketed products developed and manufactured only at General Electric and/or Westinghouse. Therefore, RCA did not even have the learning base on which to develop technical and functional capabilities in research, product development, and manufacturing of radio products.

Sarnoff's first move to achieve the necessary integration was to convince RCA's principal owners, GE and Westinghouse, to permit his company to purchase the Victor Talking Machine Company. That firm, a U.S. first-mover, was established in 1901 to commercialize Thomas Edison's invention of the phonograph but had been suffering from radio competition. Victor's managers and Sarnoff saw the potential of combining their closely related radio and phonograph learning paths into a single enterprise. Thus for Sarnoff, the primary attraction of the acquisition was the critical set of facilities that Victor offered. These included its impressive manufacturing facilities in Camden, New Jersey, and its long-established worldwide sales and distribution organization for phonographs and records operated by full-line subsidiaries in Britain, Canada, Latin America, and Japan. Through this acquisition then, RCA entered the only preelectronic sector, a sector dominated since the turn of the century by Victor and one other American company, Columbia Phonograph. In addition, Sarnoff persuaded the senior managers at GE and Westinghouse to turn over their manufacturing facilities and personnel to RCA.

On April 4, 1930, the RCA board approved the acquisition of Victor. At the same time, GE turned over its Harrison tube plant in New Jersey and Westinghouse its lamp works and radio products plant in Indianapolis. RCA also received GE's and Westinghouse's patents and the royalties in the fields of radio equipment, phonographs, and motion pictures. Finally, GE and Westinghouse relinquished their stock holdings in RCA and NBC, and canceled internal loans that they had made to RCA for the purchase of the Victor Company. In exchange, GE and Westinghouse received RCA securities valued at $6.5 million.[10]

With the transactions recorded on April 4, 1930, Sarnoff had achieved his goal of having an integrated independent enterprise with its own product development, production, marketing, and distribution. But RCA still did not have a learning base that integrated the technical and functional capabilities, for these had been learned under the auspices of three different enterprises. For this reason, the managerial staff in the radio production unit at the Indianapolis works, that at the tube and component plant in Harrison, New Jersey, and that of the recording and phonograph activities at Camden, New Jersey, remained relatively independent of one another. Moreover, RCA's only research organization had been part of its small licensing program housed in New York City.

Three weeks after RCA had acquired this worldwide, still to be fully integrated learning base, the U.S. Justice Department indicted it for antitrust violations and thus precipitated the final step in achieving RCA's corporate independence. That step came in November 1932 when RCA, GE, and Westinghouse finally agreed to a consent decree, By that decree, GE and Westinghouse agreed to reduce by one-half RCA's debts to them and to distribute their equity holdings in RCA to their own shareholders. They were to have no representation on the RCA board and were not to compete in radio or related products for two and a half years. Finally, they agreed to give RCA unrestricted, albeit nonexclusive, rights to all of GE's and Westinghouse's radio-related patents. The agreement was an impressive win for Sarnoff. RCA's complete independence was assured. In addition, RCA retained control of the licenses it held.

The Impact of the Great Depression

By the time the consent decree was signed, RCA, the industry, and the country were engulfed in the nation's most serious economic crisis of the twentieth century. After the stock market crash at the end of 1929, national sales of radio receiving sets fell from $842.5 million in 1929 to $300 million in 1934. Every major firm reported losses. RCA, with the industry's largest factories, suffered the most from the cost of unused capacity. It sold off its British and continental European (but not its Japanese) holdings that had come with the acquisition of Victor, including 50 percent in Britain's Gramophone and 29 percent in Britain's Electrical & Musical Instruments (EMI). As early as 1930 NBC had become RCA's most profitable division. However, broadcasting and licensing carried the company through to the economic recovery that began in 1934.[11]

With the onslaught of the Great Depression, the radio industry's structure matured. The collapse of its market drove out hitherto successful firms like Atwater Kent and Grisby/Grunow. Those that remained were already industry leaders before the Crash. RCA's most successful challenger in receiving sets was Philco (formed in 1893) and, in components, Sylvania (formed in 1901).[12]

During the 1930s marketing became central to competitive success in radio manufacturing. The Philco Corporation, RCA's most successful U.S. rival, was a newcomer, having entered the industry only just as the Depression struck, again indicating the value of long-established and market-tested functional capabilities. As the Philadelphia Electric Storage Company, Philco had come of age with the auto industry. It made batteries for electric cars, then batteries for self-starters in motor vehicles, and then radio batteries, which is why in 1928, when Philco began to produce radio receiving sets, it marketed them through its large national distributing network of more than 300 wholesalers and 175 large retailers. During the 1930s the Philco Corporation focused on the high end of the market. Its console sets "made a radio an ambitious piece of furniture."[13]

Second to Philco as an RCA competitor was the Zenith Radio Corporation, one of the very few successful start-ups. Like Philco, it focused on the high end of the market, concentrating on product design and aggressive advertising. Crosley competed in much the same manner, while Emerson concentrated on the lower end of the market, developing a "pee-wee" clocklike radio that sold for less than $10. Another successful challenger, Galvin Radio, took the lead in a niche market—radios for automobiles—changing its name to Motorola. Colonial produced for Sears, Roebuck. In 1935 General Electric returned to the market, first selling RCA products under its label and then producing its own name-brand radios. By 1940, ten leaders accounted for just under 75 percent of the total sales in radio receiver sets (listed in Appendix 2:1).

The more costly and complex production of tubes and other components remained even more concentrated than radios themselves. Of the fifteen RCA tube licensees in 1930, only eight remained in 1941. Sylvania Electric Products, a long-established producer of light bulbs and other electrical equipment, became RCA's primary challenger in vacuum tubes and other components. By having smaller plants in small towns, Sylvania benefited from lower wages and less scale dependence. Despite royalty payments to RCA, it prospered by becoming the major supplier of radio tubes to Philco and Zenith. The only other tube maker that survived, and barely did so, was Raytheon. A 1922 start-up refrigerator maker that turned to the production of tubes, Raytheon made a profit in only two years between 1930 and 1940. In speakers, the most successful producer was Magnavox, established in 1910, which competed in much the same manner as Sylvania. Except for Zenith, none of these firms was an entrepreneurial start-up. They had established their integrated learning bases before they began to produce radios.[14]

Nevertheless, RCA remained the industry's only enterprise producing a broad range of products. The makers of receiving sets did not produce components in large quantity, nor did the component makers produce receiving sets. RCA, in addition to its profitable tubes and components, its licensing, and its successful NBC, produced broadcasting equipment and remained the leading maker of phonographs and records. It also was still the leader in wireless telegraphy, an activity that kept RCA in the business of global communications. In addition, through its investment in Radio-Keith-Orpheum (RKO), it began in 1928 to produce sound equipment for motion pictures. RCA's Photophone system was second in this field to Western Electric's Vitaphone, which provided in 1927 the first talking film, Al Jolson's *The Jazz Singer*.[15]

Although World War II was to bring technological breakthroughs in electronics plus mass funding and the commercializing of new products, RCA and its competitors that had made it through the Great Depression continued on as the industry's leaders until they and their industry succumbed to the Japanese onslaught of the 1970s. In the 1930s, these enterprises began to use their technical and product development capabilities learned in the commercializing of radio to begin the process of commercializing video broadcasting and receiving technology.

The Coming of Television

During the 1930s television became the focus of the industry's development of new products and the enhancement of corporate organizational capabilities. In the early 1920s AT&T's Bell Laboratories and the R&D facilities of GE and Westinghouse had concentrated on developing electromechanical devices, as had the most prolific of television's noncorporate inventors, C. Francis Jenkins. The electronic breakthrough came in 1928 when Vladimir K. Zworykin, a Russian émigré who had been working on television at Westinghouse since 1923, developed the basic electronic photo tube (the iconoscope). With the transfer of Westinghouse's facilities to RCA in 1930, and the centralization of RCA's research activities at Van Cortland Park, New York, Zworykin carried on there. By 1932 he had sixty persons working under him.[16]

In 1930 Philco entered the arena by hiring an inventor/entrepreneur, Philo Farnsworth, who had invented an essential component, a cathode ray camera known as the image dissector. But as Philco had neither the necessary funds nor the research personnel, its managers dropped the project in 1932. Farnsworth proceeded on his own with the continuing support of his original backers, a group of California bankers, until 1938, when his company cross-licensed patents with RCA and AT&T. After 1938, Farnsworth moved beyond patenting into product development. Another inventor/entrepreneur, Allen B. Du Mont, who invented a cathode ray oscilloscope, created a comparable enterprise, his Allen B. Du Mont Laboratories, after cross-licensing with RCA.

The long-term challengers to RCA in the development of TV, however, were not entrepreneurial start-ups. The barriers to entry (as described in Chapter 1) had become too high. Instead the challengers were major competitors of the 1920s: Philco, William Paley's CBS, and Zenith, all of whom obtained licenses for RCA's patents. Philco, revived by financing from the investment banking firm of Kuhn, Loeb & Company, acquired the Capehart Corporation, one other small radio manufacturer, and returned to its earlier television project. CBS began to make a major development effort in the late 1930s. Zenith began to work seriously on television only in 1940. With the recovery of the U.S. radio market—the number of sets sold rose from 4.4 million in 1934 to 10.7 million in 1939—RCA, Philco, and CBS had the profits to reinvest in the commercializing of TV sets and components. They had the necessary production facilities and, as important, the marketing capabilities that new entrants lacked.[17]

As the commercialization of television became a reality, the need to set standards for screens, circuits, and other components became urgent. Although committees of the Radio Manufacturers Association (RMA) were expected to determine these standards, they were in fact defined during the battle between the leading manufacturers—between RCA, on the one hand, and Philco, Zenith, and CBS on the other. In 1936 an engineering committee of the RMA, supported by the recently established Federal Communications Commission, recommended standards for channel allocation and bandwidth attuned to those advocated by RCA. Philco immediately disowned this standard and was joined by Zenith and CBS. The RMA committee then called for further field testing.

RCA Leads the Way

In October 1938 Sarnoff decided to go it alone. In the spring of 1939 he used the New York World's Fair as a platform to announce and demonstrate RCA's first television set. But the rush of customers he expected failed to materialize. The television sets were expensive, programs were limited, and television's future was still uncertain—a very different situation from the beginnings of radio and, later, of personal computers. In April 1940 the FCC urged the resumption of further testing on an experimental basis and encouraged the RMA to set up a National Television Systems Committee (NTSC) to define the standard.[18]

Again, RCA pushed ahead aggressively. The chairman of the FCC, James L. Fly, an ardent New Dealer, responded by attacking Sarnoff as a dangerous monopolist. This charge brought a Senate investigation. By then, however, television sales were rising and the demand for standards was becoming more urgent. So in April 1941 the NTSC produced a set of standards close to those of RCA, despite the outcry from Philco and its allies. "Amidst a wealth of claims and counter-claims," Sarnoff's biographer writes, "an unfettered NBC launched commercial telecasting in the United States on July 1, 1941." Less than six months later the nation was at war. In April 1942 commercial production of television equipment was officially banned.

The Impact of World War II

It would be difficult to overstate the impact of World War II on the young electronics industry, much as it impacted other high-technology industries such as the young aircraft and the older chemical and pharmaceutical industries. The extended and varied uses of electronics by the United States and its allies and opponents dramatically increased national learning, nowhere as much as in the United States. RCA became a major contractor in military electronics. With production contracts of $84 million, it was one of the Big Five, albeit the smallest, behind Western Electric (AT&T's manufacturing arm), GE, Bendix (the nation's largest maker of motor vehicle parts), and Westinghouse. In terms of the dollar value of research contracts granted by the Office of Scientific Research and Development (OSRD), it ranked fourth behind Western Electric, GE, and the Research Construction Company (a research consortium) and was followed by Du Pont (whose primary task was building the first atomic bomb fabrication plant).

Huge military demands quickly expanded RCA's production facilities and, of a more long-term significance, transformed the nature of its research and product development. The massive military contracts for radios and radio tubes brought a major expansion of RCA's existing production facilities at Indianapolis, Harrison, and Camden. Before the war's end, RCA acquired a government-funded complex at Lancaster, Pennsylvania, of twenty thousand different types of components that produced a total of twenty million tubes.[19]

The wartime research was carried out primarily by the laboratories that Sarnoff had built in 1941 in Princeton, New Jersey, financing its costs from the income from military contracts. Research became an independent department called the "RCA Laboratories." It was given the responsibility for "all research, original development and patent and licensing activities of the corporation . . . and financial control over all of RCA's research work."

The OSRD research contracts led the new department to work on radar, sonar, navigation systems, and the development of television-guided pilotless planes. It became involved in electronic devices for directing antiaircraft guns, proximity fuses, and other specialized tubes for military purposes.

War-related television research brought, in the words of historian Margaret Graham, "the replacement of the iconoscope with the much more sensitive orthicon that became the basis for the postwar camera technology." Other wartime television developments at RCA "included the high-power vacuum tube, other special tubes as display devices, mass production techniques for cathode ray tubes, and better network relay and microwave techniques."

When the war ended, RCA and its limited number of competitors gave highest priority to the introduction of long-delayed television projects. Sarnoff's strategy was twofold. First, during the transition from military to civilian products, when TV receiving sets were not yet available in volume, RCA expanded both its television broadcasting network and its still tiny portfolio of broadcast programs. Second, RCA announced in 1946 that its television technology would be open to all—thus making it the industry standard. In June 1947 Frank M. Folsom, who had just become CEO as Sarnoff moved up to be chairman, invited RCA's competitors to Camden. He wanted them to view RCA's new postwar model, the 630TS, selling at $375, and to take with them detailed blueprints of the product. In addition, to assure reliability of the new, still-untested device, Folsom created an RCA service force to maintain and repair purchased machines.[20]

Folsom's strategy worked. U.S. television sales soared in a manner comparable to those in radio between 1922 and 1925 and personal computers between 1982 and 1985. RCA's market share in receiving sets fell off, but its income from tubes, other components, and licenses took off sensationally. Even in 1948, the year after the Camden demonstration, its share of television sets was only 42.6 percent. At the same time, its total revenues from manufacturing soared from $271 million in 1948 to $476 million in 1950. Then the shakedown began. U.S. sales of television sets, which had risen from just under 1 million in 1948 to 7.5 million in 1950, fell back to 5.4 million in 1951, leveling off to an average of 6 million a year in the decade after 1953. RCA's strategy of defining the television standard through its demonstration at Camden in 1947 brought a sizable number of new entrants into the industry, but when the demand leveled off very few survived.

By 1958 RCA's U.S. market share in television sets had leveled off at 17 percent, where it remained for a decade. In these same years RCA enjoyed close to 70 percent market share of the high-volume tube and component businesses. Therefore RCA benefited from tubes and components through both licensing as well as scale economies in manufacturing. By 1950 half of RCA's income came from manufacturing television components, receiving sets, and broadcasting equipment. As growth from hardware leveled off, NBC's television broadcasting unit increased its cash flow. Until the late 1960s RCA's revenues came primarily from television-related activities.

During the 1950s RCA's major competitors remained largely the radio producers of the 1930s—Philco, Zenith, and Motorola in receiving sets, Sylvania in tubes, and CBS in broadcasting. Other competitors included Atwater Kent, which had returned to radio during the war; Magnavox, which had expanded its line during the war by making receiving sets as well as components; and one newcomer, Admiral, a wartime producer of radios and radar established in 1940, one of the very few start-ups created to exploit wartime opportunities in electronics. By 1958 the seven firms (by then CBS had turned from television production to broadcasting) accounted for 86 percent of market share for black-and-white television.

The Drive for Color Television

In the early 1950s, as black-and-white television settled into maturity, color television became the next challenge. Here the leading players were again those that had built their research organizations and their technical capabilities before their wartime expansion—RCA, Philco, CBS, and, to a lesser extent, Zenith. But the two primary contestants, those that would determine the standards for the new technology, were RCA and CBS, the two that had begun research on color before the coming of war. In 1940 CBS announced a system based on electromechanical color techniques developed by Peter Goldmark, a member of the CBS research team since 1936. Because this system was electromechanical, it was not compatible with the electronic black-and-white and NTSC standards that Sarnoff had done so much to shape. In 1941 RCA had announced a color system that used electronic technology and was potentially compatible with black-and-white television.[21]

By the time RCA and CBS returned to concentrating on color television after the war, their managers had persuaded the FCC to take over the high-frequency channels originally allocated to FM (frequency modulation) radio. FM, a major innovation, had been developed during the 1930s by

Edwin H. Armstrong, initially with the support of Sarnoff, and had reached the market by 1940. But, as in the case of color TV, the war postponed this technology's further development.

In 1944 Sarnoff persuaded the FCC to shift FM radio broadcasting to UHF—that is, the ultrahigh frequencies of 88–108—thus opening up to color television the bands originally assigned to FM radio. Shortly afterward, with a push from CBS, whose electromechanical color technology relied on these same UHF frequencies, the commission limited FM broadcasting to a relatively small local area. FM stations usually joined local AM stations, and producers equipped their products to receive the local FM and AM channels. Nevertheless, between 1947 and 1954 only 6 percent of the thirty-four million radio sets produced were equipped with both AM and FM receivers.

On completing the development of its noncompatible color television, CBS applied in 1947 to the FCC for a license. Sarnoff urged the commissioners to hold off until RCA could present the compatible system to black and white that it was developing. RCA's presentation, made in 1949, was, in historian Margaret Graham's words, "a disaster of legendary proportions." So in July 1951 the FCC approved the CBS standard. In anticipation of that approval, CBS had expanded its production facilities, integrated backward by purchasing Hytron, the nation's fourth largest tube maker, and reorganized its operating structures for large-scale production.[22]

Once again external events intervened. The Korean War of the early fifties caused the government to allocate all electronic equipment development to military purposes. However, the manufacture of black-and-white televisions continued. By the time that war was over, the number of televisions sold had grown so fast that CBS's noncompatible color receiving set could no longer become an industry standard. Between 1950 and 1952 a total of twelve million new black-and-white sets had been produced. At Philco, Zenith, and other U.S. competitors, and at those abroad, primarily Philips Incandescent Lamp Works (Philips), a shift to electromechanical technology for their color television made little commercial sense. Late in 1951 the FCC appointed a second National Television Systems Committee. In December 1953, in Graham's words, "the committee produced proposals for television systems that were compatible with, though not identical to, the system RCA had proposed in 1949." CBS made no further attempt to promote its product. Indeed, it moved out of the production of radio and television products altogether but continued to own and operate radio and television stations, to expand the CBS broadcasting group, and to enlarge its recording enterprise, Columbia Records, which it had formed in 1938.

Nevertheless, the acceptance of RCA's system did not assure RCA a market for its color TVs, even though it made a valiant effort to begin one. Its products and those sold by its competitors were large and expensive, priced at $700 to $800 a set. (In the year 2000 that would be in the thousands of dollars.) Even RCA's expanded service organization had difficulty maintaining performance. As Ralph Cordiner, General Electric's CEO, quipped: "If you have a color set, you've almost got to have an engineer living in the house." In 1956 *Time* called the color TV the year's "most resounding flop." Soon Philco, Zenith, and the somewhat smaller firms such as Motorola and Admiral withdrew their color models from the market. But RCA persisted.

The development of color television compatible for use in existing black-and-white sets was an extremely complex technological challenge. Its success was Sarnoff's supreme achievement at RCA. He pushed the scientists and engineers at the RCA Laboratories to complete a task that they often told him was impossible. He took the responsibility for the growing high costs involved. The color tube compatible with the black-and-white television set was an outstanding achievement in both basic scientific research and the resulting product development.

But the cost had been high. As Margaret Graham reports: "While competitors enjoyed the proceeds from strong black and white sales, RCA bore the entire burden of keeping the color system alive. . . . Unable to attract advertising support for color, NBC paid a substantial premium to broadcast color programming; the RCA manufacturing organizations carried large unabsorbed overheads for color tooling; and the drain on finances robbed other enterprises, such as computer development, of necessary capital."

The payoff was slow in coming. In 1959 RCA made its first profit from color television. Both RCA Labs and the consumer electronic division continued to concentrate on improving performance and lowering costs, particularly in the production of tubes. But success was heady when the payoff came, for RCA completely dominated the new technology. In 1961 Zenith broke what had become an industry boycott on color by ordering fifty thousand RCA color tubes. The next year a million sets were in use with an average retail price of $600.

As RCA's management expected, they repeated the success patterns of both the radio and black-and-white TV markets. High profits came from licensing and components, not from receiving sets. As table 2.1 indicates, by

TABLE 2.1. Shares of the U.S. Market for Color Television Sets, 1964, 1975, 1986

Brand	1964			1975			1986–1987		
	Share	Manufacturer	Nation	Share	Manufacturer	Nation	Share	Manufacturer	Nation
RCA[1]	42	RCA	U.S.	19.0	RCA	U.S.	17.5[2]	GE -> Thomson	France
Zenith[1]	14	Zenith	U.S.	24.0	Zenith	U.S.	15.8	Zenith[3]	U.S.
GE[4]	–	GE[4]	U.S.	6.2	GE[4]	U.S.	6.3[2]	GE -> Matsushita	Japan
Sears (10%)	1	RCA	U.S.	0.9	RCA	U.S.	0.6[2]	GE -> Sanyo	Japan
Sears (90%)	8	Warwick	U.S.	7.8	Warwick	U.S.	5.5	Sanyo	Japan
Emerson	4	Emerson	U.S.	–	Emerson	U.S.	1.5	Sanyo	Japan
Quasar	8	Motorola	U.S.	5.9	Matsushita	Japan	3.9	Matsushita	Japan
Magnavox	6	Magnavox	U.S.	6.6	Philips	Neth.	5.0	Philips	Neth.
Curtes Mathes	–			–			1.0	CMM Co.	U.S.
Sylvania	4	GTE	U.S.	4.4	GTE	U.S.	3.8	Philips	Neth.
Philco	–	Ford	U.S.	2.0	GTE	U.S.	1.0	Philips	Neth.
Admiral	7	Rockwell	U.S.	3.0	Rockwell	U.S.	–		
Sony	–			5.8	Sony	Japan	6.0	Sony	Japan
Panasonic	–			2.3	Matsushita	Japan	4.2	Matsushita	Japan
Sharp	–			–			3.2	Sharp	Japan
Hitachi	–			–			3.0	Hitachi	Japan
Mitsubishi	–			–			2.8	Mitsubishi	Japan
Toshiba	–			–			1.8	Toshiba	Japan
Sanyo	–			–			1.6	Sanyo	Japan

Brand		Manufacturer	Country
Fisher	—	Sanyo	Japan
NEC	—	NEC	Japan
JVC	—	Matsushita	Japan
Teknika	—	158. Itoh	Japan
Sampo	—	Sampo	Taiwan
Tatung	—	Tatung	Taiwan
Samsung	—	Samsung	Korea
Gold Star	—	Goldstar	Korea

(Manufacturer percentages: Sanyo 0.5, NEC 0.5, Matsushita 0.5, 158. Itoh 0.4, Sampo 0.5, Tatung 0.4, Samsung 1.6, Goldstar 1.5)

National Shares

			(1987 Manufacturer)
United States	94.0	67.3	United States 16.8
Japan	—	14.0	Japan 42.3
France	—	—	France 17.5
Netherlands	—	6.6	Netherlands 9.9
Taiwan	—	—	Taiwan 0.9
South Korea	—	—	South Korea 3.1
Other/Unknown	6.0	12.1	Other/Unknown 9.6
	100.0	100.0	100.0

Source: "Decline of U.S. Consumer Electronics," *The Working Papers of the M.I.T. Commission of Industrial Productivity*, vol. 2, p. 45, with permission from MIT Press.

[1] Some sets and components supplied by owned offshore factories.

[2] Brands transferred to Thomson (France) or other suppliers in 1987.

[3] Heavy losses in 1986.

[4] Matsushita supplied GE sets on an OEM basis, that is, sets were sold over the GE label.

1964 RCA's market share of color television receiving sets in the United States had dropped to 42 percent, with Zenith a distant second at 14 percent. By 1975 RCA's share had come down to 19 percent and Zenith's had risen to 24 percent. But until the late 1960s RCA dominated globally in tubes and components. As the sole supplier of the tricolor tube, a product that became a symbol of U.S. mass production during the sixties, RCA made a profit of $35 on every tube sold. "RCA was soon back-ordered in all its color plants—from cameras and studio equipment to receiving tubes and components." Between 1960 and 1965 RCA's average profitability was three times the average of all U.S. manufacturing enterprises, and its ratio of profit to revenue doubled. Its sales passed the $2 billion mark, making it the nation's twenty-sixth largest industrial enterprise in terms of sales.[23]

Yet within less than two decades RCA and the U.S. industry were no longer able to compete at home or abroad. The search for a new strategy of growth destroyed RCA's all-powerful learning base in consumer electronics.

The Search for a New Strategy

Sarnoff, his son Robert (the heir apparent), and RCA's senior managers began to search during the early 1960s for a strategy to provide growth in the manner of radio and television in the past. That search was shaped by three major developments. The first was an antitrust consent decree of October 1958. The second was the increasing independence of the RCA Laboratories from the companies' operating divisions. The third was an increasingly popular management belief in the United States that the successful path to profit was to obtain new product lines through acquisition, even if they were not closely related to a firm's existing business.

The 1958 consent decree was part of the drive by the Justice Department's antitrust division to open the new electronic-based industries to competition by making the patents of IBM, AT&T, and RCA available to all (a drive described in chapter 4 for IBM). That decree ended RCA's packaged licensing agreement that it made with the Federal Trade Commission in 1924. Not only did it end packaged licensing, but it also made licenses available to domestic companies without charge. Foreign buyers would continue to pay full freight. For RCA's Princeton Research Laboratories, the consent decree had two important consequences. First, because the decree covered all products for "radio purposes" including television licenses, it discouraged continuing research in radio-related devices. Second, and of more significance, RCA Labs, in order to maintain licensing income after the consent decree, began to concentrate on licensing to Europe's Philips and Japan's leading consumer electronics makers. These two changes sped up the transfer of RCA's achievements in color TV technology to its two major competitors.[24]

In the following years, licensing fees did remain a significant source of income for RCA. Until the late 1960s, most of the postwar Japanese consumer electronics industry was built with RCA vacuum tube technology. Not surprisingly, when Sarnoff toured Japan in 1960 he was given a hero's welcome, including the Order of the Rising Sun from the emperor. During the 1970s royalties from consumer electronics patents reached $100 million a year. The profits from such licensing may have deterred RCA from building plants or even marketing aggressively abroad.

Government contracts dropped off after 1945, but with the coming of the cold war, RCA's government business boomed. These contracts pulled the RCA Laboratories even further away from research on radio-related products. For example, RCA joined with GE and Bendix to build radar for the SAGE air defense project (mentioned in chapter 4). It also provided communications facilities primarily for military and government agencies by developing and operating a common carrier network for overseas voice and sound transmission, a heritage from its initial wireless business. That business continued to be a significant source of income, particularly after RCA orbited two satellites in the 1960s.[25]

In addition to the claim on RCA's R&D activities through government and communications contracts, Sarnoff himself had further expanded the activities of the RCA Laboratories in the late forties by asking them to develop three quite different new products—an electronic air conditioner, a light amplifier, and a videotape recorder used for delayed television broadcasting (to permit repeated broadcasting from the use of a single film presentation). All three projects ultimately failed. The air conditioner turned into an electronic refrigerator, which its developers soon termed "the most expensive ice cube in the world." (This project resulted from a postwar plan to diversify into consumer appliances that began with the acquisition of a 20 percent holding in Whirlpool, the country's leading producer of household appliances. RCA sold off its Whirlpool holding between 1962 and 1964.) The light amplifier, feasible in principle, was too costly to produce.

Of more significance was the failure of the videotape recorder, for that experience was a foretaste of a growing conflict between the RCA Laboratories in Princeton and the Advanced Development Groups of the operating divisions. The Advanced Development Group at Camden had devised a new technology for this device. RCA Labs then decided that the Advanced Development Group's technology was too complex and shut the project down. But the RCA Labs were unable to invent a satisfactory product of their own. Later another firm, Ampex, developed one similar to that of the Camden Group that became the basis of the technology used in commercializing the videocassette recorder, the contest that would determine the future of the industry, as told in chapter 3.

This controversy between the RCA Laboratories at Princeton and the Advanced Development Group at Camden revealed an essential weakness in RCA's postwar learning base: the difficulties of integrating the technical capabilities at Princeton, those of basic and applied research, with the functional capabilities developed in the operating divisions. Since their establishment in 1941, the Princeton Laboratories controlled RCA's research and funded its development activities at Princeton. And from its wartime beginnings it had been involved in a wide range of research activities besides consumer electronics projects. Moreover, since their income was based on licensing, the researchers at the RCA Laboratories preferred to concentrate on developing new nonproprietary products and processes.

On the other hand, the Advanced Development Groups were located in the operating divisions at the major plants—Indianapolis in radio and television receivers, Harrison in tubes and components, and Camden in recording and broadcasting equipment. Their task was to integrate the product development with processes of production and above all to the market for whom the improved product was destined. Not surprisingly, the divisional advanced development groups began to look to the Japanese companies, especially Matsushita, to provide technical engineering capabilities for the products for which they were responsible. Tension was heightened by a growing broader generational conflict between the younger scientists whose training had turned them to concentrate more on basic research and the engineering and problem-solving veterans whose focus had long been on product development.

Strategies Defined

Despite these tensions, after extended discussions, top management had basically agreed by 1965 on "two fields of applied research identified as having 'the most impact on RCA's future prosperity.' These were consumer electronics and electronic data-processing."[26] David Sarnoff and his son Robert, who succeeded him as CEO in 1968, and also most of the company's senior managers, agreed that the major effort should be on data-processing computers.

By 1970 close to half of RCA's R&D expenditures and 40 percent of its research personnel were allocated to electronic data processing. At the same time, RCA's continuing commitment to overseas voice/recording communications systems that had evolved from its initial commitment to the wireless spark technology called for substantial allocation of research funds and personnel.

Therefore consumer electronics received a much smaller portion of funding and attention than had radio before the war and television in the 1940s and 1950s. Moreover, this downgrading of consumer electronics at RCA came just as the large Japanese firms and Europe's Philips were beginning to concentrate on improving their electronics products and processes, many of whose technologies they had initially received from RCA.

Then, as Robert Sarnoff took command, he was persuaded by André Meyer, a member of the RCA board of directors and senior partner of Lazard Frères and one of the most respected investment bankers of his day, to embark on a second strategy of growth. That was one of product diversification through acquisition of companies whose businesses were only distantly related, if related at all, to the learned technical, functional, and managerial capabilities. In his first annual report as RCA's CEO, that for 1968, Robert announced: "In its formative years RCA's growth depended primarily on a single product or service. . . . The word that best characterizes the modern RCA is diversity." Thus, from the start of his administration Robert Sarnoff embarked on a twofold growth strategy: to challenge IBM's lead in computers; and to make RCA into a conglomerate.[27]

By the early 1970s the implementation of these twin strategies began to demonstrate their inherent weaknesses. What might be termed "the lure of the computer" and the "curse of the conglomerate" provide telling examples of the ways in which learned organizational capabilities define the direction and the limits to growth of industrial enterprises. The lure of the computer emphasizes the difficulty in a high-technology industry of catching up to the first-mover in the technology involved. The curse of the conglomerate indicates how misguided was the assumption that managing a portfolio of companies with different production technologies was similar to managing a portfolio of the securities of such companies. By 1980 it was apparent that together both strategies destroyed RCA and with it nearly all the U.S. consumer electronics industry.

The Lure of the Computer

RCA had developed technical capabilities in electronic data processing before the Sarnoffs decided to challenge IBM. But the learning process had been sporadic and tenuous. Like other high-tech postwar contractors, RCA had built computers for the government, delivering in 1947 an analogue computer to solve simultaneous equations. In 1956 it shipped its first digital analytical computer, the Bizmac, to the U.S. Army to "provide speedy and accurate information on inventories . . . and to compute forecasts of future requirements." Although only six Bizmacs were delivered, the move caused David Sarnoff to set up the Industrial Electronic Data Processing division as a way to begin to build a learning base in this new technology. In 1958 came a radically redesigned Bizmac, RCA's first transistor-powered computer. The next two product lines, based on the Bizmac, were the first designed for the nongovernmental market. Of these, the smaller 501 was a modest operating success, but it was used primarily within RCA itself. The larger 601 mainframe was a technical and financial disaster. After $100 million in development costs, only four machines were delivered. In 1963 came the 3301, "an interim product" to "take the place of the 601."[28]

In December 1964 RCA began its first full-scale move into computers by announcing its new Spectra 70 to supersede the 3301 and to be similar to IBM's System 360, which had been announced earlier that year (as described in chapter 4). The Spectra would be powered by true integrated circuits, perfected after IBM had frozen the design of those used in the System 360. RCA's strategic plan was to build Spectra models that performed at levels between those of the different IBM System 360 models at prices that made their price/performance characteristics superior to those of the IBM model below them. Because the Spectra followed IBM's overall systems layout, its designers hoped that its development costs would be lower and its production time schedule shorter.

For a time the strategy was moderately successful. IBM personnel were hired. Indeed, John Burns, who became president of RCA in 1957 (Sarnoff remained the chief executive), was a leading computer consultant who had worked closely with IBM. The Spectra ran on IBM software, except for its input-output instructions, which had to be "translated." Its processor and much of its other hardware were more advanced than those of IBM. But, as its managers soon learned, IBM's functional capabilities in production and particularly in marketing created formidable barriers to RCA's entry into the computer path of learning.

Nevertheless, because RCA was able to ship its initial products as early as 1966, before IBM's 360 was in full production, the revenues of its computer division rose from approximately $89 million in 1965 to $211 million in 1968. But during those years losses continued. When IBM in 1970 announced its System 370, based on its well-established commercializing processes, RCA countered with a new series, essentially yesterday's technology at lower prices.[29]

It was a futile gesture. Early in 1971 an internal review reported that the company needed an additional $1 billion in new capital by 1976 if it was to remain profitable, and $500 million of this would have to go to computers. One executive responded: "I can think of two dozen things I would rather spend $500 million on." As the senior managers knew, IBM in 1970 had spent $400 million on R&D, about twice the total revenues that RCA received from computers. So in September 1971 Robert Sarnoff sold the company's computer venture to Sperry Rand's UNIVAC division for $250 million.[30]

Clearly RCA simply had neither the time nor the financial resources to create an integrated learning base with the production and marketing capabilities necessary to compete with IBM. The cost of failure was high. At the critical moment when the integrated learning bases of its foreign competitors, Matsushita, Sony, and Philips, were moving into high gear, RCA's consumer electronics were deprived of both essential personnel and funding. As William Webster, the head of the RCA Laboratories after 1968, noted: "We shot a whole generation of research engineering on computers and starved the real cash-cow—color television—to do it."

On a much smaller scale, General Electric's unsuccessful move into computers (also described in chapter 4), at much the same moment and for much the same reasons, also held back the development of General Electric's consumer electronics business. That company had returned to the making of its own radio sets in 1935 and then went into television sets after

World War II. But with the failure of its computer venture, it came to rely increasingly on other manufacturers, particularly Japanese, to produce radio and television products that were sold under the General Electric label.[31]

The Curse of the Conglomerate

The lure of the computer helped to bring down RCA, the definer of the consumer electronics path of learning, and drove out GE, a significant player since the industry's beginning. The curse of the conglomerate finished off RCA, and with it the U.S. consumer electronics industry. In addition, somewhat less blatant unrelated diversification brought down Philco and Sylvania, RCA's two foremost competitors since the 1920s. These two companies were victims of acquisition by diversifiers.

Philco, before its acquisition by the Ford Motor Company in 1961, had made a successful entry into the computer business. Philco, like RCA, had expanded its electronics capabilities in World War II and then had gone into data processing for the military during the Cold War. Philco, unlike RCA and Sylvania, had not been a major producer of vacuum tubes, but after 1952 it began to develop and commercialize transistors on license from AT&T. In 1955 it pioneered in developing the first transistor airborne computer for the air force, and in the next year the "world's first all-transistor computer" for the National Security Agency. Improved products quickly followed. By 1960, writes Kenneth Flamm: "The Philco 210 and 212 were among the largest most powerful computers of their day." Philco not only pioneered in supercomputers for the scientific market, but it also produced transistors, peripherals, and other components for the fledgling computer industry. For example, an infant, Digital Equipment Corporation, used Philco transistors in the first of its PDP series. Philco also continued to be an effective competitor in the related businesses that it had entered in the 1920s—air conditioners and refrigerators—as well as the nation's number two producer of radio and TV sets.[32]

When the Ford Motor Company acquired Philco in 1961, it did so as a means to increase its defense business. Ford placed Philco computer activities in its Space and Defense Division but kept Philco's consumer electronics and household appliances in separate operating units. As Ford managers had little incentive to fund fully the acquired radio and television business, and as they had much less experience than GE and RCA in those fields,

Philco's competitive strength in consumer electronics quickly disintegrated. In 1973 Ford managers decided to spin off most of Philco's activities. They sold its U.S. brand name and its national sales and distribution organization and two of its plants to GTE Sylvania, a wholly owned subsidiary of General Telephone & Electronics (GTE), but they kept Philco's operations in Canada and Latin America. In this way Ford's acquisition of Philco dissolved the organizational capabilities of what was becoming one of the nation's most innovative learning bases in electronics.[33]

Sylvania Electric Products, the nation's second largest producer of consumer electronics components after RCA, had been acquired in 1958 by General Telephone, which had then changed its name to General Telephone & Electronics. General Telephone had begun by merging scattered local phone systems in rural areas during the 1920s and 1930s. By 1950 it had become the largest independent telephone service provider, although it still had only 5 percent of the nation's business. It acquired Sylvania as part of an effort to produce its own switches and other telephone equipment.[34]

As in the case of Ford, GTE's managers paid relatively little attention to Sylvania's R&D and had little commitment to funding it. But unlike the Philco operations at Ford, Sylvania remained an autonomous operating subsidiary, GTE Sylvania Incorporated. It continued to produce lighting products and electrical components and defense communications electronics, as well as to carry on the Philco television activities it had acquired from Ford in 1973. Nevertheless, with little financial and managerial support and commitment during the seventies, Sylvania's television capabilities deteriorated and profits turned into losses. In 1981 GTE sold its holdings in both Philco and Sylvania to Philips North America, the subsidiary of Europe's standard-bearer.

By then RCA's own strategy of diversification through acquisition had decimated the nation's core technical learning base in consumer electronics — the learning base that had since 1920 led the world in commercializing new products and processes. The Sarnoffs had embarked on the strategy of diversification even before Robert took his father's place as chairman and chief executive officer on January 1, 1968. At a time when RCA's research organization was focusing on the Spectra, the Sarnoffs concurred with André Meyer that such acquisitions could provide funding for the computer venture as well as supporting research and development in the company's other high-tech activities. They also agreed that a portfolio of operating companies, like a portfolio of securities, would balance risks involving different businesses and different fluctuations of demand, income, and profits.

In May 1966 the father, David, made the first acquisition, Random House, one of the best-known American publishing houses, headed by Bennett Cerf. Here Sarnoff did make the argument that RCA's business, broadly conceived, was communications and entertainment, so publishing was an activity that RCA understood. But this rationale could hardly cover the purchase early in 1967 (by NBC) of Arnold Palmer Enterprises, marketer of golfing gear and a line of sports clothing. In May of 1967 came a much more massive acquisition, Hertz, the nation's largest car and truck renter. After an attempt in 1968 to take over the St. Regis Paper Company, one of the nation's largest in that industry, RCA in 1969 purchased Alaska Communications Systems from the U.S. Air Force for $28.4 million. Becoming part of RCA's Global Communications Unit, it was the only one of these acquisitions that related closely to RCA's existing capabilities.[35]

Still committed to the computer, RCA management carried out another round of acquisitions in 1970. In March it acquired F. M. Stamper Co. (renamed Banquet Foods), a leading producer of frozen-food packages. In April it acquired Cushman & Wakefield, a New York enterprise with large real estate holdings. In 1970, too, negotiations were begun for the purchase of Coronet Industries, a leading carpet manufacturer, a transaction that was completed in February 1971. With the write-off of the computer venture later in 1971 and the coming of an economic recession, RCA called a halt to major acquisitions except for adding in 1974 two British frozen-food industry producers—Oriel Foods and Morris James Jones, Ltd. But even as early as 1970, RCA's acquisitions, although paid for by exchanges of stock and the sale of bonds, had raised the company's debt from $266.4 million in 1966 to $973.5 million in 1970.[36]

By 1974 RCA's balance sheets began to reveal the disastrously high costs of implementing the two strategies of growth. Appendix 2:2 indicates their impact on the nation's leading consumer electronics enterprise. Net income from consumer electronics dropped from $57.7 million in 1972 to $48 million in 1973. After plummeting to $11.1 million in 1974, it rose again to $25.1 million in 1975, out of a total net income of $158.1 million, $183.7 million, $111.3 million, and $111.0 million. Thus by 1975 consumer electronics accounted for only slightly less than a quarter of RCA's net income, Hertz slightly more, and broadcasting equal to their combined income (appendix 2.2). The rest came from communications systems, a small amount of government business, and "others" (not defined), including Coronet and other smaller acquisitions.[37]

Its declining income and rising debt were accompanied by loss of market share. The most severe losses occurred in "commercial electronics," which included broadcasting equipment, TV tubes, and components for color and cable TV and communications systems. At the same time, interest expenses rose, reaching $55.6 million in 1974 and $62.0 million in 1975. More ominously, Japanese firms were launching their powerful drive into U.S. and then European markets, as described in detail in chapter 3.

The collapse of Robert Sarnoff's strategies of growth led the RCA board to remove him as CEO in November 1975. His immediate successor, Anthony Conrad, planned to sell off most of the recent acquisitions except Hertz, but he was forced to leave the company in September 1976 because of his failure to pay his personal income tax. His successor as CEO, Edward Griffiths, who had been the head of the electronics division, focused on cost cutting and downsizing. He sold off RCA's X-ray business, aircraft radar, land mobile radios, and some of its commercial products. But, in his cost cutting, Griffiths concentrated on consumer electronics, including the closing down of the Harrison, New Jersey, tube plant (taking a $40 million write-off). He did so just at the moment that RCA's Japanese competitors, led by Matsushita, were investing heavily in both physical and human capital in the improvement of existing consumer products. Griffiths's efforts did, however, succeed in impressively raising RCA's revenues and profits in 1977 and 1978.[38]

Nevertheless, Griffiths remained a conglomerator. His model was Harold Geneen, whose doctrine of management by the numbers and growth through unrelated acquisitions had made him an icon in the financial community. (In passing, I mention that Geneen's use of this strategy at ITT, the 1926 spin-off of Western Electric's international operations, led to the quick demise of this company's integrated learning base in international telephone equipment.) In 1978 Griffiths hired Maurice Valente, a fourteen-year veteran of ITT and its executive vice president, to be RCA's president. At the same time, Griffiths was planning to purchase a financial services company, which, like Hertz, would be a source of retained earnings to finance current and future operations.

Valente lasted only a few months as president, but the search for another major acquisition led Griffiths to the purchase of a financial conglomerate,

CIT Financial Corporation, a purchase that included taking over CIT's debt of $4.7 billion. That enterprise operated several savings and loan companies, a major life and health insurance firm, a maker of office furniture and electric outlet boxes, and a leading greeting card company. To fund this transaction, Griffiths sold off Alaska Communications in June 1979 and Random House in early 1981, then the frozen-food businesses, and then the greeting card and electric outlet box companies. These sales did little to reduce RCA's huge consolidated debt of $2.6 billion in 1981 ($1.4 billion of which belonged to Hertz), which contrasted sharply with RCA's listing of $1.1 billion (including Hertz's $422 million) of consolidated debt in 1975.

By 1981 the board had had enough. On July 1, 1981, it replaced Griffiths as chairman and chief executive officer at RCA. His successor was Thornton Bradshaw, a longtime board member and the chairman of Atlantic Richfield, a corporate descendant of John D. Rockefeller's Standard Oil. By then RCA's core learning base in consumer electronic products was collapsing. In 1980 it accounted for only 13 percent of RCA's profits. That year 43 percent came from Hertz and CIT's financial services. The rest came from broadcasting, commercial electronics and communications, government business, and licensing.[39]

Nevertheless, the consumer electronics division's top executives still had high hopes of recovery. Their hopes rested on success in commercializing a videocassette recorder based on their new videodisk technology, even though by the mid-1970s RCA had fallen behind its competitors—Philips, Matsushita, and Sony—in this critical technological race.

In reality, RCA had already lost that race by 1981. Because the outcome of that contest assured Japan's overwhelming dominance in today's consumer electronics business and because RCA's role and its ultimate failure can be understood only in relation to the activities of its major competitors, I review in chapter 3 the details of that path-defining story. The remainder of this chapter describes the evolution of RCA and the U.S. consumer electronics industry in the aftermath of this contest.

RCA Disintegrates: The Japanese Move In

When Thornton Bradshaw took office at RCA in 1981, he and his managers were still optimistic. One of Bradshaw's main objectives was "to refocus the company on its three core businesses—electronics, communications, and entertainment." To do so, Bradshaw would put CIT Financial, Hertz, and Coronet Industries up for sale. But first he had to fight off a takeover threat headed by William Agee, whose takeover talents as head of the Bendix Corporation had led to Allied Chemical's disintegration as a major chemical company. In 1983 Bradshaw successfully disposed of Hertz and CIT. But by then it was far too late to revive RCA's core capabilities in consumer electronics. Early in 1984 Bradshaw had shut down its VideoDisc project, on which the company had lost more than $500 million.[40]

Bradshaw, who had already announced his coming retirement, began negotiations in the autumn of 1986 for the sale of RCA's consumer electronics division and NBC to General Electric. This acquisition was arranged by Felix Rohatyn, the senior partner of Lazard Frères. The sale price was $6.28 billion—$66.50 a share. Jack Welch, GE's CEO, remarked: "Maybe two American manufacturers can together beat the competition. . . . We will have the technological capabilities, the financial resources, and the global scope to be able to compete successfully with anyone, anywhere, in every market we serve."[41]

Eighteen months later, in 1988, Welch swapped RCA's consumer electronics division for the medical diagnostics business of France's Thomson SA plus $800 million in cash from the French company. By then Welch had shut down or sold off the RCA units that Bradshaw had not been able to dispose of, including Coronet, Nacolah (a life insurance business), RCA Records, the existing NBC radio network, and the RCA New Products division. He retained the profitable NBC division. Welch then donated the RCA Laboratories at Princeton to Stanford University and added a commitment of $250 million spread over five years to support research.

Welch's biographer reports, "The Thomson-S.A. swap was, Welch said, 'the chance of a lifetime.' The opportunity to dump one of the businesses Welch liked least, Consumer Electronics, and to pick up a potential jewel for GE's crown."[42]

Welch's evaluation, made without a note of irony in the light of his comments upon acquiring RCA, was a fitting epitaph for the U.S. consumer electronics business. After 1981 only one sizable American producer of TV sets remained, Zenith. Between 1984 and 1994 Zenith showed a net income in only one year, 1988, when it reported income of $5 million on sales of $2.7 billion. In 1986 Zenith, the one remaining U.S.-owned and -operated company, enjoyed all of 15.8 percent of the U.S. color television receiving set market; France's Thomson SA, 17.5 percent; Philips's U.S. acquisitions, just under 10 percent; the Korean companies, 3.1 percent; and the Japanese companies, close to 50 percent (table 2.1, page 32—it does not record Matsushita's sales of sets to GE to be sold over the GE label). As Zenith had neither the technical nor the functional capabilities needed to remain a profit-producing enterprise, Welch's sale of RCA's consumer electronics division to Thomson SA marks the death of the U.S. consumer electronics industry.[43]

The rest of the U.S. consumer electronics industry had already succumbed to the foreign onslaught by the time Bradshaw had become chairman and CEO of RCA. Between 1974 and 1981 the smaller U.S. radio and television firms were swallowed up by foreign competitors. The buy-outs began in 1974 when Philips acquired Magnavox (as well as Philco and Sylvania in January 1981) and Matsushita acquired Motorola's Quasar production and distribution facilities. By then Japan's giant Matsushita, which had in the 1960s and early 1970s built an extensive organization in the United States to distribute and market its Panasonic brand, was supplying GE with its television products on an OEM (original equipment manufacturer) basis. In 1976 Sanyo, which since 1963 had been Sears Roebuck's primary supplier of television equipment, acquired full control of Warwick, which had replaced Colonial as Sears's U.S. assembler. In the same year Emerson Electric sold Sanyo the controlling interest in its Fisher Radio Division (chapter 3, page 68). Emerson had acquired Fisher in 1969 but had been unable to stay Fisher's rapidly increasing loss of market share and revenue. In 1978 Rockwell International, a defense-related conglomerate, spun off parts of Admiral (which it had acquired in 1974), selling off Admiral's Mexican operations to a Mexican company, those in the Far East to a Taiwanese company, and the rest to a Canadian company.[44]

Acquisitions provided one form of entry into the U.S. market. The other was direct foreign investment. In these same years several Japanese producers were building American manufacturing facilities. Sony led the way in 1972 with the construction of a large color television plant in California with an annual output of 450,000 units. The leading multipathed Japanese electrical engineering computer companies, which were already moving into the production of color television, entered a little later. In 1978 Toshiba built its

200,000-unit color television plant in Tennessee, and Mitsubishi Engineering built its 120,000-unit plant in California. Three years later Hitachi completed its 100,000-unit works in California, and the Sharp Corporation, the strongest Japanese challenger to Matsushita and Sony, built a 120,000-unit facility, also in California. By the end of the decade the Japanese-owned companies equipped with the newest manufacturing and processing equipment dominated American consumer electronics (see pages 58–59).[45]

These Japanese companies were much larger than the U.S. firms they purchased. Unlike the Japanese companies and Philips, the U.S. makers (except for RCA) were largely single-product enterprises, makers of receiving sets or tubes or other components. Their functional capabilities were based on that one product or very limited product lines. They did not benefit from economies of scale and scope or from the financial resources that their acquirers enjoyed. Because of RCA's long-established licensing policy, that enterprise remained the source of the U.S. industry's technical capabilities. For much the same reasons, no large supporting nexus of small independent enterprises developed in the United States. So when RCA collapsed, so did the U.S. consumer electronics industry as a whole.

The Causes of Death

RCA's attempt to challenge IBM's System 360 and at the same time to follow the corporate fashion of the time by becoming a conglomerate were the major factors in the disintegration of RCA and, with it, the death of the U.S. consumer electronics industry. Nevertheless, there was a more fundamental reason that reflects the basic concepts of this book. In market economies, the competitive strength of industrial firms rests on learned organizational capabilities. These capabilities in turn begin with the creation of a learning base that integrates the technical and functional capabilities required to commercialize for global markets the products of a new technology and to enhance those of existing technologies.

RCA did not have an integrated learning base until the 1930s, after its acquisition of Victor Talking Machine. From its beginnings in 1919 until the 1930s, it controlled the flow of U.S. radio technology through its monopoly of patents; yet it had no research facilities essential for the development of its own technical capabilities. It sold radios but had no development or manufacturing facilities essential to building its functional capabilities. That learning occurred at the radio production units of General Electric and Westinghouse. Since RCA only marketed its products, produced in different distant locations, it acquired little learning in the essential activity of guiding the flow of products from their initial concept to its final market.

In addition, RCA's control of patents had deprived other U.S. enterprises of the application of new technological learning from developing new products or processes. As a result of this limited learning base, most U.S. companies remained single-sector specialists producing receivers or components.

Once it had an integrated learning base, RCA did begin in the 1930s to commercialize new technologies by expanding the former Westinghouse research unit in New York City. Nevertheless, the continuing enhancement of product development and production capabilities remained based in the leading operating units of its predecessors, at the plants that it had acquired from General Electric, Westinghouse, and Victor.

At the moment that television reached the market in 1940, the demands of World War II transformed the RCA research learning base by expanding the number and variety of products produced. Of critical importance, to meet these war demands, Sarnoff built the RCA Laboratories in Princeton; its plural name signifies the range of the electric products initially developed. For during their initial years, they developed military and industrial as well as consumer electronics. As significant, the new RCA Laboratories from the start were given the responsibility for and financial control over all RCA's research work. Although the budgets of the operating units allocated funds for product development, this sharply defined administrative and financial distinction between the roles of the central laboratories and those of the operating divisions clearly hindered the essential integration between research and development so critical to commercializing a new technology for global markets.

During Sarnoff's focused commitment to commercializing black-and-white television, reflecting his total drive, his betting of the company, on color television, the potential inherent conflicts with RCA's management rarely appeared. But with the search for new strategy, the entrance into the computer path, and the decision to become a conglomerate, the coordination of this division of administrative and financial control raised continuing sets of difficulties that were at the base of the failure of RCA's videodisk project. If RCA had resisted the lure of the computer and avoided the curse of the conglomerate, if it had continued to concentrate, as did its Japanese competitors, on the consumer electronics market, the one that it knew best, then it might have remained the industry's path definer. Instead, RCA failed and the Japanese quickly ascended as the dominant commercializers of consumer electronics.

3

CONSUMER ELECTRONICS: JAPAN'S

PATHS TO GLOBAL CONQUEST

As the critical contest to commercialize the videocassette recorder began in 1970, RCA had fully embarked on its disastrous strategies. At the same time, the two Japanese leaders, Matsushita and Sony, had fully established their integrated learning bases and were taking the initial steps to expand their penetration into the U.S. and then the European markets. The organizational capabilities that had evolved through cumulative learning in improving existing and commercializing new technologies provided models of competitive success in global markets. Matsushita's experience exemplifies the model of successful creation and enhancement of functional capabilities. Sony's experience is a model of becoming a path definer by integrating technical with functional capabilities. Few enterprises have been more successful in commercializing a succession of major new technologies.

The evolution of the European consumer electronics industry provides still another perspective. After World War II, Philips Incandescent Lamp Works developed close ties with both of the Japanese first-movers. From the 1950s on it provided Matsushita with its technical knowledge in return for

35 percent of Matsushita's equity. In the 1970s it became Sony's partner in commercializing the new disk technology. Nevertheless, Philips was unable to build a consumer electronics business large enough to provide the economies of scale and scope comparable to those of the Japanese firms, or to attract a supporting nexus of small and large enterprises comparable to that on the island of Honshu.

Therefore, this chapter begins by describing the evolution of Japan's two path definers before the coming of the global VCR race. That race, in turn, marked the beginnings of the global dominance of Japan's consumer electronics industry and the end of the U.S. industry's capabilities to commercialize new technology and improve existing ones. By the late 1970s that contest had become one between the two Japanese leaders, Matsushita's Video Home System and Sony's better-performing Beta. Both were based on the development and commercialization of a new tape technology.

After reviewing the details of the winning strategy that eventually eliminated the U.S. industry from world markets, I consider Sony's success, as it worked with Philips, in creating and bringing to market the new disk technology that produced the audio compact disk (CD), the CD-ROM (combining both consumer electronics and computer technologies), and finally in the 1990s the digital videodisk (DVD), I next describe the evolution of Japan's two major consumer electronics followers—Sanyo and Sharp. Then, after considering Philips's inability to maintain its competitive functional and technical capabilities in consumer electronics, I observe the French government's futile attempt to build a global enterprise by acquiring RCA and a number of smaller European musical recording enterprises.

MATSUSHITA: CREATING COMPETITIVE FUNCTIONAL CAPABILITIES

Konosuke Matsushita entered the radio path of learning after creating an organization to market electrically powered consumer products. He formed his first establishment in 1918 in Osaka. His initial product was an electric bicycle lamp that he assembled using batteries and components. To sell his products, he went directly to retail bicycle dealers. By 1928 his monthly output had climbed to thirty thousand lamps and by 1930 to fifty thousand. As his retail distribution and marketing capabilities grew apace, the company began to market in volume electric irons, home heaters, other plugged-in electric appliances, dry-cell batteries, and, after 1930, radios and tubes. All were identified with the National brand name. By 1931 the company had acquired manufacturing enterprises to supply its National marketing network.[1]

By 1933 Matsushita's volume was large enough to permit the company to pioneer in the creation of a multidivisional management structure. The enterprise consisted of three autonomous divisions, each with its own integrated learning base, in three product sectors—one for lamps and dry-cell batteries; another for irons, heaters, and other plug-in electrical devices; and then for the youngest National line, the tube-based radio. The managers of these divisions had full responsibility for operations and profit and loss. In December 1935 their company was incorporated as the Matsushita Electric Industrial Company (MEI).[2]

When World War II brought government control, MEI appears to have continued to produce much the same products, but unlike the U.S. electronics companies and Japan Victor, RCA's former Japanese subsidiary that Matsushita would soon acquire, it did not enhance its electronic capabilities through war production. Instead, the military assigned it to produce wooden ships and propellers for reasons not explained in readily available sources. At the war's end, Matsushita's primary set of capabilities remained in distribution and marketing. Then in April 1950 the Allied Occupation authorities with their antitrust commitment split the firm into two independent enterprises, Sanyo Electric Industrial headed by Konosuke Matsushita's brother-in-law, and his own Matsushita Electric Industrial Company.[3]

With the coming of the Korean War and the end of the Occupation, Konosuke Matsushita once again became the senior executive at MEI. He reinstated the divisional system, putting himself in charge of the radio and vacuum tube division. Following a trip to the United States in 1951, he laid out his strategic plans to create a learning base in consumer electronics as well as to rebuild his earlier one in consumer electrical appliances. His first move came in 1952 with the formation of a joint venture with Philips called Matsushita Electronics, of which Philips held 35 percent until 1992. Philips provided the technology for, and Matsushita the management of, the new company, whose plant in Osaka was soon producing radio tubes, other radio components, and fluorescent lights on the basis of Philips's technical capabilities.

Konosuke's next step came in 1954, when his company, after setting up its first research and development laboratory, acquired 50 percent of the Japan Victor Company (JVC), the only advanced, well-established, integrated learning base in consumer electronics that had existed in Japan before World War

II. As described in chapter 2, RCA acquired JVC in 1929 as part of its U.S. parent company, American Victor. In the 1930s this integrated enterprise became an effective Japanese learning base, as 541 of its 555 employees were Japanese. In 1937 RCA, under strong pressure from Japan's government and business community, sold off its equity in JVC, which in turn was eventually acquired in 1940 by Shibaura Electric, which in turn sold it in 1952 to Matsushita.

Matsushita wisely kept JVC as an autonomous integrated learning base to provide it with "managerial direction and capital infusions." As Asia's only prewar learning base that integrated technical capabilities with functional ones, JVC focused increasingly on the commercialization of new consumer electronics products, including stereo phonographs in 1957, audiotape recorders and color TVs in the 1960s, and VCRs in the 1970s. Meanwhile the parent company, relying on Philips's technical expertise, concentrated primarily on enhancing its processes of mass production and global mass marketing, thereby benefiting from powerful economies of scale. As Matsushita was entering the consumer electronics path of learning created by Philips and RCA, it also began in 1954 to expand its electrical appliance base with the acquisition of one of Japan's leading producers of refrigerators, and the expansion of its older lines in batteries, lamps, wiring, and insulation.[4]

Matsushita had implemented its basic growth strategy just as Japan's urban and suburban housing and its broader urban and industrial construction industry entered a continuous period of boom. Encouraged, Konosuke Matsushita announced in January 1956 plans to quadruple the company's sales in five years. As the output of its electrical equipment product sectors soared, the company added washing machines, vacuum cleaners, and then in 1960 air conditioners to its prewar line of household appliances. It also expanded into personal items such as hair dryers and shavers.

In anticipation of this growth, it began in 1964 to enlarge its prewar distribution network of franchise dealers as well as its own exclusive chain of retail stores. The result was, in Mark Fruin's words, "a formidable national sales-force of 9 regional-sales offices, 19 branch-sales offices, 620 distributors, and 33,000 federated retail outlets." This was as massive an integrated marketing organization as any developed by American and European manufacturers in their home markets.[5]

At first Matsushita concentrated on the Japanese market with its National brand, remaining the leader in its markets, including radio and television. In 1959 it began moving overseas by building its own marketing organization in the United States to sell and distribute its products under the brand name Panasonic. A second Panasonic organization for Europe quickly followed. In 1968 JVC established a U.S. subsidiary (JVC America) and in 1971 a West German one (Nippon Victor [Europe] GmbH), in order to continue to market its lower-volume, more specialized, higher-quality products separately from the parent. There is little available in English on the building of these global marketing organizations, but clearly the creation of the impressive organization in Japan itself provided learning for Matsushita's swift and successful development of distribution and marketing networks in the United States and then in Europe.[6]

In 1960 Matsushita also turned to computers, joining the efforts of the Ministry of International Trade and Industry (MITI) to develop a Japanese computer industry (as described in chapter 6). But with the announcement in 1964 of IBM's system 360, it withdrew from those cooperative efforts. In the same years, therefore, as RCA began to challenge IBM at the cost of $1.4 billion and acquire business enterprises unrelated to their core capabilities for another billion or so, Matsushita began to plow back earnings into its consumer electronics products and processes.

In the 1960s, to meet the growing demand for its products, Matsushita built plants in Taiwan and the Philippines as wage scales and other costs rose rapidly in Japan. As European demand increased, Matsushita completed other plants in Great Britain and Spain. In the 1960s Matsushita was leading the Japanese invasion of the U.S. color television market as well as the smaller market in Europe. By 1965 imports of radios into U.S. markets were already impressive. But those of color television had not yet begun (appendix 3.1). By 1975, however, U.S. color TV imports had risen to a value of $200 million. In 1974 Matsushita further expanded its market share by acquiring Motorola's Quasar. By then Matsushita was also providing its products to General Electric on an OEM basis—that is, to be sold over the GE brand name. This addition to its Panasonic brand and its recently acquired Quasar brand meant that in 1975 Matsushita was supplying more than 8 percent of the U.S. color TV market, as well as a larger share of radio and black-and-white television sets.

SONY: CREATING COMPETITIVE TECHNICAL CAPABILITIES

In these same years that Matsushita was perfecting its functional capabilities—product development, production, and marketing and distribution—Sony was cultivating its technical capabilities in applied research and advancing its product development capabilities. In the 1950s Sony commercialized Japan's first audiotape recorder and became the world's first-mover in miniaturization technologies. In the 1960s it led the way in bringing integrated circuit technology to Japan and produced the Sony Trinitron color television. In the late 1970s it introduced its Walkman, the culmination of its capabilities in miniaturization and tape technology. In the 1980s it took the lead in a new disk technology by commercializing the CD, the CD-ROM, and in the 1990s the digital videodisk.[7]

In 1946 Akio Morita and Masaru Ibuka formed a partnership, Tokyo Telecommunications Engineering Co., Ltd., in war-devastated Tokyo. Before 1953 they had produced Japan's first audio magnetic tape recorder. In 1953 they acquired from Western Electric for $25,000 one of the very first licenses issued to foreign firms to produce the transistor. From the start, under the technologically talented Ibuka, the company focused on the opportunities for miniaturization. In 1955 it became the first to mass-produce small transistor radios, which it sold under the trade name Sony. That product's success, particularly in the U.S. market, gave the company its name in 1957. By 1959 Sony had introduced the first transistor-based microtelevision receiving set.

As Sony's technical capabilities expanded, so did its marketing and distribution capabilities. From the start Morita had his eyes on the overseas market. In 1955 Morita had traveled to New York, where he rejected an initial offer by Bulova Watch to sell one hundred thousand radios under its label. He turned instead to distribute and sell his own brand through a large retail chain, Delmonico International. With the introduction of a portable micro-TV, Morita again visited New York in 1960. Aware of the importance of integrating distribution with production, Morita ended the agreement with Delmonico and spent two years in the early 1960s setting up a U.S. sales subsidiary, the Sony Corporation of America. He then created a comparable marketing and distribution organization for Europe, Sony Overseas, based in Switzerland.[8]

During the 1960s, as its output of radio and television sets as well as audiotape recorders rose swiftly and steadily, Sony enhanced its learning base by integrating backward to create Sony Chemicals to produce plastic and adhesives, and by forming a joint venture with a Japanese firm to make oscilloscopes. Of more importance, Sony's engineers concentrated on improving components whose patents had been licensed from RCA. One result was the introduction in 1968 of the Trinitron television tube, which was superior to

RCA's tricolor tube, the latter a symbol of U.S. mass production in consumer electronics. Sony's Trinitron quickly became color television's most successful product. In 1972 Sony built a new television plant with an annual production of 450,000 units in California. By 1975 Sony already had 5.8 percent of the U.S. color television market (table 2:1).[9]

In 1968 Sony also negotiated a set of agreements with the American firm Texas Instruments that permitted all Japanese electronics firms to license Texas Instruments's integrated circuits. Sony then immediately applied the new technology to improve its production processes. Other Japanese electronics firms followed suit. They did so, in the words of Gene Gregory's study of Japanese electronic technology, by "maximum application of solid-state technology to reduce the number of components used in the final product; design changes which reduce the number and complexity of assembly operations; and extensive automation, which reduces the number of workers required." (For Sony's negotiations with TI, see page 125.)[10]

Also in 1968, Sony entered the industry's one nontechnical path, the recording sector, still based on the vinyl disk, by forming a fifty-fifty joint venture with CBS, Sony/CBS Records. With all this accomplished, Morita and his senior managers turned to commercializing a basic new product, the videotape, pitched for the market created by the booming sales of color television.

Commercializing the Videocassette Recorder

The initial efforts to develop a video recording device had begun in the United States at RCA. It was one of Sarnoff's three postwar goals set for the RCA Laboratories to develop a device to provide for prerecordings of television broadcasts. This was the project, described in chapter 2, developed by the Advanced Development Group at Camden and that was canceled by the Princeton Laboratories. Ampex, a California start-up, used much the same technology to introduce successfully a prerecording device in 1956. After Ampex had produced fifty thousand machines, RCA signed a cross-licensing agreement with it that divided the commercial TV broadcasting market, two-thirds going to Ampex and one-third to RCA.[11]

In the late 1960s Sony and Matsushita's JVC began to concentrate on miniaturizing the large Ampex recorder, which sold for over $50,000 apiece. In 1970 Sony and Matsushita signed a cross-licensing agreement. In the next year Sony succeeded in designing a cassette-based model using a three-fourths-inch tape named the U-Matic for the home market. Then, on the basis of this standard, Sony commercialized its Betamax format and JVC its Video Home System (VHS) format.

In 1970 two other Japanese companies, Sanyo and Toshiba (a computer maker), formed a partnership toward the same end, and Philips began to develop its V-2000 format. RCA never got beyond producing a prototype tape-based videocassette. RCA turned instead to developing a radically different proprietary product, one based on a capacitance disk rather than on a cassette. Philips also turned to a new optical disk, as it was continuing to develop its V-2000 tape cassette. By 1975 the competitive battle for the videocassette recorder had narrowed to four contestants: Sony's Betamax, JVC's VHS, Philips's V-2000, and RCA's VideoDisc.[12]

By 1975 Sony had introduced its elegant Betamax, a triumph of technical capabilities. Matsushita, after turning down Sony's proposal to adopt the Beta standard, held off for another year until it could begin to mass-produce its Video Home System. Sony entered the marketplace first, produced a superior product, and increased its playing time from one to two hours. Nevertheless, Matsushita's functional capabilities permitted it to win the race. Indeed, by 1984 VHS outsold Betamax by four to one. By that time the overwhelming market success of Matsushita's VHS also doomed both RCA's VideoDisc and Philips's disk and tape ventures. How then did Matsushita achieve this smashing victory?

That victory was based on strategic use of its functional capabilities and financial resources. Table 3.1 records the results of what can be termed Matsushita's OEM (original equipment manufacturer) strategy. Matsushita and its subsidary JVC commercialized the VHS—that is, they brought it to market—with JVC concentrating on its initial product development and Matsushita on its advanced engineering. Matsushita focused on the American market through its Panasonic sales and distribution organization as well as that of Quasar, recently acquired from Motorola. JVC's European organization did the same in Europe. Both continued to supply the domestic market through their existing outlets.

Next, Matsushita licensed the two other leading Japanese producers of consumer electronics, Tokyo Sanyo and Sharp. (At this time Sanyo was divided into two companies; I review their histories shortly.) In addition, two computer makers that were beginning to make televisions, Hitachi and Mit-

TABLE 3.1. Matsushita OEM Strategy
Group Alignments of VCR Formats, 1983–1984

Function	Japan	United States	Europe
VHS Group (38 Companies)			
Develop, Produce, & Market	JVC Matsushita		
Produce & Market	Sharp Hitachi Mitsubishi Electric Tokyo Sanyo		
Market	Brother (MI) Ricoh (H) Tokyo Juki (H) Canon (MA) Asahi Optical (H) Olympus (MA) Nikon (MA) Akai Trio (J) Sansui (J) Clarion (J) Teac (J) Japan Columbia (H)	Magnavox (MA) Sylvania (MA) GE (MA) Curtis Mathes (MA) J. C. Penney (MA) RCA (H) Sears (H) Zenith (J)	Blaupunkt (MA) Saba (J) SEL (J) Nordmende (J) Telefunken (J) Thorn-EMI (J) Thomson-Brandt (J) Granada (H) Hangard (H) Sarolla (H) Fisher (T) Luxer (MI)
Beta Group (12 Companies)			
Develop, Produce, & Market	Sony		
Produce & Market	Sanyo Toshiba NEC		
Market	General (TO) Aiwa Pioneer (S)	Zenith (S) Sears (SA)	Kneckerman (SA) Fisher (SA) Rank (TO)
V-2000 Group (7 Companies)			
Develop, Produce, & Market			Philips
Produce & Market			Grundig
Market			Siemens (G) ITT (G) Loewe Opta (G) Lorting (P) B&O (P)

Source: Michael A. Cusumano, Viorgos Mylonadis, and Richard S. Rosenbloom, "Strategic Maneuvering and Mass-Market Dynamics: The Triumph of VHS over Beta," *Business History Review,* 66, no. 1 (Spring 1992): 73 (table 5), with permission. To be cited from this source.

Note: Suppliers are indicated by initials: J = JVC, MA = Matsushita, H = Hitachi, MI = Mitsubishi, T = Tokyo Sanyo, S = Sony, TO = Toshiba, SA = Sanyo, P = Philips, G = Grundig.

Matsushita and its subsidiary, JVC, developed, produced, and marketed the VHS. Sharp, Hitachi, Mitsubishi Electric, and Tokyo Sanyo manufactured and marketed it. The rest sold the VHS over their own labels. Sony commercialized the Beta, the three computer makers produced and marketed it. The others were marketing outlets. Philips and its subsidiary Grundig commercialized the V-2000. The rest were marketing outlets. The companies listed in the table represent nearly all the significant players in the industry worldwide. In spring 1984 Zenith switched from the Beta group to VHS.

subishi Electric, were called on to volume-produce and -market the VHS through their global distribution organizations. In other words, the VHS was produced, distributed, and marketed by six Japanese companies and one Japanese-owned American company, each with its own integrated learning base: Matsushita, JVC, Sharp, Tokyo Sanyo, Hitachi, Mitsubishi Electric, and Quasar.

The major producers of the rest of the world then obtained the VHSs on an OEM basis—that is, they sold the products they received from their suppliers over their own label, as one of their own products. Table 3.1 lists these suppliers. In the United States these potential marketing outlets included General Electric; RCA; Philips's Magnavox and Sylvania; two mass retailers, J. C. Penney and Sears; and a niche producer, Curtis Mathes. In Europe, JVC's marketing organization and that of Hitachi became the primary VHS suppliers (table 3.1) to Europe's foremost electronics companies. In Japan, Matsushita had its own marketing force, while in the United States and Europe, it had its own Panasonic marketing force and, by 1975, the marketing force of its acquisition, Quasar.

To meet this onslaught, Sony had only one worldwide integrated production and marketing organization. Moreover, as Sony's chairman, Akio Morita, had declared in 1976: "Sony is not an OEM manufacturer."[13] Nevertheless, as table 3.1 shows, it did follow Matsushita's lead, signing up two major Japanese computer companies, Toshiba and NEC, as well as Sanyo (Tokyo Sanyo's allied enterprise), to volume-produce and -market the Betamax, as well as Sears, Roebuck; Zenith; and three electronics companies in Europe to market it. The third contender in the videotape recorder battle, Philips, along with its smaller ally, Grundig, supplied its V-2000 on an OEM basis to five European companies.

Matsushita's OEM strategy had a twofold impact. First, it assured that Matsushita would benefit as fully as possible from the resulting powerful economies of scale and scope in both production and distribution. Second, it prevented its non-Japanese rivals from continuing to experiment in producing and marketing a major innovation of their own.

As emphasized in the excellent analysis of the Matsushita/Sony rivalry by Cusumano, Mylonadis, and Rosenbloom, Matsushita succeeded "by utilizing its huge engineering and manufacturing resources to offer a product line with more combinations of features and prices. Compared to Sony, Matsushita introduced both less and more expensive VCRs between 1978 and

1981 and manufactured about twice the number of model types Sony produced during the same time period."[14]

As the authors further note, Matsushita also "made low cost production a major priority as it modified the VHS design and prepared its own plants. . . . Matsushita not only emphasized a reduction in parts but also invested in manufacturing automation and scheduled large production runs, anticipating that its vast distribution system would enable it to sell a great number of VCRs." Matsushita's ability to deliver low-priced VCRs with an increasing variety of features permitted it to undercut Sony's prices and win contracts to supply machines to overseas distributors—arrangements that further increased Matsushita's scale of operations and provided it with funds for additional investments in product improvement and automation.

At a critical moment in carrying out its strategy, Matsushita received an unintended boost from RCA that ironically assured its success. When Edward Griffiths became RCA's CEO in the fall of 1976, he called for a review of its videodisk project, which was falling behind that of its major challenger, Philips. The senior managers involved still assumed that the videodisk was superior to the videotape. Griffiths asked them if it made sense to continue. The project's supporters argued with passion that they "wished to keep open a continuing source of leading technology in the future." One executive wrote in his response, "In recent years our technical image has been somewhat tarnished. We have gone out of one electronic business after another, from computers to audio. Success in a high technology business would arrest this decline." Moreover, as reported by Margaret Graham, they argued that the success of their videodisk would keep the Japanese videotapes out of the huge U.S. mass market, one in which Beta in 1976 had not yet become an obvious challenger. If the videodisk launch could come quickly, the Japanese cassette onslaught could be met. The vote at the final meeting was one in favor of withdrawal, five abstentions, and eleven for continuing the program. Griffiths agreed to continue the project until the spring of 1978. As a compromise measure, while waiting for its completion, "RCA would negotiate with Matsushita for a videotape recorder that it could market through its own (RCA) dealer network as soon as possible."[15]

The product development unit at RCA's Indianapolis radio and television plant first approached JVC but quickly learned that JVC did not have the manufacturing capabilities to supply the volume and price range that it wanted. In February 1977 the group turned to Matsushita's other learning base, Matsushita Electronics, to the product development engineers with whom it had long been in contact, requesting a three-hour tape that "could record a football game." In late March Matsushita's engineers agreed on a crash program to supply RCA with approximately 50,000 four-hour tapes by the end of the year. Even before the four-hour tapes came onstream, RCA's consumer electronics division was reporting "astonishing success in marketing Matsushita's VHS format player." In this way RCA itself assisted in the successful implementation of Matsushita's strategic plan for global domination, a plan under which Matsushita captured not only the U.S. market, but also Europe's. This unintended irony resulted from the fact that RCA from the start had concentrated on the disk technology and had no choice but to go to Matsushita for the development of a tape product.[16]

As Gene Gregory indicates, the years 1978 and 1979 were a critical period of transition for Japanese electronics-based industries. In consumer electronics, "video tape recorders replaced color television as the principal export item. Moreover, since exports of videotape recorders to Europe are growing much faster than those to the United States, for the first time Europe . . . emerged as the major growth market for Japanese consumer electronics products." In fact, Japanese exports of VCRs rose from 973,000 units in 1978, of which 60 percent were exported to North America and 28 percent to Europe, to 15.2 million units in 1983, with 41 percent going to North America and 38 percent to Europe.[17]

The unexpectedly swift growth of the video market during the first years of the 1980s doomed both Sony and Philips as competitors in videotapes and destroyed the RCA and Philips videodisk challenge. The continuing demand for prerecorded tapes of television and movie programs and the rapid rise of rental stores as a new outlet were responsible for Matsushita's soaring VHS sales from 1982 to 1984. In 1984 the shift of Zenith from Beta to VHS marked the end of the Beta in the U.S. market. In that same year, RCA's CEO, Thornton Bradshaw, shut down RCA's videodisk project. Only 550,000 units had been sold—at a loss of more than $500 million. Philips had already abandoned both its videodisk and videotape projects the year before and had licensed the VHS technology from Matsushita Electronics, in which it still held 35 percent of equity.[18]

Consider the implications of Matsushita's OEM strategy. First and most important, it intentionally set the standard for videotape cassettes worldwide. In addition to setting the standards worldwide for the videocassette, it deprived its Japanese rivals of the learning experience of expanding their production and marketing capabilities. It also brought Japanese computer makers, but not foreign computer makers, into the production and marketing of consumer electronics.

Finally, Matsushita's OEM VCR strategy had by 1985 all but assured Japan's conquest of world markets in electronics. For example, Appendix 3:1 lists the value of imports and exports into and from the United States of the three major consumer electronics products. By far the largest amount of imports were produced by Japanese companies. By 1985 the Japanese dominance in videotape recorders produced imports into the United States valued at $4.65 billion. This figure was more than twice the value of color television's imports of $1.1 billion and radio's $0.6 billion. Moreover, by 1985 the major share of U.S. exports was produced by Japanese-owned factories.

Matsushita and Sony after the VCR battle

Matsushita's functional capabilities, not its technical competencies, had led to the victory over Sony. But Sony, not Matsushita, was the long-term victor in the battle to commercialize the VCR. After its triumph, Matsushita used its superior functional capabilities and worldwide facilities to produce and market a range of electronic-based products. For through the years it had received its technical knowledge from Philips. Sony, on the other hand, focused on using its superior technical capabilities. Even before the defeat of its Beta, Sony had begun working with Europe's Philips on the first step to commercialize the disk technology that had lost out to the videotape cassette. By so doing, Sony remained the world leader in commercializing technological advances in consumer electronics.

MATSUSHITA: EXEMPLAR OF FUNCTIONAL CAPABILITIES

During the 1980s Matsushita, precisely because of its well-tested functional capabilities, quickly entered closely related industrial and communications electronics industries. For this reason Matsushita made little attempt to commercialize a new technology in the manner of Sony but instead was soon making and selling worldwide—robots, welding machines, automated systems based on point-of-sales devices, bar code recorders, pagers, cordless telephones, fax machines, copiers, and a variety of computer products. By

1991 consumer electronics accounted for only 31 percent of its revenues—23 percent video (largely its VHS) and 8 percent audio (largely licensed from Sony). Its JVC learning base did attempt to enter the disk-based path but with little success. The company's post-VCR commitment to industrial and communications equipment accounted for 23 percent of its revenues, electronic components 13 percent, and the older pre–World War II lines, batteries and home appliances, only 5 percent. "Other products" (unlisted) accounted for 8 percent. In addition, a brand-new line, "entertainment," accounted for 8 percent.[19]

In 1991 Matsushita paid $6.13 billion to acquire MCA Inc., a major U.S. Hollywood producer of motion pictures (owner of Universal Studios), records, and radio and television programs and an operator of concession stands. Here it was following Sony's lead. The management's rationale behind this major strategic move into what for Matsushita was an unrelated industry was one of integration—acquiring the "software" that used its electronic hardware. But as Matsushita's outstanding functional capabilities were not relevant to this very different business, serious losses quickly mounted. Matsushita's net income dropped from $1.8 billion in 1991 to $1 billion in 1992, then to $33 million and $2.8 million in the next two years. By 1995 management welcomed an offer of $5.7 billion for 80 percent of MCA by the younger Edgar Bronfman, who had recently become CEO of the family-owned Seagram, a leading producer of distilled liquors, and who sold his family holdings in the chemical giant, E. I. du Pont de Nemours to finance the deal.[20]

By 1996, despite its losses in income from its misstep into film and entertainment, Matsushita's sales had risen to $64.1 billion. Such giant global revenues rested on its production and especially, distribution and marketing capabilities developed at its original learning base in electrical equipment and home appliances in the 1920s, in radio during the 1930s, and then in the 1950s on the product development capabilities in electronics acquired after its joint venture with Philips and its acquisition of Japan Victor. These, in turn, supported Matsushita's move into semiconductors and other electronic components, as well as into television, and then again, in the 1980s, into industrial and communications technology.

The failure of its attempt to enter the global film and entertainment business reminded its managers that the boundaries of a profitable firm are based on its organizational capabilities in closely related products that have been nurtured over decades of growth and experience. Nevertheless, there are also limits on the ability to enter even closely related markets, as illustrated by Matushita's lack of success in computer peripherals and networking hardware. Here the barriers established by the powerful first-movers in computers proved to be too much even for Matsushita's considerable capabilities in electronics technologies, as reviewed in chapter 7 (page 231).[21]

SONY: EXEMPLAR OF TECHNICAL CAPABILITIES

As Matsushita provides an illustration of the successful evolution over the decades of functional capabilities, so Sony provides an unparalleled example of the evolution of creating and maintaining effective technical capabilities and integrating them with its functional capabilities. From the late 1960s on, Japan's first-mover in electronic tape–based products and world pioneer in electronic miniaturization was also primarily responsible for commercializing of the industry's major new products. In 1968 Sony's Trinitron surpassed color television products developed earlier at RCA. In 1970 Sony, not Matsushita, produced the U-Matic, the technological base for both the Beta and the VHS cassette recorders. Then in 1979 came Sony's Walkman, the end product of its capabilities in tape and miniaturization technologies, which combined a tiny AM-FM radio, a small audiotape player, and a portable headset. One of the industry's most successful products, it helped fund the research on Sony's next move, working with Philips, to commercialize the compact disk.[22]

In bringing the CD to global markets, Sony provided the breakthrough in pulsed code technology that made possible digital sound reproduction. Philips pioneered in the new optical laser technology that it had developed in commercializing its VCR. In 1975, the same year that Sony introduced its Betamax and Philips its laser disk VCR, Norio Ohga, a trained musician, who had since 1968 headed Sony's operations in CBS/Sony Records, put his optical and audio research teams to work on a project recording digital audio information directly on a laser disk. At almost the same time, Philips had begun to meet the same challenge. In 1979 the two research teams joined forces, meeting regularly in Tokyo and Eindhoven. Two years later Sony built a mastering plant near Tokyo, paid for by the income received from CBS/Sony Records.

Sony and Philips introduced their CD player in 1982. As demand soared, Sony built a CD player plant in Terre Haute, Indiana, and then one in

Salzburg, Austria. Sony and Philips thus defined the world standard for the CD, which they maintained through a complex set of licensing and manufacturing agreements with producing companies. These contracts assured a tighter technical control over their product than did Matsushita's OEM strategy over its VHS.

By 1985 the sales of CD players in the United States exceeded one million units, greater than that of sales of the VCR in its initial years. Within the briefest period of time, the CD had replaced the vinyl disk that the Victor Talking Machine Company had made the standard some eighty years earlier. In addition to audio recording, its optical and digital properties made it a most effective delivery mechanism for photographic images, software publishing, and data storage.

The next year, Sony and Philips introduced the CD-ROM (compact disk-read only memory) that provided the computer with audio and video capabilities as well as with storage for written text, and so transformed the data processing computer into a multimedia device. Microsoft and the leading personal computer and workstation producers quickly licensed the CD-ROM technology. In 1985, Sony entered the computer industry by acquiring Apple Computer's hard disk drive operations.

These moves into CDs and CD-ROMs led Sony in three directions. It entered a new market—computers—expanded its entertainment business, and began commercializing a follow-up product, the digital video disk. In the early 1990s the differences in its performance in these three product sectors dramatically reflect the strength and weaknesses of Sony's learned organizational capabilities. The DVD, a technological achievement, became highly successful. The computers and the entertainment business were not, although in the end, both were successful.

The first, the move into computers, was less than successful. The barriers to entry were too high. By 1991 Sony had withdrawn from computers (but would return in 1997). The entry into the entertainment business reflected the success of its 1969 joint venture with CBS.

By the mid-1980s CBS/Sony Records had become Sony's most profitable subsidiary. John Nathan's *Sony* describes it as "an unstoppable money machine," so in 1987 Sony acquired full control. Two years later it purchased Columbia Pictures (which CBS had sold to Coca-Cola in 1982) for $4.9 billion. As the decade of the 1990s began, Sony had become a major Hollywood film producer.[23]

Then in 1995 Sony registered a net loss of $3.3 billion. The losses were concentrated in the entertainment sector. Musical entertainment maintained revenues, but Sony's massive losses in the film business provide, as does Matsushita's experience, powerful evidence of the challenges placed on learned organizational capabilities when a company moves into a new line of businesses in which existing capabilities have limited application.

I make no effort to review Sony's adventures and misadventures in Hollywood. They are well told in John Nathan's *Sony*, chapters 8 to 10. Instead I conclude the Sony experience with a brief review of its success in commercializing the digital videodisk. Work on a next-generation disk technology may have been delayed by both Philips's heavy losses in the early 1990s (a story I tell shortly in reviewing Philips history) and Sony's misadventures in Hollywood. But when in January 1993 Nimbus, a leading British producer of disks for storing data, demonstrated an improved disk format with much higher storage capabilities, Sony and Philips came to attention. Sony and Philips insisted that the innovation "bent" the standard established by their manufacturing and licensing agreements. So Nimbus returned to producing storage disks, while Sony and Philips immediately concentrated on developing a high-density disk aimed at the "professional publishing market," primarily producers of motion pictures. At the same time, Toshiba set a team of one hundred engineers to develop a double-sided disk, targeted at the home market. Toshiba then wisely joined with Time Warner, the world's largest media company, as a partner to commercialize a second standard. The resulting battle between the two rivals over the standard ended in a compromise in August 1994. Both camps then concentrated on commercializing the new technology. The first DVD players reached the U.S. market in 1997. In 1998 a million units were sold, and in 1999 3.5 million, a record that far surpassed sales of VCRs and CD players in the first years of their availability.[24]

Sony and Toshiba–Time Warner, but not Philips, benefited from the soaring demand for the innovation that was replacing the CD and the CD-ROM. As I describe shortly in reviewing Philips's evolution, in the early 1990s Europe's leader was suffering for the first time in its history from heavy financial losses. In addition, in 1992 its own attempt to commercialize its multimedia CD-interactive for television users, comparable to earlier CD-ROMs for PC users, failed at a cost of $1 billion. So, as the Philips/Sony DVD came onstream, Philips's managers decided that the company could not afford the huge billion-dollar plant needed to assure the necessary scale economies. Sony then authorized "Philips to handle the licensing to other manufacturers," including Toshiba, Matsushita, Sharp, Korea's Samsung, and France's Thomson SA. The licensing and manufacturing agreements were apparently as tightly controlled as they had been for the initial CD.

By 1996 Sony's technical capabilities and its supporting functional ones were restoring its income flows. In December 1993 it entered the home video game market with its PlayStation. By the end of 1998, with fifty million units sold, the PlayStation had become the world's best-selling home video game system. In the same years came a second try in computers, this time a successful entry into personal computers, first in laptops and then in desktops.[25]

Matsushita and Sony's Japanese Competitors

As Matsushita with its powerful functional organizational capabilities and Sony with its uniquely successful technical capabilities supported by its long-tested functional ones led the way in Japan's global conquest of the consumer electronics industry, its domestic competitors quickly followed them into the U.S. and European markets. I now review the fortunes of the two largest: Sanyo, a follower, and Sharp, an innovator. The competitive interaction among these leaders continually strengthened the capabilities of the overall Japanese industry and rapidly expanded its supporting nexus. By 1990 that industry concentrated in the small regional area between Tokyo and Osaka, to become the world's leading producer of consumer electronics and the only place that possessed the capabilities required to develop innovative technologies from which new products could be commercialized for world markets.

SANYO: FOLLOWING MATSUSHITA'S PATH

The evolution of Matsushita's offspring, Sanyo, provides a different but valuable example of how existing integrated organizational capabilities help to define strategies of continued growth and profitability. On April 1, 1950, the Allied Occupation's antitrust division separated Sanyo from Matsushita. Sanyo's product line thus evolved without the benefit of the technical knowledge that Matsushita was able to acquire and build on through its joint venture with Philips and product development skills from its acquisition of

Japan Victor. As one 1990 report noted: "Sanyo has traditionally relied heavily on existing technology in product development, concentrating on marketing and price competitiveness." At first it sold much the same lines as Matsushita—bicycle lamps, batteries, consumer appliances, and radios at the low-price end—and focused on markets in less developed countries. In the late 1950s it moved into television.[26]

As the demand for radios soared, Sanyo expanded its sales in East Asia and entered the American market "as a 'low-end' manufacturer" on an OEM basis. In Japan its electronic goods were sold with Matsushita's National brand label. In 1959, to meet expanding market demand, Sanyo set up a separate allied enterprise, Tokyo Sanyo, building a plant in Tokyo to produce electric fans, refrigerators, and washing machines for Sanyo's marketing and distribution network. In the 1960s Tokyo Sanyo continued to produce these same lines, as its Osaka parent expanded its output of air conditioners and television sets.

Sanyo's opportunity to become a significant player in the U.S. television market came in 1963 when RCA and Zenith tried to persuade Sears, Roebuck to sell their consumer electronics with their own brand names rather than that of Sears. Sears then turned to Sanyo, which agreed to supply black-and-white televisions at lower prices than U.S. companies. Sanyo's next strategic step was to build its own U.S. base. It began by acquiring Sears's largest supplier, Warwick, in 1976. Then came the move in the early 1970s to assist Emerson Electric in improving manufacturing capabilities of Fisher Radio (acquired by Emerson in 1969) when Emerson moved Fisher's production facilities to Hong Kong. Such assistance led to a fifty-fifty partnership in Fisher between Sanyo and Emerson in 1976 and then full control of Emerson by Sanyo in 1977. This expansion into the U.S. market helped Sanyo to increase its sales from $71.4 million in 1972 to $855 million in 1978.[27]

In 1975 Sanyo entered the VCR race as a manufacturer of Sony's Beta. Tokyo Sanyo began manufacturing and selling Matsushita's VHS. In 1977 Osaka-based Sanyo became a producer and marketer of VHS. Both were marketed in the United States through the Fisher subsidiary. Then in 1982 the two companies—Sanyo and Tokyo Sanyo—formally rejoined.

After the remerger, Sanyo continued to follow Matsushita's path into industrial and communications equipment, including cellular telephones, where in 1992 it held 20.5 percent of the Japanese market. By 1991, 31 percent of Sanyo's sales came from home appliances and batteries, its oldest line of products. Consumer electronics accounted for 28 percent, including 19 percent in video and 9 percent in audio; industrial and commercial equipment, 17 percent; and information systems and electronic components, 23 percent.[28]

With revenues during the 1990s roughly one-quarter of Matsushita's, Sanyo was not in the same league as Matsushita, but its story makes two important points. First it illustrates the difficulty of catching up with the technological leader in commercializing new lines of products and processes, for it suggests what Matsushita's revenues might have been had it not tied into the Philips and the JVC learning paths. As a follower, Sanyo had neither the opportunities nor the flow of income necessary to create its own technical and product development capabilities. Nevertheless it was able to build its production and its marketing and distribution capabilities by producing cheaper goods for less lucrative markets, and that, in turn, permitted it to become a global competitor. Thus it may provide a model for entry into global markets by path followers established in less industrialized nations.

SHARP: FOLLOWING SONY'S AND MATSUSHITA'S PATHS

The experience of the Sharp Corporation, the youngest of Japan's Big Four in consumer electronics, indicates the opportunities created for smaller enterprises as the evolving learning bases of the first-movers and the growing nexus that supports them come together, become fused, into a growing and therefore dynamic industry. Sharp had its start before World War II as a competitor to Matsushita in radio. After the war it turned to more specialized niche products. In the 1970s it returned to the industry's primary products by commercializing a new technology that became basic to television and related products. Sharp thus followed Sony's pattern, in that it built on technical capabilities and followed Matsushita's path relying on functional capabilities to enter new product lines.[29]

Sharp's founder was Tokauji Hayakawa. He began to build his initial organizational learning base in 1925 when he formed the Hayakawa Electric Company in Osaka to produce crystal radio sets. The earthquake of 1923 had forced him to leave Tokyo, where he invented the first mechanical pencil, which he named the "Ever-Sharp." After turning in 1929 from the production of crystal sets to the production of vacuum tube radio sets, his company became one of Matsushita's strong competitors. Following the war he introduced, on the basis of RCA's industrywide licenses, a black-and-white television set to which he gave the brand name Sharp in honor of his first product. In 1960 the company began to move into color television. As the company entered overseas markets, it changed its name from Hayakawa Electric to Sharp in 1970.

Under the shadow of Matsushita and Sony, Hayakawa Electric turned to transistor-based niche products, developing microwave ovens, the first electrical solar cells in 1963, and then in 1964 the first electronic desktop calculators powered by transistors. Next in 1967 came a new C-34 desktop calculator using an integrated circuit produced by Mitsubishi Electronic. Well before, in 1962, the company, following Matsushita and Sony, had set up its own sales subsidiary in the United States.

In 1968 Sharp's existing learning base produced two technological breakthroughs. One was in components, the first gallium arsenide light-emitting diode (LED), a tiny chip used for displays first in calculators, then in computers, and, in time, in televisions. The other was a product using that component, a powerful calculator the size of a pocketbook. By 1970 the manufacturing plant to produce LED chips came onstream. By 1973 the mass production of LEDs began. These production facilities, in turn, became the learning base that made Sharp a first-mover in liquid crystal display (LCD) technology soon thereafter.

In 1973 Sharp introduced the liquid crystal display calculator, in 1976 a solar-powered calculator, and in 1979 its first credit card calculator. At the same time the firm had moved vigorously into the production of digital watches. Of more significance, in 1979 it joined the Matsushita camp in the Beta/VHS battle, producing VHSs for its own worldwide distributing outlets. That year it also acquired and rebuilt an RCA television plant in Memphis, Tennessee. In these same years Sharp, following Sony's example, established both manufacturing and development facilities in the United States and then in Europe. By 1986 it was operating thirty-four plants, including twelve research units in twenty-seven countries, with its employees divided equally between Japan and overseas facilities.

In the 1980s the improved LCD technology began to replace the cathode tube in television, making Sharp the world's largest maker of LCDs and a major producer of television sets as well as videocassette recorders. A new stream of LCD products followed—an LCD color television (1987), an

LCD device for projecting television and video on large screens (1989), and then a simplified high-definition television set priced at $8,000—one-quarter of the price of its competitors (1992). In the 1980s, too, Sharp began to move into electronic office and telecommunications equipment. In 1984 it marketed its first color copier and then began to produce computers. In the early 1990s the company introduced the first cordless color fax machine. In the next year came a cordless pocket telephone that could operate continuously for over five hours. By 1991, 26 percent of Sharp's sales came from television and video equipment, 18 percent from its initial home-cooking appliances, 11 percent from its follow-up audio and communications devices, and 45 percent from information systems and electronic components.[30]

Again, Sharp's successful expansion of its product portfolio and development of a multipathed enterprise reflect the value of a growth strategy that rests on constant and highly focused enhancement of technical, development, production, and marketing capabilities, financed by the income from earlier commercialization of new products. As important, it demonstrates anew how Japan's corporate capabilities in both computers and consumer electronics were by the 1960s producing a national base that encouraged the growth of major new increasingly global enterprises through the development of closely related technologies and product lines.

The Growing, Dynamic Supporting Nexus

After the VHS/Beta battle, Japan's core learning bases in consumer electronics were the two first-movers, Matsushita and Sony, and the two followers, Sanyo and Sharp. Also, three of the giant computer enterprises—Hitachi, Mitsubishi Electric, and Nippon Electric Company (NEC), whose evolution I review in chapter 6—had become significant players. In the late 1970s and early 1980s, the continuing rapid takeover, first of the U.S. and then of the European markets for radio and television, as well as the flow of new products—Matsushita's VHS and Sony's CD and CD-ROM—brought an explosive growth in the essential network of suppliers of materials and services, the nexus, which flourished in ways that did not exist in the United States and Europe.

By the mid-1980s these suppliers had themselves become large enterprises. They included such companies as Pioneer Electronic, incorporated in 1947, a maker of speakers, stereo systems, compact disks, and a variety of components; TDK Electronics, the world's largest producer of tapes, which introduced one of the first recording tapes in 1952; and Kyocera, established in 1959, a producer of ceramic components. Their revenues in 1998 were $3 billion, $2.4 billion, and $1.9 billion, respectively.[31]

Gene Gregory in his *Japanese Electronics Technology*, published in 1985, emphasizes the "prevalent burst of innovative activity throughout the industry. Specialized research laboratories at Fujitsu Fanuc [see chapter 6], Sony, Japan Victor, Pioneer, Omron (a control equipment manufacturer), Canon [see chapter 5], TDK, Kyocera, and a legion of smaller manufacturers of new materials, components, instruments and machinery, add further innovative force to the development of new high-technology electronic products and production processes."[32]

The continuing growth of the nexus, in turn, provided fertile soil for the commercialization of basic new technologies such as Sharp's liquid crystal display or even for the creation of entire new industries, such as electronic video games. Both Sharp and a younger competitor, Casio, were niche firms in the early postwar years. Together they became world leaders in electronic calculators, using a technology initially developed by Texas Instruments. While Sharp emerged as a core company, Casio remained a niche producer of calculators and digital watches, albeit a worldwide leader in the low end of these markets.[33]

The video game industry also had its beginnings in the United States (just as did the LCD technology), but by the 1980s Japan's Nintendo and a younger Sega completely dominated world markets. Their major challenger became, as might be expected, Sony, which by the mid-1990s was the industry's number one revenue producer.

In contrast, by then the United States had only one maker of consumer electronics products, Zenith, which was reporting losses year after year. In Europe, too, no comparable supporting nexus had developed. However, Philips still retained a strong technical capability, although its functional ones had become less effective.

PHILIPS: EUROPE'S LEARNING BASE

Before World War II, Philips Incandescent Lamp Works and Telefunken had been Europe's two consumer electronics learning bases. After World War II, neither Telefunken nor its parent, AEG, which had acquired Siemens's share of Telefunken in 1941, was able to obtain the personnel, facilities, and funding essential to maintain its earlier role in the development of new products and processes. So Philips became Europe's core consumer electronics learning base.

Philips did so after it and Siemens received their transistor licenses from AT&T's Western Electric in April 1952. Philips then concentrated on using the new electronic technology in consumer markets, while Siemens focused on using it in telecommunications, industrial products, and the new data-processing computers. According to John E. Tilton, Philips "by 1960 probably accounted for half of all semiconductor sales in England, France, and Germany, particularly dominating the consumer market," while Siemens concentrated in the 1950s and 1960s on semiconductors for the new electronic data processors. Philips and Siemens, focusing on their own spheres of interest, became and remained Europe's largest producers of semiconductors and the leaders in their respective new industries, consumer electronics and data-processing digital computers.[34]

Philips, formed in 1891 to produce incandescent lamps, was by 1900 Europe's third largest producer of light bulbs. Under the guidance of the two Philips brothers, Gerard and Anton, the enterprise established in Eindhoven, Holland, continued to build an effective learning base. During World War I, when the German electrical equipment leaders were unable to reach global markets—that is, from 1914 until the end of the period of great inflation in 1924—Philips established its first research laboratories and began to commercialize wireless radio equipment, argon gas lamps, and X-ray equipment. In 1919, shortly after the war's end, it began to rebuild its marketing organization in Europe and then a smaller one in the United States. In 1924 it entered the production of radio tubes and in 1927 radio receiving sets on the basis of Telefunken's licenses. Hard hit by the Great Depression of the 1930s, the Philips management made no concerted effort to begin to commercialize television.[35]

During that decade, Telefunken, the joint venture of Siemens and AEG, as Europe's learning base, became the primary developer of television with one competitor, Fernseh. However, in the words of the industry's early history: "By 1939 Telefunken had emerged as the dominant firm in the German television." In 1941 AEG acquired Siemens's half ownership. After World War II, AEG was unable to recover fully from war damages, remaining, unlike Siemens, in Berlin.[36]

Philips had also been damaged by the war. Its management moved to Britain with the German invasion of Holland in the spring of 1940, and it then moved on to the United States. Its facilities were bombed by the Allies in 1944 and then by the Germans until the end of the war in 1945. It did not benefit, of course, from the huge war contracts that so enlarged RCA's research and operations. After the war, Philips focused on recovery. In the early 1950s it rebuilt its extensive marketing organization largely in Europe and concentrated its manufacturing and research at its Eindhoven headquarters. Its managers then expanded its existing businesses in electric lighting, medical equipment, testing and measuring devices, and semiconductor and related components and entered into electric shavers. It also made a major move into household appliances by forming a joint venture with Whirlpool, called Whirlpool International.[37]

But Philips concentrated primarily on expanding its semiconductor business based on its transistor license from AT&T in 1952 and commercializing consumer electronics products based on its technical alliance with Matsushita in 1954. Here, relying largely on the basis of RCA licenses and its growing technical capabilities, Philips moved ahead in the production of television and then color television. In these years it continued to concentrate its research and production in Holland.

After the establishment of the European Common Market in 1958, in the words of the *International Directory*, "Its factories were gradually integrated and centralized in International Production Centers—the backbone of its product divisions—as it made a transition from a market-oriented business to a product-oriented business." That is, it adopted a multidivisional form of organization with integrated product divisions for each of its major businesses.[38]

Then came more diversification in 1968, when, with its small competitor, Grundig, it entered the industry's one preelectronic learning path, that of voice and music recording on vinyl disks. In 1973 it joined with the French firm C11 and Germany's Siemens to build a pan-European IBM plug-compatible computer, Unidata (see chapter 6). Well before the collapse of that project in 1975, Philips turned to enhancing its television capabilities and had entered the VCR race, working with both tape and disk technologies.

Philips's only significant European rival in consumer electronics was Germany's Grundig AG. Max Grundig established his company in Furth, West Germany, in 1948. During the 1950s and 1960s the company produced radios, receiving sets, speakers, and other components as well as phonographs and recordings. In the early 1970s its fifty-fifty joint venture with Philips's PolyGram group acquired recording and musical publishing companies in the United States and Europe. By the mid-1970s Grundig employed a work-force of over thirty thousand, with plants not only in West Germany, but also in Austria and Poland. Until the mid-1970s the revenues of both Philips and Grundig remained steady.[39]

Before Philips entered the VCR contest, it had enhanced its learning ca-pabilities, much as had its Japanese rivals, by using the color television tech-nology licensed from RCA to expand its technical knowledge and then to improve and integrate functional capabilities. Its central laboratories and its production headquarters remained concentrated in Eindhoven, as were the headquarters of its strong European marketing organizations.

Its American activities were carried on by North American Philips (NAP), formed when the Philips management moved to New York during World War II. During the postwar years, its CEO, Peter Vink, insisted that his en-terprise was "totally independent" from Eindhoven. While it clearly was not, it did go its own way, concentrating during the 1970s on expanding its elec-tric lighting business through acquisition. By 1983 it made seven significant acquisitions, culminating with the purchase of Westinghouse's lighting divi-sion, making it the number two competitor to General Electric, the long-established integrated global leader. It built its much smaller U.S. consumer electronics business in the same manner, acquiring Magnavox in 1974 and purchasing unprofitable Sylvania and Philco from General Telephone & Electronics in 1981. As table 2:1 indicates, these acquisitions gave it close to 10 percent of the market. In the mid-1980s all three continued to report losses. At the same time, its much larger electric lighting business continued to lose market share to General Electric.[40]

By the late 1970s Japan's juggernaut had moved into high gear, through both acquisitions and then large-scale direct investment in production plants and marketing facilities, first in the United States and then in Europe. Be-cause of this competition, Grundig's financial situation deteriorated even more quickly than Philips's. To keep Grundig alive, Philips acquired 24.5 percent of Grundig's equity in 1979. In 1982 it raised its share to 32 percent in order to forestall a takeover by France's Thomson SA and shortly after-ward raised it to 37 percent.[41]

In 1981 Philips responded to the challenges by beginning a radical reconstruction of its corporate structure and personnel. Indeed, the losses incurred from the V-2000 VCR led its board in 1983 to consider "the possibility of withdrawing from consumer electronics altogether," but it did not, "because the rest of the company was crucially dependent on its consumer activities."[42]

But Philips, unlike RCA, still had a powerful set of technical capabilities. Its central laboratories had since the 1920s been improving electric and then electronic devices, not only for itself but also for Matsushita. In the 1960s the only comparable research laboratories in the world were those of RCA and Sony. As the RCA Laboratories turned away from consumer electronics and Sony and Philips began to lose out in the VCR contest, Sony and Philips joined forces to commercialize the CD. Introduced in 1982, the *International Directory* reported that "it spun off tremendous profits for Philips." In 1984 Philips and Sony began working on a follow-up technology, CD-interactive (CDI), a multimedia disk to be used in television sets. Sony continued to be involved because the major part of the development work involved digital sound technology, but Philips took the primary responsibility for its development and financing. The commercializing of the CDI for television was far more complex than creating the CD-ROM for the PC. For the PC was an intrinsically interactive device, with systems for user input placed within the computer, whereas in television they were not. CDI development, therefore, called for complex software, new optical hardware, the development of CDI studio systems, and much more. The net result was a marketing disaster, costing Philips at least $1 billion.[43]

If the CDI had succeeded, it might have offset the deficits that were resulting from Philips's inability to meet the Japanese onslaught and its attempt in the early 1980s to grow by acquisition. In 1990 the company recorded a loss of $2.7 billion, the most serious in its history. That year the consumer electronics division still accounted for 47 percent of total sales, but only 37 percent of income. In 1993 Philips reported overall losses of half a billion dollars, reflecting the failure of its CDI. By then another massive organizational restructuring, including the spinning off of major product lines, was under way. In 1991, in order to meet its deficits, Philips sold its 47 percent share of Whirlpool International back to Whirlpool. In 1992 it turned to Matsushita, which agreed to buy back the 35 percent of its equity Philips had held since 1952. In addition, Matsushita acquired Magnavox, the core of Philips's U.S. subsidiary.

Philips's deplorable financial situation explains why in 1994 top managers decided that they could not afford to build the costly plants needed to produce the DVD and why they continued to sell off their long-established product lines. In 1996 Cor Boonstra, president and chief operating officer of food company Sara Lee, became top manager at Philips. He accelerated the restructuring efforts begun in the aftermath of the losses in the early 1990s. From 1996 to 1999 Boonstra sold off myriad noncore businesses, including Grundig and PolyGram. By 1999 its major remaining money-making consumer electronics products were LCD monitors for televisions and computers.

Philips also restructured its research activities. In 1988 it switched from funding the central research laboratories directly to requiring the labs to generate their own funding through "contracts" with Philips's product divisions. Given the reduced profile of consumer electronics within Philips's 1990s portfolio, consumer electronics research remained only a small part of the labs' activities. Finally, in order to shake up the company's culture, Boonstra moved the headquarters from Eindhoven to Amsterdam, leaving the labs behind. The move to Amsterdam marked the demise of Europe's consumer electronics industry. In chapter 7, which reviews the status of both consumer electronics and computers in 1996, I have a brief obituary of Europe's two industries, including the final passing of Philips as a producer of consumer electronics.[44]

THOMSON SA: FRANCE TAKES THE LEFTOVERS

In the same decade that senior managers at Matsushita, Sony, and Philips were defining their positions in global markets, government officials were deciding the fate of France's consumer electronics business. In 1982 François Mitterrand's Socialist government nationalized the industry. (De Gaulle had done much the same in the 1960s with computers.) The Mitterrand government chose Thomson-Brandt, a descendant and longtime technical ally of General Electric, to become France's national champion. The government then divided Thomson-Brandt into two units, Thomson SA (later renamed Thomson Multimedia) for consumer electronics and Thomson CSF for defense electronics.[45]

The French government had favored Thomson-Brandt since World War II, but now, as the national champion, Thomson SA received the ample funding needed to build a global empire. It immediately began by acquiring the German radio, television, and recording companies—Telefunken, Saba, and Nordmende—and attempted to take over Grundig, the move that pushed Philips into taking stronger control of its smaller ally. Then in 1987, one month before obtaining RCA's consumer electronics division from General Electric, Thomson purchased Britain's Thorn-EMI. The British company had been a merger of Britain's two largest makers of consumer electronics—Thorn (which began as the British distributor of the U.S. company Sylvania) and EMI (which began as a subsidiary of Columbia Phonograph, Victor Talking Machine's major rival in the 1920s). By 1988 Thomson SA had become, in terms of revenue, the world's fourth largest producer of consumer electronics behind Matsushita, Sony, and Philips.

Thomson's challenge remained primarily that of consolidating and rationalizing its diverse and scattered properties. It had invested as little in research and development as had the companies it acquired. The resulting financial record was dismal. In the six years between 1990 and 1995, its annual losses in billions of francs were 2.5, 0.7, 0.5, 3.0, 2.2, and 2.7. These figures included those from Thomson CSF, by 1996 one of the world's largest defense electronics companies, which accounted for 49 percent of total sales. Given the different nature of their markets, one arranged by government officials, the other determined by the powerful Japanese competitors, Thomson Multimedia must have accounted for more than half of the company's losses. Obviously Thomson Multimedia had neither the technical nor the functional capabilities required to commercialize new consumer electronics products or improve existing ones.

By the mid-1990s Japan's conquest of global markets was complete. By then only Japanese enterprises had the integrated technical and functional—development, production, and marketing—capabilities and facilities so essential for maintaining competitive strength in existing technologies and, of even more importance, commercializing the products of new technologies. Only they had the continuing income from past products to finance the creation of new ones. Only they had a large and technically sophisticated supporting nexus to provide the wide variety of essential components, equipment, and services.

The Ingredients of Global Conquest

What, then, were the ingredients of Japan's epic conquest of global consumer electronics markets? First, Japan's industry included more core enterprises, and second, they each produced a larger number of products. Except for RCA itself, by 1960, the time of RCA's world dominance in color television, the U.S. enterprises were primarily single-sector enterprises, producers either of receiving sets or of components. By the early 1960s, the leaders—Philco in the first (sets) and Sylvania in the second (components)—had been acquired by Ford and GTE, respectively. The new management paid little attention to maintaining capabilities for the development of new markets. In addition, CBS had become primarily a broadcasting company. By the mid-1970s the remaining smaller companies had been acquired by either the Japanese or Philips or else had been disbanded.

On the other hand, Japan's Big Four—Matsushita (with its JVC subsidiary), Sanyo, Sony, and Sharp—had become full-line producers. From the start, they used their integrated learning bases to commercialize products of new technologies and to enhance existing ones. They also employed these capabilities to enter into closely related electronics-based industries, where their technical and functional capabilities provided a competitive advantage. Matsushita and, to a lesser extent, its post–World War II spin-off, Sanyo, did so by perfecting their functional capabilities. Sony and, later, Sharp did so by continuing to improve both their technical and their functional capabilities.

Matsushita became the worldwide exemplar of how to reap the rewards of continuing learning in product development, production, and, in particular, marketing and distribution. From its beginnings in the 1920s, it grew by moving into closely related industries based on both electricity and electronics. Its conquest of world VCR markets provides an outstanding example of achieving the economies of scale and scope made possible by these functional capabilities. So, too, does its continuing growth strategy. After its VHS victory, it made little effort to commercialize new technologies. Instead it quickly became a major competitor in existing industrial, office, and telecommunications equipment markets. Sanyo followed much the same strategy, on a smaller scale.

At the same time, Sony became the worldwide exemplar of continuing learning in technical capabilities, resulting in successful commercializing of new products and the continuing enhancement of old ones. Few companies have a more impressive record. Beginning with its tape and miniaturizing technologies in the 1950s, it continued to innovate with its Trinitron color TV in the 1960s, its Walkman in 1979, its U-Matic video recorder (the basic innovation for its Beta and Matsushita's VHS), its CD with Philips, its CD-ROM, and, again with Philips, its DVD.

Sharp provides a variation, in a sense combining the strengths of Sony and Matsushita. A niche firm that produced transistor-based microwave ovens and desktop calculators, it commercialized the LED technology, a chip used for displays in electronic products. On the basis of Sharp's resulting innovation in the broader LCD technology, it became a world leader in video displays (including television). In addition, it moved into information technology and telecommunications equipment, including faxes and color copiers, and maintained its components business.

The third and most important ingredient of all for Japan's success was the nexus that began to grow rapidly as these Big Four successfully invaded the U.S. and then European markets. This nexus became a nurturing soil for the maturing not only of Sharp, but also of Casio, Nintendo, Sega, Pioneer, and other global electronics competitors. As important, when the Japanese computer companies became competitive in worldwide markets in the late 1970s, the nexus concentrated in the adjoining Tokyo and Osaka industrial districts and provided them with sophisticated, tested electronic devices as well as information and services.

No such nexus existed in the United States, where components and receiving and broadcasting equipment were produced in a number of cities and facilities scattered throughout the nation. When an electronics nexus did appear, it grew to meet the needs of computers alone, first along Massachusetts's Route 128 and then in California's Silicon Valley, a central story of chapter 4. Nor did such a breeding ground appear in Europe.

To turn to Europe, Philips in the 1960s and 1970s, like Sony, relied on RCA licenses to develop color television technology. Like Matsushita, it continued to operate in electrical and other electronics industries—lighting, medical equipment, testing and measuring instruments, and semiconductors. By the 1970s Philips had perfected its color television technology and entered the VCR battle with both a tape and a disk technology. But its electronics products were sold primarily in Europe.

Nevertheless, Philips's primary contribution to the evolution of the consumer electronics industry was to provide essential technological knowledge to both Matsushita and Sony. In 1952, shortly after both Japan and Europe had recovered fully from World War II, Philips became the provider of Matsushita's technical knowledge as well as its major shareholder. That arrangement lasted for forty years, until Philips's financial collapse—a collapse that resulted from Japan's conquest of the European market, spearheaded by Matsushita and Sony. From the mid-1970s on, Philips's technical staff in Eindhoven had a long and intimate relationship with Sony's engineers in Tokyo, as together they commercialized the CD and, in the 1990s, the DVD. Certainly one of the most significant areas for research by historians of business, technology, and industry is the story of this enigmatic relationship among these three builders of the infrastructure of the Electronic Century.

In the epic story of computers, no such enigma exists. There the story is, from the beginning, that of IBM. Within less than a decade after the creation of the first electronic computer, IBM had approximately 80 percent of U.S. and world markets, a historically unprecedented achievement. By comparison, Henry Ford's famous Model T reached only as much as 50 percent of the U.S. market in one year, 1921.[46] More significant, by the late 1960s and through the 1970s, IBM's major competitors worldwide were producing plug-compatibles of IBM's System 360 and System 370—that is, they were using both IBM's licensed hardware and software. Then in the 1980s, after the microprocessor revolution, IBM's new competitors were producing and marketing clones of IBM's PC. It is to this story that I now turn.

4

MAINFRAMES AND MINICOMPUTERS:

THE COMPUTER INDUSTRY CREATED IN

THE UNITED STATES

The evolution of the data-processing digital electronic computer industry provides a strikingly different evolutionary story from that just told about consumer electronics. Here, instead of four firms interacting to shape the industry over the decades of its evolution, a single enterprise, International Business Machines, became and remained the path definer from the industry's beginning in the 1950s until the 1990s. In addition, the contrast between the roles of the two U.S. leaders, RCA and IBM, could hardly be more dramatic. Where the decisions of RCA's executives led to the destruction of the U.S. consumer electronics industry, those of IBM's managers continued to define the evolution of not only the U.S., but also the European and Japanese computer industries. As a result, European-owned and -operated computer companies were unable to challenge those of the United States and by the end of the century had died. On the other hand, the Japanese, with initial guidance from their government, became and remained strong competitors in world markets.

I begin this chapter with IBM's success as the first-mover in business and commercial—that is, nongovernment—markets by providing a brief review of World War II military projects that laid the foundations of the basic digital technology from which so much of the industry's technical knowledge initially evolved. (Appendix 4:1 provides a chronology of the U.S. Computer Industry.)

The First Computers: Analytical Devices for Military Purposes

The first modern computers were not designed for the broad business and scientific and engineering markets that they came to serve. They were invented in order to meet the demands of the Second World War. Wartime innovations in high-speed calculators, in cryptoanalytic devices (for code breaking), and in servomechanisms (as used in controlling gunnery fire) set the stage for the invention of instruments to carry out complex mathematical calculations at unprecedented speed and accuracy for very specific military needs. Today's computer technology evolved in the United States from four wartime projects. Three of the four were carried out at major universities— Harvard, MIT, and the University of Pennsylvania. The fourth had its roots in the navy's cryptoanalytical unit.[1]

The first of these four was the Harvard Mark I calculator, a collaborative project between a Harvard professor, Howard H. Aiken, and IBM that began in 1939. Aiken provided the broad concept. IBM carried out the detailed design, provided the components, engineered the machine, and brought it to Harvard in 1943; there it was taken over by Aiken, who had earlier been inducted into the navy, and thus became a navy project. After Aiken and IBM's president, Thomas J. Watson Sr., quarreled over the funding of and the credit for the invention, Aiken built a Mark 2 for the Naval Proving Grounds at Dalgren, Virginia, in 1947, where it was used for ballistic research. By then, however, it was already obsolete. But although Aiken's Harvard Mark series had relatively little impact on contemporary computer technology, it played an important role in exposing graduate students and academic associates to the complexities of inventing the computer.[2]

MIT's contribution was more significant. In 1944 Jay Forrester's Servomechanism Laboratory began working with the air force on what would become the Whirlwind Project. Whirlwind's initial task was to build a "simulator" of an aircraft cockpit to be used for training pilots. One for commercial pilots followed. With Whirlwind's completion in 1951, Forrester and his MIT group became the air force's major organization for computer development after the selection in 1952 of MIT's Lincoln Laboratory as the contractor for the goverment's SAGE program.[3]

The most fruitful university contribution to the creation of the digital computer took place at the Moore School of Engineering at the University of Pennsylvania. Two of its faculty members—J. Presper Eckert and John W. Mauchly—began in April 1943 to build for the army an Engineering Numerical Integrator and Computer (ENIAC). Their goal was much the same as Aiken's—to provide ballistic tables, this time for the army's Aberdeen Proving Ground. During the next summer, the mathematician John von Neumann, at the Institute for Advanced Study in Princeton, joined the project. The ENIAC was delivered to the Aberdeen Proving Ground early in 1946. The year before, von Neumann published an article that still remains today the definitive description of the basic architecture of the computer.

The fourth pioneering enterprise had its beginnings when at the war's end two reserve officers in the navy's cryptoanalytical unit formed, with strong support from senior naval officers, the Engineering Research Associates (ERA). It initially produced special-purpose machines for the navy. Then in 1947 ERA focused on developing a general-purpose computer (Atlas 1) for the purpose of reducing the costs and increasing the accuracy of cryptoanalytical techniques.[4]

In 1950 and 1951 the first fruits of these initial computer projects appeared. ERA's Atlas went into full operation in 1950, only a week after its delivery to the navy. Twenty more were produced during the early 1950s. In 1951 the Eckert-Mauchly team, creators of the ENIAC computer, handed over their second creation, UNIVAC I (Universal Automatic Computer), to the U.S. Census Bureau.

With the completion of ENIAC, Eckert and Mauchly formed their own enterprise in March 1946, Electronic Control Company (ECC). In the following October they signed a contract with the U.S. Census Bureau. They expected that by its use of magnetic tape, their UNIVAC would replace millions of punched cards used by the bureau. But they severely underestimated their development costs. To acquire funds, they took on a smaller project with the assistance of Northrup Aviation to provide a computer for the National Bureau of Standards. By 1950, as their debts increased rapidly, they had to sell their company to Remington Rand, the nation's largest producer of business machines.[5]

As members of Remington Rand's operating division, Eckert and Mauchly completed UNIVAC. With its delivery to the Census Bureau, it became an instant success. Its achievement in predicting the 1952 presidential election of Eisenhower over Stevenson made it a household name. By the end of 1954 General Electric, Metropolitan Life, Du Pont, U.S. Steel, and other industrial and insurance leaders had purchased this huge complex analytical computer. By 1955 the digital computer had entered American business and the era of commercial computing had begun.

Commercial Computing and the Rise of IBM

With the success of UNIVAC, James Rand's Remington Rand was poised to dominate the production of computers for nonmilitary purposes. James Rand had formed Remington Rand in 1927 by merging his Rand Kardex, the world's largest supplier of record-keeping systems, with Remington Typewriter, the oldest of the American office machine enterprises, and with two smaller companies—an adding machine maker and Powers Accounting Machinery, producers of punched-card tabulators. That is how Remington Rand became the world's largest producer of office machinery.[6]

James Rand had vision. As a successful empire builder, he decided in 1947 to dominate the new electronic computer industry even before its potential had been tested. First he recruited General Leslie Groves, who had been director of the Manhattan Project, to set up Remington Rand research laboratories near the company headquarters at Norwalk, Connecticut. Groves quickly hired a team of computer specialists. After acquiring the Eckert-Mauchly enterprise in 1950, Rand purchased ERA (developer of the Atlas computer) in the spring of 1952. "Thus Rand," wrote computer industry historian Kenneth Flamm, "had no less than three different computer development groups, together accounting for a good part of the stock of knowledge and experience in the world at that time. It also had a three year head start over any other firm in shipping a commercial computer product."[7]

Where Rand was a visionary, IBM's managers were realists. In the next year, 1953, IBM introduced its first digital computer, the Defense Calculator. A decade later, in 1963, Rand's revenues from data-processing computers totaled $145.5 million, those of IBM $1.24 *billion* (table 4.1). By then IBM had become the industry's world leader, while Rand (Sperry Rand after Rand acquired the Sperry Gyroscope Company in 1955) was producing specialized machines primarily for the military and government. For Rand had

TABLE 4.1. U.S. Revenues of Major
Computer Manufacturers, 1963

Firm	1963 Revenues ($ millions)
IBM	1,244
Sperry Rand	145
AT&T	97
Control Data	84
Philco	74
Burroughs	42
General Electric	39
National Cash Register	31
Honeywell	27
RCA	NA

Source: Fisher et al., *IBM and the U.S. Data Processing Industry: An Economic History*, p. 65, with permission from Praeger Publishers.

failed to build an integrated learning base, whereas IBM had succeeded in doing so. The success and failure of the first two entrants into the new electronic-based office machinery industry demonstrates dramatically the value of achieving a path-initiating learning base. After reviewing the process by which IBM became the industry's path definer, I return briefly to the fate of Sperry Rand.

Before 1952 IBM had pioneered in developing new analytical computers. Indeed, by building Aiken's Harvard Mark I, it had been in at the industry's very beginning. In 1947 it had brought forth a selective sequence electric calculator (SSEC), a hybrid half computer/half punched-card machine. But only after the UNIVAC success in the 1950s did IBM turn seriously to developing giant commercial computers using magnetic tapes for storing information.[8]

The 701 Defense Calculator, announced in May 1952 and delivered that December, was similar to the UNIVAC—that is, a costly machine primarily for military use. Improvements in the form of the 702 and 703 followed. Then an IBM development team headed by Gene Amdahl created the 704. Introduced in 1956, it was, in Flamm's words, "in its day the fastest and largest general purpose computer sold commercially." By 1955 orders for the IBM 700 series were already exceeding those for Rand's UNIVAC. By then IBM had acquired the learning capabilities needed to become the leader in the new analytical and scientific digital computer technology that had been born in the 1940s.[9]

The 650: "Computing's Model T"

But the source of IBM's rapid dominance worldwide in the 1950s did not come from this new learning. It came from a much smaller and much less expensive computer that was delivered in 1954 and leased out for $3,250 a month. This was the 650 (not to be confused with System 360 of the next decade). The capabilities that led to the development of the 650 and the resulting 600 series evolved from the long-term functional learning IBM had accumulated since its formation in 1911 in developing, producing, and marketing punched-card data processors. As President Thomas Watson Jr. later stated, "[W]hile our great million dollar 700 got the publicity, the 650 became computing's Model T."[10] For the 650 linked the new electronic power with the long existing punched-card tabulating technology.

From IBM's beginning as the Computing-Tabulating-Recording Company (CTRC) in 1911, it had been the first-mover in that technology. CTRC was a merger of a small producer of business clocks and another of business scales with the Hollerith Company. Henry Hollerith had formed his company after he had invented the punched-card tabulating device at the request of the U.S. Bureau of Census to process data collected for the census of 1890.[11]

In 1914 Thomas J. Watson Sr. became CTRC's president. Ten years later his company built a large manufacturing plant in Europe and changed its name to International Business Machines. When James Rand formed Remington Rand in 1927, he acquired Powers Accounting Machinery, Hollerith's only competitor. Neither before nor after becoming part of Remington Rand had the Powers enterprise been able to overcome Hollerith's first-mover competitive advantages—that is, those resulting from building that product sector's initial integrated learning base. By 1935 IBM had 85 percent and Remington Rand 15 percent of the world's market for what had become the most sophisticated of the existing office machinery technologies.

The predecessor of IBM's 650 computer was its 601 "multiplying punched card tabulator," first marketed in 1935. It was replaced in 1946 by the 603, the "electronic multiplier," the first to be powered by tubes, and then in 1948 by the 604, an electronic product whose sequential capabilities had been developed in the tabulators built during the war for the Aberdeen Proving Ground. Over five thousand of these 604 tabulators were sold between 1948 and 1955. In the final step, the transformation from tabulator to computer was carried out at IBM's plant in Endicott, New York, during the early 1950s. In the 650, delivered in 1954, IBM used a drum storage technology it had acquired from Rand's ERA division. Fees from the rental of more than two thousand of the 650 series produced more revenue for IBM than the entire 700 series of large computers over the initial ten years of their production.[12]

The culmination of this transformation was the 1401, initially delivered in 1960. Transistor powered, it rented for $2,500 a month, the price of a medium-size punched-card installation. The goal of its designers was to replace both the 650 and the existing tabulating machines by incorporating improved peripherals, new card punchers, magnetic tapes, and storage drives and also printers capable of printing six hundred lines a minute. Moreover, it was a system rather than a single device, so its configuration could be adjusted to the different needs of different markets—insurance, banking, retailing, or manufacturing. The 1401 was overwhelmingly successful. More than twelve thousand machines were produced, and they brought in revenues of $2 billion. While producing its 1400 series, IBM brought out a smaller 1620 for scientific uses.

By the early 1960s IBM was marketing seven different classes of computers. The world's leading producer of electromechanical punched-card technology had become the world's leader in the new electronic digital computer. In 1960, after IBM shut down its punched-card operation, over two-thirds of its revenues came from computers, software, and peripherals. The remaining revenues came from electric typewriters and other office equipment.

The person most responsible for this basic strategic transformation to electronic computing was Thomas J. Watson Jr. His father, Thomas senior, had been attentive to the possibilities of the new technology, as attested to by IBM's contribution to Aiken's Harvard Mark I and later to the development of the hybrid SSEC calculator of 1947. But Thomas senior remained committed to the punched-card tabulator. The younger Watson turned to the new technology as soon as he returned to IBM in January 1946 after wartime service in the U.S. Army Air Corps. He pushed for the 603 electronic multiplier with its vacuum tubes. The surprising success of the 604 electronic calculator convinced him that IBM's future lay in electronics. Upon becoming executive vice president in 1949, he concentrated on bringing the first 650 to market. Even before he became president in 1952, he had helped put together the team that developed the 701.[13]

As the younger Watson knew so well, IBM's competitive functional capabilities rested on its tabular punched-card learning base. This was particularly true in the development of peripherals. No company had developed a broader range of devices by which one basic machine could be used to meet the varied customers' needs in different industries and businesses. As Kenneth Flamm notes:

> The card readers and punchers used with early computers, even those not built by IBM, were often IBM products. An ambitious development program for printers, magnetic tape drives, and magnetic drums and disks added strength to traditional expertise. The availability of quality peripheral equipment for IBM computers was crucial to its phenomenal growth.[14]

IBM's worldwide marketing and distribution organization was prepared to lease and service the new and more powerful and versatile data-processing devices to much the same corporate customers as before, in much the same information-intensive industries. Moreover, in product and process development IBM had long routinized its underlying strategy of continually improving existing product lines and using the learning and the profits from those lines to commercialize new ones.

Nevertheless, the shift from electricity to electronics called for the building of two new sets of capabilities. One was the development of software, without which the hardware was useless. During the late 1950s about one hundred programmers at IBM began to develop this essential software, including pioneering work on one of the first major high-level programming languages, FORTRAN, also known as the IBM Mathematical Formula Translating System, for scientific and mathematical applications. At the same time, IBM worked with the rest of the industry on COBOL (common business oriented language).[15]

The other need was to build the company's technical capabilities in the new electronic technology. In the early fifties the younger Watson raised the number of engineers and technicians the company employed from five hundred to five thousand in six years. In 1955 he recruited Emanuel R. Piore, formerly the chief scientist of the Office of Naval Research, who had been intimately involved in wartime and immediate postwar developments in electronics and electronic computing. By the end of the 1950s IBM's technical capabilities in commercial computers far surpassed those of any competitor.[16]

The U.S. government, both through its massive defense contracts and through an antitrust action, further propelled IBM's transition from tabulating machines to computers. In the early 1950s over half the company's research funds came from government agencies. The SAGE air defense program, for which, beginning in 1952, IBM built fifty-six specialized computers for $30 million apiece, provided ample funding (ultimately half a billion dollars) for, as well as an invaluable technical learning experience in, the development of its scientific lines. So, too, another government program, Project Stretch, which began in 1956, led to the development of new components technology that was used in IBM's large 700 systems, delivered in 1961 and 1962, as well as in its smaller 1400 computers. Thus, Project Stretch was central to the development of the all-important System 360 in the 1960s.

Project Stretch grew out of IBM's development work to improve its large 704. Two government agencies agreed to help fund the project if the final product could meet the needs of each agency. One of these agencies was the Los Alamos Laboratories of the Atomic Energy Commission (AEC), the other the National Security Agency (NSA). The design was "stretched" to provide the high-precision "scientific" requirements of the AEC and the broader "business" ones of the NSA. Its requirements for compatibility led to advances in basic circuit logic, high-speed core memories, common interface standards, standard operating systems, and, the leading historian of IBM, Emerson Pugh, adds, "multiprogramming, memory protect, generalized interrupt, interleaving of memories, look ahead, the memory bus, a standard interface for input-output equipment, and the eight-bit character called the byte."[17]

The government's antitrust action, mentioned above, hastened the transformation of IBM's product line from punched card to computers by a consent decree negotiated with the Justice Department in January 1956. As the suit focused primarily on IBM's dominance of the punched-card record-keeping business, the younger Watson, whose commitment was computers, persuaded his father to agree that IBM would reduce its investments in plants producing tabulating cards to 50 percent of the industry's total capacity. It would sell as well as lease its machines, and would do so on terms that were comparable to its existing lease arrangements. IBM was also to assist other enterprises in servicing installed tabulator machines. But the decree did have profound implications beyond tabulating cards, for IBM further agreed to license its "existing and future patents" to any "person making written application."[18]

The Justice Department had obtained at almost the same moment a comparable clause in similar consent decrees with RCA and AT&T that had as great an impact on the future of their industries as the IBM decree had on the computing industry. As the chief of the antitrust division emphasized, these decrees provided the Justice Department with a way "to open up the electronics field." And indeed they did open the three major fields—data processing, consumer electronics, and telecommunications—opened them not just to U.S. competitors, but also to foreign ones, particularly Japanese. In fact, as I will stress again later, this decree, along with the threat of a second antitrust suit that led IBM to "unbundle" its software in 1969, thus making both IBM's hardware and software available to all applicants, became and remained central to the evolution of the computer industry worldwide.

The System 360

In 1961, when the low-priced 1401 business computers and the giant 700 scientific computers were taking commanding positions in their markets, IBM's management began to plan its next generation of computers. Its seven classes of computers bracketed the industry's price/performance range; but one was not compatible with another. Each used different peripherals, components, and architecture, thus depriving IBM of the potential of scale economies. Even more serious, each had its own operating software and applications for that software. With a major model change, the software had to be rewritten. By then IBM was beginning to encounter increased competition from companies that concentrated on only one or two lines in the overall price/performance range. By then, too, customers often wanted a mix of business and scientific applications. In addition, growing internal rivalries between the producers of IBM's large scientific machines in Poughkeepsie and those of IBM's business lines in Endicott were delaying product development. These pressures, as well as the experience in Project Stretch and other developmental activities, emphasized both the need and the potential for achieving increased economies of scale and scope by making IBM systems compatible with one another.[19]

In October 1961 Vincent J. Learson, Watson's second in command, created the SPREAD task group of senior managers to establish an "overall IBM plan" for the third generation of data-processing products. In its final report of December 1961, the task group recommended a family of compatible computers that would bracket the performance/price range using standard interfaces for input/output equipment, tapes and disk storage, card readers, printers, terminals, and other peripherals, as well as software. This was the System 360. It was to consist of five (then six) new processors spanning a two hundred-fold range in performance and priced accordingly.[20] This plan had broad similarities to the one devised by Pierre S. du Pont and Alfred P. Sloan at General Motors in 1922. Sloan reorganized existing product lines into a family of motor vehicles "for every purse and purpose." But the technological challenge of creating compatibility at IBM for achieving economies through using compatible parts, materials, and accessories in the production of several lines was far greater than that at General Motors.

The execution of the task group's charge demanded unprecedented innovation in both product and process. Most daunting were the changes required by the senior managers' decision to rely on the still untested integrated circuit technology, rather than on the existing transistor technology, for the source of computer power (note: the System 360's processor would not be quite what the industry would soon define as a true integrated circuit). Previously the company had purchased its transistor-based processors from outside suppliers, primarily Texas Instruments. Now the task force agreed not only to develop this new processor technology that increased the speed of the system's operation and decreased the cost of manufacturing by half, but also, in order to meet the large anticipated output of these processors, to design and then invest in a giant works project to produce them. In the words of James Cortada: "The decision to base the System 360 on this new technology was perhaps the riskiest ever taken by the company, but it paid off."[21]

Other innovations called for by the planners were less risky, for they rested more on the capabilities IBM had learned and expanded during the previous decade. One was to have their systems meet the needs of both the scientific and commercial markets. This led to improvement and expansion of the company's ferrite high-speed core memories. Input/output (I/O) interfaces were standardized, and a new and improved set of peripherals was developed. The most daunting challenge of all was to standardize software so that it was compatible, not only between the new family of machines, but, where possible, between new and existing ones.

To meet these unprecedented challenges and risks, Thomas Watson Jr. (now chairman) poured all the services and financial resources available to the company into the creation of the new family of compatible computers. Implementation required in time the hiring of sixty thousand new employees, an increase of IBM's population by a third in four years. The project quickly fell behind schedule, and costs soared. The development of the new processors outran all estimates. The creation of new software was even more costly. In 1964, the critical year for development, more than a thousand persons were involved in developing the new operating system alone. In that year more money was spent for software development than had been planned for the entire project.

Nevertheless, on April 4, 1964, the date originally scheduled for completion, the company announced the appearance of the System 360. It did so in part at the insistence of the sales organization, which feared the loss of customers to competitors if the announcement were delayed. The first products began to reach the market in 1965. But the manufacturing and software crisis continued. In 1966 some $600 million was tied up in work-in-process inventory. By 1967, however, the multitude of new products began to emerge. In 1963 IBM's data-processing revenues had been $1.2 billion; by 1973 they had soared to $8.7 billion.[22]

By then the System 360 was defining and rapidly enlarging the mainframe computer's path of learning. Flamm makes the point: "The introduction of the concept of compatibility proved a turning point in the economic history of the industry." As he stresses, that concept "created a unified market that greatly stimulated the commercial use of computers. . . . By drawing the boundaries of this large, unified market (IBM had roughly 70 percent of the world market at that time) with a proprietary, internally controlled standard, IBM created serious obstacles for current and potential competitors."[23]

The barriers to entry were indeed formidable. In production, the System 360's scale economies came not only from a greater output of computers, but also from the volume production of peripherals and other components. In research and development, as in the production of hardware, "the unit cost of designing a product declines with the number of units sold. All other things being equal, the firm with the largest share of the market will then have the lowest unit cost." Of more importance, Flamm points out, "companies have focused on economies of scope in product development in order to use the results of fixed investments in R&D in the widest array of products." But he stresses that in the commercializing of the System 360, software "emerged as the primary areas in which to exploit the economies of scope." Because software had to be written for specific hardware, "the fixed cost of writing a complex program could now be spread over a much wider market, and the cost of implementing such an application for an individual user greatly reduced." Software, the computer technology's unique characteristic (hardware was useless without software), remained one of the industry's most challenging technical problems and became one of its greatest sources of scale and scope economies.

In marketing, through its policies of renting and servicing its machines, IBM had direct contact with more potential buyers of computers than did other office machinery companies and certainly more than any entrepreneurial start-up. Its intimate knowledge of the requirements of different types of customers, both commercial and scientific, permitted it to meet the needs of a larger number and a broader range of customers than did its competitors. Moreover, customers whom IBM had long serviced welcomed the new services it provided to bring them into the computer age.[24]

In these ways the IBM System 360 defined the computer industry's mainframe path of learning and did so on a worldwide scale. That achievement required half a decade of intense development work and a cost of $6 billion to $7 billion. This figure, besides including the development of hardware and software, included the construction of five new plants that themselves cost $4.5 billion. Surely no other company or government agency in the world had technological and functional capabilities and the financial resources needed to carry out such an immensely innovative project.

IBM's Competitors

Table 4.1 lists the electronic data-processing revenues of IBM and its leading U.S. competitors in 1963, the year before IBM announced the coming of the System 360. In addition to IBM, nine firms are listed. Of these, two were no longer developing new computers. AT&T had agreed by the aforementioned consent decree not to produce commercial computers. Philco, a leading maker of consumer electronics, had built powerful analytical computers for the navy and air force, which were then sold in the commercial market and later produced for scientific and engineering computing by nongovernment enterprises. In 1960 Ford Motor Company acquired Philco as a way to increase its defense business, as described in chapter 2. In 1963 it shut down Philco's production of computers for commercial markets. (See page 86 for Table 4.1.)

The other seven of IBM's competitors on the list became known as the Seven Dwarfs. The three office machinery companies—Sperry Rand, National Cash Register (NCR), Burroughs—and Honeywell, the producer of temperature control systems, attempted with little success to build organizational capabilities similar to IBM's. Two others, General Electric and RCA, were the only companies in the United States, and indeed in the rest of the world, that had the broad technical capabilities and the functional resources to challenge IBM's System 360. General Electric had been the nation's leader in the production of electrical equipment since the 1890s, producing a wide range of electrical products. RCA, the definer of the U.S. consumer electronics path of learning in the United States since its beginnings in the 1920s, had as told in chapter 2 just triumphed in the commercializing of color television. Both companies waited until the early 1960s to enter seriously into the production of commercial computers. The seventh, Control Data Corporation (CDC), was an entrepreneurial enterprise established in 1957 by William Norris, who had been an original partner in the pioneering Engineering Research Associates in the 1940s, had gone into Remington Rand with ERA in 1952, and had left that company to start Control Data.

The evolution of these seven competitors during the 1950s illustrates the challenges facing enterprises attempting to enter the path defined by its firstmover. A comparison of the histories of Sperry Rand and Control Data illustrates underlying reasons for failure and for success in the initial creation of an integrated learning base. The response of the three closely related office machinery business companies indicates the barriers to entry that IBM's dominance in punched-card tabulating had already created. Finally, the story of GE and RCA emphasizes the nature of the barriers that even the potentially most powerful competitors, in terms of technical capabilities and financial resources, were unable to overcome.

Sperry Rand and Control Data: Failure and Success in Building Competitive Capabilities

In 1952 Remington Rand, IBM's only major competitor in punched-card tabulators, already accounted for a good part of the world's knowledge and experience in computers. It had a three-year head start on the production of commercial products. Yet within three years this head start had evaporated. As has so often occurred in industrial history, the empire builder (in this case Jim Rand) was not an organization creator. Sperry Rand's three R&D computer teams remained located at Norwalk, Philadelphia, and St. Paul. Their work was not coordinated or integrated. They continued to have "fragmented, rivalrous and squabbling relationships with one another." The Remington sales force had little interest in or understanding of the operations or uses of the new products. Rand and his senior managers were reluctant to invest heavily in developing a successor to UNIVAC I.[25]

Not surprisingly, Rand, the empire builder, responded to the rising challenge from IBM through acquisitions rather than internal investment. In 1955, as said earlier, he merged Remington Rand with Sperry Gyroscope to form the Sperry Rand Corporation. Sperry had been established in 1910 to produce Elmer Sperry's invention, the gyroscope. It turned to making torpedoes and bomb sights in World War I and produced gunnery-fire control and aviation equipment in World War II. By 1955 it had become the country's leading instrument maker. The rationale for the merger was that Sperry would provide research capabilities, as well as income, and Remington Rand would provide access to business markets. Although three product development units were placed in a single unit headed by William Norris, a founder of ERA, they remained in their separate locations. Conflicts continued. In less than two years a disgruntled Norris and several close Engineering Research Associates colleagues left to start Control Data.

The Rand division of Sperry Rand continued to be organized on functional lines, with the production and sales managers responsible for all office products, of which the new computer was only one. The sales force failed to develop close relationships with either the production or the development departments. It had little understanding of computer technology and how such technology might be used by their customers. Few computer-oriented capabilities were created. There was no steady stream of new products. UNIVAC II finally appeared in 1957 and UNIVAC III in 1960. The next versions, UNIVAC 1004 and UNIVAC 1008 II, were not announced until 1963 and 1965, respectively.

So as IBM moved to capture the commercial markets, Sperry Rand continued to rely on designing and building computers for the government, particularly the air force and the Atomic Energy Commission. It did little exploratory work along the lines of IBM's Poughkeepsie research laboratory. Its strategy became one of concentrating on government contract work and then spinning off commercial products when the opportunity presented itself. By 1963, before IBM's System 360 was announced, Sperry Rand had not yet built an integrated learning base essential for the development of technical and functional capabilities in the new electronic-based path of learning. This helps explain why its revenues that year were only $145.5 million, less than one-eighth of IBM's $1,244 million.

Whereas the senior managers at Remington Rand and then Sperry Rand failed to transform the capabilities of individuals into organizational ones by creating an integrated learning base, William Norris at Control Data succeeded brilliantly.

In the fall of 1951, when Jim Rand offered to acquire ERA, Norris, who headed ERA operations, opposed the move. But ERA was badly capitalized, so its president, James Parker, who had been responsible for raising much of the initial capital, insisted that selling out to Rand was necessary if the Parker-Norris team was to remain in the computer industry. Norris stayed on. After five years as general manager of Rand's UNIVAC division, frustrated by the failure of senior managers at Remington Rand and then Sperry Rand to support his development work, Norris and most of his team embarked on an enterprise of their own, Control Data Corporation.

When Norris established Control Data in 1957 with $600,000 and twelve employees, he laid down two strategies for building this fledgling start-up into a major computer enterprise. The first strategy was to develop machines for government agencies at the high end of the price/performance spectrum, then spin off commercial products from them—as he had done at Sperry Rand. However, in contrast with Sperry Rand, which was inefficient and essentially noncompetitive from the start and relied on government contracts simply to stay alive, Control Data used these contracts as a source of both initial technical learning and funding for acquiring essential production facilities. In Norris's words: "We picked out a particular niche of the market, the scientific and engineering part of the market, by building large, scientific computers with a lot more bang for their buck." Norris's CDC achieved this goal primarily by developing high-performance hardware—a supercomputer—with the customer creating most of its software. Norris's other strategy was one of vertical integration. In time, his company came to produce its own components—processors, memories, peripherals, and the like. At the same time, it built a computer-knowledgeable sales force in the United States and abroad.[26]

The new company's initial commercial product, the CDC 1604 for scientific and engineering applications, was a 1960 spin-off from computers shipped to military customers. Its CDC 160, a small-scale machine for scientific and engineering purposes, followed shortly thereafter. In that same year, the company enlarged its scientific and engineering lines through the acquisition of Bendix Aviation's computer business and Control Precision's Liberscope division. Bendix's G-15 and Liberscope's LGP-30 were small-scale computers similar to the 160.

Control Data had announced its first supercomputer, the 6600, in 1962. It was designed by Seymour Cray (who had joined ERA in 1950 immediately after graduating from the University of Minnesota) and was to be delivered to the Atomic Energy Commission's Livermore Laboratory. IBM immediately responded by announcing that it would produce an even more powerful system. The announcement of the 6600 was made as the contract was signed, but the first 6600 computer was not delivered until 1964. Nevertheless, since IBM was in the throes of creating the System 360, it was unable to fulfill its challenge. The 6600 and its successors gave Control Data and its designers dominance of the supercomputer market until 1972, when Cray left to start his own company.

In transforming this pioneering entrepreneurial start-up into a powerful industrial enterprise, Norris and his associates relied on acquisitions. These acquisitions differed strikingly, however, from those of James Rand. In the production of the initial 1604 and then the 6600 the company had had to rely on outside suppliers, including IBM, for nearly all its peripherals and on National Cash Register to market its 1600 in the United States and the British firm Ferranti Ltd. to market the 1604 abroad. Between 1963 and 1969 Control Data purchased thirty-eight small producers of data-processing equipment. Nearly all were entrepreneurial start-ups. Their careful integration into the design and production activities of the larger operating units provided the company with its initial product development and production capabilities and learning base.

Thus Control Data also became, by the end of the sixties, in addition to the supercomputers, a major producer of display terminals, printers, disk drives, storage units, tape transports, disk files, and other peripherals, not only for itself, but also for GE, RCA, NCR, Honeywell, Germany's Siemens, Britain's International Computers Ltd. (ICL), and others. In 1966 it began to produce its own integrated circuits, which until then it had purchased primarily from Texas Instruments. To expand the market, Norris began providing customized software applications, solutions to specific customers' needs, and other computer services.

Control Data, one of the two successful entrepreneurial computer firms to become a major mainframe producer, did so by focusing on a niche where no first-mover had entered and by vertically integrating through the acquisition of small start-ups. This careful strategy of consolidation provided the "critical mass" needed to provide the scale economies and broad learning base that permitted Control Data to become a global leader in the production of peripherals and services as well as supercomputers (table 4.2, page 118).

NCR, Burroughs, and Honeywell: Initial Attempts to Enter the IBM Path

Unlike Sperry Rand, the two other office machinery companies—NCR and Burroughs—and Honeywell, a producer of control systems and components, did not attempt to build giant scientific computers but focused rather on smaller commercial machines for markets in which they had long operated. None of them, however, had made a serious move into computers by the time IBM's System 360 was announced in 1964.

National Cash Register, the nation's first-mover in that business machine industry, gingerly moved into computing by purchasing in 1953 the Computer Research Corporation, a California company producing small machines for military markets. NCR's initial model, the 303, was designed in California and produced at the company's central factory in Dayton, Ohio. Next, after temporarily taking over the marketing of Control Data's 160, NCR developed its 315 and 390, primarily for its banking customers. NCR continued to sell these products through its cash register sales force. By 1962 only 2 percent of its revenue came from electronic data-processing products. In 1963 this revenue stood at $30.7 million, as compared with the six-year-old Control Data's revenue of $84.6 million. (The 1963 computer revenues for all these firms are listed in table 4.1.) Moreover, in these same years, NCR's management held back on making a commitment to transform its electrical/mechanical cash register and related processes of production into electronic ones. In 1964 NCR was still much the same company producing much the same products in much the same manner as it did before World War II.[27]

Before World War II, the Burroughs Adding Machine Company was the fourth largest office machine maker in the United States in terms of sales. The first-mover in adding machines, it broadened its line during the 1930s to cash registers and machines for accounting and bookkeeping. Its initial involvement with computers began in 1953 with the production of a static magnetic memory for ENIAC. Burroughs experimented in building small computers for the government before it purchased Electrodata in 1956. Like NCR's acquisition, Electrodata was a small California producer that had built, in collaboration with the Jet Propulsion Laboratory of the California Institute of Technology, a vacuum tube–based computer named Datatron. Datatron was a failure; but Burroughs's transistor-based follow-up was more successful. Sold largely to its bank and accounting customers, it began to lose out to IBM's 700 series and its 1400. In 1963 Burroughs's total revenues from electronic data processing were $42.1 million. As was the case at NCR, Burroughs before 1964 had made no serious attempt to transform its primary products and processes into electronic ones.[28]

Honeywell's story differs largely in that its move into computers came through a joint venture with Raytheon, a prewar producer of radio tubes that had grown enormously during World War II making radar and other military electronics. After the war, Raytheon began to work on computers for the navy. In 1953 it designed a commercial transistor-based computer that became the Datamatic, which sold for $2 million apiece. In 1955 Raytheon joined with Honeywell (60 percent Honeywell and 40 percent Raytheon) to complete and market the machine. The Datamatic performed so poorly that Raytheon decided in 1957 to pull out of the venture and the industry. More successful were Honeywell's next transistor-based systems, the 800 series and then, in 1962, the 200 series, which were similar to IBM's 1400 "punched card" series. Honeywell's 296, sold to chemical, oil, and other energy-related firms, did particularly well. In 1962 the company negotiated an arrangement under which Japan's Nippon Electric Company manufactured and sold Honeywell's computers in Japan. Nevertheless, the total revenues from Honeywell's electronic data-processing products reached only $27 million in 1963—just 5 percent of the company's total revenues. In 1964 Honeywell, like NCR and Burroughs, still considered itself a producer of electro-mechanical products by mechanical processes.[29]

In 1963 the total revenue from electronic data-processing products for these three long-established makers of office machinery was just under $100 million, as compared with IBM's $1,244 million, Sperry Rand's $146 million, and Control Data's $85 million. Nevertheless, small as their share was, they were able to survive the impact of IBM's System 360 while the nation's two electrical/electronics giants, RCA and GE, were not.

Challenges by the Giants—GE and RCA

The challenges by General Electric and the Radio Corporation of America in the early 1960s were entirely different from those of the established office machinery companies. These world leaders in the creation of twentieth-century electronics industries were much larger. They had broader technical capabilities and stronger financial resources. Both had hesitated during the 1950s to enter the commercial computer market. Lured by IBM's extraordinary success with its 650 and 1400 series, GE made its first move in 1961, before the announcement of the System 360 in 1964. RCA's full-scale entry began shortly after that announcement.

In 1963 General Electric's computer revenues were $38.6 million, only half as much as those of the then six-year-old Control Data (table 4.1). GE's total was produced largely by its 200 series of small, general-purpose machines. At the end of 1963 it announced two new lines, the 400 series of small commercial machines to compete with IBM's 1400 transistor series and its 600 series of large computers to compete with IBM's latest 700 models. At the same time, GE's technicians began working with MIT and the Bell Telephone Laboratories to develop the first time-sharing systems, an important new technology that enhanced the use of individual computers.

In the spring of 1964 General Electric revealed its grandiose plans to become a world leader in the mainframe industry, and to do so by creating a world-wide product line that would cover the main portions of the product spectrum. The ambitions of GE's senior executives were not based just on vision like those of James Rand. They were based on the organizational capabilities GE had learned in building its international competitive strength in electric lighting in the 1890s and in electrical appliances in the 1920s. Its managers began by purchasing the computer business of two of the four major European producers, France's Machines Bull and Italy's Olivetti. In Japan they turned to Toshiba, a 1937 merger of Shibaura Electric and Tokyo Electric. Both these predecessors began as joint ventures with GE during the first decade of the century (as reviewed in chapter 6). In the early 1960s GE was helping to finance Toshiba's postwar recovery.[30]

By 1968 GE's computer division had established research, engineering, and production facilities at thirteen locations in five countries. It had set up an international marketing and service organization of approximately eight thousand employees. As it expanded, it brought out a new 100 and 200 series of business computers. In that year, 1968, the division's managers reported that sales of information systems were "well above those for 1967 and with operating losses substantially reduced." To improve GE's competitive position, its senior executives approved plans to spend $400 million to develop an advanced product line (APL).

Late in 1969 GE's chairman, Fred J. Borsch, formed a New Venture Taskforce to evaluate the prospects of the company's three major high-technology businesses—nuclear power, jet engines, and computers. After a careful review, the task force recommended maintaining the first two but urged the closing down of computers. "Faced with a lack of earnings growth . . . General Electric cannot, in our opinion, undertake *any* half-billion-dollar venture such as APL, that produces substantial intermediate net income losses."[31]

Furthermore, the review continued, IBM was "a moving target." By the time GE caught up, IBM would be much further along its learning trajectory. IBM's announcement of the System 370 assured approval of the task force recommendations. In May 1970 GE's top management sold its computer hardware business, including Bull and Olivetti, to Honeywell in a transaction that led to the formation of Honeywell Information Systems, in which GE held 18.5 percent. A complex financial exchange of notes and shares appear to have covered GE's losses of $164 million in computers. The 18.5 percent holding was sold off during the 1970s.

An underlying reason for GE's failure, the task force reported, was managerial. The computer division's managers did not have the training and experience in computers necessary to pursue long-term product development.

The reported litany of errors, breakdowns, false starts, and failures to follow through document the difficulties in building an integrated operating division in a new high-technology path of learning, even by the most technically experienced enterprise. Moreover, as one of several major businesses, the computer business did not receive the attention and commitment of top management. Finally, in the words of the New Venture Taskforce: "For the first time in our generation, at least, we faced the necessity for the allocation of corporate resources which are not adequate to meet our readily identifiable needs. . . ."

As for RCA, its disastrous attempt to become a computer maker was the most crucial episode in the disintegration of the U.S. consumer electronics industry. Since this story is reviewed in chapter 2, it is summarized only briefly here. RCA's entry into the commercial computing market differed from GE's, in that it specifically chose to produce an IBM plug compatible. In December 1964 it announced its Spectra line. Its product lines were to perform at levels between those covered by price/performance levels of the System 360. By using the IBM model, RCA would achieve lower unit costs because of lower R&D expenditures and shorter production schedules and could then underprice IBM's products. In addition, its use of advanced chip technology gave the Spectra performance advantages.[32]

Nevertheless, because of its lack of long-tested production and marketing capabilities, its strategy failed. Although RCA's products were technically superior to IBM's in some respects, RCA was unable to produce and market them profitably. Despite its heavy losses in computers, RCA continued to attempt to compete until an internal review in 1971 indicated that the cost of becoming competitive would require at least half a billion dollars more. The company then sold its computer business to Sperry Rand. RCA was never able to recover from the financial losses in computers and from its failure to maintain its basic core capabilities in consumer electronic products as its R&D personnel concentrated on computers.

Minicomputers: The Creation of a Second Path

IBM's most successful challenger was neither of the nation's two electronics giants, nor any rival in office machines, but an entrepreneurial enterprise that created a new product for a new market. This was Kenneth H. Olsen's Digital Equipment Corporation (DEC), established in 1957. Although by

1963 DEC had not yet produced enough revenue to be listed in table 4.1, it was coming up fast as a major competitor.

Ken Olsen, like William Norris at Control Data, targeted a niche on the boundary of IBM's mainframe path. But whereas Norris's niche was super-computers selling for $2 million to $3 million apiece, Olsen's niche was low-priced, high-powered, volume-produced minicomputers for scientists and engineers working in their own shops and offices, a still untapped market. His product was the program data processor (PDP). Olsen's success rested on his ability to transform individual capabilities into organizational ones as he quickly commercialized his PDP series of computers.

Olsen's own learning, like that of Norris, began with the birth of the computer industry. After completing his service in the U.S. Naval Reserve in 1947, he entered MIT. While an undergraduate he worked in Jay Forrester's navy Whirlwind Project. Between 1953 and 1956 he got to know (and dislike) IBM as a liaison man for Forrester's Lincoln Laboratory during the development of the SAGE computer. In 1957, with Harold Anderson, a colleague at Lincoln Laboratory, Olsen began operations in a former textile mill in Maynard, Massachusetts. From the start he had the financial backing of one of the country's earliest venture capitalists, Georges Doriot, founder of American Research and Development (ARD).[33]

At DEC, Olsen's PDP-1 went on the market in 1961. It and the next three products were, in James Cortada's words, "little more than tailor-made devices, assembled almost to order." They were an immediate success in the academic community of Cambridge, Massachusetts. In 1963 came the PDP-5, which in Kenneth Flamm's words "quickly carved out a whole new market," for it permitted the placing of computers on the shop floor and in engineering and research laboratories. The PDP-6, delivered in 1964, was the first computer with a commercially available time-sharing system that permitted a number of users to process data at the same time on a single computer.

The PDP-8, introduced in 1965, was Digital's initial masterpiece—the first mass-produced minicomputer. It sold for the extraordinarily low price of $18,000. It consisted "of processor, control panel, and core memory in a package small enough to be embedded in other equipment." Indeed, 30 to 50 percent of the PDP-8 and its successors were sold to either original equipment manufacturers, who embedded them in their own data-processing systems, or to what were termed "value-added resellers" (VARs), who combined them with other components to produce their own specialized products.

The rest went to university laboratories and engineering and design companies. These customers used the computers for only a small number of specialized applications, and many for only a single one, so customers developed most of their own software. Because of this, DEC did not need to provide a full line of software applications to compete with IBM but could instead focus on providing high performance at a low price.

The strategy of low price/high performance succeeded brilliantly. In the single year 1966 DEC's revenues ascended from $15 million to $23 million, and from 1965 to 1967 its profits rose sixfold. Although its marketing force was much smaller and more specialized than IBM's, DEC by 1966 had twenty-four sales offices in six countries. By then Olsen had already brought together an impressive management team and designed a matrix organizational structure to integrate the activities of the functional and product development departments.[34] Nevertheless, DEC did have a strong rival, very much a potential first-mover.

In 1961 two engineers, Max Palevsky and Robert Bell, established Scientific Data Systems (SDS). They had received their training on army missile development at Bendix and then in organizing Packard-Bell's military computer manufacturing operations. SDS's initial product for the scientific and engineering market (SDS 910), delivered in 1965, was technologically superior to DEC's PDP-6. It too pioneered work in developing time-sharing techniques. For a brief period, it was the primary supplier of small time-sharing systems. In 1965 it was growing at a rate even faster than that of DEC, doubling production by 1967. Yet despite this "remarkable growth" (Flamm's words), by the early 1970s SDS was no longer a major competitor.[35]

SDS, unlike DEC, moved quickly into the development of larger computers in competition with IBM, and so fell behind developing high-volume production of minicomputers. And, again unlike DEC, it concentrated on the government market. During the late 1960s an estimated 40 percent of its production went to the National Aeronautics and Space Administration (NASA). Because it relied on the government market, it did not build a national and international marketing organization so essential to learning the needs of commercial customers. In 1969 Xerox, which had earlier invested in SDS, acquired full control. Unable to supply it with the necessary production and marketing capabilities, Xerox, in 1975, after incurring a loss of $1.3 million, sold off the SDS division to Honeywell. Thus DEC, not SDS, became the path definer for the engineering and scientific market because it had built—and SDS had not—an integrated learning base.

The Evolution of the Paths of Learning in the 1970s

With the IBM mainframe and the DEC minicomputer paths of learning established in the second half of the 1960s, the young data-processing industry came of age. The following tables placed as appendices are intended simply to illustrate this point. Appendix 4.2 shows its growth in the United States and worldwide during that decade. Appendix 4.3 pinpoints the expansion of U.S. exports worldwide of computer equipment during the critical years 1967–1971. Appendix 4.4 emphasizes the dominance of the mainframe sector, while indicating the rapid growth of the much smaller minicomputer sector; the relatively limited "small business market" met in good part by IBM's production unit that was not part of the System 360; and the very beginning of the sales of personal computers between 1955 and 1979.

Because I concluded the creation of the industry's two paths with the evolution of the minicomputer, I carry on this chronicle of the U.S. industry in the 1970s with the story of DEC and its followers. (As the only challenger to Control Data in the 1970s was Norris's chief designer, Seymour Cray, the supercomputer niche is not a broad path of learning.) Next I review the path of IBM's mainframe and its competitors during that decade.

THE EVOLUTION OF THE MINICOMPUTER PATH IN THE 1970S

By the early 1970s DEC was becoming the most dynamic enterprise in the computer world. In the late 1960s it had begun to move into larger machines designed to compete with the lower end of the IBM System 360 line. But after 1970 it pulled back to concentrate on its initial market by developing the PDP-11 family. Elegantly designed, versatile, and powerful, that series came to be considered the most technologically advanced minicomputer of the 1970s. In 1977 DEC introduced a new product line, the VAX-11/780, to compete with a larger IBM 3031 and 3032. This enhanced minicomputer quickly made impressive inroads on the low end of IBM's mainframe markets and in time spurred Olson on to compete directly with IBM in mainframes.

Unlike Control Data, DEC quickly had its followers. DEC's initial major rival was Data General, formed in 1968 by Edson de Castro, a senior designer of the PDP-8, who took with him a group of DEC's most talented engineers. They quickly applied the technical and functional knowledge that they had learned in commercializing the PDP series to develop, produce, and market a competitive minicomputer of their own. Their primary product, the low-cost NOVA (priced at $8,000), was the first to have a 16-bit processor with improved memory capability. It was followed in 1974 by the larger and more sophisticated Eclipse series. The systems could be linked together and had interfaces for linkages with IBM's System 360. Data General, like Control Data, sold peripherals and some software and services, focusing on VARs.[36]

Next came Prime Computer, established in 1971 by William Poduska and other senior executives of the Computer Control Corporation (CCC), specialists in scientific and electronic switching applications. In 1966 Honeywell acquired CCC. Then, frustrated by Honeywell's failure to support their efforts to develop a minicomputer, Poduska and his group formed their own company to commercialize the product they had been developing. Prime grew quickly during the 1970s, commercializing state-of-the-art systems, but its competitive strength declined after Poduska and much of its top management, disturbed by the failure of Prime's board of directors to invest in product development, left the company to start Apollo, the first to apply the revolutionary new microprocessor technology to the engineering and scientific market in the form of the workstation—a story for the next chapter.[37]

The most successful of DEC's followers was Hewlett-Packard (HP), a producer of electronic analytical instruments. Formed in 1938, it expanded the output of its initial line during World War II. In the following years, new products were commercialized, including in 1966 its first processor to provide computational support for its instruments. It then led the way in handheld electronic calculators. In 1968 it began cautiously to develop a minicomputer, bringing out in early 1972 its highly successful HP 3000. This versatile minicomputer performed broader general-purpose computations than its rivals. Upgraded in 1976, it did time-sharing, multiprogramming, batch, or on-line processing and supported various computer languages used by large mainframes. Because HP had experience in commercializing electrical and electronic equipment, its move into the minicomputer learning path was highly successful. In time it became second only to IBM in maintaining its worldwide competitiveness in the new product sectors that evolved with the coming of the microprocessors, again a story for chapter 5.[38]

After 1972 the new entrants in minicomputers were specialized producers, not general-purpose ones. Of these the most successful was Wang Laboratories, formed in 1951 by An Wang, a student of Howard Aiken's, whose company specialized in office automation. In June 1976 his company introduced the Wang Word Processing System (WPS), the first screen-based word processor. It was an immediate success. Wang's revenues rose from forty-fifth in data-processing computers in 1976 to eighth in 1983. The two other specialized computer makers, Tandem Computer and Stratus Computer, built fault-tolerant systems, computers with a number of processors so that if one failed, the other would take over, thereby eliminating the risk of system failures and damages to databases by electronic malfunctions. Tandem shipped its first fault-tolerant computer in May 1976. Stratus became its primary competitor in 1980.[39]

During the 1970s, as the minicomputer firms began to challenge mainframes successfully in broader commercial markets, mainframe producers responded by entering the minicomputer business. IBM did so successfully with its 4300 midrange series. Burroughs and Sperry Rand were somewhat less successful. By 1985 IBM was first, ahead of DEC, with Hewlett-Packard third, albeit a distant third, in revenues generated in the minicomputer sector, followed by Wang, Data General, Prime Computer, and Tandem (table 4.2). Together these seven accounted for roughly 70 percent of the revenues generated in the minicomputer market. At that time this market accounted for 30 percent of the total computer revenues.[40]

THE CONTINUING EVOLUTION OF THE MAINFRAME PATH DURING THE 1970S

The continuing evolution of the mainframe path during the 1970s began with IBM's decision to build the System 370. In keeping with their long-held policy of using the knowledge and income from one major product line to commercialize the next, the senior managers at IBM began to focus on their next line of computers even before the System 360 reached the market. In January 1965 John W. Haanstra, who had headed the SPREAD task group, was appointed president of the new Systems Development Division. He immediately began to plan for the creation of a system as revolutionary as the System 360 had been, one based on the promise of greatly increasing the number of circuits on an integrated chip. At a time when the challenge was to fabricate a chip with five circuits, Haanstra set a goal of ten to one hundred. That great leap forward in chips would require entirely new operating systems. But 1965 was the year of the System 360 crisis at IBM. In the management reshuffling that resulted, Haanstra was dropped as head of product development. When planning was renewed in the following year, his successor and senior managers agreed that evolution, not revolution, was the most promising course.[41]

So the System 370, whose first models were announced in June 1970, was an evolutionary extension of the System 360. Improvements in both the integrated circuits and the central processing unit (CPU) brought a fourfold increase in the performance of the processors and much greater reliability. Semiconductor memories replaced all the ferrite core ones. The improved peripherals included faster printers, greater disk storage capacity, and "virtual memory" (a combination of hardware and software that expanded the capacity of the main memory).[42]

The System 370 also enlarged the number of computer lines IBM produced, particularly at the high end. However, at the low end the designers were still unable to produce a computer that was compatible with the System 360/370 basic operating system. The technological complexities remained too challenging. So in October 1969 the company established a separate unit to manufacture its small business system, noncompatible with System 360—a unit that was to become the entry level systems division that spawned the IBM PC (see chapter 5).[43]

IBM Falters

As the System 370 entered the marketplace, senior management created the Future Systems (FS) task force, with John R. Opel as its chairman, to meet the challenge of future growth. At that moment a business recession had brought a sharp decline in orders. At the same time, long-term projections indicated that because of the continuing drop in costs and prices of computers, new products and new applications were needed if the company was to maintain its target of 15 percent annual growth. One of the goals set by the task force was to reduce the customers' costs of developing their own application software. Another was to develop interfaces that were more user-friendly for professional programmers and novices alike. More radical was the goal of consolidating all memories and memory storage so that information stored anywhere in the system could be retrieved more quickly and easily. Central to the program was the development of high-powered, high-density, very large-scale integrated (VLSI) chips, which Haanstra had proposed in 1965. But despite intensive continuing effort, the developers were unable to overcome the technical challenges involved. As one consultant, Fred Brooks, reported in June 1973: "Complexity is the fatal foe."[44]

In the spring of 1974 the expected time before formal announcement of the System FS was forty-five months, precisely what it had been in the fall of 1971 when Opel's task force completed its work. Top managers then agreed to terminate the FS and instead "to extend the architecture of the System 360/370." Although much of the hardware developed for System FS was used in later models, Emerson Pugh points out that "most of the system designs, microcodes, and software were discarded. It was the most expensive development failure in the company's history." It was often referred to as IBM's Vietnam. IBM's FS may be an example of the limits to further commercializing an existing broad technology for a well-established market.[45]

IBM Plug-Compatible Peripherals and Mainframes

During these years when IBM was attempting to develop innovative architecture for its mainframe computers, competition increased. Although IBM remained the global giant, its market share in the computer industry declined from 1970 on. Competition came less from its rivals of the 1950s and early 1960s and more from the makers of the low-priced minicomputers and the high-priced supercomputers. But most serious from IBM's perspective were the companies that on the basis of the 1956 consent decree were able to produce and market their own versions of the peripherals and mainframes of the Systems 360 and 370—that is, the companies that produced IBM "plug-compatibles," or, in later terminology, clones. These manufacturers could undersell IBM because they did not have the first-mover cost of developing the hardware and related software. In other words, in computer hardware IBM's primary competitors were producing IBM-invented devices.

Even before 1970 a number of existing enterprises had begun to produce IBM plug-compatible products. They usually started by producing on an OEM basis—that is, selling directly to other manufacturers to be used in those producers' final products. Soon, however, they were marketing them over their own labels to computer users as replacement parts. Telex, a prewar hearing aid producer that had begun to manufacture tape drives in 1962, marketed its first IBM plug-compatible tape drive in 1967, which it sold at a 50 percent discount to IBM's price. In 1968 Memorex, established in 1961 as a maker of magnetic and then tape drives, began making plug-compatible disk packs and drives. In the same year, Ampex, the established maker of tape drives that had pioneered the videocassette recorder (see chapter 3), began producing plug-compatible tape drives and in 1969 plug-compatible core memories. In addition, twelve IBM engineers left in 1967 to form Information Storage Systems, and shortly thereafter four others started Storage Technology Corporation.[46]

The coming of these IBM clones enlarged the incipient supporting nexus of small enterprises in the data-processing industry, often entrepreneurial start-ups producing peripherals and other components. The most aggressive of such competitors became Control Data in peripherals and the Amdahl Corporation in mainframes.

Control Data, which in the early 1960s produced a full line of peripherals for its own computers and then sold them to others on an OEM basis, quickly began to make IBM plug-compatible disk drives, then "add-on memories," and shortly a full line of such IBM peripheral clones. Each time IBM announced a new peripheral, Control Data quickly followed by bringing one out at a lower price. Through the practice of retroengineering and making slight changes, it could stay abreast of IBM without incurring similar development costs. By 1970 Burroughs, NCR, and Sperry Rand, as well as RCA and GE, were producing plug-compatible peripherals. Britain's International Computers Ltd., Germany's Siemens, and Japan's Fujitsu soon followed.[47]

In mainframes, RCA (as described in chapter 3) and computer makers in Europe and Japan (as told in chapter 6) attempted with little success to build plug-compatible computers during the 1960s. Not surprisingly, the first to succeed was Gene M. Amdahl, a chief designer of the 704, the System 360, and then the 370. He did so when he resigned from IBM in 1970 to form his own company. He left because in the development of the System 370, top management insisted that its high-end computer had to conform to the price/performance relationship defined for the rest of the 370. Amdahl was certain that the high-end computer could be produced at a profit, but not at what IBM considered its "normal" (that is, impressively high) profit level. As

Amdahl wrote, he recognized "that IBM's desire to optimize its financial return represented an Achilles' heel, which I could exploit if I were to leave and go into the large computer business in competition with IBM." His firm would build the central processor, obtaining the peripherals from the rapidly growing plug-compatible market.[48]

Amdahl's challenge, however, was finance. His business plan called for raising only from $33 million to $44 million. But in that year of economic depression, 1970, he was unable to find a venture capitalist to provide the necessary funds. So in 1971 Amdahl turned to the leading Japanese computer maker, Fujitsu, which, with other Japanese companies and the government agency MITI, was making little headway in its efforts to build an IBM plug-compatible. Fujitsu's management responded immediately to Amdahl's proposal. It then acquired 24 percent of Amdahl's equity, in return for an exchange of technical information. Three years later Fujitsu announced that it would make Amdahl computers in Japan to be sold through Amdahl in the United States. As Kenneth Flamm notes: "This was the turning point for the Japanese computer industry. At last it would acquire the ability to produce computers competitive with the latest IBM models."[49] The story of how Amdahl's move permitted Japan's computer industry for the first time to challenge the U.S. industry provides a basic theme of chapter 6.

IBM also had to compete with its own machines on another front. In the 1960s independent companies began to purchase IBM computers and lease them out to their own customers. As the System 360 came onstream in the late 1960s, its leasing immediately became a big business. These firms purchased IBM machines, leasing them at a lower price and offering more financing alternatives than did IBM. They did so in good part by depreciating them over a longer time period. When the System 370 appeared, they sold their System 360s as they bought the new machines. Some of the leasing enterprises were units of large established enterprises, but most were start-ups, including such firms as Itel, Diebold, Leasco, Levin-Townsend, and MAI. Their sharp increases in revenues were astonishing. For example, from 1967 through 1969 Diebold's revenues rose from $268,000 to $30.8 million; Itel's from $1.4 million to $38.7 million; and Leasco's from $8.5 million to $37.7 million. Those of Greyhound, the pioneering lessor, rose from $17.3 million in 1965 to $49.9 million in 1969 In leasing, as in peripherals, the coming of the System 360 led to the beginning of these new lines of business in the data-processing industry's supporting nexus.[50]

IBM's U.S. Mainframe Competitors in the 1970s

In addition to the new competition from the makers of cloned IBM products, IBM continued to be challenged by its well-established competitors. Of these, after the withdrawal of General Electric and RCA, Control Data was the most successful. Not only was it a major rival in plug-compatible peripherals and services, but it continued to hold the lead in its chosen path of large-scale supercomputers. In that high-end scientific market IBM was unable to catch up. Control Data's 7600 followed the 6600. Then came the Star in 1969 and the Cyber 205 in 1981. As in the past, the first models were delivered to government customers. Control Data's major competitor in the superconductor market became and remained its brilliant designer, Seymour Cray, who left in 1972 to form Cray Research, much as Amdahl resigned from IBM to form his own company and de Castro departed from DEC to establish Data General.[51]

Of the remaining four, Sperry Rand and Honeywell expanded their lines through acquisition, Sperry Rand by acquiring those that RCA discarded and Honeywell by acquiring those cast off by General Electric and then Xerox's Scientific Data Systems. On the other hand, Burroughs and National Cash Register concentrated on adapting the new electronic technology to their established markets. Their existing product lines provided them with the competitive advantage of well-learned functional capabilities in production, marketing, and product and process development. The success of Burroughs and NCR and the relative failure of Sperry Rand and Honeywell—in terms of revenues, income, and financial strength—emphasized that continuing profitability comes from enhancing existing internal capabilities through internal investment and rarely through acquisition.

SPERRY RAND AND HONEYWELL DECLINE

With the coming of the IBM System 360, Sperry Rand's UNIVAC division continued to lose market share in mainframes. As earlier in the 1950s, it did little exploratory research and continued to rely heavily on government agencies, particularly the air force, for the sale of its products—initially its UNIVAC series and then its general-purpose computer, the 1100, announced in 1970. The acquisition of RCA's computer business in 1971 significantly increased revenues, but its performance did not improve. Little effort was made to make its two commercial computing lines compatible.

The company continued to produce RCA's SPECTRA and its own 1100 series. By the end of 1974 only 5 percent of RCA's customers had installed UNIVAC equipment, and 77 percent still had their RCA machines. By 1973 Sperry Rand, which had been number two in computer industry revenues for much of the previous decade, dropped to fourth place despite the increase in size through the RCA purchase. Merger brought no new capabilities and diluted existing ones.[52]

Honeywell's initial response to the System 360 was an attempt to market its 200 line and then its 800 line to users of IBM's 1400, which had been displaced by the 360. The strategy was not successful. Most of Honeywell's sales continued to come by providing updated versions to purchasers of its earlier models. So in 1966 it turned to the strategy of growth through acquisition.

First came Honeywell's purchase of Computer Control Corporation. But, as mentioned earlier, its failure to support CCC's technical staff in the development of its minicomputer project led to their departure and the formation of Prime Computer. Then in 1970 Honeywell doubled its electronic data-processing business by acquiring GE's computer hardware unit, including GE's 66 percent interest in France's Machines Bull. It continued to maintain GE's lines for its existing customers in parallel with its lines for its own long-term users. Its acquisition of Xerox's Scientific Data Systems in 1975 was even less successful than that of CCC. After 1975 Honeywell continued to handle three noncompatible computer lines but made little attempt to improve any of the three.[53]

Not surprisingly, Honeywell, which in 1973 had the second largest data-processing revenues, had dropped by 1982 to seventh, and in 1984 to ninth. In the late 1970s it had moved back to the military market. In 1986 it exited altogether from the computer business but retained a minority stake in France's Machines Bull. On the other hand, as it moved out of data processing, Honeywell did successfully make the transition from electromechanical to electronic products and processes in its core lines of control systems and components and restored its leading position in the computer-based temperature control systems industry.

BURROUGHS AND NCR SUCCEED

As the computer fortunes of Sperry Rand and Honeywell declined during the late 1960s and 1970s, those of Burroughs and NCR recovered. For both, continuing success rested on applying recently learned technical capabilities to the markets they knew best. They reshaped their product-specific functional capabilities, particularly in product development and, to a lesser extent, marketing, and they did so with existing personnel and conservative external financing. The strengthening of capabilities in their initial primary markets, in turn, permitted them to begin to produce competitive data-processing computers for a broader range of markets. By 1979 NCR was the second largest U.S. mainframe producer behind IBM, and Burroughs was third, both producing revenues of well over $1 billion.

Burroughs began a corporate restructuring immediately after IBM's announcement of the System 360. A team headed by Ray W. MacDonald, who would become the company's CEO after leading its marketing organization, was formed "to establish a set of clearly defined product development objectives" and to reshape its functional activities so as to implement the new definition. In defining the company's strategy, the team took on "the line of business approach," focusing on the needs of its specific business markets in industry, banking, and government. Its accounting machines were transformed from electrical-mechanical to fully electronic products, including electronic memories. Manufacturing was decentralized with the building of several new plants, each producing different machines for the different markets. The sales force was reshaped along the same lines. Computers were now sold not by accounting machinery salesmen, but only by those trained in electronic data processing and procedures. Burroughs improved its computer lines by using new monolithic integrated circuits. By the end of the 1960s it produced a new generation of low-end general-purpose computers and was competing successfully with IBM, particularly in the banking and accounting markets.[54]

Restructuring paid off. Revenues almost doubled from 1963 to 1969—$392 million to $760 million—with net earnings rising more than fivefold from $10 million to $55 million. R&D expenditures more than doubled, growing from $15 million to $35 million (and to $102 million in 1977). Over $670 million had been raised through increases in debt and equity. The renewed earnings permitted the debt/equity ratio to drop from 52 percent in 1970 to 20 percent in 1976. During the same period assets had risen over 75 percent and earnings over 110 percent.

By 1973 Burroughs's increased revenues made it the third largest mainframe producer, just behind Honeywell (which had more than doubled its income through the acquisition of GE's computer hardware business in

1970). During the 1970s Burroughs continued to grow through the development of two new series of general-purpose computers, as well as low-cost smaller computers, word processing, and facsimile systems. At the same time, the continuing government work made it a major producer of computers for the army's ballistic missile systems. For Burroughs the road to profit was one of continuing the development of improved and new products for much the same well-defined, closely related markets that it had long served.

NCR waited almost a decade before refining its competitive strength with a comparable strategy. Indeed, if its board had not brought the head of its Japanese subsidiary, William F. Anderson, to Dayton as CEO in 1972, the company might well have gone under. By then Singer, Pitney-Bowes, Litton, and other firms had, largely through acquisitions, become powerful competitors in the new electronic point-of-sales cash registers. In 1972 Singer alone held 50 percent of the market. Within two years Anderson transformed NCR from a mass producer of high-precision mechanical parts machines into a high-quality assembler of purchased electronic components. Manufacturing, which had been centered in Dayton, was spread out in the United States and overseas in small new plants. The NCR marketing organization was also transformed in the Burroughs manner.[55]

In 1973 NCR delivered seventy-five thousand of its new electronic cash registers. The next year Pitney-Bowes exited from the industry. By 1975, as NCR rounded out its complete line of electronic point-of-sale cash registers and closed down the production of its electromechanical machines, its market share of cash registers had risen to 61 percent. Given NCR's existing worldwide marketing strength and its new technological abilities, Singer and two smaller competitors abandoned the market. By 1976 a new line of computers with its own peripherals, software, and services for retailing and banking customers was coming into production. Three years later NCR had caught up and was number two in mainframe revenues, just ahead of Burroughs. IBM, of course, was first.

Three of four of IBM's major U.S. competitors were first-movers in their respective sectors of the office machinery industry, as was the fourth in the heating and control industry. All had created their initial integrated learning bases in the 1880s, three decades before IBM established its base. All four had become followers in the learning path that IBM defined. Two, Burroughs and NCR, were successful in entering the path because they concentrated on applying the new electronic technology to products for much the same markets, markets they had initially created and operated in for decades. They did so through direct investment in facilities and personnel. Sperry Rand and Honeywell were not successful primarily because they grew through acquisition and failed to consolidate their acquisitions into their learning base. At the same time, they attempted to compete with IBM in the broader market for commercial computing. Both stayed alive primarily by the orders they received from government bureaus.

The Computer Industry in 1980-1985

The years 1980 to 1985 were critical in the evolution of the U.S. data-processing computer industry and, indeed, of the larger U.S. electronics industry. In that half decade, when the Japanese consumer electronics industry had all but completed its conquest of world markets, the Japanese computer industry had all but destroyed the U.S. memory chip business, shutting down the main facilities of Intel, Advanced Micro Devices, and National Semiconductor, the core enterprises of the Silicon Valley nexus. However, the introduction of the microprocessor at the same historical moment swiftly recast the industry worldwide. It permitted the U.S. industry to meet the Japanese challenge and to retain its position of global dominance.

To begin the review of this critical period, I summarize the status of the established U.S. computer industry in 1984 and 1985, reviewing the situation in mainframes, minicomputers, peripherals, and services. Similarly, I next review the Japanese computer industry as recorded in table 4.2. Then I turn to the evolution of the semiconductor industry, an industry on which the computer industry's evolution depended. I first review the rise of the U.S. semiconductor manufacturers, then turn to the Japanese challenge in semiconductors. Finally, I introduce the coming of the microprocessor, the savior of the U.S. industry and the subject of the next chapter.

MAINFRAMES, MINICOMPUTERS, AND PERIPHERALS IN 1984-1985[56]

In mainframes, IBM was still overwhelmingly the world leader. IBM was represented in all four of *Datamation*'s categories, being number one in all but services. Control Data was the leading supercomputer maker. Sperry Rand and Honeywell still enjoyed large revenues resulting from their acquisitions of RCA's and GE's cast-off businesses but had smaller incomes. Bur-

TABLE 4.2. The Leading Computer Companies Worldwide by Product Sector, 1982–1985

Rank for 1985; Company	Country	1982	1983	1984[2]	1985
Mainframes					
1 IBM	U.S.	10,662	11,443	13,131	14,010
2 Sperry Rand	U.S.	729	700	1,451[2]	1,891
3 Fujitsu	Japan	—	1,050	1,536	1,619
4 NEC	Japan	—	777	1,077	1,217
5 Control Data	U.S.	705	775	813	856
6 Hitachi	Japan	—	679	745	837
7 Honeywell	U.S.	1,060	1,000	665[2]	775
8 Burroughs	U.S.	2,000	2,000	747[2]	747
9 Machines Bull	France	—	—	500	574
10 NCR	U.S.	1,100	1,000	486[2]	486
11 Amdahl	Japan / U.S.	412	571	400	434
12 Siemens	Germany	—	686	351	374
13 ICL	U.K.	—	—	363	370
Minicomputers					
1 IBM	U.S.	2,945	2,627	3,500	3,500
2 Digital Equipment	U.S.	2,500	2,700	1,527[2]	1,600
3 Hewlett-Packard	U.S.	660	736	950	1,050
4 Wang Laboratories	U.S.	655	893	971	871
5 Data General	U.S.	670	705	840	800
6 Prime Computer	U.S.	351	417	479	564
7 Tandem Computer	U.S.	295	400	477	533
8 Harris	U.S.	—	—	410	470
9 Fujitsu	Japan	—	—	384	439
10 Nixdorf Computer	Germany	—	—	340	408
11 Sperry Rand	U.S.	—	—	410	401
12 Burroughs	U.S.	900	950	400[2]	400
Microcomputers					
1 IBM	U.S.	500	2,600	5,500	5,500
2 Apple Computer	U.S.	664	1,085	1,747	1,603
3 Olivetti	Italy	—	252	497	885
4 Tandy	U.S.	466	598	574	797
5 Sperry Rand	U.S.	—	386	503	743
6 Commodore International	U.S.	368	927	1,000	600
7 Compaq Computer	U.S.	—	111	329	504
8 Hewlett-Packard	U.S.	258	399	500	400
9 Convergent Technologies	U.S.	—	163	362	395
10 Zenith Electronics	U.S.	—	—	249	352

Estimated Revenues ($ millions)[1]

TABLE 4.2. (*Continued*)

Rank for 1985; Company	Country	Estimated Revenues ($ millions)[1]			
		1982	1983	1984[2]	1985
Peripherals					
1 IBM	U.S.			11,652	12,676
2 Digital Equipment	U.S.			2,500	2,750
3 Burroughs	U.S.			1,412	1,479
4 Xerox	U.S.			1,180	1,430
5 Hitachi	Japan			1,049	1,416
6 Control Data	U.S.			1,314	1,270
7 Wang Laboratories	U.S.			1,106	1,229
8 Hewlett-Packard	U.S.			900	1,100
9 Fujitsu	Japan			932	1,064
10 NEC	Japan			882	1,053
11 NCR	U.S.			950	1,000
12 Siemens	Germany			701	816
13 Toshiba	Japan			521	759
14 Machines Bull	France			605	699
15 Honeywell	U.S.			600	656
Computer Services					
1 Automatic Data Processing	U.S.	—	816	958	—
2 Control Data	U.S.	—	1,030	931	—
3 EDS (General Motors)	U.S.	—	719	786	—
4 General Electric	U.S.	—	600	725	—
5 Computer Sciences Corp.	U.S.	—	719	710	—
6 McDonnell Douglas	U.S.	—	525	608	—
7 Martin Marietta	U.S.	—	154	362	—
8 Boeing	U.S.	—	250	260	—
9 Cap Gemini Sogeti	France	—	184	206	—
10 IBM	U.S.	—	175	200	—

Source: Compiled from *Datamation*, June 15, 1986, pp. 44–46; June 1, 1985, pp. 38–39; June 1, 1984, pp. 55–56. Excerpted with permission of *Datamation* magazine. Copyrighted in 1986, 1985, 1984, by Cahners Publishing Company. Figures for U.S. companies are drawn solely from the 1984 and 1986 *Datamation* reports; the 1985 report was used solely for foreign company revenues in 1983.

[1] For 1982, figures are available for U.S. companies only. In case a company does not publish separate revenue figures for different market sectors or if a company's fiscal year is different from the calendar year, estimated calendar-year figures are presented. *Datamation*'s definitions of product sectors change periodically, leading to occasional large jumps in estimated revenues. The table, therefore, indicates rankings across companies and the change in those rankings reasonably accurately. However, the figures are not a reliable indicator of a given firm's specific sales growth (or decline) over the period.

[2] Between their 1984 and 1986 reports, *Datamation* began reclassifying significant amounts of revenue out of Hardware categories (i.e. mainframes and minicomputers) and into a separate Maintenance category. Thus, for several mainframe and minicomputer manufacturers (Sperry, Honeywell, Burroughs, NCR, and Digital), 1983 revenues differ markedly from 1984 revenues. Reclassified maintenance revenues constitute the bulk of the difference. IBM, however, is not affected by this discontinuity, as IBM's maintenance revenues were classified separately even for the 1982 and 1983 estimates.

roughs and NCR had smaller revenues but higher incomes by profitably meeting the demands of their niche markets. In minicomputers, Digital and its followers had been joined by IBM and three other mainframe makers, one of them Japanese.

In peripherals, the leading producers were still large computer makers. These major computer producers had followed the Control Data model by producing IBM plug-compatibles for use in their own systems as well as for sale in the broader market. Xerox, with its copiers, was the exception. By 1984 the smaller peripheral producers—Telex, Memorex, Ampex, Information Storage Systems, and Storage Technology—which had pioneered in exploiting the 1956 consent decree, had not yet grown to rival the peripheral revenues of the major computer companies.

SERVICES (INCLUDING SOFTWARE)

Services was first listed in *Datamation* in 1983. The companies in Table 4.2 performed two distinct types of service. One was providing data processing services. Six of the ten listed in table 4.2 included two start-ups, Automatic Data Processing (ADP) and Electronic Data Systems (EDS, acquired by General Motors in 1984), whose primary business was providing data-processing services; one industrial giant, GE; and three aerospace companies—McDonnell Douglas, Martin Marietta, and Boeing—which were basically leasing unused capacity on their own computer systems. The other four provided technical-based activities of installing and maintaining computer systems and writing software for those systems. These included two start-ups, Computer Sciences Corporation in the United States and Cap Gemini Sogeti in Europe, and two mainframe makers, Control Data and IBM.

The revenues of the new start-ups in computer services rose as fast as did those mentioned earlier in leasing. Those of Automatic Data Processing, the pioneer established in 1948 to handle payrolls in firms using existing methods and machines, went from $187,000 in 1957, to $2 million in 1963, to $20 million in 1968, to $37 million in 1970. H. Ross Perot, who left IBM to start Electronic Data Systems in 1962, sold it to General Motors for $2.5 million in 1984. By 1976 some 1,560 service companies were producing revenues of well over $3 billion. Appendix 4.5 documents the rapid expansion of the industry's service sector. Between 1965 and 1979 the estimated revenues for the service sector increased tenfold from just over half a billion dollars to $5.5 billion.[57]

A significant component of this dramatic rise was the growth of packaged software, whose emergence again reflects the epic role of IBM as the path definer. The modern software industry can be said to have had its beginnings in the 1970s, as packaged software overtook custom programming. While a few software firms did exist before 1970, they represented only a minor piece of the data-processing industry. In the earlier years, software, aside from that written by the computer companies themselves, had been produced by the buyers of computers or by individuals for hire.

According to Lawrence Welke, a publisher of catalogs of available packaged software, almost no capital was required: "All you need is a coding pad and a sharp pencil." By one estimate 85 percent of the production costs were for salaries to programmers and system analysts, 5 percent for developing new programs, and 10 percent for buying software packages and services.[58]

It was IBM's unbundling of its software in 1969 that hastened the shift from software designed for customer-specific needs to packaged software to handle specific functional services such as payrolls, ledgers, income tax preparations, and the like. This unbundling was the result of an antitrust case brought by the Justice Department in January 1969. The grounds for that suit was that IBM had "impaired" the development of independent electronic data-processing companies. Hoping for a quick settlement, IBM announced in June of that year that it would respond to one of the major charges—the charge that it sold hardware, software, and services only as a single package—by unbundling its software. (Its hardware had been available since the consent decree of 1956.) It would now sell, in Watson's words, at "à la carte prices for engineering services, customer training and some of our software." This opened up a market for companies hoping to sell independent software applications for the System 360 and 370.[59]

Revenues from packaged software rose from $100 million to $1.5 billion between 1968 and 1980. In these same years, those for custom programming only doubled from $300 million to $600 million (Appendix 4.6). Individual companies producing packaged software, including Computer Sciences Corporation, Informatics, Inc., and Applied Data Research, grew as fast as did those in leasing and services. For example, the revenues of Computer Sciences Corporation, established in 1959, rose from $5.7 million in 1965 to $82 million in 1970; to $452 million in 1980; and to $709.4 million in 1984.

By 1980, in addition to the software produced by computer makers, service bureaus, leasing companies, and in-house units of industrial, commercial, and military enterprises, over one thousand different firms were producing two thousand different products with estimated sales of over $2 billion, and by the mid-1980s sales had doubled again.[60]

THE JAPANESE CHALLENGE

In addition to recording the status of the U.S. computer companies in terms of revenue, table 4.2 records the arrival of the Japanese in world computer markets. That industry, created by the five Japanese core computing companies—Fujitsu, Hitachi, NEC, Toshiba, and Mitsubishi Electric—became competitive in the mid-1970s. It did so by exploiting first the opportunities of IBM plug-compatible hardware, and then, after 1960, IBM's unbundled software. But most important of all was the acquisition of Gene Amdahl's plug-compatible mainframe that incorporated both IBM hardware and software into a complete system. This story, of course, provides a major theme of chapter 6. But a few words are needed here to understand the industry's powerful challenge in the early 1980s.

By then, Japan's computer companies had become the primary producers of mainframes not only for their own rapidly growing market but also for the European market. They did so in the following manner. In 1973, three European companies—Siemens, Philips, and a French government-owned enterprise—joined together to build a plug-compatible mainframe, the Unidata. After the project had collapsed in 1975, Siemens, Europe's most successful computer maker, turned to Fujitsu to acquire its Amdahl-made plug-compatible on an OEM basis. In 1982, Britain's ICL did the same. Similarly, France's Machines Bull got a comparable product from NEC, and Olivetti got one from Hitachi. In other words, three Japanese companies—Fujitsu, NEC, and Hitachi—accounted for not only their own mainframe revenues on table 4.2, but also for those of the European firms listed thereon. The same holds for the peripherals sector as well, with the addition of Toshiba.

But in 1985 the United States was faced with an even more serious Japanese challenge. By then, five Japanese core companies had all but destroyed the U.S. producers of memory chips. In order to understand the significance of this challenge, I next review the history of the semiconductor industry, a history that shaped the evolution of the computer.

SEMICONDUCTORS

Semiconductors differed from peripherals and other computer hardware from the start because they were used in a wide variety of industries—in telecommunications equipment, appliances, medical devices, and automated production equipment—and a wide range of military devices. When the industry began, the government market accounted for 55 percent of integrated circuit production, while commercial computing accounted for 35 percent, consumer products 1 percent, and industrial uses 9 percent. By 1978 government was 10 percent, computers 38 percent, consumer products 15 percent, and industrial uses 38 percent.[61]

The beginnings of the semiconductor industry can be precisely dated. In April 1952 Western Electric, the manufacturing arm of AT&T, invited the representatives of twenty-five U.S. and ten foreign firms to its Bell Laboratories to attend an eight-day symposium on the electronic transistor that three of the Bell engineers had invented in 1948. Each representative paid $25,000 in advance royalties to AT&T. AT&T made this move because it was intending to concentrate on its use in commercializing switches and other telecommunications devices. It also did so because of a continuing threat of an antitrust suit from the U.S. Department of Justice.

The attendees of the April conference included large established firms and smaller niche ones. The producers of radio transmission and reception equipment, including GE, Westinghouse, RCA, Philco, Sylvania, and Raytheon, as well as Europe's Philips and Siemens, soon began to produce and improve the transistor and related diodes and rectifiers. These firms, however, remained committed to the older vacuum tube technologies as described in chapter 2.[62]

Therefore the more aggressive pioneers in the broad application of the new transistor and then the integrated circuit technology were smaller firms that had not produced vacuum tubes for the market. These included Motorola, a maker of car radios since 1927 and of walkie-talkies and other radio communication products during World War II; Texas Instruments (TI), producers of geological instruments for the oil industry since 1930 and of airborne magnetic detectors during the war; Hughes Aviation, another wartime producer; and two start-ups, Transitron, established in 1952, and Fairchild Semiconductor, established in 1957. Fairchild was an offshoot of a company that William Shockley, one of the transistor's inventors, had organized near Palo Alto in 1955, Shockley Semiconductors Inc.

By 1963 Hughes had dropped out and Transitron, which had 20 percent of the transistor market in 1957, had fallen back to only 3 percent. Texas Instruments, the supplier of IBM's semiconductors until the commercializing of the System 360, enjoyed 18 percent, Motorola 10 percent, and Fairchild 9 percent. GE, RCA, and Westinghouse together accounted for another 20 percent (8 percent, 7 percent, and 5 percent, respectively). By 1957 TI and Motorola were the two world leaders in transistors in terms of revenue and would remain so in the subsequent business of integrated circuits until the 1980s, when the Japanese producers began to drive the U.S. companies out of the market.

Both TI and Motorola had the advantages of retained earnings, which Transitron and Fairchild did not, and of capabilities learned in the development, production, and marketing of electronic products, which Transitron, Fairchild, and Hughes did not. At TI, Motorola, and Fairchild, transistors quickly became a major product line, which was not the case at GE or Westinghouse. Nor did they have, like RCA, a dominant position to maintain in vacuum tube–based radio and television. So I review very briefly the history of the three leading U.S. producers of semiconductors—that is, transistors and then integrated circuits—Texas Instruments, Motorola, and Fairchild Semiconductor.

Of the three, Texas Instruments was the most successful. From 1946 on it enhanced its electronics capabilities by producing radar and sonar systems for the military. Then in 1952, after signing the group agreement with AT&T, it began to volume-produce transistor radios. As the first to commercialize the silicon junction transistor (1954) and the diffused transistor (1956), TI quickly dominated silicon-based products. Its success led IBM in December of 1957 to enter a joint licensing and development agreement that, for all practical purposes, made TI the component supplier (until the System 360 began to be shipped in the 1960s) to the computer industry's fastest-growing enterprise. TI's position was further strengthened in 1959 when Jack Kilby, one of its engineers, patented an integrated circuit in the same year that Robert Noyce patented Fairchild's integrated circuit.[63]

During the 1960s TI, after making large investments in production and marketing facilities at home, began rapidly to expand by building plants and marketing networks abroad, an expansion financed almost entirely by retained earnings. By 1965 it was operating fifteen plants in ten different countries, all wholly owned. Those in Europe placed manufacturing close to customers but, of more importance, where skilled technicians and workers were available to build and operate complex fabrication plants. Those in

Latin America and Asia used cheap labor for assembling the final product. By 1968 TI was the largest producer of semiconductors in Britain (with 23 percent of the British market) and France (with 22 percent) and the third in Germany (with 16 percent). Throughout the 1970s TI led the semiconductor industry with worldwide market shares of 11.5 percent in 1972 and 12.8 percent in 1974.[64]

This overseas expansion was carried out by direct investment through the creation of wholly owned subsidiaries. Japan was the one exception. There TI was forced to enter a joint venture. Negotiations with Sony lasted from November 1963 until April 1968. They were completed only after TI agreed to license the Kilby patent and other IC technologies, not just to Sony, but to *all* Japanese firms. The delay and the deal itself, according to Marie Anchordoguy, the historian of the Japanese computer industry, provided the Japanese producers of electronics "a crucial opportunity to build up economies of scale before encountering foreign competition."[65]

Motorola was less of a radical innovator than TI, but more successful in maintaining its technological leadership in product development through continuous learning. The 1952 AT&T license freed Motorola from its dependence on RCA for radio tubes. It immediately began to produce transistors both for internal use (in its production of radios and televisions) and for external sales. After 1958 the company's senior managers, under the leadership of Robert Galvin, the son of the founder, began to move more aggressively into semiconductors. It expanded abroad, though somewhat more slowly than did TI. By 1968 it had 5 percent of the semiconductor market in Britain and 4 percent in West Germany, two countries where it had built no plants, and 5 percent in France, where it had. By 1970 it had factories in Britain and West Germany as well as in Latin America and Asia. As in the case of TI, Motorola wholly owned all these overseas operations except in Japan, where it had an even more difficult time than TI in gaining entry through a joint venture. Thus by 1972 Motorola was the world's second largest producer of semiconductors behind TI, with 9 percent. But by then their major global competitors had become Siemens, Philips, and the rapidly expanding Japanese producers.[66]

In the U.S. semiconductor market, according to the estimates of Mariann Jelinek and Claudia B. Schoonhoven, TI and Motorola together held just over 70 percent, with TI having 37.4 percent and Motorola having 33.3 percent for the five-year period 1975–1979. Their closest competitor in that period was the leading California start-up Fairchild Semiconductor with 8.3 percent.[67]

The third of these three leaders, Fairchild, had an auspicious beginning. This 1957 spin-off from Shockley Semiconductors came into being when eight engineers headed by Robert Noyce departed to form Fairchild Semiconductor with the financial backing of the Fairchild Camera and Instrument Company, in nearby Palo Alto. Noyce had spent three years at Philco after getting his Ph.D. at MIT. He had joined the Shockley outfit in 1956. In 1959 at Fairchild, he patented the integrated circuit almost simultaneously with Jack Kilby of Texas Instruments, as just mentioned above. By 1963 Fairchild Semiconductor had 5 percent of the semiconductor market, and in 1966 its 13 percent moved it ahead of Motorola's 12 percent. Fairchild also expanded overseas. In 1961 it entered a joint venture with Olivetti and another Italian business machine company. In 1963 it built a plant in Hong Kong, followed by one in Singapore. In 1965 it restructured its marketing organization with separate units for the four major markets to which it was selling semiconductors—military, industrial, consumer electronics, and computers.[68]

But whereas Texas Instruments and Motorola continued to grow, Fairchild declined. In 1968 it sold its share of its Italian joint venture to Olivetti. Its own market share fell off. In 1979 it was acquired by the French firm Schlumberger. By 1982 Fairchild had fallen back to be the tenth largest producer worldwide.[69]

Fairchild failed precisely because its managers were unable to build a functionally integrated learning base. They were unable to transform individual capabilities into organizational ones. But for that very reason Fairchild played an essential role in the creation of the computer industry's entrepreneurial seedbed, Silicon Valley, a region some thirty miles south of San Francisco with its center in Palo Alto and Stanford University.

SILICON VALLEY EMERGES

The exploding growth of the computer industry after IBM's System 360 and DEC's PDP-8 transformed the production of chips from custom-designed into standardized, volume-produced devices, just as it transformed the production of software from primarily custom-designed to packaged products. As a consequence, the cost of a fabricating plant rose from $500,000 in 1960, to $2 million in 1972, $5 million in 1978, $10 million in 1980, and $200 million by the mid-1980s. In 1993 the cost of Intel's new plant came to $1.3

billion. The rising cost of facilities reflected the increasingly complex technology involved in chip production and the increasing need for close supervision in coordinating the processes involved from design to delivery of the final product. By 1980 the industry had already become, as AnnaLee Saxenian notes, "seven times more capital-intensive than the U.S. average." As costs of facilities burgeoned, so did output, and the prices of semiconductors dropped dramatically. Many entrepreneurial enterprises disappeared. As *Dataquest* reported in 1980, "Of the 35 semiconductor companies started between 1966 and 1975, only seven remained independent in 1980."[70]

The most successful of these were established in California's Silicon Valley. There, between 1967 and 1969 three companies built their large-scale integrated learning bases—National Semiconductor, Advanced Micro Devices (AMD), and Intel. These three companies and their suppliers, Saxenian reports, "contributed to the creation of more than 200,000 new technology jobs in the region during the 1970s, more than quadrupling local technology employment."

In 1967 Peter Sprague, heir of the Sprague Electric Equipment fortune and owner of National Semiconductor Corporation with a small plant in Danbury, Connecticut, made the move to Silicon Valley. Sprague hired Charles Spork, the general manager at Fairchild, to become National's president. One authority has written that National Semiconductor, by building a large fabricating plant in Silicon Valley, "positioned itself as the low-cost, efficient producer of integrated circuits," both linear memories and logic chips. In 1969 W. Jeremiah Sanders, formerly a salesman (not an engineer) at Fairchild Camera (not Fairchild Semiconductor), formed Advanced Micro Devices. Sanders moved into the volume production of chips designed and usually licensed by other chip specialists.[71]

The third of these start-ups, Intel Corporation, was established in 1968 a few months before AMD, by Robert Noyce, one of the founders of Fairchild Semiconductor, and Gordon Moore, who was Research Director at Fairchild Semiconductor. Noyce became Intel's CEO and focused on management, and Moore became director of research. Andrew Grove, who joined Fairchild in 1963 after receiving a Ph.D. from the University of California, became Moore's assistant. The challenge at Fairchild, as Moore has written, was not innovation but how to commercialize the innovations and get them to market before a spin-off from Fairchild did. The problem was that the new ideas developed in Moore's laboratory at Fairchild were "spawning new companies rather than contributing to the growth of Fairchild," he wrote.[72] Intel succeeded where Fairchild failed and did so by creating an effective integrated learning base.

At Intel the founders began by manufacturing, in volume, complex random access memories (RAMs) based on the metal-on-silicon (MOS) technology developed at Fairchild. Their success was followed by the production of DRAMs (dynamic-RAMs) and then the first erasable programmable read only memories (EPROMs). By 1972 Intel's success rested on its 1K DRAM. This first standardized, mass-produced DRAM made Intel the world leader, accounting for 90 percent of its $23.4 million in revenues that year.

Intel also pioneered in commercializing the microprocessor, the innovation that would so transform the industry in the 1980s. In 1971 one of its engineers, Ted Hoff, combined into a single integrated circuit "all the basic registers and control functions of a tiny, general-purpose stored-program computer." This "computer on a chip" was, like the earlier integrated circuit, under development at TI at the same time. Both Texas Instruments and Motorola quickly developed and commercialized their own powerful microprocessors. But, as Gordon Moore points out, until 1980 the microprocessor was used primarily in dedicated control systems for automobiles, appliances, automated production lines, and the like. During the 1970s, when Intel's revenues from memory systems were much greater than from microprocessors, the company expanded its marketing organization and capabilities and improved and speeded up its manufacturing processes. The resulting scale economies reduced costs and prices. The price for its 8-bit 8080A was $110 in 1975 but only $20 in 1977. By 1980 a standard 8-bit processor sold for between $5 and $8, setting the stage for the microprocessor revolution. Nevertheless, the primary product of the U.S. semiconductor industry in the 1970s was memories, not microprocessors.[73]

TI and Motorola, using mass-production techniques comparable to those of Intel, had surpassed Intel by 1976 in their shares of the DRAM market. Motorola did concentrate on perfecting the new microprocessor, and soon its 6800 processor was considered superior to that of Intel's 8080. TI and Motorola in 1980 were still the world's largest producers of semiconductors, with 11.2 percent and 7.8 percent of the global semiconductor market.[74]

THE NEXUS BEGINS TO CONSOLIDATE GEOGRAPHICALLY

During the 1970s existing mainframe makers continued to produce their own peripherals, software, and services. But as they and others began to produce and sell IBM clones and IBM's unbundled software, the industry's supporting nexus began to come together geographically. In the West it flourished in Silicon Valley after the establishment of the three new semiconductor companies. But the initial geographic concentration had come in the late 1960s around Route 128, a new highway that connected Boston's northern and western suburbs. In the East, MIT provided the academic stimulus; in the West, Stanford. In the East, the Route 128 nexus began as DEC's stripped-down PDP-5 was introduced, for it required outside suppliers to provide it with peripherals, software, and services, and it was sold to other companies for their own uses and to value-added resellers. Its growth expanded rapidly as DEC, Data General, Prime, Wang, and others built their plants and expanded the new minicomputer path in the late 1960s and early 1970s.

Silicon Valley's growth came in these same years after its new semiconductor companies went into full production. The Valley soon took over from Route 128. In 1965, according to Saxenian, high-technology employment along Route 128 was three times that of Silicon Valley. In 1970 it was still almost 50 percent larger. By 1975, however, Silicon Valley's high-technology employment had risen to approximately 120,000, while Route 128's was approximately 100,000. By 1980 Silicon Valley's had risen to over 200,000, while Route 128's was approximately 135,000. In the 1980s Silicon Valley rose to above 250,000 employees, while Route 128 remained close to 150,000.[75]

As the Valley's historian, James C. Williams, records, with the coming of Fairchild in 1957, "Silicon Valley was born." Fairchild became a "corporate vocational school for young engineers." Once trained, most moved on "to replicate the founders' experience in new ventures." By Williams's count, 141 new companies were founded by the employees of Fairchild. At a 1969 conference in Sunnyvale, AnnaLee Saxenian reports, "fewer than two dozen of the 400 men . . . had never worked for Fairchild."[76]

One of the greatest differences between the evolution of computers and consumer electronics was that in consumer electronics there was no such concentrated center of technical capabilities. A consumer electronics nexus comparable to Route 128 and then Silicon Valley did not appear in either the United States or Europe. But it did in Japan—and this growing concentration of electronics firms also contributed to competitiveness in the computer industry.

THE JAPANESE CHALLENGES IN SEMICONDUCTORS

In the early 1980s Silicon Valley and the U.S. computer industry were suddenly feeling the challenge of the long-established Japanese electronics companies in both consumer electronics and computers, supported by their ever growing nexus of small and large firms. In the U.S. computer industry the initial challenge came from Japanese semiconductors. Indeed, the Japanese semiconductor producers destroyed the U.S. memory chip sector in the briefest of periods. The production of semiconductors evolved in the United States and Japan in a very different manner. In Japan there were no enterprises that produced only semiconductors in the manner of Intel, Advanced Micro Devices, and National Semiconductor. They were produced by the major computer companies and, to a lesser extent, the consumer electronics ones.

The Japanese industry became competitive after Sony acquired the Kilby patent in 1968. It grew rapidly in the 1970s with the expansion of the consumer electronics industry and after the computer manufacturers began to build their IBM plug-compatibles, as described in chapter 6. In 1975 the five Japanese computer companies joined forces in a three-year project, supervised by the Ministry of International Trade and Industry, to develop a very large-scale integrated circuit. The project focused on DRAMs. In 1972, when Intel introduced the first standardized mass-produced chip, its 1K DRAM, the U.S. market share of memories was 95 percent to Japan's 5 percent. With the coming of the next generation, the 4K DRAM, the U.S. share dropped to 83 percent, with Japan's rising to 17. Then, following the example of the consumer electronics companies, the Japanese semiconductor producers perfected the high-volume production processes of high-performance technology products for the follow-up, 16K DRAM. By 1979 the Japanese market share of the 16K DRAM had risen to 48 percent.[77]

By the end of the 1970s the semiconductor divisions of these Japanese firms were operating at a scale that spewed forth high-performance products at prices that permitted them to sweep global markets. But the American industry remained relatively complacent. Then in 1980 Hewlett-Packard sounded the alarm for the American industry by announcing that the Japanese 16K DRAMs were of far higher quality than those made in the United States: "At first glance the impression is that the Japanese are using low-cost and domestic production as levers to build a strong base for exports. On closer inspection, this premise does not hold up. The Japanese semiconductor companies are using superior product quality to gain competitive advantage of enormous magnitude." Their impact was indeed devastating.

In the four years 1980–1984, as the next-generation 64K DRAM was followed in 1982 by the 256K DRAM, the U.S. industry was destroyed. By 1985 Motorola, Intel, National Semiconductor, Advanced Micro Devices, and MOSTEK (a spin-off from TI based in Colorado Springs) had dropped out of the memory chip business. Only a weak TI with production facilities in Japan and a tiny start-up, Micron Technology, hung on. At the end of the 64K generation the Japanese market share had risen to 71 percent and then, with the coming of the 265K, to 92 percent.

I end this chapter by returning to table 4.2, to the one category I have not yet discussed; the microcomputer. Table 4.2 indicates the rising Japanese mainframe challenge by showing that the Japanese had become more serious competitors to IBM in mainframes than any U.S. rival. But the more striking point is made by the record of the new microcomputer sector. Between 1982 and 1984, the years of the successful Japanese challenge in semiconductors, the new microcomputer, powered by the microprocessor, created a new sector overnight. In its first three years on the market IBM's personal computer rose from $500 million to $5,500 million in revenues. This development reshaped the industry worldwide by opening not only a huge new commercial market but also the first home market. The coincidence in timing between these two developments—the Japanese challenge and the coming of the microprocessor, which had no direct relationship to each other—caused the Japanese challenge to fade away.

5

THE MICROPROCESSOR REVOLUTION:

THE COMPUTER INDUSTRY RECAST

IN THE UNITED STATES

An understanding of the fading away of the Japanese challenge calls for an awareness of the recasting of the computer industry in the same first five years of the 1980s. In commercial computing, the microprocessor created the industry as it came to be known by the late 1980s—a world of small computers used by individuals in offices, connected by networking systems, and using a wide array of software applications for all types of data processing. In addition, it created a new market: the home.

Again, IBM became the initial path definer. It was not a first-mover, but its mass-produced personal computer, followed by its multitude of clones, opened up a huge commercial computing market that swiftly reduced the demand for mainframes.

The microprocessor affected the scientific and engineering path in a different way. Here the minicomputer makers continued to serve the same scientific and engineering customers but increasingly replaced their minicomputers with microprocessor-based workstations, a technology perfected by the innovative start-up Sun Microsystems. The workstation, however, contributed to the development of increasingly powerful networks, as it was well suited to the emerging client-server technology, in which a number of desktops or workstations were connected to a central workstation or minicomputer within an office, department, or large institution.

I begin this review of the recasting of the industry with the coming of the personal computer, followed by the development of the workstation, and then the new supporting sectors, those in hardware and software, with references to changes in the service sector. Then I indicate how the commercial and home paths and the engineering and scientific paths melded together and were then connected with the public Internet to complete the basic technological infrastructure of the Electronic Century. Then, in chapter 6, I return to how the recasting of the computer industry in the United States transformed the national computer industries of Europe and Japan, bringing about the death of the European industry while permitting the Japanese industry to launch a second powerful challenge to the U.S. industry in the 1990s.

The Coming of the Personal Computer

The microcomputer revolution began in the late 1970s. This timing reflected the two basic long-term developments of the industry during the previous two decades. First, the rapidly increasing production volumes of peripherals had greatly reduced their prices. At the same time, development and commercializing of the microprocessor at Intel, Texas Instruments, and Motorola in the 1970s, described in the previous chapter, had greatly increased the power and lowered the price of the computer's engine.

The increasing availability of components and their low cost encouraged young hobbyists to make their own personal computers, much as hobbyists had done in fashioning the first radio receiving sets. In 1975 Edward Roberts, maker of radio kits for model airplanes in Albuquerque, New Mexico, produced the Altair 8800, a kit for computer hobbyists. The Altair, using an Intel 8080 chip, had no keyboard, monitor, or storage device and had a tiny memory (256 bytes). Roberts priced it at $395 and $495 fully assembled. The marketing of the Altair and its imitators created the demand for software. In 1975 William Gates and Paul Allen moved from Boston to Albuquerque and founded Microsoft, as part of an effort to write a version of the BASIC programming language for Robert's Altair. In the next year Gary Kildall, another hobbyist, developed the first operating system based on the Intel 8080, the CP/M (control program for micro computers).[1]

The Initial Learning Bases

The year 1977 marked the spontaneous beginnings of the microcomputer industry. That year three enterprises had sufficiently integrated production and marketing capabilities to commercialize a complete personal computer. They were widely separated geographically—Apple in California, Commodore in Pennsylvania (a producer of electronic calculators), and Tandy in Texas (the largest mass retailer of electronic goods in the United States)—and all had different origins. Two of these offerings, the Apple II and Commodore PET, were launched simultaneously at the West Coast Computer Faire (*sic*) that spring.[2]

The story of Apple is legendary, the classic one of a garage-born enterprise combining the brilliance of a computer designer and the creativity of an entrepreneur. The major achievement of Apple's founders, Steven Wozniak and Steven Jobs, twenty-year-olds who had grown up in Cupertino in the heart of Silicon Valley, was not that they had designed a technologically advanced machine. It was, as Richard Langlois noted, "rather one that was a compromise between technology and marketing, the Apple II." Apple II used an MOS (metal-on-silicon) 6502 chip designed and produced by Chuck Peddle. Peddle had worked at Motorola, where he had helped develop its successful microprocessor 6800 before establishing his own enterprise, MOS Technologies, in West Chester, near Philadelphia. He introduced his first microprocessor product in 1976. Nearly all the components were obtained from outside sources, except for its disk and disk drive, which were Wozniak's most significant innovation. As Adam Osborne, a competing start-up entrepreneur, noted, Apple's key to success was "that this company was the first to offer real customer support and to behave like a genuine business." Apple's success was assured when in October 1979, Daniel Bricklin, a former DEC employee now attending the Harvard Business School, developed VisiCalc (*Visible Calcula-tor*), the first spreadsheet application, for the Apple II, thus permitting Apple to enter the commercial market.

In contrast with Apple's legendary story, the origins of the industry's two other first-movers are less known. Commodore was a growing electronic enterprise even before introducing a microcomputer. Jack Tramiel, Commodore's founder, had established the company in Toronto in 1956 to produce handheld calculators. In 1975 he acquired Chuck Peddle's MOS Technologies to have an assured supply of chips for calculators. Peddle, in turn, urged Tramiel to begin producing microcomputers. So Commodore's PET computer, produced in Peddle's Pennsylvania plant, was announced in January 1977. From the start Tramiel and Peddle remained focused on the home computer market.

In 1977 the Tandy Corporation of Fort Worth, Texas, was the largest mass retailer of electronic goods in the United States. Established in 1927, it became a national chain retailing leather craft products after World War II. In 1962 Charles Tandy, the son of the founder, decided to enter the electronics business by acquiring the Boston-based mass retailer Radio Shack. Radio Shack had grown from 172 stores in 1968, to 2,294 in 1973, to 7,353 by 1979 (as compared with McDonald's fast-food chain of 5,353 stores). In response to the suggestion of one of its merchandise buyers, Don French, Tandy's Radio Shack decided to enter the new microcomputer market. French brought an engineer who had worked for National Semiconductor to Fort Worth to assist in commercializing its TRS Model (using a 280 processor produced by Zilog, a spin-off in 1974 from Motorola). Like Commodore and Apple, Tandy developed its own proprietary operating system. Tandy sold its product primarily through Radio Shack's outlets at low prices for home education and amusement, particularly for video games.

After 1977 Apple, Commodore, and Tandy improved their product lines. Apple's upgraded VisiCalc spreadsheet and its customer service organization enhanced its strong competitive advantage in business markets. By one estimate, the three firms enjoyed 72 percent of the new microcomputer market in 1978—Tandy with 50 percent, Commodore 12 percent, and Apple 10 percent. Established enterprises began to enter the industry. By 1980 Apple led with 27 percent, Tandy had 21 percent, and Commodore 20 percent, followed by Hewlett-Packard with 5 percent and Japan's NEC with 9 percent. When IBM's management decided in the spring of 1980 to enter the field, the industry was still in an embryonic stage.

IBM Enters—The Revolution Begins

Entering with an impressive, well-executed strategy, IBM almost immediately laid down the industry's new foundations. That move began when the senior managers at IBM directed William Lowe, the manager of its Entry Level Systems Division (that is, small computers), based in Boca Raton, Florida, to organize, in the usual IBM manner, a task force to study the feasibility of mass-producing and mass-marketing a desktop computer in as short a time as possible. In July 1980 Lowe carried the task force's report to IBM's headquarters at Armonk, New York.[3]

The report stressed that the project was feasible only if IBM set up a completely autonomous unit that operated outside IBM's existing organization (and its business culture) to develop, produce, and market the new system. The implementation of the report required a totally new approach on a number of dimensions. For one, the task force recommended "an open architecture." It would have a modular "bus" (to connect and communicate with its internal parts and other components) that would permit the customer to use desired "add-ons." As Langlois has written: "The IBM PC was a system, not an appliance; an incomplete package, an open box ready for expansion, reconfiguration and continuing upgrading." Here there is a parallel to DEC's PDP-8.

More significant, the computer would not be built with proprietary components, developed within IBM. Instead, in the interest of speeding the product to the mass consumer market and in order to benefit from the recently created availability of low-cost components, these items would be purchased from outside suppliers unless IBM units could supply them immediately. Thus the computer would not be protected by patents, as were those of its competitors. In addition, the software would be developed independently of the hardware. Once the prototype was completed, the software would be developed as the assembly plant was being built at Boca Raton. Last, the unit would create its own sales and service force to support a national and then a worldwide marketing network of both franchised dealers and large mass-market retailers.

IBM's Central Management Committee approved Lowe's report, upgraded the task force to a full-scale project development group, appointed Philip "Don" Estridge its chief, and gave him precisely *one year* to have the product on the market. Estridge quickly recruited the management team to head its engineering, materials, production, and marketing units.

For their microprocessor, Estridge's team chose Intel's older 8-bit chip, rather than the state-of-the-art chips of Motorola or its clones that were then used by Apple, Tandy, and Commodore. Indeed, IBM even avoided Intel's new, much more powerful 16-bit chip, the 8086. The IBM task force agreed that the PC did not need the computing power of the 16-bit processor. The cheaper 8-bit 8088 could accommodate nearly all the application software then available for the personal computers. Estridge next asked Intel to sign a standard nondisclosure agreement and, in addition, stated that Intel must license the chip to its competition so that the Boca Raton plant could be sure of a steady supply. Intel, as a contemporary noted, "readily accepted the offer" for its "commercially unpopular chip," which was "losing out to competing products from Motorola, Zilog and others." As Gordon Moore, then its research director, later pointed out, that IBM decision "changed the entire course of Intel's history."[4]

Once the chip decision had been made, Estridge approached Gary Kildall, who had written the pioneering CP/M, which by 1981 had become the dominant operating system for microcomputers. Kildall, however, was unwilling to sign the standard nondisclosure agreements on which IBM insisted. So Estridge turned to Bill Gates, who had moved Microsoft from Albuquerque to Seattle in 1978.[5]

Gates quickly accepted IBM's offer with its nondisclosure clause. He then purchased for an initial $75,000 an operating system from Seattle Computer Products, a company owned by a nearby fellow computer buff, Rod Brock. One of Brock's employees, Tim Paterson, had developed the operating system for the Intel 8086. Gates failed to reveal the reason for the purchase to Brock, later citing his nondisclosure agreement with IBM. Gates then turned Brock's "Quick-and-Dirty Operating System" (QDOS) into the Microsoft-Disk Operating System (MS-DOS).

Once DOS was fully developed, IBM agreed to let Microsoft license it to others. The reasoning was that although the move would allow competitors to enter, it not only assured the availability of software, but also would help to make that software the industry's standard. In this way, Intel and Microsoft received what became the most lucrative franchises in the history of American industry. If Kildall had been willing to accept the nondisclosure clause, and if Motorola's chip had been the first choice over Intel's commercially unpopular one, the underlying history of the personal computer during the critical decade of the 1980s might have remained much the same. But the industry's two most powerful players in the 1990s might not have been Intel and Microsoft.

Once those two had been signed on, Estridge completed contracts with suppliers of components. Tandon made the disk drives in California; Zenith the PC power supplies in Michigan; the Silicon Valley division of SCI Systems (a contract manufacturer) the circuit boards; a Japanese firm, Sieko Epson, the printers; IBM's plant at Charlotte, North Carolina, the board assemblies; and its plant at Lexington, Kentucky, the keyboards.

The marketing and servicing of the new low-cost mass-produced computer obviously had to be as new and different as its manufacturing. As directed, Estridge's group made arrangements with such mass-retailing chains as ComputerLand and Sears Business Centers and built a national and then international marketing unit to recruit and then support a network of franchised dealers. Nevertheless, Estridge also decided to let the sales forces of other IBM divisions sell and then service PCs to corporate and government customers.

William Lowe's directive was impressively implemented within the allotted year. As two members of Estridge's team wrote, this success made real a strategy that believed IBM's entry into the market would cause "a dramatic explosion in demand for personal computers." As a consequence, IBM's operating system "would be the internationally accepted standard for all desktop computing."[6]

But no one anticipated just how explosive that demand would be. It rose far above anticipated sales. Though its automated production lines were spewing out one PC every forty-five seconds, IBM was unable to keep pace with demand. In 1983 IBM's Central Management Committee created an entirely new Entry Level System Division to manage this explosive growth. The announcement of this organizational change noted that more systems were shipped over the first five months of 1983 than in all of 1982. "Daily manufacturing volumes increased 600% with high quality. Retail outlets have doubled. Sales have risen to the point that would rank ESD eligible for the Fortune 500 index." The committee further stated, "Some 6,000 application programs for the IBM PC were being written by more than 2,000 software houses." And it added that plans were being completed to sell the division's products in seventy-four countries. In 1984 soaring revenues had reached an estimated $5 billion, equivalent to those of the seventy-fifth largest company on the *Fortune* 500 list. They leveled off at $5.5 billion in 1985. The organizational and management challenges driven by a $5 billion increase in revenue in four years were truly unprecedented.[7]

Although in 1980 IBM's managers were not aware of the far-reaching implications of the mass production of microcomputers, several sensed that the "microprocessor based PC was a very real threat to the core of IBM's business." They saw it as "a Trojan horse within the Big Blue walls." Their opposition was strong enough to force John Opel, the CEO, constantly to protect the project during its development. In one way the critics were right, for the coming of the PC did mark the beginnings of the disintegration of IBM's core mainframe business. On the other hand, by commercializing its PC in the way it did, IBM was assured of a major role in the industry's new microprocessor sector.[8]

Computing and the Computer Transformed

Consider the profound, but largely unintended and certainly unexpected, consequences of IBM's Boca Raton venture.

First, it revealed a mass consumer market for computers. Hitherto the market had been institutional—corporations, government offices, universities, research laboratories, and the like. Now the users were individuals, not only in the office, but also in the home.

Second, by entering the market with a nonproprietary system and applying the classic techniques of mass production and mass marketing, IBM set a de facto standard for the personal computer. This sudden growth of a single standard created barriers to entry because it provided IBM with significant scale and scope economies. Had it, like its existing computer enterprises, entered the market in a comparable manner with a competitive proprietary system, then the personal computer market would likely have grown more slowly and also allowed for the entry of other proprietary systems from other existing companies.

Third, by making its PC nonproprietary, IBM created an unprecedented opportunity for both existing and start-up companies to enter this new market by cloning its product, an opportunity Apple and other PC makers denied with their proprietary systems. The PC clones indeed poured in. As *Business Week* reported in July 1986, "Now more than 200 clone suppliers using the same software and working with the same hardware" were challenging the standard's progenitor. The number of microcomputers shipped to business rose from 344,000 in 1981 to 3,290,000 in 1985. This solidified the IBM PC as the de facto standard.[9]

Fourth, because the essential components of any IBM clone were the intimately tied microprocessor and operating system, Intel and Microsoft enjoyed far larger scale and scope economies and thus became critical learning bases for this multibillion-dollar market. The focus of technological innovation moved from computer platforms to chips and software. By the early 1990s the near monopolistic position of Intel and Microsoft provided them with far greater funding and broader learning bases for continuing research and product development than was available to any of their competitors. After the mid-1980s they increasingly became the industry's path definers.

Fifth, the swift proliferation of desktop computers created a demand for new types of application software for individual use in offices and also at home rather than packaged software for corporate information technology managers. That demand led to what *Datamation* referred to as the beginning of "pure software companies." Such independent application software producers, usually entrepreneurial start-ups, first came in spreadsheets (VisiCalc and Lotus), then in management databases, word processing, graphics, desktop publishing, finance, and other data-processing tasks. Software applications for personal computers became the industry's fastest-growing sector.

Sixth, the sudden appearance of personal computers on a multitude of desks within corporations and other institutions demanded creation of internal enterprise networks to connect individuals within and between offices and departments and between corporations and other institutions. As early as 1983 start-ups, led by Novell, were beginning to provide software for what had become termed Local Area Networks (LANs).

Seventh, and most significant, the sudden and unexpected creation in the early 1980s of a multibillion-dollar market defined by IBM's product became the savior of the U.S. computer industry. In itself unique in industrial history, the PC market underlines the epic fashion in which the computer industry evolved. Just at the moment when the Japanese consumer electronics companies had finished off their U.S. competitors and the Japanese computer companies were shutting down the U.S. memory chip plants, IBM's revenues from its new personal computer soared from $50 million in 1982 to an estimated $5.5 billion in 1984. With IBM, its clones, Microsoft, and Intel, the U.S. computer industry quickly dominated the world. Nevertheless, the Japanese did continue to lead in memories as well as in providing Europe with its large systems. During the 1990s, when new technologies were creating demands for far greater computer power, the Japanese industry once again challenged the United States. Table 5.1 (page 142) lists the sectors of the recast computer industry whose histories I now review.

Personal Computers: Recasting the Earlier IBM Defined Path

The boom that created the huge new market could not last. Late in 1984, as output began to catch up with demand, an industry shakeout occurred. Many of the start-ups disappeared, including the initially profitable Sinclair, Osborne, and Corona. Texas Instruments left the field (returning in the late 1980s by putting its label on clones made in Taiwan), and Hewlett-Packard began to concentrate on producing workstations. Nevertheless, when demand began to grow again, the opportunity to build clones with improved performance and lower price reappeared. They were so successful that by the end of the decade IBM's PC market share worldwide had dropped from around 50 percent in 1985 to 22.3 percent in 1989.[10]

Again following the premises of chapter 1, IBM's major competitors in PCs became the industry's most successful first-mover, Apple, and the first IBM clone producer, Compaq. In this competition, IBM may have been handicapped because the PC remained only one of its several major products. Finally, the successful followers to these three major revenue producers were entrepreneurial firms whose successful learning bases relied primarily on marketing rather than on technological innovations—Dell, Gateway, Packard-Bell, and AST Research (table 5.1).

The Leaders in Personal Computers—Compaq, Apple, and IBM

Compaq, which became and long remained the most successful clone in terms of market share, revenue, and profit, was the very first to build an integrated learning base, one that transformed individual capabilities into organizational ones. Rod Canion and two other engineering managers from Texas Instruments established Compaq in 1982. The three were frustrated, not only by their company's failure in the new desktop market, but also by its inability to compete with Japan's Sharp and Casio first in calculators and digital watches, both of which it had initially developed, and then in semiconductor memories. They were also well aware of Motorola's capabilities. TI's rival, Motorola, moved successfully into new electronic products, including

TABLE 5.1. The Ten Largest U.S. Information Technology
Companies by Product Sector, 1994

Rank; Company	Estimated Revenues[1] ($ millions)
Large Systems (Mainframes)	
1 IBM	5,957
2 Unisys[2]	1,243
3 Amdahl[3]	819
4 Cray	571
5 Intel	461
6 Silicon Graphics	163
7 Convex	76
8 Digital (DEC)	40
9 Control Data	5
Midrange Systems (Minicomputers)	
1 IBM	5,764
2 AT&T [NCR]	5,042
3 Hewlett-Packard	2,688
4 Tandem	1,538
5 Digital (DEC)	1,174
6 Motorola	616
7 Data General	536
8 Sun Microsystems	534
9 Unisys	497
10 Apple	477
Workstations	
1 Sun Microsystems	3,262
2 IBM	3,207
3 Hewlett-Packard	2,880
4 Silicon Graphics	1,223
5 Digital (DEC)	1,080
6 Intergraph	833
7 Motorola	593
8 Unisys	435
9 Control Data	31
10 Data General	23
PCs	
1 Compaq	9,018
2 IBM	8,775
3 Apple	7,161
4 Dell	2,870
5 Gateway 2000	2,700
6 Packard-Bell	2,600
7 AST Research	2,311
8 AT&T [NCR]	1,718
9 Digital (DEC)	1,350
10 Hewlett-Packard	1,152

TABLE 5.1. (*Continued*)

Rank; Company	Estimated Revenues[1] ($ millions)
Peripherals	
1 IBM	8,583
2 Hewlett-Packard	6,336
3 Seagate	3,465
4 Quantum	3,286
5 Xerox	3,126
6 Conner Peripherals	2,352
7 Western Digital	1,900
8 Digital (DEC)	1,620
9 Lexmark [IBM]	1,215
10 Storage Tek	1,121
Software	
1 IBM	11,529
2 Microsoft	4,649
3 Computer Associates	2,148
4 Novell	1,998
5 Oracle	2,001
6 Lockheed Martin	1,242
7 Digital (DEC)	1,215
8 Lotus	971
9 AT&T [NCR]	916
10 Unisys	683
Services	
1 IBM	16,653
2 EDS	10,052
3 Digital (DEC)	6,345
4 Hewlett-Packard	4,608
5 Unisys	3,108
6 Computer Sciences	3,085
7 KPMG Peat Marwick	2,300
8 Andersen Consulting	2,206
9 Entex	1,300
10 Deloitte & Touche	1,041

Source: Compiled from "Datamation 100, 1995," *Datamation,* June 1, 1995, pp. 47, 48, 57, 61, 62, 66. Excerpted with permission of *Datamation* magazine. Copyright 1996 by Cahners Publishing Company.

[1] Revenue figures represent worldwide revenues for each segment. These estimates do not necessarily match precisely with actual reported revenues both because companies do not always publish sector-specific results and because their fiscal years may not match the time frame of the estimates. Nonetheless, the estimates still represent the relative magnitude of various competitors. For the Software category, revenue figures for firms whose actual revenue is presented in appendix 5.1. have been adjusted to match figures reported in annual reports.

[2] Formed as a merger of Burroughs and Sperry Rand in 1986.

[3] Fujitsu was dominant stockholder

modems and telecommunication equipment, and built and maintained a competitive position in microprocessors, becoming the primary supplier of Apple and other proprietary personal computer makers.[11]

Canion stressed that his goal was not to start a little company expecting it to grow large, but to begin by laying the foundations of a big company. He explicitly rejected the Silicon Valley model of relying on individual entrepreneurial capabilities (which was the same source of Gordon Moore's concern about Fairchild, as noted in chapter 4). Instead Compaq would focus on developing and maintaining the organizational capabilities of the company as a whole. "Above all," he insisted, "we want team members and not individualists." The founders raised a record amount of venture capital, $30 million, and developed strong financial controls and a forecasting system even before production began. They recruited design and production engineers from TI and lured "Sparky" Sparks and James D'Arezzo, who had built Estridge's PC marketing organization at IBM, to do the same at Compaq. Such preparations made it possible for Compaq to become the new sector's seventh largest revenue producer by 1985 (table 5.1).

Compaq's strategic goal was as straightforward as its organizational one: Build an IBM clone, add extra features to the finished model, and sell it at a higher price. Its first product was a portable rather than a desktop personal computer, a niche that IBM had not yet entered. This strategy permitted it to have R&D costs of 4 percent of revenue, well below those of IBM and Apple. The national retail organization that Sparks and D'Arezzo created consisted principally of a network of authorized dealers supported by a strong marketing and distribution organization with an impressive market research staff. Unlike IBM, it had no direct sales staff of its own, so its franchised marketers did not have to fear competition from company sales reps. Another former TI executive, Eckhard Pfeiffer, then built a similar marketing network abroad, setting up subsidiaries in eleven European nations in 1983 and 1984.

In 1985, as Compaq developed its new desktop, Deskpro 386, its engineers worked closely with Intel and Microsoft. At Intel's request, Compaq tested that company's next generation—80386, a 32-bit microprocessor—to assure that it met all software requirements written for systems already using the 80286. Rod Canion then persuaded Intel to adjust the chip to meet Compaq's requirements. At the same time, Bill Gates for a year assisted Compaq, as *Fortune* reported, "mainly by writing software that increases the amount of computer memories current programs can use when they run on a Deskpro 386."[12]

Introduced in September 1986, the new product provided Compaq with revenues that made it the third largest maker of personal computers behind IBM and Apple. In Europe, where Compaq was number two, ahead of Apple and Olivetti, its sales exploded from $20 million in 1984 to $733 million in 1988. In 1987 Compaq built the first U.S. overseas PC clone works. This was a large plant in the Glasgow/Edinburgh area, Britain's so-called Silicon Glen, which already housed plants of IBM, Honeywell, Digital, NEC, Motorola, and Sun Microsystems. By then Compaq was listed among *Fortune*'s top five hundred companies, the fastest a start-up had ever made that list. By 1988 Compaq was the third largest producer of personal computers worldwide, with revenues of $2.1 billion and 7.4 percent of the world market.

Meanwhile, Apple was preparing for success. During the first half of the 1980s its management effectively solidified the company's organizational learning base. In 1981 A. C. "Mike" Markkula, who had worked for Fairchild and then Intel and was the major initial investor in Apple (holding one-third of its equity), took over the administrative reins as CEO. In 1983 Markkula and Steve Jobs persuaded John Sculley, the president of Pepsi-Cola, to become Apple's president. In 1985 Sculley became chairman and CEO. That same year both of the individualistic, idiosyncratic founding engineers, Jobs and Wozniak, left the firm. As Langlois notes: "It was only under the administration of John Sculley that the Macintosh took off."[13]

Jobs himself, a talented visionary who was inspired by the fruitful electronic innovations at Xerox's PARC (Palo Alto Research Center), introduced the Apple Macintosh in 1984, a low-cost version of its Lisa, the successor to Apple II. Jobs had taken Apple's best talent from the rest of the company and personally headed the development team. The "Mac" became the PC industry's premier product, the model others would follow. Powered by a Motorola chip, it provided the best graphical interface of all personal computers. As Paul Ceruzzi points out, its "elegant system software . . . displayed a combination of aesthetic beauty and practical engineering that is extremely rare." That excellence made it the leader in the publishing and educational market. But for business management uses, its operating system had drawbacks. It was much slower than what Microsoft-DOS developed for the IBM PC, and even more difficult for programmers developing application software. Thanks to the Macintosh, Apple long remained the one major personal computer maker with its own proprietary operating system. The rest of the sector consisted primarily of the IBM PC and its clones.

As Compaq and Apple began to build their global enterprises, IBM's Entry Level System Division was becoming integrated back into the long-established, relatively centralized operating structure of one of the world's largest industrial enterprises. As a child of IBM, the PC division benefited from its parent's powerful financial and managerial strengths. Nevertheless, within IBM's hierarchy, the division remained something of a sideline of the mainframe business, which in 1985 had revenues of $14 billion and enjoyed much higher profit margins.

The difference in circumstances in the evolution of IBM's PC unit and its major independent start-up competitors appeared in the development of new products. In 1983 designers at Boca Raton had their first failure, an inexpensive "PC Jr.," which was to compete with Commodore in the home market. They failed in part because it was an area in which they had no learning. But the PC/AT it introduced a year later for the business market, based on a 16-bit Intel chip rather than its 8-bit, remained the new sector's largest revenue producer.

In the development of its next generation, the PS/2, conflicts within IBM and uneasy relationships with its suppliers, particularly Microsoft, plagued commercialization in ways that were rarer in small start-up enterprises. One error was the decision, made partly at Gates's urging, to use the 16-bit Intel 80286 instead of its 32-bit 80386—a decision to be discussed later in the chapter. Another was the failed attempt to develop a new proprietary "bus" that would provide IBM's PC with competitive advantages, a dud that Compaq and other competitors quickly overcame with a 32-bit "bus" of their own.[14]

By 1988 IBM, Apple, and Compaq were the world's three largest producers of personal computers. Together, by *Datamation* estimates, they received 43.4 percent of total revenues. IBM's 25.5 percent share was followed by Apple with 10.5 percent and Compaq with 7.4 percent. With the exception of Tandy/Radio Shack and a British firm, Amstrand, their competitors were still large, long-established companies. Fifteen firms accounted for 85 percent of the revenues of that sector. Of these, the other U.S. firms besides those just listed were as follows: Hewlett-Packard, Unisys (the merger of Burroughs and Sperry Rand in 1986), AT&T (which sold under the AT&T label the products of the only European pioneer in microcomputers, Olivetti), and Zenith—the remaining U.S. radio and television maker. The six others were foreign firms—four Japanese: Toshiba, Fujitsu, NEC, and Matsushita; and two European: Olivetti plus Amstrand.[15]

Nevertheless, given the competitive advantage of the IBM PC and its clones based on the low cost and high performance of Intel chips and Microsoft operating systems, IBM and Compaq would continue to be the industry's two leaders. Except for Toshiba, the other multiproduct computer companies still relied on their own proprietary systems. Even Apple, which had the advantages of being a first-mover, struggled to keep its proprietary system competitive with that of the two leaders.

Because technological innovation in the PC rested primarily in the microprocessor and operating system, entry and growth in the PC clone business itself after 1985 was based increasingly on innovations in marketing and distribution. Here the pioneer was Michael Dell of Austin, Texas. He began in 1984 to differentiate his product from other clones by developing a direct-marketing business. Dell's machines were ordered to meet the customer's individual specifications and delivered directly to the customer. In this way, inventory costs were reduced below those of its competitors, while the steady introduction of new components kept the average selling price high. Repairs were guaranteed in twenty-four hours. In 1992 Dell's revenues placed it among the top fifteen PC producers.

In 1985 three more start-ups built their enterprises on marketing strategies. Gateway 2000 of North Sioux City, South Dakota, followed Dell's direct marketing strategy. Packard-Bell of Sacramento, California, sold through Wal-Mart and other mass-retailing discount stores. AST Research marketed through multiple channels, including PC dealers, computer chain stores such as Sears Business Systems, and value-added retailers.[16]

By the mid-1990s personal computers had become the leading revenue-producing sector in the computing industry (table 5.1). Compaq and IBM were contesting for first place, with Apple following. Then came the four marketing-oriented producers. Of the top ten U.S. computer pioneers in 1985 listed in table 4.2, only the three major first-movers plus Hewlett-Packard remained. The two other computer makers listed in 1994 were NCR, recently acquired by AT&T, and DEC. In that year, both enterprises reported heavy losses (see chapter 7).

Workstations: Recasting the Minicomputer Path

The evolution of the workstation path differed sharply from that of the path of the IBM PC and its clones. Here there was no sudden, unanticipated opening of the new market. Instead the story provides another example of the successful application of a new technology, in this case the microprocessor, to an existing market, that of engineering and scientific computers, much as IBM had used the new electronic technology to move from tabulating punched cards to digital computers. The workstation was developed to provide engineers and software developers with powerful graphics and processing capabilities. But it soon came to be used as a "server" in the networks that were being developed both inside single departments, enterprises, or institutions as well as across institutions. For these new workstations, the minicomputer companies created their own operating systems based on their own chips. After 1985 they turned to a new chip technology, reduced instruction set computing (RISC) and used variations of UNIX for their operating software.[17]

John Cocke of IBM had initially developed the RISC processor in the 1970s, but IBM never attempted to commercialize it. It was then fully developed in the early 1980s by a project at Stanford called MIPS (millions of instructions per second), headed by John Hennessy. In 1984 members of that project formed MIPS Computer Systems to commercialize their invention. The RISC technology increased the power of the chip and reduced its costs by simplifying and streamlining the instruction set so as to meet the more specialized high-power needs of engineering and scientific computation.

AT&T's Bell Laboratories had initially developed what was termed "the UNIX operating system." As the earlier antitrust consent decree had prohibited AT&T from engaging in commercial computers, after UNIX was released in 1969, AT&T licensed it free to all comers. By 1982 three thousand mainframes and minicomputers, largely in universities and government agencies, were using UNIX operating systems.

THE FIRST-MOVERS: APOLLO AND SUN

William Poduska was the first to exploit the potential of the new workstation technology. Poduska was the leader of a small group of engineers who had left Honeywell to form Prime Computer in 1971. In 1981, once again, he and his senior management team had become frustrated with the failure of Prime's board to invest sufficiently in the new microprocessor technology. So Poduska and his senior managers departed Prime in 1981 to start Apollo. Apollo developed its own processors (based on Motorola's) and wrote its own proprietary software system but purchased most of its peripherals from outside sources. For Poduska and his managers: "The competitors to worry about are IBM, DEC, and Hewlett-Packard. The start-ups are not a threat to our existence—which is not to say that we don't look over our shoulder to see what they are doing." Apollo began production in 1983.[18]

Poduska should have looked harder, for Sun Microsystems was about to define the shape of the new workstation technology. In 1982 two young Stanford MBAs, Scott McNealy (who became Sun's CEO) and Vinod Khosla, had formed the company to commercialize a workstation designed by a Stanford graduate engineering student, Andreas Bechtolsheim. The three then recruited William Joy, a UNIX expert at the University of California (Berkeley), to develop the operating system. Like Apollo, Sun purchased its peripherals from outside suppliers, used a Motorola-based chip, and began with a UNIX operating system. Like Apollo and also DEC, in its early years a large portion of Sun's sales went to value-added resellers, who added their own software applications and specialized equipment, as well as to third-party application software developers. Sun's workstation, like DEC's minicomputer and IBM's PC, thus created new opportunities for entrepreneurial start-ups. Sun's production began in 1984.[19]

Once established, the four entrepreneurs set forth an ambitious strategy. They would use their Stanford contacts to set the standard in workstations by developing an open system much as IBM had done in personal computers. The authors of *Sunburst: The Ascent of Sun Microsystems*, published in 1990, make this point:

> Sun tenaciously pursued the vision of open systems because it gave the company an immediate distinction over its competition. The company also saw that riding the open system wave was the most effective way to become a long term major player in the computer industry. . . . In the view of Sun's management, if the company were to survive into the next century, it would have to establish itself as a multi-billion organization that offered a clear and desirable alternative to the competition. In the minds of some at Sun, with McNealy as the most vocal and visible proponent, the workstation's arena

would be reduced to four, maybe five, serious players consisting of IBM, DEC, Apple, Sun, and perhaps Hewlett-Packard.[20]

Sun's founders had taken three steps to carry out this goal. First, they took advantage of the existing MIPS project at Stanford and began working with MIPS Computer Systems to develop a superior RISC microprocessor. Second, they turned to Robert Metcalfe's 3Com Corporation for its coaxial Ethernet cables to connect its workstation into networks. (Metcalfe, an inventor of the Ethernet technology at Xerox's PARC research unit, joined with Xerox in 1980 to commercialize his technology.) Third, they looked to AT&T to develop what they hoped would become the standard UNIX operating system.

Choosing UNIX was fortuitous. Many of the computing systems used by universities and government agencies and the minicomputer systems used by corporations ran on some variant of UNIX. Thus Sun's workstations could be easily networked into existing computer systems. In fact, Sun's workstations, initially intended for focused scientific and engineering processing, began to be used as servers in these UNIX-based networks.

By 1987 these moves had paid off. That year Sun Microsystems introduced its SPARC chip, along with the advertisement "The network is the computer." RISC-based servers became the standard to which Sun's competitors moved. That year AT&T assured continuing support for Sun's efforts to standardize UNIX software. It did so by purchasing $450 million in Sun stock and set up a joint development project.

Then in order to expand rapidly the number of software applications written for Sun's product, McNealy immediately licensed the SPARC chip and proprietary UNIX operating system for that chip to Fujitsu in Japan, Philips in Europe, and, in the United States, to Texas Instruments as well as to more specialized semiconductor and component makers in the industry's nexus, Cypress Computer, Bipolar Integrated Technology, and LSI Logic. At the same time, the company expanded its manufacturing facilities and quickly put together a national and international marketing organization.

McNealy's strategy worked. Supported by aggressive financial moves, Sun quickly became the workstation sector's leader. By the end of the eighties 2,800 software packages had been written for its machines. Fifty-one percent of the company's sales were outside the United States. Sun had built a plant in Scotland's Silicon Glen even before Compaq did. By 1987 Sun led the U.S. companies in workstation revenues, with 29 percent as compared with Apollo's 21 percent. By then McNealy's prediction as to the potential five "serious players" in the sector had been fulfilled, with the exception of Apple. In 1989 Hewlett-Packard acquired Apollo. After that, four firms—Hewlett-Packard, Sun, DEC, and IBM—accounted for over two-thirds of the U.S. companies' revenues from workstations.[21]

Nevertheless, McNealy did not reach his ultimate goal of making Sun's "open" RISC/UNIX architecture into an industrywide standard, as IBM had done in personal computers. For one thing, in May 1988 Sun's major competitors formed the Open Software Foundation, with the aim of wresting UNIX from the AT&T-Sun combination. But more important, as these competitors continued to produce their own versions of UNIX and their own MIPS-designed RISC chips, the convergence to a single standard did not happen. Thus such an alliance was not needed and quickly fell apart.[22]

THE FOLLOWERS: HP, IBM, AND DEC

Hewlett-Packard had introduced its first workstation in 1982, the year Sun was established. This was the HP9000, termed "a desktop mainframe," and it resulted from $250 million in development. Four years later came the RISC-powered Spectrum, which HP licensed to Hitachi, Samsung, and others to enhance the numbers of software applications and packages using the Spectrum. HP's growth was held back briefly by its acquisition of Apollo in 1989 and the resulting absorption of Apollo's personnel into its restructured operating organization; but then, after the development of an improved combination of RISC chip and UNIX software, HP's revenues began to rise again slowly, from just under $1 billion in 1990 to $1.52 billion in 1992, bringing a market share worldwide of 11 percent.[23]

IBM's initial entry, its RT-PC workstation introduced in 1986, was a failure. By 1990 IBM had only 4 percent of workstation revenues worldwide. IBM's senior managers responded by forming an independent business unit similar to the one that had created the PC to commercialize its much more powerful RS600. Introduced in February 1991 and made available with either UNIX operating systems or IBM's own OS/2, it quickly elevated IBM to second place behind Sun. At the same time, IBM introduced its highly successful advanced minicomputer, the AS/400, which rapidly increased its revenues as those from mainframes began to fall off sharply.[24]

As IBM and HP moved forward, DEC fell behind. Because DEC remained focused on its mainframe and minicomputer businesses, served by its VAX technology, which had so successfully replaced its initial PDP series,

it was slow in developing a workstation line. In 1984 that company introduced its VAX Station 1, based on VAX technology. In 1988 DEC did turn to
the dominant technology by purchasing 20 percent of the equity of MIPS
Computer Systems and then producing a RISC/UNIX system.[25]

In 1994, as table 5.1 indicates, Sun, IBM, and Hewlett-Packard were the
three top American workstation producers. DEC had fallen to fifth. The
other workstation makers among the top ten included Silicon Graphics, Motorola, and Intergraph, in addition to two mainframe makers and another
minicomputer producer.

Silicon Graphics evolved from another Stanford project, headed by
James Clark. It was a niche producer that was the first to commercialize
three-dimensional computer graphics primarily for technical and scientific
market. The company was established in 1981, and its first products appeared in 1984. Then, in 1987, with a MIPS-developed RISC chip and its
own UNIX software, it quickly doubled its revenues. In 1992 Silicon Graphics acquired RISC-chip maker MIPS Computer Systems. By then Motorola, the second largest producer of microprocessors and supplier of Apple
and later IBM, integrated forward into workstations. Intergraph, formed in
1969 in Huntsville, Alabama, became during the 1970s a major producer of
computer-aided design/computer-aided manufacturing (CAD/CAM) products. Output of these workstation producers was smaller than that of Sun,
IBM, and Hewlett-Packard. They did not become what McNealy had earlier termed "serious players."[26]

Although much smaller in terms of revenues by the mid-1990s, the networked workstation began to overtake PCs as the industry's dynamic sector.
Indeed, network servers became central to Japan's renewed challenge to
U.S. worldwide dominance, as reviewed in chapters 7 and 8. But an understanding of the developments of the 1990s requires an awareness of the rapidly evolving supporting hardware and software sectors that were recast by
the coming of the personal computer.

The Supporting Sectors: Hardware and Software

Here I follow the pattern used in chapter 4 by considering first the rapid growth
of the supporting hardware—peripherals and semiconductors—and then software—operating systems and applications. Additionally I include a brief review
of the changing service sector. The most obvious and immediate impact of the

microprocessor revolution was that the makers of U.S. semiconductors, especially the first-movers in microprocessors, became world leaders once again. Nevertheless, the Japanese maintained their strength in memory chips. In the United States, both in peripherals and software, large specialized independent producers appeared for the first time, particularly dramatically in software, where several entrepreneurial start-ups became world leaders almost overnight.

PERIPHERALS

The unprecedented expansion of personal computers and the more modest growth in workstations meant that American producers were the first to acquire the cost advantages of scale in the production of microprocessors and other peripherals. However, as minimum efficient scale in production of hardware components was often lower than in semiconductors, the microprocessor revolution did increase the number of small and medium-size enterprises in the United States and East Asia (though far less so in Europe) making modems, scanners, terminals, network cards, ancillary chips, and the like.

On the other hand, the explosive demand brought into being new large-scale mass producers of such basic peripherals as printers and disk drives. Before the early 1980s the major producers of printers for the merchant market had been the giant first-movers in copiers, Xerox in the United States and Canon in Japan. From the early 1970s these firms had produced printers for mainframes (primarily IBM plug-compatibles) and minicomputers. Although IBM awarded the Japanese firm Epson the initial PC franchise for printers, Hewlett-Packard, already an established producer of peripherals, was selected as a much-needed second source. As the demand for personal computers soared, it seized the opportunity offered. Working with Canon, HP brought out the first low-priced laser printer (at $3,500) for the new PC market. After making the investment necessary to assure the cost advantages of scale, HP continued to work with Canon to introduce the Laser Jet II. With the Laser Jet II, HP became and remained the leading producer. Xerox continued to lag behind. Apple, using a Canon engine, went on to make its own printers. By the early 1990s Hewlett-Packard was producing 60 percent of global printers, with Epson staying in second place on printers and Canon enjoying a 70 percent share of laser printer engines.[27]

The coming of the personal computer reshaped the disk drive business in the same manner. By 1994 five entreprenuerial start-up makers of disk drives for PCs were among the top fifteen peripheral producers worldwide. These five were Seagate Technology, Storage Technology, Quantum Peripherals, Western Digital, and Connor Peripherals. Although Tandon had received the initial IBM franchise, IBM's second source, Alan Shugart's Seagate Technology, quickly took the lead. Shugart had been one of the IBM team that invented the floppy disk. He left IBM in 1969, taking more than a hundred IBM employees to establish Memorex, one of the first producers of plug-compatible IBM equipment. In 1973 he formed Shugart Associates, which Xerox purchased in 1977. Finally, in 1979 he and others of his team, including Finis Connor, founded Seagate Technology. The firm was thus positioned to miniaturize mainframe hard disks for IBM and IBM clones in a way that permitted the drive to have thirty times more storage than a floppy disk. By 1984 Seagate, exploiting economies of scale, became the nation's high-volume, low-cost disk drive producer.[28]

The other two leading disk drive producers, Quantum, a small start-up, and Connor Peripherals, were established to meet the needs of Apple and Compaq. In 1990 Apple still accounted for 41 percent of Quantum sales. By then Quantum was also selling to Matsushita as well as to IBM and IBM clones. In 1985, when Compaq's output began to take off, Rod Canion asked Finis Connor, who had left Seagate to form a company of his own, to supply Compaq, providing a $12 million investment in its stock to assist the start-up. At first 90 percent of Connor's output went to Compaq, but soon, like Quantum, he was supplying other PC makers. Under such competition, Tandon, IBM's initial choice for PC disk drives, fell behind. In 1988 Western Digital, a producer of storage control systems, acquired Tandon, but it was unable to make a reasonable profit until the beginning of the second computer boom in the mid-1990s.[29]

The two other enterprises listed in table 5.1, ranking nine and ten, were Lexmark and Storage Technology. Lexmark International Group was a 1991 spin-off from IBM that produced printers. It reported annual losses until 1995 and then registered a small profit in 1995. Storage Technology was established by four IBM engineers in 1969 and began as a niche producer of IBM-compatible tape drives. Then it became a full-line supplier of peripherals, but, unable to compete, it filed bankruptcy in 1989 and subsequently limped along, with losses in 1993 and 1995. The successful firms in this category were therefore either long-established enterprises or the first entrepreneurial firms to enter the market.[30]

THE MICROPROCESSOR AND IBM SAVE INTEL

In microprocessors, the franchise IBM had given Intel quickly made Intel the world's largest producer and so permitted it to define a standard for personal computers. But this occurred only after Intel weathered the Japanese challenge in memories.

In the early 1980s Intel's managers were in shock as the Japanese onslaught was destroying its major market, memories. In 1983 Intel lost $114 million in the third quarter. By 1984 Intel had only one DRAM plant left in operation. In 1982, to save its critical supplier, IBM had provided $250 million through the acquisition of 15 percent of Intel's equity. By 1984 IBM had raised its stake to $400 million and a total of 20 percent of Intel's stock. That aid permitted Intel to weather the losses in memories and position itself to benefit from the explosion of PCs.[31]

By 1983 the microprocessor began to have its impact on Intel and its Silicon Valley rivals. As Andrew Grove, Intel's CEO, noted in the company's 1986 annual report:

> In 1983, demand for semiconductors exploded, fueled in large part by the expansion of the personal computer business. No one could get enough semiconductors, especially Intel Microprocessors, which had emerged as the standard for personal computers. . . . We licensed other semiconductor manufacturers to produce Intel microprocessors, peripherals, and microcontrollers. We met our customers' needs and helped expand the total market for our products, though we lost control over a generation of our products and created our own competition.[32]

Again, as in disk drives, IBM called for a second source, specifically Advanced Micro Devices. Soon that firm, Cyrix, and several other small, specialized chip makers were producing Intel's 8088, 8086, and 80286 under license. In time Advanced Micro Devices came to have an even larger share of these early PC processors than did Intel itself. In fact, IBM's second sources ultimately commanded over two-thirds of the 8088/86 and 80286 market. With this experience, these second sources would ultimately be able to develop their own versions of Intel's later 386 and 486 microprocessors, despite Intel's decision not to license these later chips.[33]

By 1985 Intel's survival was reasonably assured as a producer of microprocessors. Thus, when the Japanese further reduced DRAM prices in 1985, Intel could choose to abandon the memory business altogether. Not only that, Intel could also make plans to solidify its leadership in microprocessors by developing a next-generation chip and investing in enough capacity to avoid the need to license its rivals. This effort involved not only construction costs, but also a planned $250 million for "a massive program to build design expertise and CAD tools," for the designing, as well as the production, of volume-produced microprocessors required different equipment and skills than those for volume-produced memories.[34] Because the onetime cost for shutting down the memory operations came at precisely the same moment that the company began to retool for its next-generation microprocessor, its profits dropped from $198 million in 1984 to $2 million in 1985 and to a loss of $173 million in 1986. Still, Intel's survival seemed secure, so IBM sold off its 20 percent stake in 1986 for a profitable $625 million.[35]

By 1985 all agreed that Intel's continued leadership depended on the success of its investment in the new, far more powerful, volume-produced 32-bit 80386 microprocessor. That year IBM, after negotiation, agreed to have Intel continue to provide the 80386 microprocessor for its PC on the condition that IBM could develop compatible versions for its own use. According to a senior IBM executive, the company decided not to take up the option because Intel was already far ahead in the development of the new microprocessor. So the development of an Intel clone that used Microsoft software would not warrant its costs. Intel's managers then asked Compaq to test the processor to meet the requirements of all existing personal computer software. That processor, used by Compaq and nearly all the PC clones as well as IBM's second-generation PS/2, assured Intel's continuing dominance. Revenues doubled from just under $2 billion in 1987 to just under $4 billion in 1990, and net income rose from $248 million to $650 million. In 1989 the company brought out a still higher-powered microprocessor, the 486. By then it was producing over 70 percent of microprocessors for desktops, portables, notebooks, laptops, and other personal computer products.

As *The New York Times* reported in April 1992, Intel's increase in revenue between 1986 and 1991 was "a gain that alone is responsible for the American market share [in semiconductors worldwide] being 5% higher than it would have otherwise been." Intel was then fighting legal battles with AMD, its major competitor, which had cloned the 386 and 486. Its only other strong competitor was Motorola, which made a proprietary processor for Apple and continued to be a major producer of dedicated chips for a wide variety of industries. Texas Instruments had not yet recovered from its series of mishaps in calculators and digital watches during the 1970s that led to the departure of Compaq's founders. Furthermore, the company moved into personal computers in 1979, only to have its sales collapse with the coming of the IBM PC.[36]

The first serious challenge to Intel's overriding dominance came in October 1991. IBM, Apple, and Motorola announced an alliance to develop a RISC processor, the Power PC, to be the engine for IBM's PC, Apple's Macintosh, and systems using UNIX operating technology. This alliance had evolved from Apple's interest in IBM's RS/6000 workstation as the basis for a new faster processor. For IBM, it promised an alternative to the Intel/Microsoft alliance, which had led in 1990 to the smashing victory of Gates's Windows over IBM's OS/2, a story that will be told shortly.[37]

This alliance reshaped Intel's decade-old relationship with IBM. Motorola's Power PC, supported by IBM technology, now became Intel's most significant competitor. Intel quickly responded. In 1993 it released the Pentium, a far more powerful chip to be fabricated in plants that cost $1.3 billion. Like the Power PC, it was to support UNIX as well as Microsoft's Windows. It assured Intel's continuing dominance. By 1994, of the worldwide market for microprocessors, Intel held 74 percent, followed by Motorola with 12 percent, Advanced Micro Devices with 7 percent, and Texas Instruments with 3 percent.[38]

A return look at Intel's brief history provides a striking example of the competitive advantages resulting from building an integrated learning base at the very beginning of commercializing a major new technology. Two of its founders, Robert Noyce and Gordon Moore, who had entered the field at its very beginning by joining the inventor of the transistor, William Shockley, left him to form Fairchild Semiconductor. There Robert Noyce invented the integrated circuit. Moore and Noyce then departed Fairchild to establish Intel, where they quickly built an integrated learning base to commercialize memory chips using the new MOS technology developed at Fairchild and to pioneer in the invention of the initial microprocessors. The development of the 386 and the 486 microprocessors required the funds, the knowledge, and the skills that were not available to other entrepreneurial start-ups. In addition, Intel enjoyed a powerful advantage of having its product become the de facto market standard for personal computers, thus locking in customers whose existing applications rested on Microsoft's operating software.

The Supporting Sectors: Services and Software

The most revolutionary aspect of the microcomputer revolution was software, beginning with the growth of Microsoft, the other primary beneficiary of IBM's move into personal computers. Before I take up the Microsoft story in detail, a word needs to be said about the data-processing industry's service sector.

SERVICES

Datamation first included services as a separate sector in its 1983 and 1984 listings of industry leaders. If software was the most changed sector with the coming of the microcomputer, the service sector was the least changed, and for very good reasons. The computer services continued to be provided to corporations and other large institutions rather than to individuals. And the services provided were broadly the same provided a decade earlier—either the provision (that is, outsourcing) of data-processing services on the service provider's systems or the provision of technical consultants for the creation and maintenance of the customer's own computing systems. This sector did change in two ways. First, the technical consulting business became much larger than the outsourcing/data-processing side. Second, as a consequence, the industrial companies that had been leasing spare computing capacity, and even the top revenue producer in 1984, Automatic Data Processing, had been replaced on the list of leading producers by additional computer makers as well as large accounting firms that were providing technical consulting.

Of the ten largest U. S. producers in the service sector in 1984 (table 4.2), four were entrepreneurial start-ups that began operations in the 1960s— Automatic Data Processing (#1), Electronic Data Systems (by then a subsidiary of General Motors) (#3), Computer Sciences (#5), and the U. S. subsidiary of the French firm Cap Gemini Sogeti (#9). Two were mainframe makers, Control Data (#2) and IBM (#10). The remaining four were giant industrial corporations—three aerospace companies and General Electric.

By 1994 two of the pioneering start-ups, EDS and Computer Sciences, remained among the sector's leaders. They provided technical consulting and outsourcing of data processing. So did IBM, who had moved from tenth to first place and had been joined by fellow mainframe maker, Unisys (the 1986 merger of Burroughs and Sperry Rand), and two minicomputer/workstation makers, DEC and Hewlett-Packard. Three large accounting firms, who had replaced the aerospace companies, primarily provided technical services. One new start-up, ENTEX, had appeared to serve PC users. Table 5.1 shows the 1994 ranking of the suppliers of services and the increasing volume of their revenues. By the mid-1990s the service sector produced more revenue than did any of the industry's seven sectors.

To some degree, the microprocessor had influenced the nature of this technical consulting. Since institutional customers increasingly came to own a range of computing platforms—mainframes, minicomputers, and PCs—the challenge of tying them all together into enterprisewide systems created large demand for "systems integration" services. By 1994 the leading revenue producers in services all generated significant revenues from systems integration. Only in 1993 did ENTEX Information Services begin to offer comparable services for the users of personal computers and client-server networks.[39]

SOFTWARE—MICROSOFT, THE FIRST-MOVER

The history of Microsoft provides a stunning example of the creation of competitive advantage based on the economies not only of scale and scope, but also of de facto standard setting. Bill Gates's comment on his company's strategic strength was: "It is all about scale economics and market share. When you are shipping one million units of Windows' software a month you can afford to spend $300 million a year improving it and still sell it at a small price." Cusumano and Selby, in their book *Microsoft Secrets*, describe Gates's benefits from the economies of scope in much the same terms as Flamm outlined those of the System 360. By competing in both the operating system and application markets, Microsoft could exploit innovations and expertise developed for one product across several others.[40] But Microsoft had an additional first-mover advantage, even more powerful than those enjoyed by Intel. Its franchise from IBM permitted it to define the standards for PC operating systems, which gave it not only a de facto monopoly in operating systems, but also a significant competitive advantage in developing software that ran on top of the operating system—that is, application software, a new product, based on, in the words of software historian Edward Steinmueller, "a new and revolutionary organizing principle, mass production of packaged software."[41]

The writing of the new operating systems and applications transformed the production of software. Before IBM's PC had reshaped the data-processing industry, the leading software producers had written software for mainframes and minicomputers. By 1987, the first year that *Datamation* listed software as a separate sector, of the fifteen largest revenue producers Microsoft was #11, Lotus (the producer of spreadsheets) #12, Oracle (databases) #13, and Computer Associates, a services firm that acquired several start-ups in application software, #7. The remaining eleven included IBM, Unisys, DEC, and long-established Japanese and European competitors in mainframes and mini-computers. By 1994 (table 5.1) Microsoft was #2 behind IBM (still producing software for the older large-scale systems), Computer Associates #3, Novell (networking software) #4, Oracle #5, and Lotus #8. Of these, Microsoft was the only new entrant to produce major operating systems, which nevertheless further highlights how the PC recast the industry, where traditionally operating systems were produced by hardware manufacturers.[42]

Microsoft Breaks with IBM

Microsoft, like Intel, got off to an impressive start. It effectively met the challenge of the huge unexpected demand by playing a major role in the development of the disk operating systems of DOS 1.0 and then DOS 2.0, which appeared in 1983. By 1985 it had licensed close to two hundred companies, largely start-ups. Clearly Microsoft's learning in responding to the challenge was critical to the continued development of IBM's PCs.

Early in 1985 senior IBM managers, headed by William Lowe (who took over the Entry Level Systems Division on Estridge's death in an airplane crash), began negotiations with Gates to determine Microsoft's role in the development of the next generation of software. Under the Joint Development Agreement signed that June between the two companies, Gates was to participate in the development of OS/2. Gates agreed to develop OS/2 and its follow-up for "essentially nothing," if Microsoft received the royalties from licensing the other makers—that is, the clones. Gates would retain the rights to the DOS source code. In the agreement no mention was made of the Windows operating system that Gates had begun to develop in 1981. As Paul Carroll wrote in *Big Blues*, before the signing of the joint agreement "Lowe and IBM had plenty of leverage over Microsoft. Afterwards they had none, and they would never get it back."[43]

Tensions quickly arose between the signers of the agreement. The underlying reason, Ferguson and Morris point out in *Computer Wars*, was that each had a different goal. "Microsoft's ambition was to become the software standard setter; to do so, it needed to treat all hardware platforms equally. But

IBM was aiming at hardware supremacy that served its own ambitions, not Microsoft's." Other conflicts occurred. For Gates these included IBM's internal confusions, bureaucratic struggles, and resulting delays and mistakes. IBM managers were, in turn, troubled by Gates's aggressive, petulant attitude and, most important of all, his concentration on Microsoft's own products.[44]

This last concern reflected the different goals. Gates had tied the development of the new OS/2 operating system to Intel's older 16-bit 286, rather than the 32-bit 386. He had played a part in the commercializing of the 386 by working with Compaq and Intel, since he planned to use it for his Windows 1.0. Why, then, write OS/2 based on the 286 chip? Ferguson and Morris suggest two reasons. One, "OS/2 would have been a serious learning exercise," as Gates was developing his own Windows system. Two, "Bluntly, if Gates expected ultimately to break with IBM, he had every interest in ensuring OS/2's failure."[45]

Gates's strong protests against IBM's negotiations with other firms concerning software further reflected their different goals. Gates was incensed when in the spring of 1988 IBM joined with DEC, Apple, and Hewlett-Packard in the Open Software Foundation to combat the Sun/AT&T combination's attempt to set the client-server technology standard. Fearing that the association might bring into being a single UNIX standard that would challenge DOS, OS/2, and ultimately Windows, Gates "mounted a brief spirited counterattack against IBM's involvement." He returned to IBM's headquarters at Armonk the following October, where he "blew up again" because IBM had paid Steve Jobs $50 million for the rights to Jobs's innovative operating systems for workstations. (After leaving Apple, Jobs had formed a company called NeXt.) In the summer of 1990 Gates was again at IBM headquarters, asking for its support in his plans to challenge Novell, the leading networking software producer, with his Windows NT, a challenge that I describe shortly. Again Gates was rebuffed.[46]

Later that same year, 1990, six months after Microsoft introduced Windows 3.0 in May, Gates broke openly with IBM. The OS/2 for IBM had appeared in late 1987, receiving a chilly reception. By 1990 it had only about 1 percent of the installed base of operating systems. It was clearly a failure. Windows 3.0 became an instant success. It had "a vast array of supporting third-party software," Ferguson and Morris report, "including a long list of excellent applications from Microsoft that somehow never got developed for OS/2."[47]

Gates had achieved his goal. Windows had emerged as the standard for personal computer software, worldwide. From 1989 through 1991 revenues zoomed from $804 million to $1,843 million, and net income from $171 million to $466 million. Its 1991 growth of 56 percent made Microsoft one of the fastest-growing firms among the Fortune 500. This was only the beginning, as documented in appendix 5.1 and appendix 5.2.

By 1995, before the introduction of the next-generation operating system, Windows 95, Microsoft's revenues had soared to just under $6 billion and net income to just under $1.5 billion, thus maintaining a steady growth in revenue of 25 percent a year from 1990 through 1995—an achievement comparable to IBM's revenues and net income in the late years of the 1960s after the introduction of the System 360. These remarkable revenues rested on Microsoft's technical and functional, as well as managerial, capabilities, learned during the late 1980s in all three of the new software sectors' major businesses—operating systems, applications, and networking software.

By 1991, when Microsoft had acquired its near monopoly in personal computer operating systems, 51 percent of Microsoft's revenues came from applications, 36 percent from operating systems, and the rest from related hardware and electronic books. By then Microsoft was well on its way to becoming the leading producer of networking software, not only for PCs but also for workstations. The learning base for all three of these software activities—operating systems, applications, and networking—had been put in place in the late 1980s. I now briefly review Microsoft's accomplishments in building learning bases in the three different data-processing activities in the new software sector.[48]

Building Microsoft's Learning Bases

OPERATING SYSTEMS: THE EVOLUTION OF WINDOWS

From the start, Gates had his eye on creating his own operating system, Windows, which would ultimately rival DOS. Windows 1.0, which featured a graphical user interface (GUI), was introduced in 1985 but was not a success. By then the popularity of Apple's Macintosh, released in 1984, confirmed the value of a GUI and so led Gates to John Sculley. On November 25, 1985, only five months after signing the Joint Development Agreement with IBM, he and Sculley signed an agreement by which Microsoft secured a license for visual characteristics of the Macintosh's graphical user interface. These included pictures, or icons, with a mouse to point to the icon and a click to perform the tasks required. In return, he would broaden Apple's application software base by developing Macintosh versions of Microsoft's spreadsheet, word processing, and other applications. This learning became incorporated not only into its spreadsheet and word-processing products for the PC but also into its own Windows 2.0, introduced in 1988. Windows 2.0, however, was still incomplete. But the success of Windows 3.0 in 1990, with its impressive set of complementary Microsoft applications, was testimony to Gates's choice of technology on which to build Microsoft's technical capabilities.[49]

After removing the final "bugs" from, and adding improvements to, Windows 3.0 during 1991, Microsoft's researchers turned to developing the next generation, Windows 95. That project broadened and improved the system's uses. It required as much investment in research as had Windows 3.0—and even more time to complete. In 1994 a substantial part of the $830 million Microsoft spent on research went to Windows 95. Even so, that project ran almost two years late, appearing finally in late 1995.

APPLICATIONS

The dominance of Microsoft's application software was another direct result of the November 1985 licensing agreement. Gates had begun writing software applications as he was developing his Windows operating system. Microsoft introduced its word-processing application, Word, in 1983 and quickly followed it by a spreadsheet, Multiplan. Both were less than successful. Two start-ups, WordPerfect and Lotus, quickly captured these markets for the PC. But as the result of the 1985 agreement with Sculley, Microsoft developed GUI-based versions of Microsoft Word and Multiplan (renamed Excel) long before its competitors. As Microsoft's Windows operating systems gained share from DOS, Microsoft's Windows-friendly applications rapidly began to take market share from the non-graphics-based products of WordPerfect and Lotus. In 1990 Windows 3.0 gave Microsoft dominance in word-processing and spreadsheet applications. In addition it entered database applications by the acquisition of Access in 1992. Other applications followed, such as Money in personal finance and PowerPoint in graphics.[50]

NETWORKING

Microsoft's initial forays into networking software in the early 1980s were no more successful than its spreadsheet and word-processing applications of that time. Here its learning base began with the development of Windows NT, a long-term project of a highly innovative order. That project began in November 1988 when Gates invited David Cutler, the leading operating system developer at DEC, to join Microsoft. Cutler had been DEC's chief architect for the VMS operating system for the VAX minicomputer, which replaced the PDP-11 in the late 1970s. In the early 1980s he began to design a RISC-based operating system for DEC's workstations. In 1988 DEC's top managers unexpectedly shut down his project. Gates, on learning of this decision, invited Cutler to come to Microsoft with his team to develop a competitive workstation operating system. G. Pascal Zachary, in his splendid book, *Show-Stopper!*, writes that Gates from the start allowed Cutler to create his own company within Microsoft.[51] As the learning progressed, the project's goal broadened. The operating system would run not only on Intel and Motorola processors, but also on RISC technology.

Microsoft introduced Windows NT at the end of July 1993. "By fall 1993, IBM, Apple, Hewlett-Packard, and Motorola began adapting NT to their own chips," according to Zachary. "After NT was just a few months on the market, plans were in place for it to work with virtually every major computer, putting it on the path towards becoming the first universal operating system."[52]

By 1993 Microsoft's investment and learning in the late 1980s had assured its dominance in operating systems, applications, and networking. By then, as Zachary's statement indicates, the two primary data-processing paths of learning were beginning to meld into each other. Gates was producing operating systems for engineering and scientific computing as well as for commercial and home computing. The IBM-Apple-Motorola alliance was making Power PC chips that could power UNIX systems. Moreover, Novell was moving in the same direction. Its Netware 386 software, released in 1989, ran on both UNIX and Macintosh systems, as well as on Intel's 386 chips. By 1993 the fastest-growing data-processing market was for wide area networks (WANs) used by large corporations and other institutions to connect and coordinate their hundreds of thousands of computers at home and abroad.[53]

Before turning to the story of the merging of those two paths of learning—commercial/home and engineering/scientific computing—I need to review the impact of Gates's success on the independent producers of applications software, including Novell.

The Application Software Companies

The leading producers of mass-produced application software, enterprises that *Datamation* initially termed "pure software companies"—that is, "making no other products"—built their learning bases in the U.S. industry's critical years 1980–1985. Like Microsoft, they became worldwide leaders in the shortest time. Their fate, however, rested on the extent of their bondage to a Microsoft operating system, as appendices 5.1, 5.2, and 5.3 illustrate. Those that were not so bonded—Oracle, Computer Associates, and Novell—grew apace. Those that were—Lotus, WordPerfect, Borland, and Ashton-Tate (acquired by Borland)—were pushed aside in the late 1980s by Microsoft. Nevertheless, there were exceptions. The somewhat smaller Adobe provides an impressive example of the creation of a learning base with barriers to entry high enough to ward off a Microsoft attack.

Of the new application software companies, Oracle was the first to market specialized application products. In 1978 Lawrence J. Ellison and Robert Miller, two experienced computer experts (Ellison had worked with Gene Amdahl on the development of IBM's System 360), began to commercialize an IBM innovation, the relational database system (RDBS). That innovation permitted computers of different sizes and from different manufacturers to use a standardized database management system for management controls, special-purpose inventory, purchasing, and the like—activities previously handled by a wide variety of packaged software producers. The two men marketed their product for two years for mainframes and minicomputers before IBM introduced its own RDBS system.[54]

Oracle's growth was impressive. In 1982 the company had twenty-four employees and seventy-five mainframe and minicomputer customers. After the development of a portable RDBS, the customers by 1986 had risen to two thousand mainframe and minicomputer users, including major national corporations. By then it had established seventeen international subsidiaries to market its products in thirty-nine countries. By then, too, its managers were working with Apple and Lotus to develop programs for personal computers, a promising source of potential growth.

Such uncontrolled growth had its price. In 1990 came a loss of $12 million, followed by an extensive management and financial reorganization. Back on track, Oracle launched new products, including Oracle 7, a network-compatible database. It reached the $2 billion mark in sales in 1994. By then it was the world's largest producer of database management systems. Large systems remained its major market.

If Oracle prospered because it fully established its initial learning base in markets in which Microsoft did not compete, Computer Associates (CA) maintained stable growth, in terms of sales and income, first by maintaining its initial corporate learning base in services as it moved into PC applications, and second by focusing on database software for PCs, a market that Microsoft entered only in 1990. Computer Associates, like Oracle, evolved from an IBM seed, but a very different one. Charles Wang, a Chinese-born New Yorker, had acquired Computer Associates in 1980. At the time, it was a small systems integration service company for which he and his brother had worked and which, at the time, concentrated on improving the performance of IBM's equipment for its customers. By retaining that business as its core, CA was able to enter the applications market largely through the acquisition of small start-up companies.[55]

In 1983 it purchased a word-processing producer, and in the next year it acquired Super Calc, a spreadsheet application. It purchased an application for financial securities in 1985 and one for accounting in 1987. Then came a major move into database software. As at Oracle, a management reorganization followed, a move that more carefully defined its three major lines — its new database management products, its earlier spreadsheets and other PC applications, and its original system integration activities. In 1994 sales at Computer Associates were $2.4 billion, with net income of $401 million. Computer Associates' performance in terms of its relatively high income as a percent of sales provides an effective example of growth through carefully chosen acquisitions in the beginning years of a new industry. Its success was similar to that of Control Data, which grew through acquisitions of start-ups in the early years of the evolution of the mainframe sector.

The successful start-ups that provided applications just for personal computers — Lotus, WordPerfect, and Borland — suffered a very different fate from that of Oracle and Computer Associates. Lotus, formed in 1982 by Mitchell D. Kapor in Cambridge, Massachusetts, was the first "pure" software company to be listed in *Datamation's* one hundred largest computer revenue producers. Within a year its spreadsheet, Lotus 1-2-3, had overtaken Daniel Bricklin's VisiCalc. In 1985 Kapor purchased Bricklin's company, Software Arts. By 1986 Lotus had the highest revenue among the new software companies, well ahead of Microsoft. With the appearance of Apple's Macintosh in

1984, Lotus made a relatively unsuccessful attempt to develop for Macintosh a combined spreadsheet and word-processing program called Jazz. Then in 1988 Gates became a competitor when he bundled his Excel into Windows 2.0. Windows 3.0 followed. By 1991 Lotus's market share dropped from 75 percent in 1988 to 55 percent, with Microsoft's Excel accounting for most of the difference. Lotus never really recovered. In 1995 IBM acquired Lotus primarily to obtain Lotus Notes, a new category of software called groupware, which permitted groups of computer users to collaborate from distant locations, a product line that Microsoft had not yet entered.[56]

The story of WordPerfect was much the same. After Satellite Software International, formed by Bruce Bastion and Alan Ashton, introduced WordPerfect in 1982, it quickly became the nation's best-selling word-processing application. The corporation's name was then changed to WordPerfect. The product was far superior to Microsoft's Word and Wang Laboratories' MultiMate, the minicomputer maker's initial move into software applications. The first version of Word that Microsoft wrote for Apple's Macintosh was not a success. So WordPerfect continued to lead. But the much improved version in Windows 3.0 assured Microsoft's dominance. By 1992 Microsoft controlled more than half the market, with WordPerfect holding less than a third. In 1994 WordPerfect was acquired by Novell, which then sold it to Corel within a year, as Novell dealt with its own crisis (to be covered shortly).[57]

The collapse of Borland International reflects more than just Microsoft's late entry into database applications. It provides another example of the difficulty of attempting growth through large-scale acquisitions instead of through internal learning. Philippe Kahn, who had formed Borland in 1983 to produce niche software products, decided in 1986 to build a diversified software application enterprise. His strategy was to follow what he called "the Honda way"—that is, to begin by producing low-priced goods and then expand market share with improved, higher-priced products. Kahn began by acquiring Ansa Software, which produced a database product called Paradox. He then introduced his Quattro Pro spreadsheet, followed by the acquisition of a word processor, and finally in 1991 he bought a much larger database leader, Ashton-Tate, just as Microsoft was introducing its Access. Appendix 5.1 registers the disastrous results of Borland's "Honda" strategy.[58]

If Borland's fate suggests a strategy for failure, Adobe's provides one for success, based on continuing enhancement of its own development and marketing capabilities. Between 1982 and 1984 Adobe's founders, John

Warnock and Charles Geschke, developed a computer language for desktop publishing. Next, working with Apple, they produced a desktop printer that was able to publish nearly everything produced by a computer. Then came the creation of a marketing organization, first in the United States, then in Europe in 1987, and finally in East Asia in 1989. A steady increase in sales and income provided funds for improving existing products and developing new ones. Its lines soon included Adobe Illustrator, TypeManager, Photoshop, and others. So when Microsoft entered the desktop publishing market in 1992 with its Microsoft Publisher, the barriers to entry created by Adobe's completed learning base were so high that Microsoft quickly withdrew.[59]

Before turning to networking software, I mention the one major producer of application software outside of the United States, Germany's SAP AG. Its story parallels that of Oracle, for it, too, had IBM roots and its product was introduced even earlier than that of Oracle. In 1972 four German technicians in IBM's German unit, working on a project called Systems, Applications, and Projects (SAP), left to form their own enterprise, naming it SAP for the project in which they had learned their technical skills. In 1978 they introduced a mainframe-based "enterprise resource planning" system, their R/2, which integrated various business functions, such as financial accounting, inventory management, and production scheduling, into a single database application. SAP's financial success, however, had its beginnings in 1988, when its managers decided to invest a massive $650 million in R&D to develop a client-server based architecture. In 1992, as the sales of its mainframe-based R/2 software lagged, it introduced its client-server based R/3. Its revenues tripled from $634 million in 1993 to $1.7 billion in 1996. SAP was the only major enterprise in Europe to benefit from the microprocessor revolution. The implications of this success are reviewed in chapter 7.[60]

Software: Networking

Novell, the only networking software producer on appendices 5.1, 5.2 and 5.3, led the way in the development of technology for linking desktop computers within a department, corporation, or some comparable institution, that is, for building a local area network (LAN).

After Raymond J. Noorda acquired Novell, a nearly bankrupt maker of peripherals, in 1983, he began, in the manner of Adobe's founders, to put together an integrated learning base around networking technology. He first produced an operating system that permitted personal computers to share printers, disk drives, and other peripherals. Then he created a file server, usually a PC with generous storage and "I/O capacity." Next came the acquisition of Santa Clara Systems, a manufacturer of data storage systems and other LAN hardware. At the same time Noorda built what one analyst termed "a first class distribution network." Novell's sales jumped from $82 million in 1986 to $281 million in 1988, giving Novell 50 percent of the networking market. Noorda's major achievement came with the introduction in September 1989 of NetWare 386, which could simultaneously serve UNIX, Apple's Macintosh, and Microsoft's Windows.[61]

In 1991 Noorda was ready to challenge Microsoft's dominance in software. He set up an "entrepreneurial arm . . . to develop Wide Area Networks (WAN) needed by large corporations to link together hundreds of small and large computer systems, many of them not in the same building, or even in the same country." To achieve these goals, Noorda expanded Novell's learning base by acquisition, purchasing a maker of UNIX operating systems and also AT&T's UNIX Laboratories (initially created for the AT&T-Sun alliance). He formed alliances with IBM, H-P, and Compaq. In addition, by purchasing WordPerfect and Borland's Quattro Pro spreadsheet, Novell became the second largest producer of PC software applications in the world.

But Noorda's attempt to challenge Microsoft as a software leader failed abruptly. In August 1993, as just pointed out, Microsoft introduced its Windows NT, which could be incorporated in every major computer platform. Windows NT had a slow start, with sales of three hundred thousand units in the first year. But an improved NT 3.5 introduced in September 1994 had, by the end of December, sold seven hundred thousand units, with total sales for the year of about one million units.[62] Gates's victory led to Noorda's retirement. Noorda's successor drastically reorganized the company and sold off WordPerfect and other acquisitions. Income continued to rise during the boom that accompanied the connection of private corporate networks with the public Internet in 1995. But Novell's networking software market share fell from 70 percent in 1993 to 50 percent at the beginning of 1997.

Microsoft's victory over Novell marked the blending of the two paths of learning—one for commercial and home computing, the other for scientific and engineering computing. By 1994, as indicated in the timeline in Appendix 4.1, the industry's first two paths of learning had come together. By 1994 Intel, Microsoft, and Novell were producing existing and developing new products for both sets of markets. So too were IBM, Apple, and Motorola. As part of this merging, the client-server technology was becoming increasingly used for the expanding corporate LANs and WANs.

Connecting Private Networks to the Public Internet

The next step in the evolution of the digital computer industry was the development of the hardware and software required to connect the expanding private networks to the rapidly evolving public Internet. That connection was fueled by the coming of the router, the World Wide Web, and the browser. Once the connection was made, digital computing was transformed in an even more revolutionary manner than it had been by the coming of the IBM 360 in the late 1960s and the opening of the mass market of personal computers in the 1980s.

Although corporate networks and the Internet shared many of the same technologies, the Internet evolved along a very different course from the two computing paths—that for commercial/home and that for engineering/scientific—that led to the coming of corporate networks. The latter were private, to be used primarily by the employees of the for-profit institutions that created them. The Internet was public, open to interested users, but not for commercial purposes.[63]

Today's Internet had its start in 1969 when the Department of Defense's Advanced Research Project Agency (ARPA) funded its ARPANET. In the next year four universities—Stanford, the Universities of California at Los Angeles and Santa Barbara, and the University of Utah—tested the initial pilot program. Each switching center, or, as it was termed, "node," had a specialized interface message processor (IMP), usually a small minicomputer, that connected mainframe computers to telephone lines, which in turn transmitted the messages to their destinations. Each IMP in a system had the same software program, called "the host," that collected and directed the flow of information between each node. Thus the same software program was used by all the IMPs in a single network. By December 1970 eleven universities and research centers had installed these nodes and hosts that made up the initial ARPANET. A major conference held by the ARPA in Washington in 1973 gave its ARPANET widespread publicity. By the end of 1973 forty-five hosts were operating; and by 1977, 111. From the start, the ARPANET was restricted to noncommercial uses.[64]

Other such networks soon appeared, developed by institutions that did not have access to the ARPANET. In 1975 Telnet was formed to provide commercial computer services. Large corporations developed their own private networks for proprietary use. Several informal, noncommercial networks were created by university users, such as USENET, which was described as a "poor man's ARPANET." With the coming of the personal computer, even individual users, unaffiliated with an institution, could join on-line communities using their own telephones to connect to other computers. As Campbell-Kelly and Aspray note: "Electronic mail was the driving force behind all these networks." The personal computer also stimulated the creation of the commercial on-line services—CompuServe, Prodigy, and America Online—that set up central systems to which individuals could connect over telephone lines to access a variety of information. In order to make communication among these different networks possible, the ARPA established in 1977 a single common protocol, Transmission Control Protocol/Internet Protocol (TCP/IP). In 1983 the Defense Department required all host computers on the ARPANET to use TCP/IP. That protocol became the common language of today's Internet.[65]

During the 1980s, as the microprocessor revolution was getting under way, the public Internet became accessible to many more institutionally affiliated users and acquired a civilian rather than a military orientation. First, the National Science Foundation (NSF) began to create additional public networks for noncommercial research purposes. In 1980 NSF embarked on a five-year program to provide sustained support for a new Computer Science Research Network (CSNET). In 1985 the NSF, at the close of its five-year program, funded five supercomputer centers that became the core of the National Science Foundation network (NSFNet). In 1983 the Defense Department divided the ARPANET into two, the smaller ARPANET focusing on civilian activities and MILNET for military and government uses. By 1989 the ARPANET was incorporated into the NSFNet, bringing NSF oversight of the public noncommercial Internet and closing out the Defense Department's connection.

During the first half of the 1980s the growth of the ARPANET had been modest—from fewer than 200 hosts in 1980 to about 1,000 in 1984. But then the numbers rose sharply to 28,000 at the end of 1987 and to 159,000 in 1989 as the multiple research networks and scores of LANs within ARPANET-connected institutions became attached to the public Internet. But at this point, the Internet was still under government oversight and explicitly restricted to noncommercial uses. In the meantime, separate private networks—built and operated by start-ups like CompuServe, Prodigy, and America Online and telecommications providers like MCI and Sprint— were growing in parallel to provide network services for commercial users. These networks, too, began adopting the TCP/IP protocol.[66]

By the early 1990s the completion of the basic infrastructure of the Electronic Century still required the marriage of corporate private networks and the networks of other commercial services with the public, noncommercial Internet. That interconnection required both hardware, to provide high-speed switching, and standard, cross-platform operating software. Cisco, a pioneer in data-network switching equipment, provided the former. The World Wide Web and the browser came to provide the latter.

Cisco Provides Switching Hardware

Cisco Systems pioneered the development of the router, the necessary switching hardware for these growing public and private networks. The evolution of that enterprise provides another classic example of first-mover advantages. Cisco was established in December 1984 by a husband-and-wife team at Stanford who had assisted in building a local area network for the university. They introduced their first product, a TCP/IP router, in 1986 for ARPANET users. By the following July, when sales reached $1.5 million, Cisco Systems still had only eight employees.[67]

In 1988 came the creation of an initial learning base. The founders turned to a venture capitalist, Donald T. Valentine, who raised the initial capital. He hired an experienced computer executive, John Morgridge, as CEO. Together the two built a direct-marketing organization in the United States and reinforced it with what became a model customer support service. By 1990 the entrepreneurial founders had departed. From 1988 on Cisco quickly moved beyond its initial customers, those that used TPC/IP protocols and UNIX-based computers for Internet communication. By developing reasonably priced, high-performance routers, Cisco was able to secure a larger primary market, that of major corporations building their internal networks—local and then wide area.

By 1993 Cisco was the leading worldwide supplier of routers for private networks as well as the Internet. By then its managers were working with IBM, Microsoft, and Novell to improve the performance of their products. In these years Cisco's sales and income soared, the sales from $183 million in 1991 to $649 million in 1993. The firm expanded its overseas marketing by using foreign distributors rather than its own sales department. By 1993, 39 percent of the sales came from overseas. Again, as in the case of Microsoft's Windows 3.0, this was only the beginning. With the coming of the World Wide Web, Cisco's sales in 1994 doubled, and in 1995 they were three times those of 1993. While Cisco provided the essential Internet and private network hardware, the World Wide Web and the browser provided the essential software.

The World Wide Web and the Browser Provide Software

By the end of the 1980s a major challenge had become, in Paul Ceruzzi's words, "a sudden and unexpected need to navigate through [the Internet's] rich and ever-increasing resources. . . . The Internet began to feel like a library that had no card catalogue, or a used book store that had a number of great books at bargain prices but with the books piled up at random on the shelves." The first step in organizing this massive, expanding network was the creation of the World Wide Web (WWW). This came in 1990, the year that Bill Gates introduced his triumphant Windows 3.0. In late 1990 Tim Berners-Lee wrote the first prototype of the Web at CERN, the European particle physics laboratory. Roughly, Berners-Lee's WWW system provided a common way of labeling or addressing any information on the Internet, as well as a format for locally organizing that information. The analogy might be that of providing everyone with a standard telephone number and the means to organize local directories. As Ceruzzi notes, "[T]he World Wide Web got off to a slow start."[68]

The Web's usability was vastly improved by the evolution of the browser. The essential browser software, Mosaic, was initially written at the NSF's National Center for Supercomputing Applications at the University of Illinois, Champaign-Urbana. There in January 1993 Mark Andreesen and Eric Bina wrote an early version that permitted full graphical exploitation of the WWW's hypertext. The university released Mosaic in November 1993. As Janet Abbate, the historian of the Internet, notes, "Once Mosaic became available the system spread at a phenomenal rate. In April of 1993 there had been 62 Web servers; by May of 1994 there were 1248." Earlier that year James Clark, the former Stanford professor who had created the successful workstation company, Silicon Graphics, joined with Andreesen to form an enterprise, named Mosaic, to commercialize the innovative software. After the University of Illinois protested the use of the name, they called it Netscape Communication Corporation. In September 1994 they introduced their Netscape Navigator, offering it free of charge in order to create a market. The company's revenues began in December when it started to sell improved software packages for $40 apiece.[69]

A few months earlier the Internet had been privatized. It was no longer owned by the U.S. government and operated by the NSF. Once privatized, it no longer carried the prohibition against commercial usage. In 1991 the NSF embarked on an advanced network project named MERIT, to be implemented in 1994. That year NSF contracted with four service providers to operate the network. On April 30, 1995, as Janet Abbate reports: "MERIT formally terminated the old NSFNet backbone and ended the U.S. government's ownership of the Internet's infrastructure." Now all the private and public networks could be connected into a single Internet, available for all purposes.[70]

Bill Gates, who had been skeptical about the potential of the Internet, now responded quickly to this extraordinary new opportunity by obtaining a license for a browser from Spy Glass, another spin-off from the Mosaic project. In December 1995, Microsoft bundled it into Windows 95 as Microsoft Explorer 2.0 and also distributed it free of charge on its own.

In this way a dot-com world had been created in less than three years. As 1996 began, commercial messages could be sent at minimal cost by the many millions of personal computer users. The resulting transformation of communications came more swiftly and had a more profound impact than did the coming of the IBM PC and its clones in the 1980s and the System 360 in the 1960s. It led to an explosion of demand in the already growing market for networking hardware and software. Chart 5.1 makes the point. During 1994 the number of hosts on the Internet more than doubled, from 2.2 million to 5.8 million, and in 1995 it almost tripled to 14.4 million. The impact of the commercially available Internet quickly began to transform commerce, industry, and the basic ways of life. With its appearance, the infrastructure of the Electronic Century was in place. So I consider 1996 as the cutoff date of this history.

CHART 5.1. Number of Internet Hosts, 1969–2000

Date	Number of Hosts
Dec-69	4
Dec-70	13
Apr-71	23
Oct-72	31
Jan-73	35
Jun-74	62
Mar-77	111
Dec-79	188
Aug-81	213
May-82	235
Aug-83	562
Oct-84	1,024
Oct-85	1,961
Feb-86	2,308
Dec-87	28,174
Oct-88	56,000
Jan-89	80,000
Oct-90	313,000
Jan-91	376,000
Jan-92	727,000
Jan-93	1,313,000
Jan-94	2,217,000
Jan-95	5,846,000
Jan-96	14,352,000
Jan-97	21,819,000
Jan-98	29,670,000
Jan-99	43,230,000
Jan-00	72,398,092
Jul-00	93,047,785

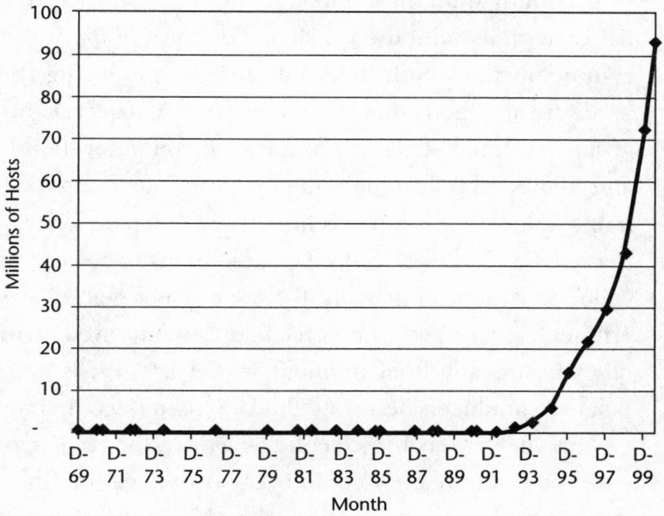

Source: Internet Software Consortium (http://www.isc.org/).

In addition, the huge increase in the demand for computing power led to a shift in the industry's technical orientation. The PC was no longer king. As the two paths of computing converged and networks tied together disparate hardware platforms, demand for mainframes and high-powered servers began to surge. This shift fueled a second Japanese challenge, based on large systems and servers.

Before turning to the evolution of the U.S. industry's foreign competitors, let me review briefly the epic story of consumer electronics and computers so far. Chapters 2 and 3 narrate the story of the consumer electronics. There the epic is the Japanese conquest of world markets. Occurring in such a brief period, less than two decades in the 1970s and 1980s, this achievement is unique in the annals of industrial, business, and technological history. It is unique because the Japanese conquest led to the death of both the European and U.S. consumer electronics industries. For the Western nations this was a tragic story in terms of national income, employment, and the loss of the technical and functional capabilities that had played a critical role in the creation of the new Electronic Century.

Chapter 4 chronicles the unique and epic story of the computer industry. Here a single enterprise, in this case IBM, shaped the global industry from its beginning until the completion of the infrastructure in the 1990s. Its initial System 360 and then System 370 became the world's standard. Its foreign competitors built their industries on producing IBM plug-compatible hardware and then complete mainframes. Chapter 4 also provides a preview of Japan's initial challenge to the U.S. computer industry, for in the 1970s and 1980s, after Europe's attempt to produce an IBM-compatible mainframe failed, the Europeans turned to the Japanese for their major computing systems. In this way, the Japanese industry became competitive. As they captured European markets, these computer makers, working with the government, focused on commercializing an improved memory chip. In yet another historically brief moment in the late 1970s and early 1980s, these Japanese producers destroyed the U.S. memory chip industry.

This chapter records a second epic story, the coming of the personal computer powered by the microprocessor. By recasting the computer industry, the personal computer assured the U.S. industry's continued world dominance. Again, IBM played the central role. By mass-producing and mass-marketing the PC, used by individuals instead of institutions, IBM set the standard. Here, too, the story was dramatic and unique. First, the use of the microprocessor in computing was initiated not by established enterprises, but by young hobbyists. Second, the primary beneficiary of scale and scope and proprietary learned knowledge made possible by the mass production and distribution of the IBM PC was not IBM, which was one of many competing PC producers, but rather the providers of the microprocessor and operating system, Intel and Microsoft. Hence, they became the primary path definers during the PC period. Nevertheless, the rise of RISC chip-based client-server networking technologies, in both private networks and the public Internet, by increasing the demand for high-powered computers, led to Japan's second challenge in the mid-1990s.

I now turn to recording the evolution of the U.S. computer industry's foreign competitors. I begin with Europe, which is essentially a history of each national industry's inability to commercialize IBM plug-compatible mainframes and then PC clones. Then I tell the epic story of the Japanese computer makers.

6

THE NATIONAL COMPETITORS: EUROPE'S

COMPUTER INDUSTRIES DIE, JAPAN'S

INDUSTRY CHALLENGES

This chapter's story of the evolving success and failure, life and death, of the U.S. industry's foreign competitors is essentially a review of the evolution of four European and five Japanese participants in data processing and then the broader information technologies. The European enterprises were International Computers Ltd., Compagnie des Machines Bull S.A., Olivetti S.p.A., and Siemens-Nixdorf, a subsidiary of Siemens AG (a descendent of Siemens & Halske AG). The Japanese enterprises were Fujitsu Limited, NEC Corporation, Toshiba Corporation, Hitachi, Ltd., and Mitsubishi Electric, a member of the Mitsubishi group. The European computer industry, except for Germany's Siemens, evolved from the office machinery path (SIC 357). The German and Japanese companies evolved from paths initially created by the global first-movers in electrical and telecommunications equipment in the United States and Europe during the 1890s. I begin with the defeats of Europe's national industries and then turn to Japan's achievements.

The European Competitors

The history of the four European competitors is straightforward. Government-sponsored "national champions," Britain's International Computers Ltd. and France's Machines Bull, simply failed to create integrated learning bases. Italy's Olivetti also failed to do so, but it did participate in the beginning of the microprocessor revolution. So it remained an international player until IBM's PC and its clones destroyed nearly all earlier personal computer companies with proprietary operating systems. Siemens, Europe's one relatively successful computer mainframe maker, did acquire Nixdorf, Europe's one minicomputer maker. Together the two German companies combined their integrated learning bases. But the volume of their joint output was too small to provide the necessary economies of scale or to permit the development of a substantial supporting nexus comparable to those of their Japanese and U. S. competitors.

INTERNATIONAL COMPUTERS LTD.: BRITAIN'S NATIONAL CHAMPION

In the 1950s Britain's commercial digital computer industry was initially a product of the licensees of the two U.S. producers of punched-card tabulators—IBM and Remington Rand. Before World War II, British Tabulating Machine Company (BTM) had been IBM's licensee for punched-card tabulators within the United Kingdom and the British dominions, except Canada. Powers Samas had played a comparable role as a licensee of Remington Rand.[1]

After World War II these two existing British punched-card tabulating enterprises became independent of their American mentors. In 1945 Vickers, Britain's largest military contractor, acquired control of Powers Samas by purchasing a large block of shares held by the Prudential Assurance Company since 1915. In 1949 IBM, already under antitrust pressure and engaged in a squabble over royalties with its British licensee, cut its ties with BTM. It did so in part to open up the British Empire to its own experienced sales force. During the 1950s BTM developed its first business computers with the help of Britain's General Electric Company (GEC—which had no connection with the American GE). On the other hand, Powers Samas made little effort to replace its electromechanical tabulators with the new electronic transistor-based machines, thus losing market share and profits. The two, BTM and

Powers Samas, merged in 1959 to form International Computers and Tabulators (ICT), with Vickers holding 20 percent of the merged company.

After the 1950s Britain's computer industry grew almost entirely through mergers and acquisitions. Between 1961 and 1963 ICT purchased the military and analytical computer divisions of Britain's General Electric Company and also those of Electrical Musical Instruments. In 1963 ICT attempted without success to merge with France's producer of punched-card tabulating machines, Compagnie des Machines Bull. At the same time, it began purchasing computers from RCA to be sold under the ICT label, and it signed a long-term nonexclusive license agreement for RCA's computer technology.

Then in 1964 came the shock of the announcement of IBM's System 360. That announcement led Harold Wilson's Labour government immediately to begin planning to create a national champion. In 1964 and 1965 it put forth several initiatives that provided ICT with £5 million for R&D. Acquisition and merging continued. The government then quickly arranged for a merger of the two remaining independent computer makers, Elliott-Automation Associates and English Electric. The new company took the name English Electric Computers. Before that merger, English Electric had acquired Ferranti, which had installed Britain's first analytical computer in 1951 but had only begun to produce computers in numbers in the late 1950s. Finally the Wilson government led the way in carrying out the last merger in 1967, that of joining English Electric Computers with ICT to form International Computers Ltd. It then funded this national champion with £35 million and gave it preference in all government procurement.

As pointed out by Kenneth Flamm, the historian of the industry's global growth: "The rash of mergers left ICL with a highly incompatible product line, unfortunately, and an agglomeration into one firm of the problems of many elements." The new national champion had little hope of becoming an effective national learning base.[2]

Nevertheless ICL tried valiantly. The government, as a major purchaser and provider of funds, continued to support ICL. The company spent £83.9 million in R&D between 1969 and 1973. Even so, by 1974 only 25–30 percent of the computers installed in Britain were produced by British enterprises. With the coming of IBM's System 370, ICL's management decided to move away from IBM's top-level mainframes and to concentrate on middle-level and small business computers. As a result, R&D spending rose to £138.7 million in 1978.

But progress remained slow, and the ICL management decided to return to the development of large mainframes. That decision led to the spending of £266 million for development between 1979 and 1981. Profits did hold up until 1979, when IBM introduced the fourth update of its System 370. That update was IBM's response to Gene Amdahl's System 370 plug-compatible produced by Fujitsu (as described later in this chapter and also in chapter 4). ICL's sales then collapsed, and the firm recorded a £50 million loss in 1981.[3]

In 1981 ICL's board of directors decided to try again. It brought in a new management team headed by two executives from Texas Instruments, Robb Wilmot and Peter Bonfield. For the recruited Americans, the only hope for ICL was Japan. The two immediately traveled to Tokyo. There in October they made an agreement with Fujitsu that defined a role for this Japanese leader in ICL's three lines of products. Fujitsu would produce and ship the largest of its IBM-compatible M-series, to be sold over ICL's label. For ICL's existing medium-size Estrial computers, Fujitsu would manufacture in Japan the completed platforms and components to ICL's design and software requirements. For ICL's smaller DM/1, Fujitsu would manufacture the semiconductors in Japan. In this way, Britain, after an investment of half a billion pounds in R&D alone, lost much of what was left of its learning base in computer production. From then on Fujitsu also provided the technical as well as the development and production capabilities for most of the products that ICL sold through its marketing and distribution organization.[4]

In 1984 Standard Telephone & Cables (Britain's direct descendant of AT&T's Western Electric) acquired control of ICL. During the late 1980s ICL responded to the microprocessor revolution by moving into client-server workstations licensed from the United States, and IBM desktop PC clones, as well as by enlarging its computer services. Then in July 1990 Fujitsu took full control of ICL by acquiring 80 percent of its shares. Standard Telephone kept the remaining 20 percent.

In 1991 Fujitsu expanded its ICL product lines by purchasing from Finland's Nokia Corporation its Nokia Data Holdings, which produced microcomputer products and services. This enhanced Fujitsu's strength in Europe in the products of the microcomputer revolution. In this way, by the 1990s Britain's computer industry had become in large part an appendage of Japan's. In the mid-1990s, for example, Fujitsu had its own marketing organization take over the selling and distribution of ICL's personal computers and servers. This left ICL to carry on only software, services, and systems integration activities, and this with little success: in 1995 ICL reported a loss of $312 million.

In Britain no core computer company with an integrated learning base evolved. The government strategy of building a national champion through mergers of several small enterprises failed. These merged enterprises, with somewhat related technical capabilities, had very little in the way of integrated functional ones—that is, product development, production, or even marketing. ICL provides a classic example of the difficulties of creating competitive strength through merger.

MACHINES BULL: FRANCE'S NATIONAL CHAMPION

France's response to IBM's System 360 was the same as Britain's—create a national champion. One difference was that in 1964 America's General Electric Company, also responding to the challenge of IBM's System 360, acquired France's only significant computer learning base, Compagnie des Machines Bull. Another difference was that the government responded not by merging existing companies, but in the classic French manner, by creating a broad, national, government-sponsored program, the Plan Calcul.

Machines Bull, established in 1932 on the basis of patents of a Norwegian engineer, Frederic Bull, had become the continent's one major challenger to IBM and Remington Rand in punched-card tabulating machines. In the 1950s Machines Bull moved energetically into the development of commercial digital computers. Its Gamma 3 quickly began to compete with some success against IBM in Europe. Then in 1960 Bull introduced a technically advanced Gamma 60, an impressive and complex machine that had been developed at a high cost—so high, indeed, that Bull was on the verge of bankruptcy when, in 1964, GE, as part of its grand plan to challenge IBM worldwide, acquired a controlling interest, as described in chapter 4. At the same time, GE purchased the computer division of Italy's Olivetti (whose story comes shortly).[5]

Before the coming of the System 360, the French government had provided little direct support of its computer industry. In fact, in 1963 it had chosen IBM over Bull for three-fourths of the public sector's computer installations. The De Gaulle government waited two years before creating its national champion by embarking on its ambitious Plan Calcul. Under this plan, a new company, the Compagnie International de l'Informatique (Cii), was to be the new leader. It was a merger of two small companies, SEA, producing for the scientific market, and CEA, for the commercial one, which together in 1966 accounted for 7 percent of the small French market. Cii was financed by government and private funds. In addition, the Plan Calcul established a new enterprise to produce peripherals; a government-funded leasing company; and a national research institution—all to be government subsidized from 1967 through 1971. Cii began producing medium-size computers based on licenses from a U.S. minicomputer company, Scientific Data Systems (see chapter 4). In 1967 the government formed a companion program for the development of semiconductors.

But little was accomplished under Plan Calcul before IBM again defined the industry's path with the introduction of the System 370. In 1970 General Electric responded by selling its computer unit to Honeywell, where it became Honeywell-Bull. In the same manner, in 1971 Siemens lost its initial U.S. ally, RCA, on whom it had relied for technology, when RCA sold its computer unit to Sperry Rand.

One response to the abrupt withdrawal of General Electric and RCA was the attempt to build a European champion. In 1973 the French champion, Cii, joined with Siemens and Philips, the Dutch consumer electronics giant, to develop an IBM-compatible system called Unidata. ICL in Britain declined to participate. Philips, with the least experience in computers, was to produce the smallest model and did so with some success. Siemens was to design two medium-size systems and moved along fairly well on its project. But Cii, given its very limited learning base, did little to meet its assignment to create three compatible medium and larger mainframes.[6]

By 1975 the frustrated French government decided that they were ready to pull out of Unidata and to regain control of Honeywell-Bull. Cii did pull out of Unidata, and after negotiations with Honeywell, Cii and Honeywell-Bull were merged into one firm, Cii-Honeywell-Bull (Cii-HB), owned 53 percent by French interests and 47 percent by Honeywell. Once again, merger failed. It brought neither the consolidation of existing technical or functional capabilities nor the creation of new ones. By 1980, even in the protected French market, Cii-HB accounted for only 31 percent of computer installations as compared to IBM's 52 percent.

In 1981 François Mitterrand's recently elected Socialist government nationalized Cii-HB, returning to the name Compagnie des Machines Bull, and strengthened an existing development alliance with the Japanese firm NEC. The French government acquired 42.5 percent of the new nationalized enterprise, while Honeywell also retained 42.5 percent, which it was to sell off at intervals. NEC got 15 percent. NEC, in much the same manner as Fujitsu at ICL, provided Bull with its mainframe (the DPS9) and the technology for its smaller computers.

Nevertheless, the effort of the Mitterrand government to establish a French computer industry was no more successful than that of Plan Calcul instituted under Charles De Gaulle's government. As one historical analyst noted, although "Mitterrand fed Bull $1 billion (U.S.) between 1983 and 1990," profits were minimal. Losses began in 1989. In the five years from 1990 through 1994 they totaled over five billion French francs.[7]

In December 1989 Bull made its initial response to the microcomputer revolution by acquiring the personal computer business of Zenith, the U.S. consumer electronics producer. In 1993 it purchased a 19.9 percent interest in Packard-Bell. As both these American firms were recording heavy losses, this was surely not the way to enter a highly competitive business in which they had no capabilities. In the mid-1990s Bull was unprofitably marketing over its label large and midrange systems produced by NEC.

The attempt of the French government to create a national industry through a national plan proved to be as futile as the British government's effort to do so by combining their leading makers of electronic data-processing equipment into a single enterprise. The futility of these efforts underlines the basic historical findings of this book. Competitive organizational capabilities can rarely be achieved except through the creation of an integrated core enterprise that becomes a learning base through which new technologies are commercialized for world markets and in so doing create high barriers to entry that continue to protect that base.

OLIVETTI: EUROPE'S ONE MAJOR PERSONAL COMPUTER MAKER

The evolution of the Italian computer industry provides a different perspective from that of the British and French, for it was left to create technical and functional capabilities on its own. Italy's best opportunity for a national champion disappeared in 1964 when General Electric acquired Olivetti's computer unit. Italy's government, like that of De Gaulle in France, had paid little attention to the country's computer industry before the announcement of IBM's System 360. But, unlike the French, the Italian government made little attempt to strengthen its potential champion, Olivetti, or to support the industry in any other way even after 1964. However, in 1978 the company's ownership and management changed hands. The new management became a pioneer in producing personal computers. Until the onslaught of the Microsoft/Intel combination took hold, Olivetti was a leading competitor worldwide in personal computers.

The company, whose formal name was Ing C. Olivetti & C. S.p.A., had been created in 1911 as a producer of typewriters. It broadened its product line in the 1930s to include adding machines, teleprinters, and other office machinery. Although it did not attempt to produce punched-card tabulators, its managers were well aware of the data-processing market. By the 1950s Olivetti was Europe's largest producer of office machines.[8]

In 1959 Olivetti formed a joint venture with France's Bull to market Bull's computers. In the same year it announced its own Elea System, a product that became Italy's first successful line of computers. After GE acquired Olivetti's computer business in 1964, Olivetti stayed in the production of electromechanical office equipment, but it did produce one competitive electronic product, a calculator.

In 1978 two entrepreneurs, the De Beneditti brothers, took over the nearly bankrupt Olivetti family firm, transformed its electromechanical products and processes into electronic ones, and put it back into the computer industry. To do so, the brothers turned to another Japanese firm, Hitachi, to provide Olivetti with its M-series IBM plug-compatible mainframes on an OEM basis—that is, to be sold as an Olivetti product.

The timing of the De Beneditti takeover was fortunate. Microcomputers had just begun to be sold in the United States, so the new entrepreneurial owners quickly developed their own personal computer and created a production and marketing organization while the field was still wide open. Olivetti became the first European company to produce personal computers in volume. By 1983 it was making personal computers on an OEM basis for AT&T and Xerox in the U.S. market and sold in the same way by Toshiba in Japan. In return, AT&T acquired 20 percent of Olivetti's stock and agreed to complete Olivetti's line by providing it with AT&T's minicomputer, also on a comparable OEM basis. Toshiba took a 20 percent holding in Olivetti's Japanese subsidiary. By 1985 Olivetti, with major U.S. and Japanese outlets, was the third largest revenue producer of PCs worldwide behind IBM and Apple.

But with the onslaught of IBM's PC and its clones, Olivetti's revenues declined, as did other makers with their own proprietary operating systems.

Nevertheless, in 1992 Olivetti was still #8 in worldwide market share in PCs (this may have included machines sold through AT&T and Toshiba), #13 in midrange computers (from AT&T's minicomputers), and #13 in software.

But Olivetti had neither the funding nor the capabilities to meet the competition from U.S. producers in midrange computers and PCs. From 1989 through 1994 Olivetti continued to record heavy losses, and losses surpassed $1 billion in 1995. In 1996, after Carlo De Beneditti was forced to resign, the Olivetti computer unit was sold to a foreign investment consortium headed by an American, ending Italy's four-decade-old effort in computer making.[9]

SIEMENS AND NIXDORF BECOME EUROPE'S ONLY INTEGRATED COMPUTER LEARNING BASE

The evolution of the German computer industry differed from that of Britain, France, and Italy precisely because it was a process of long-term learning. That learning began when Siemens & Halske AG (Siemens) became Europe's first-mover in the 1890s in electrical and telecommunications equipment. Unlike its somewhat smaller competitor, Allgemeine Elektricitäts-Gesellschaft, it recovered quickly after World War II by moving out of Berlin to Munich. In the postwar years, now incorporated as Siemens AG, it moved into data processing through internal investment and the thoughtfully planned and executed acquisition of three small companies. Other investments, too, were thoughtfully planned and executed. The introduction of IBM's System 360 led to support by the German government. Such support came not from direct funding, but from the provision of technical knowledge and equipment.

Siemens differed from other major European computer makers in two ways. From the start, as a first-mover in electrical and telecommunications equipment, it produced a wide range of products in addition to computers. Its technical capabilities in electronics far surpassed those of any other European company except, of course, Philips. It had long experience in building the functional capabilities required to make a new product competitive in international markets.

Second, during the 1920s the leading American office machinery makers—IBM, Remington Rand, National Cash Register, and Burroughs Adding Machine Company—had all set up manufacturing plants, marketing organizations, and headquarters in Germany. So there was less opportunity for the development of an indigenous office machinery industry than in France and Italy. In the 1950s the potential German competitors were Zuse and AEG-Telefunken. Zuse was a small enterprise that had produced electromechanical calculators during the 1930s and had experimented during World War II in applying electronic tubes to electrically powered calculators. AEG-Telefunken was the consumer electronics company that Siemens and AEG had formed as a joint venture before World War I. AEG had acquired full control of it in the early 1940s.

During the 1950s Siemens, Zuse, AEG-Telefunken, and a German affiliate of International Telephone & Telegraph (ITT) put commercial computers on the market. (ITT was spun off by Western Electric in 1927 to own and operate Western Electric's foreign business.) Even with these four entries into the new industry, by 1959 IBM dominated the German market with 53.5 percent of new computer installations, while Siemens held 13.1 percent, Zuse 5.5 percent, and Sperry Rand 3.3 percent. By the mid-1960s, Kenneth Flamm reports, Siemens's declining share "hovered about 5 percent."[10]

The response to the coming of the IBM System 360 in 1964 was somewhat less dramatic in Germany than that in Britain and France but was nevertheless impressive. Siemens purchased Zuse. Then, with the announcement of RCA's Spectra 70 (IBM plug-compatible), Siemens arranged to be supplied with RCA's computer technology. By 1967 Siemens was selling the Spectra 70 line as the Siemens 4004.

In that same year the West German government began its first Data Processing Program, providing financial support for the development of computer hardware. With the coming of IBM's System 370, the program was enlarged to include support for software operating systems and applications, components, and peripherals. Unlike the British and French programs, both of the German projects allocated sizable funds for research in German universities. The government also pushed for a Siemens merger with AEG-Telefunken's computer business in 1970—a move that Siemens warded off until 1973.

When RCA pulled out of computers in 1971, Siemens joined with the French Cii and the Dutch Philips to form Unidata, as told earlier. That was a last desperate and futile attempt to build a European mainframe base. When the French withdrew in 1975, Siemens turned to Fujitsu to provide it with IBM-compatible mainframes on an OEM basis and to supply the components and other hardware for the lines that Siemens had developed before the collapse of the Unidata enterprise. The timing was fortuitous, for in 1976 the first of Fujitsu's M-series came onstream. This was the M-190, the exact replica of IBM's System 370. (Fujitsu's achievement is described in the following section on Japan.)

The learning that Siemens had acquired from government-sponsored programs, from participation in the Unidata project, and from its new ties with Fujitsu permitted it to carry out what Franco Malerba, the historian of the semiconductor industry worldwide, describes as a "follower-imitator strategy" for its own corporate learning base in mainframes and semiconductors. In the late 1970s Siemens entered into the development and then the production of microprocessors. It did this by acquiring a 17 percent holding (later raised to 20 percent) of the American firm AMD, by obtaining a license for Intel's 8080 chip, and then by forming a joint venture with AMD, Intel, and Philips for that chip's production and distribution. As Malerba notes, in the 1980s Siemens focused on specialized and niche products primarily for its own use.[11]

In the meantime, Germany's Nixdorf Computer AG had become the only European learning base in minicomputers. Heinz Nixdorf had established a calculator company using electronic tubes in Paderborn, West Germany, in 1952. In introducing his general-purpose minicomputer, modeled on the PDP series of Digital Equipment, he was able to build production, marketing, and R&D organizations before DEC and its followers in the United States had begun to move into European markets. By 1972 the Nixdorf enterprise was exporting 30 percent of Germany's total computer output, largely in Europe. But at no time did the company have more than 1 percent of the U.S. market. Even before Nixdorf was able to adopt the new RISC/UNIX client-server technology, developed by Sun and then the other U.S. workstation makers, it suffered severe losses. In 1988 its profits dropped 90 percent, followed by heavy losses in the next year. The owners, the Nixdorf family and Deutsche Bank, turned to Siemens, which then acquired the company for U.S. $350 million in 1990. Siemens consolidated the two computer enterprises into a single company, Siemens-Nixdorf Information Systems AG (SNI), whose equity was held by Siemens AG in its role as the parent firm.[12]

During the 1980s Siemens survived both the challenges of Japanese competitors and those of the microcomputer revolution by continuing its "follower-imitator" strategy of developing its technological capabilities through working with its allies in the United States and with Fujitsu in Japan. However, the consolidation of the German computer industry within Siemens-Nixdorf (which included AEG-Telefunken, acquired earlier) failed to enhance its competitive capabilities.

During the mid-1990s the Japanese continued to take market share in large systems and the Americans continued to dominate in personal computers. Indeed, in the year following the merger, Siemens-Nixdorf reported losses of $583 million. *Datamation's* listings for 1992 made it #8 in terms of overall IT revenues, with $8.3 billion. It was then still listed among the top fifteen in all its product sectors except for personal computers. It was #8 worldwide in large-scale computers, #7 in midrange computers, #10 in workstations, #6 in software, and #13 in peripherals. By 1996, although it was #11 worldwide, with information technology revenues of $9.2 billion, its net income had dropped to only $2 *million*. It was still #7 in large systems and #12 in software, primarily for those large systems. By then, only 13 percent of the sales of the larger enterprise, Siemens AG, came from Siemens-Nixdorf.[13]

At this point Siemens-Nixdorf was considering exiting from computers. The company still relied on the Japanese firms for technical and product development knowledge. They were unable to develop the new RISC/ UNIX client-server technology in the ways that the Japanese were doing. Nor were they any more successful than Olivetti and the U.S. producers of proprietary systems in meeting the onslaught of IBM's PC clones, with their Intel chips and Microsoft operating systems. Moreover, the volume of Siemens-Nixdorf's activities had neither the scale nor the scope that gave its U.S. and Japanese rivals competitive advantage. Its smaller volume of activity also meant that it did not attract a growing nexus of supporting niche enterprises as developed in the Tokyo/Osaka area in Japan and Silicon Valley in the United States.

In April 1998 the managers of Siemens announced that they were accepting an offer from Acer, a Taiwanese producer of PCs, to acquire SNI's PC operations. This contract, according to *The Wall Street Journal Europe*, "removes Europe's last big player from the PC market." In the following autumn, Acer, because of the financial crisis in Asia, canceled the contract. SNI now had little choice except to turn to Fujitsu. Fujitsu's managers obliged. The result was a fifty-fifty joint venture, Fujitsu-Siemens Computers, with headquarters in Amsterdam. It began operations in October 1999, producing laptop and desktop PCs, servers, and mainframes. After that date, Europe's major computer enterprise was a part of the European operations of Japan's leading computer enterprise, Fujitsu Limited.[14]

Japan's Successful Challengers

In Japan, as in Germany, the computer industry arose from capabilities developed in long-established firms making electrical and telecommunications equipment. In this process the government provided funds as well as guidance for the creation of the new industry's technical capabilities. But it left to the individual firms the investment in and operation of the facilities and personnel used in product development, production, and distribution. The firms then competed vigorously for market share. The resulting learned capabilities thus came to differ somewhat from one another and so enhanced the competitive strength of the national industry.

From the start, all of the Japanese computer makers produced semiconductors, peripherals, software, and other related products, both for their own internal use and for external sale. They remained leaders in the electrical and telecommunications industries in which they had been Japan's first-movers. After they successfully entered the computer industry in the 1960s and 1970s, these multi-industry, multisectored enterprises moved into other sectors of the electronics industry—industrial electronics, communications, and components. By 1980 they had become some of the largest industrial companies in Japan and indeed in the world. In 1987, of Japan's largest industrials, the leading makers of computers were the second five. Hitachi was #6 in terms of overall revenues, Toshiba #7, NEC #8, Mitsubishi Electric #9, and Fujitsu Limited #10. (The first five were Toyota, Nippon Steel, Mitsubishi Heavy Industry, Nissan, and Matsushita Electric.)[15]

THE INDUSTRY BEGINS

From its very start in the 1950s, the evolution of the Japanese computer industry was defined by the actions of IBM. Nevertheless, IBM was not the first data-processing enterprise to serve the Japanese office machinery market. In the 1920s that market was dominated by IBM's American rival, Remington Rand, whose Powers Tabulating Machine was sold in Japan through the Mitsui Trading Company. IBM's punched-card tabulators made their Japanese appearance in the same decade, but at first with little success, in good part because its Japanese customers found it hard to adapt to IBM's unique renting policy. Nevertheless, because of the quality of its products, revenues of IBM Japan grew rapidly in the 1930s, quickly surpassing those of Powers. In 1937, as Japan's aggressive moves in China created international tensions, IBM took a high-risk step by establishing a manufacturing subsidiary in Yokohama. It staffed this enterprise with Japanese employees, including its managers. When Toshiba took over IBM Japan after the attack on Pearl Harbor, its Japanese staff continued to expand its learning base throughout the war.[16]

After the war ended, the return of IBM's control and the restoration of its property required negotiations with both the Allied Occupation Forces and the Japanese government. By 1950 it had received the necessary credentials to begin full-scale production of punched-card machines and related products. In 1956 IBM began a long-drawn-out negotiation with the Ministry of International Trade and Industry to build and sell its new electronic data-processing equipment in Japan. MITI insisted on a joint venture with one of Japan's five leading electrical engineering companies. IBM, in turn, insisted on working through a wholly owned subsidiary. Finally, in December 1960, MITI agreed to IBM's demands in exchange for IBM's patents.

Earlier in 1957 and 1958 the Japanese government placed a tariff ranging from 15 percent to 25 percent on imported computers. While IBM Japan remained within the new tariff barrier, it did not benefit from other government subsidies and benefits provided to Japanese-owned companies. In 1961, after MITI's agreement with IBM, MITI and the industry formed the Japan Electronic Computer Company (JECC) to finance and distribute the industry's production. JECC was jointly owned by seven companies, the aforementioned five—Fujitsu, Toshiba, Hitachi, NEC, and Mitsubishi Electric—plus Oki Electric, a telecommunications supplier like NEC, and Matsushita, Japan's leading consumer electronics producer. JECC provided funding (drawn largely from the Japan Development Bank) at below market rates to support the development of computer products and the processes of their production. JECC then purchased the finished computers built by the partners and leased them to domestic users.[17]

The availability of the IBM patents, however, did not mean the transfer of technology essential for creating a new corporate learning base. The required technical and functional knowledge had to come from alliances with or manufacturing licenses and technical assistance from U.S. companies—

that is, from IBM competitors. Five of the seven partners in JECC quickly made alliances with U.S. companies. Hitachi signed up with RCA in 1961; NEC with Honeywell in 1962; Mitsubishi Electric with TRW Inc. in 1962; and the much smaller Oki with Sperry Rand in 1963. Toshiba reinforced its long-standing ties with General Electric in 1964. Of the other two, Matsushita pulled out of computer development in 1964 (that story is told in chapter 3). On the other hand, Fujitsu, a highly focused telecommunications producer and, in time, the most successful of Japan's computer companies, decided to develop these essential technical and functional capabilities without a U.S. ally.[18]

In September 1962 MITI established the initial cooperative computer development effort, the FONTAC project, to build computers to compete with IBM's 1400 series. It assigned Fujitsu to develop the main processor and the nation's two other telecommunications producers, NEC and Oki Electric, to develop the peripherals. FONTAC failed to produce a computer. Nevertheless, it did lay the foundations for Fujitsu's later capabilities in development and production.[19]

These efforts, plus a high tariff, helped to raise the Japanese companies' share of Japan's domestic computer market from 18 percent in 1961 to 52 percent in 1966. Nevertheless, because the transfer of technology came from IBM's competitors, with weaker competitive capabilities than IBM, and because the learning process was just getting under way, Japanese computer firms made low-quality products and minimal profits.[20]

THE JAPANESE RESPONSE TO
IBM SYSTEMS 360 AND 370

The 1964 announcement of the IBM System 360 led in Japan, as it did in Europe, to a thorough rethinking of efforts to create a competitive industry. The government and the companies turned to "transforming the FONTAC experiment into a blue-print for technological development." First came a cooperative project to develop an integrated circuit, which had only just begun to be developed in Japan. (The Japanese industry did not acquire the Kilby patent from Texas Instruments until April 1968; see chapter 3.)

Then in 1966 MITI proposed the creation of another, more broad-based national computer R&D project, the Ôgata (or "large-scale project"). It was based on a detailed major report by MITI that identified, in Kenneth Flamm's words, "the computer industry, for the first time, as the single most important element in the future of economic growth of Japan." With funds provided by MITI, the companies would bring into being "a super high performance computer." MITI assigned Fujitsu, Hitachi, and NEC to develop mainframes and integrated circuits compatible with IBM's System 360, Model 67. Toshiba, Mitsubishi, and Oki were to concentrate on developing the necessary peripherals. In addition, the first three and the Industrial Bank of Japan were to form a joint venture, Nippon Software, to create the essential software — operating systems and applications.[21]

On the basis of Fujitsu's FONTAC experience and the contributions of the technical alliances with U.S. companies, the Ôgata project did create some key advances in hardware, but it completely failed in the development of software, despite a three-billion-yen subsidy made to Nippon Software. One reason was that Fujitsu and Hitachi soon preferred to license the software that IBM unbundled in 1969. Another was the unexpectedly huge cost of developing compatible software, a lesson that IBM had learned in creating the System 360. After much effort, Japan's national computer industry still had a long way to go. From 1970 to 1974 the Japanese producers' share of the domestic market fell from 59.8 percent to 48.4 percent.[22]

In 1970 the announcement of IBM's System 370 once again stunned MITI and the Japanese computer makers. Although IBM's new generation of computers incorporated relatively little new basic technology, the announcement showed the Japanese how far behind IBM they still were, just as it showed this to the European producers and to RCA and GE in the United States. The initial response of MITI was to follow the European route and call for merger. But the companies involved flatly refused. The agency then bargained for even closer cooperation than in the Ôgata program by promising to fund a "New Series Project" that would pair the industry leaders in the development work required to build the equivalent of an IBM System 370.[23]

In the New Series Project, MITI assigned Fujitsu and Hitachi to create an M-series of large computers. NEC and Toshiba would produce a series of medium-size and small-scale compatibles based on the technology that Toshiba had acquired from its ally GE (before GE sold its computer operations to Honeywell). Mitsubishi Electric and Oki Electric Industry were to develop small computers for specialized uses such as factory control based on technology acquired from Sperry Rand.

In October 1971 Fujitsu and Hitachi were the first to announce formally their cooperative arrangements. At that moment, Fujitsu was making the deal with Gene Amdahl, a leading designer of both IBM's System 360 and 370. That deal, more than any other single factor, assured the success of the New Series Project and the long-term viability of the Japanese computer industry. The history of Amdahl's departure from IBM to build his own high-end System 370 computer, his difficulty in raising funds, and his turn to Fujitsu has been told in chapter 4. Fujitsu's president, in flying back to Tokyo after meeting with Amdahl, was ecstatic about the prospect. "If this goes well," he told an assistant, "it will be incredible!" And indeed it was.

Nevertheless MITI hesitated. Its chiefs were unhappy that Japan's strongest firm was tying itself to the technology of the world's most powerful computer maker, IBM. Hitachi was also uncertain about entering into the proposal with Amdahl (not part of their cooperative agenda), primarily because of the cost, but also because of its hope that its tie with RCA would provide the necessary technology. (Negotiations with RCA took place just before RCA announced its decision to sell its computer activities to Sperry Rand.) Fujitsu went ahead, investing $56 million in the Amdahl firm. By 1976 it held 41 percent of its stock. The funds were raised from MITI, JECC, and, most of all, Nippon Telegraph & Telephone (NTT). In 1979, Gene Amdahl relinquished control when Fujitsu increased its stake to 47 percent.

Amdahl's first product, the 470 V/6, introduced in 1975, was "a one-to-one replacement" of the largest System 370 series, Model 168. Fujitsu's M-190, the first of its M-series, introduced in 1976, was its twin. Fujitsu had marketed six other models by the end of 1978. Hitachi, in developing four models of its M-series between 1975 and 1978, soon had the same architecture and hardware. But because it did not have the Amdahl connection, it did not have the necessary software. Nevertheless, instead of licensing the software from IBM, seven of its employees were caught attempting to steal the software from IBM, in what became the well-publicized "IBM sting case." Hitachi was forced to pay a substantial fine and the unpaid license fees.

In the same years, Toshiba built its systems based on the technology GE had sold to Honeywell, relying especially on Honeywell's software. But Toshiba's managers decided not to compete against Fujitsu and Hitachi's growing M-series. So they turned over the production of their medium-size mainframes to NEC but continued to produce smaller computers. Meanwhile NEC continued to produce a fairly broad line of IBM-comparable hardware with a goal of creating its own software that it was soon sending on an OEM basis to Machines Bull. MITI's third pair, Mitsubishi Electric and Oki, did make a modest number of small specialized computers but contributed relatively little to the development of Japan's computer industry.

The New Series Project, in Marie Anchordoguy's words, "made the difference between the industry's success and imminent failure." By the early 1980s the Japanese companies were competing successfully with IBM Japan at home and were beginning to ship out competitive IBM plug-compatibles to Europe's Siemens, Machines Bull, and Olivetti.[24]

The New Series Project, which was partially funded by NTT, marks the beginning of Japan's epic achievements in computers. It made possible Japan's takeover of the European market for large computer systems during the 1980s. MITI's follow-up collaborative project, the VLSI circuit project from 1976 to 1979, led to the destruction of the U.S. memory chip industry in the same few years.[25] Only the unplanned and largely unexpected mass production and mass marketing of the personal computer saved the U.S. computer industry, but not that of Europe. What, then, accounts for the organizational capabilities embodied in the integrated learning bases of Japan's five major computer companies that permitted them to take over the European and challenge the American computer industries in a little more than a decade? That question can be answered only by reviewing the evolution of the individual companies and the nature of the competition within the Japanese computer industry.

The Evolution of Japan's Major Computer Companies

The evolution of the Japanese computer makers, before they had become computer makers by participating in MITI's cooperative projects, was profoundly different from that of their counterparts in the West. During the last two decades of the nineteenth century, the Western first-movers had commercialized their new electrical and telecommunications technologies into an extensive technological and industrial infrastructure that had been developing since the late eighteenth century. Their counterparts in Japan had no such broad base on which to build their electrical and telecommunications industry. They had to start from scratch.

In the first decades of the twentieth century, Japan was just emerging from two hundred years of self-imposed isolation from the West. During the two decades after the restoration of the Meiji emperor in 1868 came the initial building of Japan's basic modern commercial, political, and social order. Then in the first years of the twentieth century came the building of its basic modern commercial and industrial institutions. The basic scientific and engineering technical knowledge that was needed to build this industrial infrastructure had to come from the West. So also did the product-specific functional knowledge required to build the learning bases essential to meet Japan's industrial needs and, in time, to compete in international markets. Understandably, the transmitters of such knowledge were the Western first-movers. They did so primarily by forming joint ventures with local Japanese entrepreneurs or existing domestic commercial enterprises.

The companies that evolved from these joint ventures—Fujitsu, NEC, Toshiba, and Mitsubishi Electric—created Japan's initial electrical and telecommunications equipment industries during the first two decades of the twentieth century. Also in that group of creative companies was Hitachi, which did not enter a joint venture with a Western company but built its learning base on its own. Those five companies played the same role again after 1945 in rebuilding Japan's production facilities and its war-destroyed infrastructures. In those years they became deeply involved in the massive expansion of hydroelectric power and the complete rebuilding of Japan's railroads, communications networks, and electrical utility systems, using the most up-to-date electrical and electronic devices. They also met the large and ever-growing demand for electrical equipment to run factories and communication systems. The housing boom that began in the early 1950s provided a comparable market for consumer electrical appliances and consumer electronics—a market into which these same firms entered. These enterprises became and remained what I term Japan's Big Five, which played the central role in computers comparable to that of Japan's Big Four in consumer electronics.

So I now review the evolution of these five companies from their beginnings at the start of the twentieth century until the 1990s and the opening of the Electronic Century, the twenty-first century. All five participants in the MITI-guided cooperative projects also participated in the Japanese industry's first entrance into worldwide computer markets. Then, except for Toshiba, they gave way to the U.S. industry, which established dominance in personal computers through the PC clones with their Intel chips and Microsoft operating systems. Toshiba ignored the Japanese market and instead quickly turned to producing clones for world markets. Then all participated in the second Japanese challenge to the U.S. industry that came with the increasing demand for high-powered computing stimulated by the expansion of corporate networks and the coming of the Internet.

FUJITSU LIMITED: JAPAN'S FOCUSED FIRST-MOVER

The learning base of the most focused of these computer companies, Fujitsu, had its beginnings in 1876 when a Siemens representative set up an office to be the sole supplier of electrical equipment to the Furukawa *zaibatsu* (the Japanese term for the family-owned, diversified enterprises that played a basic role in the industrializing of Japan). After World War I and the ensuing severe postwar depression, Siemens and Furukawa *zaibatsu* formed a joint venture, Fuji Electric, with Siemens holding 30 percent of the stock and Furukawa the rest. That arrangement took place in August 1923, and in 1925 Fuji Electric became the sole importer of Siemens products. With its marketing organization in place, it began to build its functional capabilities and enhanced its technical ones by producing, as well as marketing, Siemens light and heavy electrical equipment.[26]

During the 1930s Japan's military occupation in Manchuria and then China rapidly expanded the volume of Fuji Electric's business. In 1935, therefore, in part to reduce its administrative load at the top, Fuji Electric spun off its small telecommunications department as a subsidiary named Fuji Communications Corporation (later taking the name Fujitsu Limited). Fuji Communications then made an agreement with Tokyo Electric, a protégé of the American colossus GE, by which Fuji Communications would focus on its expanding telephone business and Tokyo Electric on broader communications technology. The agreement was reinforced by transferring 20 percent of Fuji Communications stock for a comparable share of Tokyo Electric's stock.

In the late 1930s Fuji Communications was pulled away from its primary market (in telephones) to meet the needs of military communication. Military demands during World War II reinforced the firm's technical and production capabilities even as the nation's communications system was being knocked out by Allied bombing.

After the war, Fuji Communications, which had become Fujitsu Limited, became a specialized supplier to Nippon Telegraph & Telephone (the government-owned provider of telecommunications services formed in 1952). In helping to rebuild Japan's telephone system, it further expanded and enhanced its technical and functional capabilities. During this time, Nippon

Electric Company (NEC) remained NTT's primary supplier. But as a specialized supplier, Fujitsu further expanded and enhanced its technical and functional capabilities as it focused on telecommunications electronics. NTT provided most of the funds for Fujitsu's electronics research and its development of new electronic switches and other equipment. In these same years it unsuccessfully attempted to develop a comupter system comparable to the UNIVAC. So when meeting the IBM challenge in the early 1960s, Fujitsu Limited, as Japan's most advanced electronics company, led the way in the cooperative computer projects mentioned earlier, first in the FONTAC project and then in the Ôgata one. It was the only one of MITI's participants that did not turn to IBM's U.S. competitors for technical support. During the 1960s it became the largest supplier of JECC, the new computer industry's joint leasing agency.[27]

As it moved into computers, Fujitsu also pioneered in commercializing electronic numerical controls (NCs) and other automatic control devices. By 1965 that new business had become profitable. Then in 1972 Fujitsu spun off its NC division, much as Fuji Electric had spun off Fuji Communications thirty-seven years before. The spin-off, Fujitsu Fanuc Corporation, a separate enterprise in which Fujitsu held the controlling share, soon became a world leader in NC technology and robotics. It continued to build and enhance its organizational capabilities. At the same time, its competitive position in the U.S. market was strengthened as several of its American rivals had been acquired by conglomerates. In those conglomerates the preference of the acquirers for short-term profits caused the long-established organizational capabilities of the American NC firms to disintegrate, much as occurred in radio and television during the same period.

Meanwhile the parent, Fujitsu Limited, flourished in the computer business. Its successful acquisition of IBM's System 370 technology from Gene Amdahl, plus the completion of the Fujitsu-controlled Amdahl factory in Japan in 1975 and the introduction of its own M series between 1976 and 1978 assured Fujitsu's position as Japan's leading computer maker. During the late 1970s and early 1980s it developed a full line of midlevel computers, including the equivalent of a minicomputer, as well as supercomputers; it made its agreement to supply Britain's ICL with large systems; and it became a key player in Japan's DRAM challenge, selling $2.5 billion worth of memory chips a year. Fujitsu also began to produce point-of-sale devices and ATM products. At the same time it continued to augment its capabilities in telecommunications, becoming a leader in information network systems, including the development of Integrated Services Digital Networks (ISDN), private exchanges, and digital switching systems.

But computers remained Fujitsu's primary product. By 1990 Fujitsu held 43 percent of the United States's Amdahl Corporation and 80 percent of Britain's ICL. In 1992 the company, as noted earlier, expanded ICL's European operations by acquiring Nokia Data Holdings. In 1991, 73 percent of Fujitsu's revenues still came from computer systems, 13 percent from communication systems, 10 percent from electronic devices, and 4 percent from other products.

Because Fujitsu was so concentrated on computers and because it had become the world's largest computer maker behind IBM, it suffered more than its Japanese cohorts from the microcomputer revolution. Its initial entrance into personal computers was slow and unprofitable, as will be described shortly. Fujitsu's net income dropped dramatically in 1992, then turned to serious losses of $284 million in 1993 and $366 million in 1994 (similarly, IBM's losses, far larger, were in 1991–1993).

Then, as the rapidly growing private corporate networks increased the demand for high-powered computers, Fujitsu began to concentrate on restructuring its strength in large systems (mainframes and supercomputers) and, as important, on expanding the output and quality of its workstations—a market it entered after acquiring Sun Microsystems's SPARC technology in 1988. That year it formed a joint venture with Advanced Micro Devices to build a $700 million plant in Japan to produce new "flash" semiconductors. In 1994 it tightened its ties with Sun Microsystems by investing $40 million in a joint development project to produce more powerful RISC chips. The next year it budgeted $1.7 billion for new logic chips and earmarked half of its $60 million research budget to Internet and multimedia technologies. By 1995, amid the surge in demand for computing power created by the exploding Internet, its net income had returned to its pre-1992 level. With the return of its income flow, Fujitsu moved aggressively back into personal computers, as I review in discussing Japan's PC story later in this chapter.

THE NEC CORPORATION: FROM TELECOMMUNICATIONS TO COMPUTERS

Fujitsu's history underlines the long-term advantages of continued concentration by first-movers on their core products. NEC provides another perspective, that of the ability to evolve successfully in closely related paths of learning. From its beginning, NEC was the dominant producer of telecommunications equipment in Japan, the conduit by which most American telephone technology reached Asia. In addition, it has been the only telecommunications company worldwide that became and remained a leading computer maker. NEC did so by maintaining and expanding the technical and functional capabilities learned as a participant in the MITI programs. In fact, by 1996 its sales from computers were nearly twice those from telecommunications.

In 1899 Western Electric, AT&T's subsidiary that developed and produced its equipment, formed the Nippon Electric Company, with Western Electric holding 55.6 percent ownership and the rest held by its importing agent, Iwadare Kunhiko, and an associate. They, in turn, disposed of much of the remaining 46.4 percent to Japanese investors, and Kunhiko became NEC's president.[28]

NEC's two factories, one acquired and the second one completed in 1902, produced telephones, switching and transmitting equipment, and telegraph equipment. Their output grew rapidly as Japan's initial modern economy took off and then expanded further after Japan annexed Korea in 1910. In the early 1920s, on the basis of Western Electric's technology, NEC also began producing radio tubes, receiving sets, and broadcasting equipment.

In 1925, when AT&T spun off Western Electric's non-U.S. operating activities to the newly formed International Telephone & Telegraph, NEC's senior management, increasingly made up of Japanese personnel, concentrated on building its own development capabilities and enhancing those in its other functional activities. At the same time, the Japanese government began putting pressure on NEC to reduce its American control. In 1929, just before Japan began its move into Manchuria, ITT was essentially forced to sell 15 percent of its shares to the Sumitomo *zaibatsu*'s cable manufacturing company. By 1941 ITT's holdings had fallen to 11.9 percent. These, in turn, were expropriated after Pearl Harbor and turned over to Sumitomo, which took full control. During the war Sumitomo expanded NEC's electronic capabilities by producing radar, sonar, and radio sets and components for the military. With the postwar dissolution of Sumitomo's *zaibatsu*, NEC again became an independent enterprise.

In 1951 ITT's interests were restored when it received a 32.8 percent holding in NEC, and ITT and NEC signed a new cooperative technical agreement. In the years that followed, NEC enhanced its internal organizational capabilities as it met the new postwar challenges in rebuilding Japan's communications infrastructure. Meanwhile Harold Geneen, a pioneer and leading advocate of the conglomerate movement, became ITT's CEO in 1959. Geneen's conglomerating activities quickly dissipated ITT's electronics capabilities. ITT remained NEC's largest shareholder until 1977 but paid little or no attention to NEC and sold off its shares in 1978 and 1979.[29]

During the 1950s NEC, as the major supplier of central office and switching equipment to the government-sponsored NTT, built its capabilities in the new telecommunications technologies. At the same time it entered consumer electronics and appliances with the formation in 1953 of a new subsidiary, called the New Nippon Electric. (It changed its formal name from NEC to the NEC Corporation.) In 1964 it formed a joint venture with Hughes Aircraft that became a first-mover in satellite communications systems. By the late 1960s NEC had become the world's largest exporter of radio and microwave communications equipment and a world leader in digital switching and mobile communications systems.

At the same time NEC, recruited by MITI, became a computer maker. Unlike Toshiba (its partner in MITI's New Series Project), NEC continued to play a major role in the production of medium-size and smaller IBM-like computers. In commercializing these products, its CEO, Koji Kobayashi, decided to develop NEC's own software for its IBM-compatible hardware, unlike Fujitsu. It became and remained the supplier of computer technology to France's Machines Bull, much as Fujitsu did for Britain's ICL. In the late 1970s and early 1980s its participation in the VLSI project made it a major player in Japan's initial challenge in DRAMs, and it subsequently became a world leader in semiconductors.

Indeed, by 1991 only 17 percent of its sales came from communications systems and equipment. Computers, accounting for 51 percent, had become its major business. In addition, 17 percent of its sales came from memory chips and other components and only 5 percent from consumer electronics. By then computing had become its major path of learning and telecommunications its secondary one.[30]

NEC appears to have been less affected by the PC revolution than other Japanese computer makers, for it became Japan's first-mover in the domestic personal computer market (as will be reviewed shortly). It dominated the Japanese market through the 1980s until the American companies—IBM,

Apple, Compaq—using Japanese-language operating systems, entered in the early 1990s. NEC's net income dropped in 1992, and in 1993 NEC recorded a $407 million loss. But then, thanks to the investment in client/server technology acquired from MIPS Technologies, its fortunes improved. As the increased demand for computing power spurred sales of its mainframes and particularly its servers, NEC showed positive net income in 1994 and by 1995 it recorded its largest net income for the ten years 1987–1996. Its rising net income may have led to the acquisition of the fifth largest revenue producing desktop company, Packward Bell, as briefly described in Chapter 7.

TOSHIBA CORPORATION: A BALANCED, MULTIPATHED ENTERPRISE

Whereas NEC's technical and functional capabilities evolved from AT&T's Western Electric, those of Toshiba were derived from General Electric. GE's mentorship came not only in electrical lighting and power, but also in electric consumer appliances, where GE had been a first-mover in the 1920s. After the success of MITI's New Series Project, Toshiba, in the manner of Matsushita, turned more to exploiting its functional capabilities in closely related markets, rather than further developing its technical ones, as NEC and Fujitsu did.

The Toshiba history differs, however, from that of NEC, in that GE maintained much closer ties for a much longer period than did Western Electric and its successor, ITT, with NEC. Until well after World War II, GE transferred corporate, administrative, and financial knowledge as well as functional and technical know-how to its Japanese protégé.[31]

Toshiba's origins are a bit complicated organizationally. Toshiba became the official name, after World War II, for the Tokyo Shibaura Electric Company. Tokyo Shibaura was a merger in 1939 of Shibaura Engineering and Tokyo Electric. Both of these predecessors were joint ventures between General Electric and a Japanese firm named Shibaura Electric in the first decade of the new century. Their origins can be briefly summarized as follows.

Shibaura Electric, established in 1885, first built electrical telegraphic equipment, then turned to making torpedoes and steam engines. In 1893 it was taken over by the Mitsui Bank (a creditor) and became a member of the powerful Mitsui *zaibatsu*. With this support it became in the 1890s Japan's leading producer of transformers, electric motors, and other heavy electrical equipment. As the Mitsui *zaibatsu* expanded its activities, its managers decided to turn the most successful of its varied enterprises into independent companies.

Shibaura Electric received its independence in 1904 and immediately formed its first joint venture with General Electric to produce GE's licensed light bulb technology. This joint venture was Tokyo Electric. About half its initial capital came from the Mitsui family and about a quarter from General Electric. Then in 1910 Shibaura formed a second joint venture with GE, called Shibaura Engineering, to produce heavy electrical equipment.

In the next year GE substantially increased its holdings in both ventures, Tokyo Electric and Shibaura Engineering. These two firms soon created integrated learning bases by manufacturing as well as marketing the products of their American mentor, just as Fujitsu Electric did with Siemens and NEC did with Western Electric. With the reduction of imports during World War I, Shibaura Engineering began to build its own organizational capabilities in engineering design and product development, and especially in the production and marketing of complex multiproduct electrical systems. Tokyo Electric did the same in lamps and other electric lighting products. During the 1920s and 1930s, under GE's guidance and with GE's technology, Shibaura Engineering remained Japan's leading electrical equipment manufacturer; while Tokyo Electric began producing improved tungsten fluorescent lamps, vacuum tubes, and radios, as well as electric washing machines, refrigerators, and other consumer appliances.

In the 1930s Japan's moves to overseas conquest and military self-sufficiency led to the expansion of the output, facilities, and employees of both of the companies, thus strengthening their internal capabilities, particularly in product and process development. At the same time, Japan's government and industry leaders pressed the two companies to weaken their ties with General Electric. These moves led to the merger in 1939 that formed Tokyo Shibaura. Then came the removal of GE's control immediately after Pearl Harbor.

Before the war, GE had not only been the source of the two forebears' technical and functional capabilities, but also, as Mark Fruin notes in his *Japanese Enterprise System*, "their mentor in all things managerial." After World War II, these ties were renewed with Tokyo Shibaura, the 1939 merged company.

After GE's relationship to Tokyo Shibaura was restored at the end of the Allied Occupation (and its name shortened in time to the Toshiba Corporation), the ties became more financial and advisory and less those of direct technological transfer and general oversight. Wartime bombing had destroyed much of the consolidated company's production facilities, but its technological and functional capabilities in electrical machinery and electronics were actually enhanced during the war decade and remained fully intact. After the war, Toshiba's initial financial support came from the Mitsui Trading Company, but General Electric then provided much of the sustained funding to rebuild Toshiba's facilities and complete its postwar recovery. In 1965 GE provided an "infusion of capital [that] enabled Toshiba to expand and modernize its operations." As pointed out in chapter 5, this move reflected GE's grand plan to challenge IBM's System 360 worldwide.

After the war, in the 1950s, Toshiba changed its product mix. In addition to expanding electrical machinery and equipment, it enlarged its prewar output of household appliances, adding air conditioners to its earlier lines. More than the other electrical machinery firms, it entered the production of light office machines such as cash registers, typewriters, and other office machinery. Of the electrical engineering companies reviewed in this chapter, it became, based on licenses from GE and then RCA, the strongest domestic competitor to Japan's existing radio and TV equipment makers (as described in chapter 3). Here Toshiba had the advantage over the other Japanese computer makers because of Tokyo Electric's long-established learning base in electrical consumer products.

MITI's allocation of labor in the New Series Project in 1971 helped to determine Toshiba's position in the computer industry in Japan and worldwide. It put Toshiba below Fujitsu and Hitachi in terms of building a learning base for large mainframes. Because Toshiba's partner, NEC, had a broader set of capabilities based on its telecommunications learning, Toshiba became the junior member in that New Series Project pair. NEC contributed 60 percent and Toshiba 40 percent to the joint venture they established to carry out their assigned project of medium-size computers. Because the development of their IBM-compatible computer, based on the General Electric technology (which Honeywell had acquired when GE quit the computer business), was slow in coming, Toshiba turned over to NEC its facilities for making the high end of MITI's midrange series and concentrated on developing the series' smaller computers. Settling in behind Fujitsu, NEC, and Hitachi, Toshiba became the fourth largest revenue producer of information technology products in the New Series Project—a position where it would remain into the 1990s.[32]

As it turned away from general-purpose computers, Toshiba paid closer attention than its rivals to expanding the output and number of its electronics products for consumers and businesses. By the early 1980s its color television products had become established in the U.S. market. In the same years, Toshiba moved into the production of small calculators, photocopiers, and then letter-handling and cash-handling machinery. In the 1980s it continued to hold its own in the heavy equipment industry. Indeed, in the early 1990s it built three new nuclear power plants. It maintained its strength in appliances, joining with GE in 1991 to promote cooperative ventures in large home appliances in Asia. In semiconductors, again a beneficiary of the VLSI project and a participant in drive to conquer world DRAM markets, Toshiba passed Hitachi to become the second largest Japanese producer behind NEC. By 1991 Toshiba's sales were distributed 49 percent in information and communications systems and electronic devices, 21 percent in heavy electrical equipment, and 30 percent in consumer products.[33]

In the 1980s Toshiba began to make technical alliances with Western firms. Its initial focus was its semiconductor market. In 1986 it formed two joint ventures with Motorola, one to exchange microcomputer and memory chip technology, the other to produce the U.S. company's chips in Japan. In early 1992 came another alliance, this time with Siemens and IBM to commercialize the first 256-megabit DRAM. The same year, responding to the new demand of the 1990s, Toshiba entered a joint venture with IBM and Apple to develop multimedia equipment and software. The following year, 1993, came a joint venture with MIPS Computer Systems from which it had licensed its RISC/UNIX client-server technology to develop an advanced microprocessor. By 1994 Toshiba was a world leader in large-scale DRAM chip and in liquid crystal displays, where it was behind the pioneer in that technology, Sharp (as described in chapter 3).[34]

Toshiba's revenues were affected somewhat differently from those of its three major Japanese rivals during the personal computer era. Unlike its rivals, it produced an English-language PC clone with its Intel-Microsoft combination. Another was that it had opted out of the mainframe market, concentrating on midlevel computers and entering workstations in the early 1990s. Additionally, of the four major Japanese computer producers, Toshiba was the only one to focus on consumer electronics products. It continued the development and production of television, VCR, CD players, and CD-ROM disk drives. In 1993 it entered the U.S. entertainment industry by investing $500 million in Time Warner. That investment, in turn, made Toshiba a major player in the commercializing of the DVD. Thus, while Toshiba's sales, too, leveled off in the early 1990s, unlike Fujitsu and NEC, it did not suffer losses. By 1996 its income of $853 million had returned to the level of 1989–1991.

By 1996 Toshiba's total sales of $48.3 billion were evenly divided among three major product markets. Thirty percent came from information technology products, 24 percent from semiconductors and other electronic components, 24 percent from consumer products, and 22 percent from heavy electrical equipment. Toshiba's multipathed capabilities appear to have assured it of a more stable flow of income and revenues than Fujitsu or NEC enjoyed. Its long-term performance lay in its capabilities first to absorb and then to enhance U.S. computer and consumer electronics technologies, as it had earlier done in the first decades of the century in heavy electrical equipment and electrical consumer products.

HITACHI, LTD.: THE HOMEGROWN ENTERPRISE

Although Hitachi had been Fujitsu's partner in developing Japanese IBM-compatible mainframes, it played a more limited role in the growth of Japan's computer industry during the following years. This may reflect an earlier history different from that of its major rivals. In its early years Hitachi had not participated in joint ventures with Western leaders. Nor did it begin as a member of a multi-enterprise *zaibatsu*. It relied more than the others on its own internal efforts rather than on the assistance of foreign mentors in the development of its technological and managerial capabilities. Thus its history provides a perspective on the process of indigenous corporate growth as Japan suddenly entered the industrial world of the early twentieth century.

Hitachi's founder, Namihei Odaira, opened a repair and maintenance shop for the Kuhara Mining Company in 1908. During World War I he expanded its product lines to produce turbines, generators, and electrical transmission equipment for nearby electric companies during the wartime scarcity of Western machinery. At the same time, his establishment began making Kuhara's copper metal into wire. In 1920 Odaira incorporated his business, naming it for Hitachi, the town in which he had started operations. Mergers in 1918 and 1921 brought it into the manufacturing of locomotives and other equipment and then elevators, pumps, and other mechanical goods. Simultaneously it integrated backward into the production of iron and steel parts and malleable cast iron.[35]

By that time, individual capabilities had been transformed into organizational ones. By 1930 Japan's Ministry of Post and Communications, concerned by the foreign ownership in NEC, turned to Hitachi as the only electrical machinery company not relying on foreign technology to produce telecommunications equipment. By that date, Hitachi was the nation's fourth or fifth largest electrical company, depending on the criterion used— assets or sales. As in the case of Toshiba, the demands created by Japan's imperialistic moves into China further enhanced Hitachi's organizational capabilities. Again, its lack of Western corporate ties made it a favored contractor of the government.

After the Pacific war, Hitachi grew fast as a key player in the development of the nation's new hydroelectric power system and then nuclear power plants, in the rebuilding of its transportation network, and to a lesser extent in the creation of a new telephone system owned and operated by the government. In 1956 and 1957 Hitachi started to move into consumer markets by enlarging its production of electric fans and washing machines. Next, on the basis of licensing arrangements with RCA, it began to produce radio and television sets and components. Its major vacuum tube plant came onstream in 1958. Then in the 1960s came its participation in MITI's computer projects. Between 1965 and 1970 Hitachi's managers set up four separate divisional-level laboratories to handle the commercializing of new products—that for household electrical goods in 1965, for electrical machinery in 1966, for computers in 1969, and for television and other electronic products in 1970.[36]

Hitachi's success in computers rested on its "New Series" partnership with Fujitsu to build IBM plug-compatibles. After turning down Fujitsu's offer to join in the financing of Gene Amdahl, Hitachi had to rely on its own internal development of software, an effort that led to its being caught in 1982 attempting to steal IBM's software technology, as mentioned earlier. So it fell behind Fujitsu and NEC in selling mainframes on an OEM basis to Europe and the United States. It did, however, obtain orders from Olivetti and also from a marketing subsidiary of the U.S. National Semiconductor, a subsidiary in which Hitachi in 1989 acquired 80 percent equity. Hitachi made only a limited effort to move into midrange systems. But as a participant in MITI's VLSI program, it was soon producing semiconductors for the global market on the scale of both Toshiba and Fujitsu.[37]

In the 1970s and 1980s Hitachi was more a path follower than a path definer. Its participation in Matsushita's Video Home System, the VHS (see chapter 3), made it a major player in VCRs as well as television. But Hitachi did little to develop new consumer electronic products and processes. Nor in the 1980s did it attempt to enter personal computers. It did, however, license client-server technology from Hewlett-Packard, a source for the revival of its revenues in the mid-1990s as the demand for that technology increased rapidly.

During the 1980s Hitachi maintained its capabilities in its pre–World War II lines. Indeed, by 1992 only 34 percent of its revenues came from information technology, semiconductors, and other computer and electronic devices, and 20 percent from consumer goods, including household appliances. The rest came from power plants and industrial systems, materials and cast iron and steel and copper products, and wire and cable products. Through the 1980s Hitachi reported a better record than its three major competitors, Fujitsu, NEC, and Toshiba, in income and in income as a percentage of sales, and enjoyed a lower debt ratio. But from 1991 through 1994 Hitachi's sales remained relatively flat. Its income fell off more than 70 percent because of losses in consumer products and a weakening in the demand for semiconductors. No losses were recorded, but the income drop did bring a major corporate shake-up that included a retreat from consumer products and a reshaping of the enterprise's internal structure. By the mid-1990s its revenues and income had returned to what they had been at the beginning of the decade.[38]

By 1996 only 29 percent of Hitachi's total sales of $77 billion came from information technology, and 9 percent from semiconductors, peripherals, and other components. Consumer electronics accounted for 9 percent, while its older power/industrial systems and materials businesses accounted for 25 percent and 13 percent, respectively. The balance was in services and other businesses. In the computer market, its continuing concentration on large systems and servers resulted in major profit gains, at the same time that its remaining consumer electronics division continued to report serious losses. Its success in developing innovative high-speed central processing units for its mainframes, expanding its production of servers, and its output of software for both these sectors permitted Hitachi to remain #5 in *Datamation*'s Global 100 information technology producers in 1996.

By continuing to maintain and enhance competitive capabilities in mainframes, Hitachi returned its income to the level it had enjoyed before 1991. So Hitachi, which began with the weakest initial technological input and the most government support, failed to create a multisectored learning base comparable to that of its three major multi-sectored competitors, but it was able to remain a strong competitor in its long established lines.

MITSUBISHI ELECTRIC AND OKI ELECTRIC INDUSTRY

The other two participants in the MITI New Series Project were Mitsubishi Electric and Oki Electric Industry. Before MITI's call, Oki had been a second supplier to NTT (NEC remained the primary supplier), and afterward it became a niche producer of electronic products. Mitsubishi Electric continued on in computers as well as in consumer electronics, becoming a somewhat smaller but still effective competitor. Because of their limited computer experience, MITI had assigned the two only a modest part in the big project. They were to develop the small-size set of IBM compatibles, with Mitsubishi concentrating on the central processing unit and magnetic devices, and Oki on the peripheral and terminal equipment.

Oki did not become a major player in the global computer markets. After suffering severe losses in 1978, it began to specialize in automatic teller machines (ATMs) and other banking and financial computing systems. Then came an unsuccessful move into semiconductors. The resulting large losses turned it to producing specialized chips while carrying on its core business in computer systems for banking and finance.[39]

Mitsubishi Electric evolved as a smaller path follower. In 1923, the same year that Siemens and the Furukawa *zaibatsu* formed Fuji Electric, Westinghouse and the Mitsubishi *zaibatsu* established Mitsubishi Electric in much the same manner and with much the same results. As it had less of an impact on the evolving industry, I do not review its early history. After Japan's defeat and the Allied Occupation, Mitsubishi pioneered in semiconductors even before Sony had acquired Robert Noyce's integrated circuit patents, thereby becoming a leader in their production. In the late 1970s it turned more to consumer electronics, setting up television plants in the United States, Britain, and Australia. At the same time, its income benefited, as did Hitachi's, from the production and sale of Matsushita's VHS cassettes.[40]

In 1996 Mitsubishi's information technology revenues of $5 billion and net income of $559 million, produced in all six sectors, made it #30 in *Datamation*'s top IT one hundred list. By then, 77 percent of its information technology revenues came from large systems, servers, peripherals, and the new networking switching equipment. Even so, these information technology products accounted for only 3 percent of the total revenues of the larger Mitsubishi group, much smaller than its revenues from metals, machinery, foods, fuels, chemicals, and textiles. As part of a giant *zaibatsu*, Mitsubishi kept its electronics products as something of a sideline. Nevertheless, it did remain a significant competitor in global markets.

THE SOURCES OF JAPAN'S COMPUTER INDUSTRY'S COMPETITIVE STRENGTH

The most obvious difference between the Japanese and the U.S. and European computer industries lay in the number, size, and age of Japan's core companies. By 1990 the five core companies had from seventy to ninety years of continuous learning in the intricacies first of electrical and then of electronic engineering as they continued to enhance existing and commercialize new products for national and international markets. In the United States, only IBM had a similar continuing learning experience in electrical and electronic data-processing equipment; and in Europe, only Siemens.

The four Japanese giants, Fujitsu, NEC, Toshiba, and Hitachi, and the somewhat smaller Mitsubishi, created their initial learning bases by building Japan's very first electrical and communications infrastructure. They did so as Japan made its extraordinary leap into the modern world of the late nineteenth century after more than two centuries of isolation from the West. Moreover, except for Hitachi, these companies acquired their technical and functional capabilities through joint ventures with leading Western first-movers that initially commercialized the inventions of Thomas Edison and others. The building of that initial modern infrastructure began in the first decade of the twentieth century and was completed in the 1920s. With its completion, Japan's leaders in electrical equipment had incorporated the most advanced technology of the day into their integrated learning bases.

During the 1930s these firms continued to learn as Japan's political and military leaders began to expand their nation's control over Asia's mainland.

In September 1931 the Japanese army occupied much of Manchukuo. In 1937 came the next move into China, with the taking of Nanking in December. The publication of the New Order of East Asia in November 1938 promised further occupation in East Asia. In the conquered areas, these five firms expanded the limited existing electrical and telecommunications infrastructure. Besides enlarging markets for Japanese firms, these moves also led to a strong commitment by both government and business to reduce Western participation in these enterprises. That participation was, of course, eliminated after the bombing of Pearl Harbor and the powerful Japanese military drive to the south and southeast in Pacific waters.

When Japan surrendered in August 1945, months of Allied bombing had destroyed much of its physical infrastructure. But organizational capabilities remained. The same five enterprises played the major role in rebuilding Japan's electrical and telecommunications infrastructure. Again they installed the most advanced technology. When the Japanese government decided to make a major effort to enter the new computer industry in the late 1950s, these five companies, plus the smaller Oki and Matsushita, the radio and TV maker, constituted all the available candidates for the task. Unlike the British government, the Ministry of International Trade and Industry did not plan for merger. Nor did it, like the French government, sponsor a national plan. Instead it set up a project that permitted the participants to work together, and thus by 1970 five large enterprises with tested integrated learning bases were ready to compete for national and, of much more importance, international markets.

With the technical and functional capabilities learned over decades, and an extraordinary piece of good fortune (the fact that Gene Amdahl was unable to raise $40 million in the United States to finance his plug-compatible), the five Japanese leaders were by the early 1980s supplying Europe and challenging IBM and other U.S. producers with a range of plug-compatible mainframes. But at the very same moment, these five had to face the impact of the microprocessor revolution. They were far less successful in meeting the challenge of the IBM PC and its clones, with their Intel chips and Microsoft operating systems, during the 1980s and early 1990s than they had been in meeting those of IBM and its plug-compatibles in the 1970s.

To summarize, chapter 4 described the initial Japanese challenge in the 1970s and 1980s. Chapter 5 reviewed how the personal computer reestablished the dominance of the U.S. computer industry. In this chapter I have indicated that the Japanese embarked on their second challenge, based on the new demand for high-powered computers created by the rise of networks. Before reviewing the status of the computer and consumer electronics industries as the Electronic Century begins in chapter 7, I here review, in the briefest manner, Japan's response to the coming of the PC. In addition, I consider the coming of the computer industry in other East Asian nations. For with the death of Europe's industries, these nations remained the only potential challengers to the United States and Japan in commercializing major new computer systems.

Japan's PC Industry

By 1980 NEC, Fujitsu, and Toshiba, but not Hitachi, had moved into the production of PCs. Indeed, by that date NEC, Japan's first-mover, was already accounting for 5 percent of the U.S. market. With the coming of the IBM PC, these three responded in different ways.

NEC and Fujitsu turned to the Japanese domestic market. NEC assured its dominance over Fujitsu and other competitors by introducing in 1982 the first Japanese-language IBM clone, its PC98. Two moves quickly gave NEC over 80 percent of Japan's PC market. First, it implanted Japanese characters into its hardware rather than into its software, terming its operating system JDOS. Second, it then mass-marketed the product through "a vast distribution network, including 7,000 retail outlets" and developed a broad set of user-friendly manuals and assisted software vendors in adapting new applications. After Fujitsu and IBM Japan, with an English-language operation system, and the much smaller Seiko Epson (the initial supplier of printers for IBM's PC) entered the market, NEC's share of the Japanese market had fallen to 52 percent in 1991 and 1992.[41]

Toshiba, on the other hand, focused on producing an Intel-Microsoft clone for global markets. By the end of the 1980s it had become a world leader in laptop computers by capitalizing on its strength in miniaturization engineering and precision manufacturing. But it was slow in moving from laptops into notebooks, and its U.S. market share dropped from 43 percent in 1989 to 12 percent in 1993.

In the early 1990s the American companies began their invasion of the Japanese market. In 1991 IBM introduced its DOS/V, an operating system that handled Japanese characters entirely in software, and licensed it to Fujitsu and Toshiba. Apple followed with a Japanese version of its Macintosh with its proprietary software. Then in 1993 Microsoft's Windows 3.1 offered a Japanese-language operating system that ran both on NEC's JDOS and IBM's DOS/V. As a result, Compaq, with its Windows 3.1 operating system, quickly entered Japan's market. By 1994 the three U.S. firms had 29 percent of the Japanese market (IBM 10 percent, Apple 15 percent, and Compaq 4 percent), and the three Japanese firms held 56 percent (NEC 43 percent, Fujitsu 9 percent, and Toshiba 4 percent). The other Japanese competitor, Seiko Epson, accounted for 5 percent, and the remaining 10 percent came primarily from Taiwan.[42]

After the U.S. invasion, the Japanese companies renewed their PC efforts in the mid-1990s. By 1994 Toshiba had regained a world position in notebooks. Also by 1994, Fujitsu, using profits from its growing output of large systems and servers, entered the PC market, first within Japan and then worldwide, so that by 1996 Fujitsu had become the third largest PC revenue producer in the world. It expanded production by reorganizing its global marketing organization. This included taking over from its British subsidiary, ICL, the production and sales of PCs as well as servers. Finally, in 1996 NEC acquired Packard-Bell. By then Fujitsu, Toshiba, and NEC were the third, fourth, and fifth largest revenue producers of personal computers worldwide behind IBM and Compaq.

The "Four Tigers" as Potential Competitors in Information Technology

By 1996 Europe no longer had the learning bases necessary to commercialize new computer systems. But the Japanese multisectored and multi-industry enterprises had once again become effective challengers to the earlier U.S. dominance. Would the growing electronic industries in other Asian countries, specifically those of the "Four Tigers"—namely, Taiwan, Korea, Singapore, and Hong Kong—give rise to another set of challengers? As of 1996 the answer was, not at the moment; but unlike Europe, they certainly showed potential. Taiwan and Singapore had become a significant part of the supporting nexus for the U.S. PC sector. Taiwan provided components for desktops and Singapore on a smaller scale also peripherals, particularly disk drives. By 1996 one Taiwanese enterprise, Acer Incorporated, with revenues of $7 billion, was listed as 16 on *Datamation*'s Global 100 list. The Korean industry concentrated on semiconductors, particularly memory chips. One enterprise, Samsung Electronics, did move into information technology. With revenues of $2 billion in 1996, it was #58 on *Datamation*'s list. Hong Kong, however, remained little more than a port of entry into China's potentially huge market.

TAIWAN

Taiwan's electronics industry had its beginnings in the 1960s and early 1970s, when overseas assembly plants were established by the U.S. semiconductor producers, primarily Texas Instruments, and by the Japanese consumer electronics makers, primarily Matsushita and Sanyo. But impressive growth in Taiwan awaited the coming of the PC revolution in the mid-1980s. Then the U.S. first-movers in the new industry began to obtain their smaller peripherals and components from Taiwan on an OEM basis. Although IBM, Apple, Compaq, Dell, and Packard-Bell continued to rely on the large established firms for their printers, disk drives, CD-ROM drives, and DRAM chips, they turned to numerous small enterprises in Taiwan for mother boards, monitors, keyboards, scanners, mice, and graphical and networking cards. Soon those enterprises began to assemble PCs on an OEM basis for the same American companies. They did this as well when miniaturized laptops, notebooks, and personalized digital assistants (PDAs) made their appearance. By 1995 Taiwan had become the world's leader in the production of notebooks and remained a primary source for components.[43]

But with the exception of one firm, Acer, the leading Taiwan IT companies were assemblers, whose products were sold to leading manufacturers that would market them over their own label. Such a firm was termed an "original design manufacturer" (ODM), as differentiated from an "original brand manufacturer" (OBM) such as Acer. In fact, Taiwan's computer industry as a whole also remained dependent on foreign imports for key parts and components, for example, CPUs from Intel, disk drives from IBM, and liquid crystal displays from Japan or Korea. In general, Japan became Taiwan's major supplier of imported components and interconnected, technological expertise. In 1999 Japan accounted for one-third of Taiwan's total imports of machinery and electrical equipment. The United States share was only 17 percent.[44]

Acer, the world's tenth largest revenue producer of desktops in 1996, is historically important because it provides a relatively rare example of a nexus company that became a major core competitor. Acer Incorporated began as a producer of calculators and then built Taiwan's first large retail computer chain, selling Apple, IBM, and Compaq products. In 1980 it produced its first personal computer, and in 1982 it began to make IBM clones on an OEM basis. It built its own global marketing organization, concentrating first on the United States. But as a latecomer it found the barriers to entry high and so turned to the markets of Latin American and other developing nations. By the end of the decade it had established a U.S. subsidiary to produce UNIX systems. By 1996 desktops accounted for 65 percent of its revenues, peripherals 30 percent, and servers only 5 percent. Then, as described earlier in this chapter, in April 1998 came the contract to acquire Siemens-Nixdorf's PC unit. Although that transaction did not go through, it foreshadowed the enfolding of Siemens-Nixdorf into Fujitsu's European operations as told in chapter 7.[45]

SINGAPORE

Singapore evolved as a comparable adjunct to the U.S. PC industry in much the same manner as Taiwan, but there the product was peripherals. Singapore's electronics industry began in the 1970s, a little later than Taiwan's, at a time when Texas Instruments, Fairchild, and National Semiconductor built Singapore assembly plants. But its impressive growth began in 1982, when Seagate Technologies, the leading U.S. producer of PC disk drives, chose Singapore as its primary overseas manufacturing location. Its major competitors, including IBM, Conner, and Tandon (later acquired by Western Digital), quickly followed. In the 1980s Compaq and Apple built plants for PC assembly and for producing PC components. By 1994 Seagate, which had acquired Conner, had 17,000 employees in Singapore, the other disk drive producers between 4,000 and 4,800. At the same time, Compaq accounted for 4,000 workers and Apple 1,800. By then the disk drive industry had become a much larger employer in Singapore than the semiconductor industry, which had come earlier in the 1970s.[46]

KOREA

Neither Korea nor Hong Kong has played a significant part in the production of computers and peripherals. The Korean story, however, has been one of impressive success in semiconductors. Beginning in 1993, three of the Korean *chaebol* (comparable to the Japanese *zaibatsu*)—Samsung, LG, and

Hyundai—quickly challenged the Japanese leaders in the production of DRAM memory chips. By 1996 Samsung was the largest with 15 percent of the world market, LG with 9 percent, and Hyundai with 7 percent. Of the three, only Samsung made an attempt to enter Korea's home PC market. In 1996 only 24 percent of its $2 billion information technology revenue came from desktops and 60 percent from peripherals. In 1994 it made its major move into the world PC market by acquiring 40 percent of AST Research. In 1996 it took over the remaining 60 percent, "feeling that if it was going to keep pumping money into the company, it should have complete control." In 1996 Samsung was still the only Korean company on *Datamation*'s list of one hundred worldwide IT producers. As for Hong Kong, by 1996 it had become a commercial intermediary, not a manufacturer—the link between East Asian producers and China's market.[47]

By the year 2000, Taiwan, Singapore, and Korea had not yet developed industries that could challenge that of the United States or Japan in commercializing major new technologies. The concentration of technical knowledge and functional capabilities evolved during the past decades in the United States and Japan had created powerful barriers to entry. Nevertheless, as a supporting nexus for the U.S. and, more recently, Japanese core companies, it seems certain to grow and prosper, particularly in Taiwan and Korea. As the East Asian markets grow—particularly in China—new core companies may emerge as challengers to the U.S. and Japanese competitive dominance, but as the new century opens, such a contender has not yet appeared.

This chapter brings the details of the epic and unique stories of the computer/information technology industry up to 1996, the year that the basic infrastructure of the Electronic Century had been completed. In the following chapter I review the status of the major players in both the consumer electronics and computer industries whose evolution has been the subject of this book. I focus on the developments of the early and mid-1990s that set the stage for the continuing evolution of these two increasingly interrelated industries as the Electronic Century begins.

7

THE CONSUMER ELECTRONICS AND
COMPUTER INDUSTRIES AS THE
ELECTRONIC CENTURY BEGINS

The privatizing of the Internet and the ending of the prohibition on its commercial use completed the basic infrastructure of the Electronic Century. Continuing evolution of the two industries whose history has been recorded in this study must evolve from this base, and certainly their activities will become increasingly interrelated. In making this review of the two industries as the Electronic Century began, I rely on a listing, a "program," of the industry's largest players in 1996. For consumer electronics, table 7.1 (a reprint of Table 3.1) illustrating Matsushita's OEM strategy, provides a listing of fifty-seven players during the 1980s. For computers in the 1990s, I use the term "information technology" (IT) and rely on table 7.2, *Datamation*'s listing of the top ten revenue producers in the industry's seven product sectors in 1996.

I first review the evolving product lines of the consumer electronics leaders in the late 1980s and early 1990s. This review is brief because by then the Japanese had all but completed their conquest of world markets and the number of players was so small. Then comes the much longer examination of the evolving product lines in information technology, with a particular focus on the Japanese challenges beginning in the 1990s. There, more companies are involved and more detailed information is available.

Because the two European champions, Philips and Siemens, withdrew from their industry at almost the same moment, I follow the review of consumer electronics with an obituary of Europe's two industries. I then turn to Japan's renewed challenge to the U.S. IT industry. Here table 7.2 provides a scoreboard of the comparative status of the U.S. and Japanese leaders in terms of revenues in each of the industry's seven sectors. Then follows a broader analysis of the basic differences between the U.S. and the Japanese industries in terms of the scale and scope of the core enterprises and the nature of their supporting nexuses. I close the chapter with an evaluation of the strengths and weaknesses of the two national industries as the new century begins.

Consumer Electronics

Table 7.1 is a reminder of how Matsushita, Sony, and Philips developed, produced, and marketed their different VCRs that resulted in the rest of the world's players receiving their VCRs on an OEM basis to be sold over their labels. After that time, all but the Japanese firms were producers of niche products or members of the larger recording and musical entertainment business. These firms had relatively little significant impact on the technological evolution of the consumer electronics industry.

Table 7.1, therefore, emphasizes the dominance of the four Japanese leaders. Matsushita (with its subsidiary JVC) and Sony had developed two versions of the videocassette recorder. Matsushita licensed its Video Home System to Sharp and one branch of Sanyo, as well as two computer companies, Hitachi and Mitsubishi Electric, for production and distribution. Sony did the same for the other branch of Sanyo as well as two other computer companies, Toshiba and NEC. So I summarize briefly the pattern of the changing product lines of Japan's Big Four in consumer electronics—Matsushita, Sony, Sharp, and Sanyo—after their conquest of global markets.[1]

This pattern reflected the functional and technical capabilities that had been embodied in their initial integrated learning bases in the 1950s and 1960s. Matsushita, with its sales of $64.1 billion in 1996, continued to exemplify growth and competitive strength based on functional capabilities—that is, product development, production, and marketing. After its VCR

TABLE 7.1. Matsushita OEM Strategy
Group Alignments of VCR Formats, 1983–1984

Function	Japan	United States	Europe
VHS Group (38 Companies)			
Develop, Produce, & Market	JVC Matsushita		
Produce & Market	Sharp Hitachi Mitsubishi Electric Tokyo Sanyo		
Market	Brother (MI) Ricoh (H) Tokyo Juki (H) Canon (MA) Asahi Optical (H) Olympus (MA) Nikon (MA) Akai Trio (J) Sansui (J) Clarion (J) Teac (J) Japan Columbia (H)	Magnavox (MA) Sylvania (MA) GE (MA) Curtis Mathes (MA) J. C. Penney (MA) RCA (H) Sears (H) Zenith (J)	Blaupunkt (MA) Saba (J) SEL (J) Nordmende (J) Telefunken (J) Thorn-EMI (J) Thomson-Brandt (J) Granada (H) Hangard (H) Sarolla (H) Fisher (T) Luxer (MI)
Beta Group (12 Companies)			
Develop, Produce, & Market	Sony		
Produce & Market	Sanyo Toshiba NEC		
Market	General (TO) Aiwa Pioneer (S)	Zenith (S) Sears (SA)	Kneckerman (SA) Fisher (SA) Rank (TO)
V-2000 Group (7 Companies)			
Develop, Produce, & Market			Philips
Produce & Market			Grundig
Market			Siemens (G) ITT (G) Loewe Opta (G) Lorting (P) B&O (P)

Source: Michael A. Cusumano, Viorgos Mylonadis, and Richard S. Rosenbloom, "Strategic Maneuvering and Mass-Market Dynamics: The Triumph of VHS over Beta," *Business History Review*, 66, no. 1 (Spring 1992): 73 (table 5), with permission. To be cited from this source.

Note: Suppliers are indicated by initials: J = JVC, MA = Matsushita, H = Hitachi, MI = Mitsubishi, T = Tokyo Sanyo, S = Sony, TO = Toshiba, SA = Sanyo, P = Philips, G = Grundig.
Matsushita and its subsidiary, JVC, developed, produced, and marketed the VHS. Sharp, Hitachi, Mitsubishi Electric, and Tokyo Sanyo manufactured and marketed it. The rest sold the VHS over their own labels. Sony commercialized the Beta, the three computer makers produced and marketed it. The others were marketing outlets. Philips and its subsidiary Grundig commercialized the V-2000. The rest were marketing outlets. The companies listed in the table represent nearly all the significant players in the industry worldwide. In spring 1984 Zenith switched from the Beta group to VHS.

victory in the early 1980s, Matsushita made only minimal attempts to commercialize the new consumer electronics technologies that it had received since the early 1950s directly from its mentor, Philips, as well as from RCA licenses. Instead it concentrated on the development, production, and marketing of products in closely related industries, where its perfected functional capabilities provided competitive strengths. As a result, in 1996 only 26 percent of sales still came from audio and video equipment (8 percent from audio and 18 percent from video); 30 percent from industrial equipment, including robots and communications, a move that brought Matsushita into the production of information technology peripherals and networking equipment (table 7.2); 15 percent from electronic components; 19 percent from home appliances, including batteries; and 10 percent from other products such as cameras and copiers. Matsushita continued to be one of the world's most successful exemplifiers of growth through well-tested functional learning.

Sony, with sales of $48.3 billion, remained the exemplar of continuing growth through the commercializing of new products based on learning and by generating from the success of previous innovations. By 1996, 53 percent of its sales came from consumer electronics (20 percent from audio equipment—audiotapes and stereo systems; 16 percent from video equipment—VCRs and laser disk players; and 17 percent from television sets). Its Musical Entertainment Group (including recording, movies, and TV shows) added 11 percent. The remaining 36 percent included personal computers and semiconductors. By the late 1990s Sony had become a world market share leader in handheld computers and home video games.

The financial difficulties Sony encountered in its Hollywood ventures, as well as the billion-dollar losses of its partner, Philips, delayed the commercializing of the DVD until 1997. But then DVD sales soared in 1998 and 1999. By the end of the century Sony was carrying out its basic growth strategy in video games, using the learning and profits from its initial game product, PlayStation, to commercialize PlayStation 2, a product that could play audio CDs, DVD movies, and its new game software.

As for Sharp, that company's early evolution was comparable to that of Sony's technology-based evolution. But after it became a first-mover in a new technology, it began to follow Matsushita's functional strategy. After World War II, Sharp, the small radio maker, turned to producing solar cells, microwave ovens, and other household appliances. In the late 1960s it also began to commercialize electronic calculators, becoming the dominant firm worldwide in that product, and was soon producing other products for the business market.

In the early 1970s Sharp pioneered the new LCD technology and became a first-mover in commercializing LCD calculators and other LCD-based products. In the late 1970s Sharp's recruitment by Matsushita to produce and market the VHS expanded Sharp's existing radio and television activities. In the 1980s the company enlarged its offerings of electronic office equipment products such as copiers, fax machines, and cordless telephones. By 1996, of Sharp's sales of $15.4 billion, television and video equipment had dropped to 20 percent, and audio and communications equipment to 11 percent, while industrial and office equipment had risen to 25 percent, with components accouting for 27 percent. Its older home appliance products were still at 17 percent.

In the same manner, Sanyo, with sales of $17.1 billion in 1995 (information is incomplete for 1996), continued to follow its strategy of relying heavily on existing technology and concentrating on marketing and price competitiveness. That is, Sanyo did not attempt to enhance its product development capabilities in the manner of its three major Japanese competitors. By 1996 its consumer electronics accounted for 44 percent of sales but only 35 percent of total income.

By the late 1980s only two of these four enterprises, Sony and Sharp, had the critical combination of the applied research and the functional capabilities required to commercialize the products of new technologies and enhance those of existing ones. In 1996 they were joined by a computer company, Toshiba, which successfully commercialized a DVD product competitive to that of Sony and Philips. So with Philips's withdrawal from consumer electronics, these three would be the chief—indeed, the only—architects of the evolving consumer electronics path in the new Electronic Century. In the previous century the three creators of that path were in each of the three competing national industries. In the new century, they were again three, but all in Japan.

As the old century was closing, Philips was pulling out of consumer electronics, and Siemens, Europe's longtime leader in computers, was doing the same in computers. Their withdrawal permits the writing of a brief obituary of Europe's consumer electronics and computer industries.

An Obituary of Europe's Consumer Electronics and Information Technology Industries

In the last two years of the twentieth century, the European leader in each industry passed away as an independent producer. In 1998 Philips sold off its major remaining consumer products business, PolyGram, to the musical entertainment divisions of Seagram's, the bottled liquor producer. In 1999, to save its one remaining consumer electronics product, it formed a $1.6 billion joint venture with Korea's L. G. Electronics to produce LCD monitors. At the same time, the one consumer electronics project being carried out by Philips's once great laboratories was a competitive set-top box for connecting televisions to the Internet. To emphasize the shift of Philips's business out of consumer electronics, the CEO, Cor Boonstra, moved Philips's headquarters from Eindhoven to Amsterdam (see endnote 42, chapter 3).

In 1998 Siemens received and accepted an offer from Taiwan's Acer to purchase its personal computer business. When Acer reneged on the contract, Siemens had little choice but to turn to Fujitsu, the longtime provider of its large computer systems. After the formation of the joint venture, Fujitsu-Siemens Computers, in 1999, the new partner moved the Siemens headquarters from Munich also to Amsterdam (see endnote 14, chapter 6).

Of the three other national European producers of computer systems, Britain's ICL, a subsidiary of Fujitsu, had become little more than a marketing agent for the Japanese company. France's Groupe Bull, formerly Machines Bull, received its large systems and servers from Japan. It waited until 1989 to enter the personal computer market and then did so by acquiring the PC unit of Zenith, the collapsing U.S. consumer electronics company. That acquisition helped to account for Bull's continuing losses from 1989 to 1994, including a $1.3 billion loss in 1990. In these same years Olivetti's losses forced it to depart from the computer industry. In 1990 its income dropped to $53 million. Severe losses then followed every year, reaching over $1 billion for the year 1995. Olivetti was then acquired by a venture capital firm headed by an American and was long a viable competitor.[2]

Two other European companies are listed in 1996 on table 7.1, France's Cap Gemini Sogeti, a computer services pioneer of the 1960s, and Germany's SAP, whose growth in the mid-1990s was phenomenal. Its sales and income rose from $634 million and $84 million in 1993 to $1,875 million and $282 million in 1995. The history of each company makes an important historical point. The longevity of the first emphasizes that the wide variety of local governmental, professional, and business standards within the many European nations required custom application development *services*, rather than standardized application software. The success of the second, SAP, stemming from that company's early development of client-server-based software applications in the 1990s while its competitor, Oracle, still concentrated on large systems, documents the rapidly growing demand for networked computing.

By 1996 only six other European companies were listed in *Datamation*'s Global 100. Two, the Sema Group, a French company, and Getronic, a Dutch one, provided services and software in the manner of pioneer Cap Gemini Sogeti. Three were major telecommunications equipment companies—Sweden's Ericsson, France's Alcatel, and British Telecom. Their only IT products were, like those of Japan's NTT, networking devices that they had long been producing for their own telecommunications systems. The sixth, Oce, was a Dutch enterprise that produced peripherals and software. In this way, *Datamation* records the death of Europe's IT industries, except for software and services.

Japan's IT Industry Continues to Challenge

As Europe's national IT industries were dying, the five multisectored, multi-industry, decades-old Japanese enterprises listed on table 7.2 were again seriously challenging the U.S. industry. The Japanese firms, having fallen behind after the recasting of the industry by Intel/Microsoft-based IBM PCs and clones, were benefiting in 1996 from the demand for greater computing power. *Datamation*, in its July 1997 issue, headlined its review of large systems with "Big Iron Soars" and, in a review of servers, stressed that "Internet-based applications, such as web servers and electronic applications, fuel server sales."[3]

In fact, the year before, *Datamation* had redefined its six product sectors and added a new one to meet the new computing realities. PCs and workstations were combined into a single "desktop" category. Desktops included all portable machines, including laptops and handhelds. Servers included multiunit systems such as IBM's AS/400, Intel-based servers (those using its chips), and large-scale UNIX servers. They classified large-scale systems as

TABLE 7.2. The Ten Largest Information Technology Companies Worldwide by Product Sector, 1996

Rank	Company	Country	Estimated Revenue[1] ($ millions)	% of Total IT Revenue
Large-Scale Systems				
1	IBM	U.S.	5,316	7%
2	Fujitsu	Japan	5,052	17%
3	NEC	Japan	3,850	26%
4	Hitachi	Japan	1,829	12%
5	Unisys	U.S.	828	13%
6	Silicon Graphics	U.S.	682	21%
7	Siemens-Nixdorf	Germany	643	7%
8	Machines Bull	France	624	13%
9	Amdahl	Japan/U.S.	375	23%
10	Mitsubishi	Japan	348	7%
Servers				
1	IBM	U.S.	7,595	10%
2	Hewlett-Packard	U.S.	4,396	14%
3	Compaq Computer	U.S.	3,984	22%
4	NEC	Japan	2,502	17%
5	Toshiba	Japan	1,967	14%
6	Digital (DEC)	U.S.	1,633	12%
7	Tandem	U.S.	1,611	80%
8	NCR	U.S.	1,495	23%
9	Hitachi	Japan	1,219	8%
10	Fujitsu	Japan	1,189	4%
Desktops				
1	IBM	U.S.	12,912	17%
2	Compaq Computer	U.S.	11,228	62%
3	Fujitsu	Japan	9,807	33%
4	Toshiba	Japan	7,868	56%
5	NEC (Packard-Bell)	Japan	7,500	100%
6	Dell Computer	U.S.	7,488	96%
7	Apple Computer	U.S.	6,686	75%
8	Hewlett-Packard	U.S.	6,594	21%
9	Gateway 2000	U.S.	5,040	100%
10	Acer	Taiwan	4,550	65%
Peripherals				
1	IBM	U.S.	10,633	14%
2	Hewlett-Packard	U.S.	10,361	33%
3	Seagate	U.S.	8,075	95%
4	Canon	Japan	6,907	100%
5	Quantum	U.S.	4,950	100%
6	Fujitsu	Japan	4,160	14%
7	Western Digital	U.S.	3,550	100%
8	Toshiba	Japan	3,232	23%
9	Xerox	U.S.	3,107	60%
10	Matsushita	Japan	2,821	44%

(*Continued*)

TABLE 7.2. (*Continued*)

Rank	Company	Country	Estimated Revenue[1] ($ millions)	% of Total IT Revenue
Software				
1	IBM	U.S.	12,911	17%
2	Microsoft	U.S.	9,435	100%
3	Hitachi	Japan	5,487	36%
4	Fujitsu	Japan	4,755	16%
5	Computer Assoc.	U.S.	3,157	80%
6	NEC	Japan	2,310	15%
7	Oracle	U.S.	2,280	54%
8	SAP	Germany	1,700	71%
9	Novell	U.S.	1,225	91%
10	Digital (DEC)	U.S.	1,225	9%
Services				
1	IBM	U.S.	22,785	30%
2	EDS	U.S.	14,441	100%
3	Hewlett-Packard	U.S.	9,463	30%
4	Digital (DEC)	U.S.	5,988	44%
5	Computer Sciences	U.S.	5,400	100%
6	Andersen Consulting	U.S.	4,878	92%
7	Fujitsu	Japan	4,160	14%
8	Cap Gemini Sogeti	France	4,104	95%
9	Unisys	U.S.	3,950	62%
10	ADP	U.S.	3,567	100%
Datacom Equipment (Networking)				
1	Cisco Systems	U.S.	5,406	100%
2	IBM	U.S.	3,797	5%
3	Lucent Technologies	U.S.	3,400	85%
4	NTT Data	Japan	3,300	60%
5	3Com	U.S.	2,797	100%
6	U.S. Robotics	U.S.	2,258	100%
7	Bay Networks	U.S.	2,094	100%
8	Hewlett-Packard	U.S.	1,570	5%
9	Matsushita	Japan	1,539	24%
10	Motorola	U.S.	1,446	47%

Source: Compiled from *Datamation*, July 1997, pp. 49, 50, 55, 57, 62, 73, 71. Excerpted with permission of *Datamation* magazine. Copyright 1997 by Cahners Publishing Company.

[1]*Datamation's* revenue estimates do not necessarily match precisely with actual reported revenues both because companies do not always publish sector-specific results and because their fiscal years may not match the time frame of the estimates. Nonetheless, the estimates still represent the relative magnitude of various competitors.

IBM/S390 class and above. The new sector, "datacom equipment," included "products that allow computers to send data to each other and to peripherals over local or wide area links." The software sector continued to include all systems and applications software products not embedded in hardware. And the peripherals sector included storage devices, monitors, disk drives, and printers.[4]

I use table 7.2 as a scoreboard of the standing of the Japanese challengers, particularly the leaders—Fujitsu, Hitachi, NEC, and Toshiba—and the U.S. defenders—especially IBM, Hewlett-Packard, Compaq, Sun, Microsoft, and Intel. (Intel is not listed on table 7.1 because *Datamation* does not list semiconductor producers).

LARGE SYSTEMS

In large systems—mainframes and supercomputers—IBM and three heirs of MITI's New Series Project—Fujitsu, NEC, and Hitachi—dominated the field, while the smaller Mitsubishi Electric tagged along in tenth place. In addition, Fujitsu controlled Amdahl and provided Siemens-Nixdorf with its large systems, as NEC did for Groupe Bull.

IBM's System 390, a direct descendant of the System 360, provided revenues of $5.3 billion, which equaled the combination of Fujitsu's and Amdahl's revenues but provided only 7 percent of IBM's total IT revenues. As for the other two U.S. companies in the top ten, Unisys, the 1986 merger of Sperry Rand and Honeywell, still received 25 percent of its revenues from large-scale systems (equivalent to 0.15 percent of IBM's). Silicon Graphics, on the other hand, had entered the large-scale sector in order to provide mainframe power for its niche product of three-dimensional motion pictures.

As the revenues of three of Japan's four plus those of Amdahl and Mitsubishi Electric were three times that of the U.S. companies, Japan's industry dominated the world's large systems market. The dominance was a reward for Japan's first challenge to the U.S. industry with the successful sale of IBM plug-compatible systems, first to its own domestic market as Japan was on its way to becoming the world's second largest economy and then to the European market.

SERVERS

In servers the U.S. leader again was IBM, followed by Hewlett-Packard. HP had been one of the most successful producers of minicomputers and then workstations, in terms of revenues and the steadiness of income as a percent of sales. In 1996 H-P was listed #2 in *Datamation*'s Global 100, with worldwide revenues just ahead of Fujitsu. The third, Compaq, had just completed a highly successful move into servers. Together the three accounted for twice the revenues of the four Japanese firms. (See also table 7.3, page 232.)

Nevertheless, the Japanese were catching up as the other U.S. competitors were falling behind. The four Japanese leaders had enthusiastically embraced the new RISC chip technology. Fujitsu had immediately licensed Sun's SPARC, Hitachi licensed Hewlett-Packard's Spectrum, and Toshiba and NEC turned to MIPS Technologies. That partnership continued when in 1993 NEC and Toshiba, working with MIPS, began the development of a next-generation RISC microprocessor. In 1994 Fujitsu and Sun accounced that they would jointly spend $500 million for a new competitive RISC processor.[5]

Again the listings of the Japanese companies in terms of revenues reflect MITI's original choice of having NEC and Toshiba commercialize the middle-level systems. They were #4 and #5 in server revenues. Hitachi and Fujitsu, MITI's choices for large-scale systems, were only #9 and #10 in servers. More should be said about their activities, but unfortunately there is little information available in English on the commercializing of client-server technology in Japan.

Of the remaining U.S. computer companies listed—Tandem, DEC, and NCR—one, Tandem, the first-mover in fault-tolerant computers (see chapter 4), remained in its original market and provides a successful example of maintaining a first-mover position in a single sector. The other two, DEC and NCR, suffered serious losses in the 1990s. In addition, Sun, the workstation innovator, did not make the list of the top ten revenue producers. In 1994 it had been #9 on *Datamation*'s Global 100 list. In 1996 it had dropped to #20.

DEC and NCR were victims of their own misguided strategies. DEC's loss resulted from remaining committed too long to a successful strategy. During the 1980s it perfected its VAX minicomputer product line, which shared a single operating system and had replaced its earlier PDP line. Its commitment to the VAX architecture led DEC to enter the workstation market with its VAX technology, rather than embracing the RISC/UNIX technology. Management concentrated on bringing out its VAX9000 as a rival to IBM's major mainframe offerings. The VAX9000 appeared in 1990 just as that market was collapsing. As noted earlier (see chapter 5), its income had already plummeted from $1.1 billion in the year 1989 to $74 million in 1990, followed by heavier annual losses from 1991 to 1995, including over $2.3 billion in 1992 and $2.1 billion in 1994, and $343 million in 1996. Even so, as Paul Ceruzzi writes, "DEC probably could have weathered an assault from UNIX workstations or from the IBM PC if either occurred alone, but the combination was too much."[6]

Just as disastrous was AT&T's strategic decision made in 1991 to enter the computer business by acquiring National Cash Register through a $5.6 billion unfriendly takeover. NCR had been moving into workstations. Then AT&T, after a series of losses on the scale of those of DEC, spun off NCR, whose name had been temporarily changed to Global Information Systems (GIS), in 1995. Few better examples exist of the futility of large-scale acquisitions in the high-technology industries.

Sun's brief decline resulted from its initial response to increased competition. In the early 1990s both HP and IBM had increased their competitive strength in the scientific/engineering market, HP through the acquisition and successful integration of Apollo, and IBM with its advanced RS600 (see chapter 5). So in response, Scott McNealy, Sun's chairman and CEO, decided to diversify, to become "a one-stop technology shop." In this way, the first-mover and leader in the scientific/engineering market moved into the commercial market and expanded to produce less expensive general-purpose workstations (now listed as desktops), software, and microprocessors. By 1996, 62 percent of its revenues came from desktops, 11 percent from servers, and only 5 percent from software. The remaining balance came from microprocessors, peripherals, and services. For this reason, Sun dropped from #9 to #20 on The *Datamation*'s Global 100 list. However, by 1996 it had quickly recovered by taking advantage of the explosion of the Internet, through its commercialization of the Hot Java browser in 1995, a new Internet server called Netra, and an alliance with Motorola to develop high-speed Internet access systems for home PCs. As a result, profits rose in 1996 to $476 million on sales of $7,095 million.[7]

Also in the early 1990s, Compaq successfully entered the server market shortly before Sun moved into desktops. Compaq did so by developing, not acquiring, its own servers. Late in 1992 it introduced the world's fastest PC server, the SYSTEM PRO/XL. Then came a joint venture with Microsoft in 1993 to develop a multiprocessor computer, another with Cisco to develop PC-to-server links, and a third with Texas Instruments to commercialize high-speed networking chips. So Compaq by 1996 had become the world's third largest server producer, which accounted for 22 percent of its total IT revenue. As table 7.3 records, Compaq by 1996 had become the fourth largest information technology revenue producer worldwide, behind IBM, Hewlett-Packard, and Fujitsu. In 1997 its drive to become a "full-service computer company," the stated goal of its CEO, Eckard Pfeiffer, was achieved by the acquisition of the floundering DEC.[8]

DESKTOPS

As for desktops in 1996, listed in table 7.1, the impact of the growing Japanese challenge is clear. IBM, the industry's path definer, and Compaq Computer, the first clone to appear on *Datamation*'s microcomputer listing in 1983 (table 4.2), remained the top revenue producers, with Hewlett-Packard listed as #8. What was new in this listing was the strength of three Japanese leaders—Fujitsu, Toshiba, and NEC—in the sector that had been so dominated by U.S. firms since the PC period began. Fujitsu's increase in revenue resulted from its aggressive move into PCs after 1993, apparently financed in part by increased revenues from its large systems and servers. Toshiba's gains resulted from its initial strategy of becoming the only Japanese leader to produce IBM clones for world markets (as noted in chapter 6). NEC's entry, however, came with its acquisition of Packard-Bell in 1995.

These moves of Fujitsu and Toshiba brought large losses in market share and income to two other leading PC makers, Packard-Bell and AST Research. Packard-Bell, established in 1986, made its first profit, $5 million, only in 1991 and reported losses in 1992 and again in 1995. In 1994 NEC acquired a 20 percent stake in Packard-Bell for $170 million. A year later it merged most of its business outside of Japan with Packard-Bell, transferring $300 million in assets to the new NEC Packard-Bell. AST Research, which had losses in 1992, 1994, and 1995 that totaled over $400 million, had become by 1996 a wholly owned subsidiary of Korea's Samsung (see chapter 6).[9]

In addition to the U.S. leaders, IBM and Compaq, and the three Japanese firms, the top ten included Hewlett-Packard, the direct marketers Dell and Gateway, Apple, and Taiwan's Acer (whose story is also told in chapter 6). Hewlett-Packard had been a minor player in the sector since the initial boom of the early 1980s. Dell, the sector's first-mover in direct marketing, and its successful "follower," Gateway, continued to hold their own worldwide (unlike fellow direct marketers Packard-Bell and AST Research). To maintain its strength, Dell did have to go through a major restructuring after a loss of $36 million in 1990. Gateway completed its integrated learning base, moved in 1990 from the family homestead to North Sioux City, South Dakota, and continued to evolve in an exemplary manner. It expanded its activities abroad and was soon producing derivative products, including notebooks and its Handbook.[10]

Apple, the PC sector's most creative first-mover and the one remaining major PC producer with a proprietary operating system, had fallen back as a revenue producer. In 1992 it lost a copyright case against Microsoft for incorporating the look and feel of the Macintosh into Microsoft's Windows operating system. In the next year an 84 percent drop in earnings forced a reshaping of its technology, its working force, and its management, and this reorganization resulted in a return to the higher net income of its earlier years. Nevertheless, Apple's total IT revenues in 1996 had fallen to $8.9 billion, resulting in a loss of $867 million. Just as Sony's Beta gave way to Matsushita's VHS, the (arguably) technically superior Macintosh lost out to the cost and scale economies of PC clones based on Intel processors and Microsoft software.

SOFTWARE

In software, table 7.2 once again underlines the significance of Japan's revival in large systems and servers. IBM and Microsoft, as might be expected, ranked first and second. But the Japanese followed, Hitachi and Fujitsu ranking third and fourth and NEC sixth. (Toshiba, as a producer of IBM clones, relied, of course, on Microsoft's Windows.)

In software, table 7.2's column "Percent of Total IT Revenues" clearly defines the critical difference between the Japanese challengers and the U.S. defenders, a difference reflecting the revolution created by the mass production and marketing of the personal computer. Software revenues of these three, like those of IBM and DEC (the industry's two pioneer path makers), represented only a small percentage of their total IT revenues. By contrast, the software revenues of Microsoft and the other U.S. producers of application software, including Computer Associates and Novell, were between 80 percent and 100 percent of their total IT revenues. (Although software accounted for only 56 percent of Oracle's revenue, the other 44 percent came from services associated with its database software.)

In other words, the entrepreneurial start-ups remained primarily single-sector enterprises. The same pattern held for desktops with Dell, Gateway 2000, and Apple concentrating 75 percent to 100 percent of their IT revenue in that sector. Compaq's 62 percent reflects its move into servers. Clearly in both desktops and software the Japanese challengers and the U.S. defenders were very different types of enterprises.

PERIPHERALS, SERVICES, AND NETWORKING EQUIPMENT

In peripherals, services, and networking equipment, the Japanese challenge is less significant. But the pattern in terms of types of enterprises was much the same. In peripherals, the Japanese challengers were multi-industry, while the U.S. companies, except for IBM and HP, were single-sector enterprises, which were, in turn, first-movers in their sector. Fujitsu and Toshiba followed the pattern. The two other Japanese entrants—Canon and Matsushita—were not computer makers but still multi-industry firms that had recently entered the IT industry. Canon entered into a single peripheral, printers for PCs (in so doing, this turned Xerox to focus primarily on printers for large systems). On the other hand, the much larger Matsushita made a broader commitment, so that in 1996 it was the tenth largest in peripherals and the ninth largest in networking equipment.

The Japanese challenge had little impact on services, as this sector relies largely on local personnel to customize IT systems and applications to local user needs. Thus Fujitsu became the major supplier in Japan much as Cap Gemini Sogeti had been for thirty years in Europe. It is worth noting that between 1994 (table 5.1) and 1996 (table 7.2) ADP, a first-mover of the 1960s, had reappeared on the top ten list, displacing ENTEX Information Services, the first provider of services for the PC.

In *Datamation*'s new sector, datacom equipment, the pattern of enterprise types was much the same. The four entrepreneurial start-ups have 100 percent of their revenues in this sector, while the multisector IBM and DEC have 5 percent each. Three others were from related industries. Lucent Technologies, the name given to Western Electric when AT&T spun it off in 1996, had been a longtime producer of switching equipment. Its initial move as an independent enterprise was to concentrate on networking equipment. Japan's NTT made the same move by setting up a subsidiary, NTT Data, to develop the new technology. On the other hand,

Matsushita created new learning bases in both data communications and peripherals, as well as desktops, making it #18 on The *Datamation*'s Global 100 list in 1996. Nevertheless, its losses (table 7.3) indicate that the barriers to entry into IT were higher than Matsushita's managers anticipated. Finally, Motorola, the world's largest producer of equipment for cellular telephones, pagers, and two-way radios, was meeting the challenge of Internet access.

The three entrepreneurial start-ups followed Cisco's strong head start. 3Com, established by Robert Metcalfe, the inventor of the Ethernet, initially used by Sun for its innovative client-server technology, at first concentrated on LAN adapters, hubs, and switches and then turned to routers. But lacking Cisco's initial output for the Internet, 3Com did not develop a profitable stream of income from routers until the demands for private corporate networks surged. The same was true for Bay Networks, a 1994 merger of two smaller start-ups, Syn Optics, established in 1985, and Wellfleet, established in 1986. Both began by producing switching equipment for LANs and then WANs. U.S. Robotics, which was formed in 1976 to market modems, began to produce routers and other switching equipment in 1988.

Underlying Differences between the U.S. IT Industry and Its Japanese Challengers

As shown in this sector-by-sector scoreboard of the IT industry as the Electronic Century begins, the Japanese and U.S. firms operate in a very different manner. Table 7.3 indicates another dimension of these differences. Not only had Japanese companies become powerful competitors in multiple sectors, but also they had from the start been multi-industry enterprises, diversified beyond electronics. (As table 7.3 illustrates, 60 percent of Fujitsu's revenues came from IT; 34 percent for NEC, 24 percent for Toshiba, and 23 percent for Hitachi.) In addition, because they had entered computers from the paths of electrical equipment and telecommunications, they continued to have integrated learning bases in electrical appliances and in light and heavy electrical equipment. With the consumer electronics companies, they created the Japanese semiconductor business in the 1970s. In the 1980s and 1990s they began to produce other electronic industrial and communications devices. These five firms—Fujitsu, NEC, Toshiba, Hitachi, and Mitsubishi Elec-

TABLE 7.3. Leading Information Technology Companies
Ranked by Information Technology Revenues

	Company	Country	1996 IT Revenue[1] ($ millions)	IT as Percent of Total Revenue	Total 1996 Revenue	Total 1996 Net Income
1	IBM	U.S.	75,947	100%	75,947	5,400
2	Hewlett-Packard	U.S.	31,398	80%	39,427	2,708
3	Fujitsu[2]	Japan	29,717	63%	47,170	5,300
4	Compaq Computer	U.S.	18,109	100%	18,109	1,313
5	Hitachi[2]	Japan	15,242	23%	68,735	712
6	NEC[2]	Japan	15,092	34%	44,766	841
7	Electronic Data Systems	U.S.	14,441	100%	14,441	432
8	Toshiba[2]	Japan	14,050	24%	58,300	1,533
9	Digital Equipment	U.S.	13,610	100%	13,610	-343
10	Microsoft	U.S.	9,435	100%	9,435	2,476
11	Siemens-Nixdorf	Germany	9,189	100%	9,189	20
12	Apple Computer	U.S.	8,914	100%	8,914	-867
13	Seagate Technology	U.S.	8,500	100%	8,500	222
14	Dell Computer	U.S.	7,800	100%	7,800	518
15	Packard-Bell NEC[3]	U.S. / Japan	7,500	100%	7,500	N/A
16	Acer	Taiwan	7,000	100%	7,000	N/A
17	Canon	Japan	6,907	51%	10,430	1,000
18	Matsushita	Japan	6,410	10%	64,102	-537
19	NCR	U.S.	6,403	92%	6,960	-109
20	Sun Microsystems	U.S.	6,390	100%	6,390	447

Source: *Datamation*, July 1997, p. 45. Excerpted by permission of *Datamation* magazine. Copyright 1997 by Cahners Publishing Company

[1] Calendar year 1996 results.

[2] Figures based on fiscal year ending March 31, 1997.

[3] Includes revenue for new Packard-Bell NEC consisting of Packard-Bell, Zenith Data Systems, and NEC's PC sales outside Japan.

tric—were older than their U.S. competitors, with the exception of IBM, and had created their initial learning bases in electrical and telecommunications equipment by the time of World War I. Because of these barriers to entry established from the industry's beginning, no entrepreneurial start-ups challenged these core companies in Japan.

On the other hand, until the 1990s only three U.S. firms were multisectored, IBM, HP, and DEC. None, not even IBM, were multi-industry. By the 1990s DEC was no longer an effective competitor. The first IBM clone producer, Compaq, and the innovative Sun were beginning to become multi-sectored. The remainder were primarily single-sector enterprises, including the PC path definers Microsoft and Intel.

How, then, did these U.S. and Japanese rivals match up as the Electronic Century began? The U.S. companies had many advantages. In the early 1980s they commercialized the microprocessor and so recast the industry and continued to dominate the industry's leading PC sector for the rest of the century. In addition, Sun, followed by Hewlett-Packard and IBM, had commercialized the new RISC/UNIX technology. In the 1990s these companies, as well as their supporting nexus, led the way in uniting private corporate networks with the public Internet. Silicon Valley was well placed to be again an entrepreneurial seedbed for creating the new hardware and software for the revolutionary Internet-based communications networks, which by the beginning of the new century were radically transforming the ways of commerce, business practices, entertainment, and everyday life. As a result, the Japanese companies remained challengers in IT. Unlike their counterparts in consumer electronics, however, they were not the dominant firms in world markets.

Nevertheless, the Japanese companies did have an advantage—one that may tip the scale in their favor in the early years of the coming Electronic Century. From their initial entrance into world markets in the 1960s and 1970s, all but Fujitsu were producing and marketing both consumer electronics and IT products. That reinforcing coevolution reveals the greatest source of competitive strength of Japan's core companies, the combined supporting nexus.

The Economies of Proximity

The competitive success of what I have termed Japan's "Big Nine"—its five core IT companies—Fujitsu, Hitachi, NEC, Toshiba, and Mitsubishi Electric—and four core consumer electronics companies—Matsushita, Sony, Sharp, and Sanyo—resulted from the fact that these two industries were born and evolved in geographical proximity and in much the same period of time. Their coevolution reinforced the technical and functional capabilities in both sets of industries. They had their beginnings and matured in the relatively concentrated industrial regions of Tokyo and Osaka less than four hours apart by high-speed trains, on the island of Honshu. They evolved in what is, for the historian, a brief period from the late 1960s until the late 1980s. That generation of managers and skilled researchers matured after Japan's crushing defeat in World War II and before the burst of the financial bubble in the early 1980s. They all attended what had become among the world's best engineering schools and enjoyed a high social status.[11]

The primary benefit of this proximity was the growing size and increasing technological sophistication of the two industries' supporting nexus. That nexus first began to grow to meet the needs of the four core consumer electronics firms. Matsushita, Sanyo, and Sharp had headquarters in Osaka, and Sony in Tokyo. By the late 1960s and early 1970s Sony and Matsushita were commercializing superior television and electronic tape-based products, and Sharp those based on the new LCD technology. (By 1975 Sony and Matsushita accounted for just under 14 percent of the U.S. color television market. RCA's share was 19 percent, table 2.1.) Their growth, in turn, led to the rapid expansion of nexus firms such as Pioneer Electric, maker of speakers and other radio and television components, and TDK, which became the world's largest manufacturer of audio- and videotape.

In the same second half of the 1970s, Japan's consumer electronics companies opened up their markets to computer makers. In the critical VCR battle, Matsushita licensed Hitachi, Mitsubishi Electric, and one of the two Sanyo enterprises to market and sell its VHS system. Sony did the same for Toshiba and NEC (table 7.1). At the same time, the computer companies began to produce color televisions for the U.S. and European markets (table 2.1). Although Hitachi over time pulled out of consumer electronics and NEC's sales from consumer electronics remained about 5 percent, Toshiba by the mid-1990s had become the world's only challenger to Sony, Matsushita, and Sharp.

The impact of the computer industry on the growth of the nexus also started in the second half of the 1970s. It began after Gene Amdahl's transfer of the IBM plug-compatible mainframes to Japan permitted its industry after 1975 to become competitive in world markets for the first time. Of greater significance was the explosive growth of the nexus set off by MITI's VLSI project that during the second half of the decade of the 1970s required a vast array of new devices and services. Indeed, Gene Gregory's chapter, "Chip-Making Machinery: The Birth of a Hi-Tech Industry," provides an excellent description of the creation of a supporting nexus in high-technology industries. Many small enterprises, as well as several large ones, began to produce devices for the microlithographic, dry-etching, film deposition, ion-implanting, and other processes. In fact, by 1985 Canon had captured most of the world's market for proximity aligners, water steppers, and other specialty parts.

This explosive growth quickly made Kyocera the world's largest producer of integrated circuit packages and Alps the world's largest producer of floppy disks.[12]

The growth of this unique concentration of the electronic knowledge and organizational capabilities necessary to commercialize new products and processes and to improve existing ones helped propel the swift expansion of Japan's five core computer companies (all headquartered in Tokyo) and four electronics companies into overseas markets. The success of that onslaught, in turn, expanded the size and the capabilities of those core companies and their mutually supporting nexus.

Two Japanese scholars, Masahisa Fujita and Ryoichi Ishii, record the impressive drive Japan's Big Nine made that permitted Japan's industry to conquer the world's consumer electronics markets, to cause the death of Europe's computer industry, and to continue to challenge the U.S. IT industry. Between 1975 and 1985 these nine core companies established 60 domestic plants (17 in Tokyo and Osaka manufacturing areas and 44 in nonmanufacturing areas in what they termed "metropolitan Japan") and 92 plants overseas, as well as 25 R&D laboratories, 21 of them in the Tokyo/Osaka manufacturing area. In the five years from 1985 through 1989 they had built only 21 new plants at home but 125 overseas, as well as 17 overseas laboratories and, possibly more significant, 5 overseas regional headquarters. In these same years, leading nexus firms—Pioneer Electric, TDK, Kyocera, and Alps—made somewhat similar, if smaller, investments in personnel and facilities abroad.[13]

Fujita and Ishii further emphasize the exceptional economies of proximity created by the Big Nine in the Tokyo and Osaka manufacturing areas. By 1994 the Big Nine had dispersed their production plants throughout Japan and in overseas countries. However, their headquarters remained either in Tokyo or Osaka, as did 100 percent of their applied R&D laboratories, 70 percent of their product development laboratories, and 91 percent of their trial production plants. As Fujita and Ishii summarize, "[T]hese knowledge-intensive or information-oriented activities favor close clustering in the primary cities due partly to the convenience of face-to-face communications and more generally to enjoy the agglomeration economies which are generated by accumulated as well as newly created knowledge and information there."

Compare this extraordinary concentration within taxi distance of two railroad stations roughly four hours apart to that of the supporting areas of the U.S. leaders. IBM's headquarters and several research laboratories are centered in New York State. Microsoft is in Seattle, Dell in Austin, Gateway in North Sioux City, South Dakota, and two major semiconductor producers, Texas Instruments and Motorola, are in Houston and near Chicago, respectively. Silicon Valley remained the headquarters for only H-P, Sun, and Intel. Therefore the Japanese Big Nine would appear to have powerful advantages from the economies of proximity relative to their U.S. rivals.

There was one other striking difference between the largest U.S. supporting nexus, Silicon Valley, and that located in the Tokyo/Osaka area. In a study published shortly before this book went to press, *Understanding Silicon Valley*, editor Martin Kenney writes that to understand Silicon Valley means to understand two economies. "Part of Economy One is a dense network of specialized suppliers and often customers supporting the existing firms. . . . Economy Two is populated by organizations whose sole purpose, or a significant component of their business, is related to servicing start-ups. These organizations have evolved to provide the inputs necessary to create a firm de novo." Silicon Valley's second economy has never existed in Japan, nor have multi-industry/multisectored enterprises appeared in Silicon Valley. In the overall evolution of these two electronics industries, the main paths of learning have stemmed from firms with integrated learning bases. Silicon Valley's emphasis on creating new companies may plant the seeds of new technologies but often fails to exploit the long-term potential of those technologies by building integrated learning bases.[14]

This historian's verdict based on the historical findings outlined in chapter 1 is that the Japanese challengers have strong advantages in shaping the infrastructure of the Electronic Century. First, the multisectored, multi-industry enterprises have more of the organizational capabilities and income required to commercialize products of new technologies and to enhance products of existing technologies than do the single-sector enterprises. Second, Japan's economies of proximity and its far-wider range of electronic products and specialized organizational capabilities give the Japanese industry an edge on the development of new and improved hardware systems. These drastic differences certainly will help shape the contours of the continuing evolution of the two industries during the Electronic Century.

If their evolution continues as it has in the past, through the commercializing of new Information Technology hardware and the enhancing of existing ones, then the U.S. industry is handicapped. If, on the other hand, the central innovative thrust in the new Electronic Century is based on exploitation of the revolutionary new ways of communication, broadly defined, then the U.S. enterprises have the advantage. I return to this comparison at the end of the concluding chapter.

8

THE SIGNIFICANCE OF THE EPIC STORY

his concluding chapter on the evolution of the consumer electronics and computer industries worldwide contains two parts. Both parts deal with the unique characteristics of the two industries, a uniqueness that accounts for the epic quality of their evolution. The first part provides a summary of preceeding chapters that ties their contents to the basic concepts outlined in chapter 1. It argues that the first-movers created their industries by establishing integrated learning bases that embodied their technical and functional capabilities. Those learning bases provided the economies of scale and scope, the head start in cumulative proprietary learning, and an assured income that together created powerful barriers to entry. The result was that the numbers of successful core companies remained very few and entrepreneurial start-ups rarely became core companies.

The second part further underlines the uniqueness of this epic story by pointing to the almost complete inability of the leading Japanese enterprises to compete abroad in an older high-technology industry: chemicals and pharmaceuticals. European and U.S. enterprises dominated those two industries throughout the twentieth century. By the end of the century the Japanese companies in chemicals and pharmaceuticals had made almost no investments in facilities and personnel in U.S. and European markets, in stark contrast to the overseas success of their compatriots in consumer electronics and computers. Nor did they export overseas. The explanation for this totally different pattern of national performance across the two sets of high-tech industries provides an introduction to the main themes of book two of this two-volume series on the evolution of high-technology industries. Pointing out the basic underlying differences between the two sets of industries places the story of each in a broader historical perspective.

First-Movers and Barriers to Entry—Semiconductors

As I noted at the end of chapter 1, the uniqueness of the electronics industries was that their evolution rested on four closely related electronic devices—the vacuum tube, the transistor, the integrated circuit, and the microprocessor. From the start, very few enterprises possessed the technical capabilities to commercialize these electronic "engines."

The vacuum tube and transistor were invented in the most technologically advanced industrial research laboratories of the day. The vacuum tube was developed by General Electric in the United States and Siemens in Germany. The Bell Laboratories at AT&T commercialized the transistor, licensing it in 1952.

The integrated circuit and microprocessor were developed not by industrial laboratories, but by manufacturers working with Bell Labs licenses. In 1958 two small Bell Labs licensees—Texas Instruments and Fairchild—commercialized the integrated circuit. TI, a niche enterprise producing instruments to search for oil, built its integrated learning base during the 1930s. Fairchild was founded by William B. Shockley, one of the three inventors of the transistor, and Robert Noyce, who was soon to patent an integrated circuit. But despite these most distinguished inventors, Fairchild failed precisely because its founders were unable to create an integrated learning base. Instead Motorola, a producer of automobile radios established in 1928, became TI's major competitor. A decade later, when Noyce and Gordon Moore left Fairchild to form Intel, they immediately created a learning base in semiconductor memories and then commercialized the first microprocessor. Motorola followed quickly with a comparable achievement.

With the coming of the personal computer and its insatiable demand for microprocessors, the two Silicon Valley start-ups, Advanced Micro Devices and National Semiconductor, joined Intel to become major producers. At the beginning of the new Electronic Century, five firms remained the core U.S. producers of semiconductors.

Their major competitors became the five Japanese computer makers, themselves technological heirs of the U.S. and German first-movers in electrical and telecommunications equipment. The two European leaders, Philips and Siemens, transistor licensees of Bell Labs, fell behind after Sony acquired the Noyce integrated circuit patent for the Japanese computer industry as well as for consumer electronics.

The Japanese industry acquired its powerful competitive strength with the coming of Japan's MITI-sponsored VLSI project. The resulting swift entry into the U.S. DRAM market quickly destroyed the U.S. DRAM producers. The five U.S. producers were then saved by the unprecedented demand for microprocessors created by the mass production of personal computers. Japan's major challenge came, in turn, from Korean multi-industry enterprises. By the end of the century the U.S. companies dominated the microprocessor industry, while the Japanese and Korean companies dominated memories. Thus, except for the three thirty-year-old Silicon Valley semiconductor companies that emerged during the initial rapid growth of the computer industry, the core semiconductor producers have all been long-established enterprises. Other U.S. entrepreneurial start-ups have remained relatively small, specialized nexus producers.

First-Movers and Barriers to Entry—Consumer Electronics

The consumer electronics industry began with the continuous wave technology that emerged from the world's most technologically advanced research laboratories, those of the first-movers in the electrical and telecommunications industries. In Europe the functional learning required to commercialize the radio was developed at Telefunken, the joint venture of the two dominant electrical equipment companies, Siemens and AEG. RCA, a comparable joint venture, became the leader in the United States, but until 1930 the initial functional learning in production and marketing remained at General Electric and Westinghouse, two of the companies that created RCA. RCA acquired its integrated learning base only after the acquisition of Victor Talking Machine in 1930.

The introduction of the continuous wave technology did lead to an outburst of radio receiving sets and components manufacturers. In the early 1920s over six hundred new enterprises entered the market within a four-year span, but nearly all disappeared quickly. By 1940 ten companies accounted for close to 75 percent of sales of receiving sets. Of these, all but two were established companies in related electrical equipment industries, companies that had already integrated their functional capabilities into a learning base. The same was true of a smaller number of component makers. From the industry's beginning, long-lived entrepreneurial start-ups were very few.

In the 1930s the list of companies in Europe with the technical and functional capabilities required for the commercializing of radio's follow-up, television, had narrowed to Telefunken. The outbreak of war in 1939 ended Telefunken's commercializing capabilities. In the United States, after the creation of RCA's integrated learning base, it became the primary path definer in consumer electronics, followed by Philco and Columbia Broadcasting System. In 1941 RCA launched the first commercial television program. After a wartime hiatus, RCA announced in 1946 that it would license its improved postwar model, which became the industry's standard.

Sales of black-and-white television sets soared in the late 1940s. Again a sizable number of existing enterprises and entrepreneurial new ones entered and began producing receiving sets and components. But with one exception (Admiral), no major new competitors emerged. The barriers to entry had become too formidable. By the mid-1950s seven established producers accounted for 86 percent of the U.S. market for televisions. All but one had been among the leaders in radio products the 1930s.

Next came the commercializing of the industry's follow-up product, color television. Preparations for this had begun in the 1930s, again with RCA as the primary path definer. Philco, CBS, and then Zenith followed in the late 1940s. In Europe World War II had destroyed Telefunken's learning base. The war had forced Philips's managers to move to Britain and then the United States, thereby breaking up its integrated learning base. After the war Philips restored its integrated capabilities in Europe and moved ahead by licensing RCA technology, as did the Japanese first movers, Matsushita and Sony, in these same years.

The final steps of the commercializing of color television during the 1950s brought an exceptionally complex technical challenge. CBS, Philco, and Zenith dropped out of the race. RCA persevered, bringing onstream a most impressive technological achievement. By the mid-1960s Philips, by licensing RCA's television technology and, in turn, by providing that technology to Matsushita (in which Philips held 35 percent equity), enhanced the technical capabilities of both companies. Sony also benefited. But with its innovative miniaturization and tape capabilities, it was becoming a significant path definer in its own right. By then only four enterprises worldwide had the capabilities to commercialize products of new technologies—RCA, Philips, Matsushita, and Sony.

In the late 1960s RCA self-destructed. It turned from a virtuous path of success, using the learning achieved and income earned from the commercializing of one product to commercialize the next product. Lured by IBM's success in mainframes, RCA attempted to produce a comparable product line but failed because of its lack of learned functional capabilities, those in production and above all in marketing. At the same time, it became a conglomerate, attempting to manage activities of separate and often large enterprises in which its senior executives had little or no management experience. An attempt to manage "by the numbers" proved to be more disastrous than its computer try.

Then came the epic clash for world markets in the commercializing of the industry's next product, the VCR (videocassette recorder), whose market had been created by skyrocketing worldwide sales of color television. Matsushita won that battle among the industry's four giants on the basis of its impressive functional capabilities. Matsushita strategically opened up production and distribution of its products to a select few Japanese consumer electronics and computer producers. Thereby Matsushita created significant barriers to entry and turned the rest of the consumer electronics industry worldwide into mere retail outlets for its VHS.

Sony and Philips lost the battle, but because of their technical capabilities—and Matsushita's lack thereof—they continued to define the industry's paths of learning. At the same time, the defeat marked RCA's death and with it that of the U.S. consumer electronics industry. Shortly after GE acquired RCA, GE's CEO quickly sold the consumer electronics unit to France's Thomson and turned RCA's Princeton Laboratories over to Stanford University.

That left the world's applied research in audio and video technologies to Sony and Philips. Together they commercialized the CD in 1982 and introduced the CD-ROM the next year. Then came the disaster that led to the downfall of the Philips electronics research laboratories. Those laboratories, working with the firm's functional departments, developed a television-based counterpart to Sony's computer-based CD-ROM, the CD-interactive. But it failed commercially, incurring a loss of over $1 billion. This development failure was then followed by even larger market share and financial losses, which resulted ironically from Philips's inability to compete in consumer electronics in Europe against Sony, its research partner, and Matsushita, which had long relied on Philips for technical knowledge and applied research. To be sure, Philips and Sony did continue to work on commercializing the next major product, the DVD. But then Philips, without the funds necessary to invest in facilities to produce the DVD, withdrew from the consumer electronics industry.

Sony's domination of the world's consumer electronics industry in the 1990s exemplifies success in these epic battles as much as RCA's experience exemplifies failure. Sony's record from the 1950s to the 1990s is historically unsurpassed. It repeatedly commercialized new technologies on the basis of learning and funding produced by the previous try. The one exception was its move into the entertainment business, but even here it could afford to stay on until the necessary learning had been achieved. Matsushita, which by choice did not develop its technical capabilities, was no longer a path definer. Nevertheless, by continuing to follow its basic strategy of entering related industries where its long-tested functional capabilities gave it a strong competitive advantage, it followed another virtuous path. It turned its capabilities from consumer electronics to industrial and telecommunications electronics.

By 1996 Sony competed now only with its Japanese brethren. Sharp had an increasingly versatile learning base by the early 1970s, as did the computer company Toshiba by the early 1990s. The nexus firms such as TDK and Kyocera had growing comparable technical and functional capabilities embedded in integrated learning bases. The Japanese industry's world conquest permitted these suppliers and other specialized electronics producers, such as the video-game companies, to become the core companies in their global markets.

What, then, does this historical story imply about the future? The historical evidence is overwhelming. To bring to market the products of different technologies mentioned in this chapter required not only highly specialized technical knowledge embedded in an integrated learning base, but also extended time of concentrated study before new products reached world markets. Thus existing enterprises, not start-ups, generate the process of evolution. Therefore, the critical question is that since the U.S. and European industries no longer have lost their technical and functional capabilities to commercialize products from new consumer electronics technologies, can those industries of East Asia build the integrated learning bases required to become effective challengers?

First-Movers and Barriers to Entry–Computers

The evolution of the computer industry followed a very different pattern from that of consumer electronics. It did so because of IBM's historically unique evolution as the industry's path definer from the industry's beginnings in the 1950s until the 1990s. IBM's challengers had to create their competitive integrated learning bases within an existing IBM framework.

IBM did not become the industry's path definer and protagonist in this computer epic by inventing a new computer technology. It did so by integrating the new electronics technology with the company's long-established functional capabilities learned as the dominant first-mover in the production of punched-card tabulators, then the most sophisticated of data-processing machinery. As a result, IBM acquired close to 80 percent of the world's computer market with its 650 computer within less than a decade after its introduction in 1954.

But IBM was not the first. James Rand, the chief executive of the world's largest office machinery company, envisioned the computer's commercial potential even before the introduction of the transistor. He moved quickly to obtain control of the new industry. By 1952 Remington Rand had acquired two of the four pioneering computing enterprises. Together they included most of the world's knowledge and experience in computing. But Rand's vision collapsed because his company failed to integrate the required technical knowledge with a set of functional organizational capabilities necessary to reach the new commercial computer market.

IBM, with the profits and learning from the 650 and its successor, moved a step further with the commercialization of its System 360, a family of compatible mainframes. The System 360 required nearly half a decade of intense development work and cost $5 billion to $6 billion. In addition to greatly expanding the industry's technical knowledge, the introduction of the System 360 radically recast and defined the evolution of the computer industry in three distinct ways.

First, IBM became a primary source for creating the supporting nexus. Both existing enterprises and entrepreneurial start-ups began to produce IBM plug-compatible components and "unbundled" packaged software. I return to this point shortly.

Second, Gene Amdahl, the designer of the System 360 and its successor, the System 370, after failing to raise the $40 million in the United States to produce his own plug-compatible computer, carried it to Japan. Japanese companies became competitive only after they began producing IBM plug-compatibles in volume for their own growing market. Then, after three European companies failed in a joint effort to commercialize a plug-compatible machine, the Japanese companies began to supply Europe with its large systems.

The third impact of the System 360 was that, after IBM defined the primary paths of learning for commercial computing, the only opportunities for new entrants was outside IBM's dominance of mainstream commercial computing. Consequently two enterprises created their own new paths of learning on each side of the price and performance sector carved out by the System 360. William Norris's Control Data entered the high side with its costly supercomputer. On the low side was Ken Olsen's stripped-down PDP minicomputer at DEC. The latter met the demands of a larger engineering and scientific market than that for supercomputers. Both founders had been involved in computers since the industry's very beginning and were among its most knowledgeable practitioners. They provide relatively rare examples of successful entrepreneurial start-ups.

Clearly, as table 4.2 shows, the barriers to entry in the first three decades of the computer industry were high and had been high from the very start. With the exception of Control Data, IBM's major competitors were either office machinery companies or Japanese producers of IBM plug-compatibles.

The exception, Control Data, illustrates the experience needed by entrepreneurial start-ups to overcome existing barriers. The founder, William Norris, frustrated as head of Remington Rand's new computer division, had departed to form Control Data. There he built, through acquisition and internal investment, a strong integrated learning base in a high-priced niche. Its only significant competitor was Cray Research, established by Norris's chief designer, Seymour Cray.

The nature of the followers in the minicomputer path illustrates a common pattern of industry evolution. All, with one exception, were existing computer companies or were established by experienced computer executives. These followers are listed on table 4.2. The first was Data General, established in 1969 by Olsen's chief designer, Ed de Castro. The others had established their bases by 1974. The computer companies included IBM and three other mainframe makers. In addition, Hewlett-Packard, Wang Laboratories, and Germany's Nixdorf had already built their integrated learning bases in related product lines. Prime and Tandem, both founded by executives in computer companies producing for the government market, provide examples of entrepreneurial start-ups. On the other hand, Harris Corporation, a maker of printing presses and lighting equipment, which had just made a major move into electronics, soon withdrew from the computer industry.

Although the first-movers and their initial followers created formidable barriers to entry in the data-processing industry's mainframe and minicomputer paths of learning, the booming growth of the industry after the full-scale introduction of the IBM System 360 and DEC's PDP-8 created opportunities for a plethora of small and medium-size companies to enter the computer industry's supporting nexus. They were producers of wide varieties of components and other hardware and packaged software, much of which became available as a result of the U.S. government antitrust actions against IBM, as described in chapter 4.

IBM's mass production and mass distribution of the personal computer in the early 1980s was an even more historically unique event than the commercializing of the System 360, for it transformed commercial computing and opened a new computer market, the home. The consequences were profound. It created a multibillion-dollar mass consumer market with few barriers to entry. Existing companies and a host of start-ups entered the market, producing some two hundred IBM clones. Additionally, a new sector appeared overnight, that of application software. And in so doing, it warded off the Japanese challenge and gave the U.S. industry worldwide dominance once again.

At the same time, the PC almost destroyed IBM and the mainframe industry it had created. Except for IBM, the U.S. mainframe producers collapsed. The multisectored IBM, like the multi-industry, multisectored Japanese companies, continued to serve the much reduced large systems market, one that would become a base for meeting the expanded demands for computing power of the 1990s.

The personal computer quickly became the industry's leading sector. Even so, few of the two hundred clones that poured in between 1981 and 1985 became leading products. By 1994, only six startup PC producers remained on *Datamation*'s Global 100. Each had established its learning base by 1986. Moreover, of the producers of proprietary operating systems, only Apple remained.

Because every PC clone had to use an Intel chip and a Microsoft operating system, these two companies became the path definers of what had now become the IT industry. No start-ups challenged them effectively. As pointed out, Intel's major competitors remained its two thirty-year-old Silicon Valley neighbors; and Texas Instruments and Motorola, both over fifty years old.

In software, Microsoft enjoyed even more than Intel the benefits of economies of scope as well as scale. Through its increasing control over application software because of its operating system strength, Microsoft became the dominant enterprise in the new software sector. It was in this brand-new application software sector that entrepreneurial start-ups flourished. Again, the first-movers in that sector enjoyed competitive advantages. By 1994 (table 5.1 in chapter 5) six of the top ten revenue producers in applications were entrepreneurial start-ups; all had created their learning bases by 1985.

The microprocessor transformed the minicomputer path in a much less radical manner than it did the mainframe path. For the makers of minicomputers used the new microprocessor RISC chip and the UNIX operating system to produce workstations for their existing specialized engineering and scientific markets. The innovator in the workstation technology was a startup, Sun Microsystems. But its followers were existing computer enterprises, with the exception of Silicon Graphics, the commercializer of a profitable niche product, three-dimensional graphics.

In this workstation sector, the most significant long-term development was the quick entrance of the four leading Japanese computer makers (table 7.2 in chapter 7). By 1996 these four seventy-year-old enterprises challenged the three U.S. leaders, IBM, Hewlett-Packard, and Compaq. Supported by their continued success in large systems, they were making their second challenge to the U.S. industry. Their overall success then allowed them to become leaders in both desktops and software.

The personal computer sector, with its phenomenal growth and its closely related applications software sector, was primarily responsible for the continuing rapid expansion of the supporting nexus and the industry's many smaller and medium-size firms. The numbers and variety of enterprises supporting the U.S. personal computer industry expanded not only in Silicon Valley, but also in East Asia, particularly Taiwan.

Their number, along with a description of the many niches and services offered, is given in *Hoover's Guide to Computer Companies*. Its 1996 edition has a separate section entitled "Selected Industry Players," which provides basic standard data on 141 companies. Relatively few of these had annual sales equivalent to the one hundredth company on the 1996 *Datamation's* Global 100 list of IT enterprises, Adobe Systems, which had $787 million. The large majority had sales from $100 million to $500 million.

Industry Evolution as a Classical Epic Drama

One way to emphasize the uniqueness or the evolution of the consumer electronics and computer industries is to depict their story in the manner of a classic epic. In Greek drama, the gods set the stage for human action but the Fates often intervened to alter the course of events. In this epic drama there are two major protagonists, both U.S. companies that shaped their industries worldwide. One protagonist, IBM, follows the virtuous path of learning for maintaining the long-term profitability and growth of the enterprise. The other protagonist, RCA, after succeeding by taking the virtuous path, is lured away and falls from grace. By the 1960s each is challenged by smaller, more agile Japanese enterprises, which acquire IBM and RCA learning. IBM comes through the ensuing competitive battle with historically unprecedented success. RCA's deviation leads to its own self-destruction and that of its national industry.

From the beginnings of the computer industry in the 1950s until the end of the century, IBM remains the industry's giant. In the early years its revenues are over two and a half times the total revenues of the rest of its U.S. competitors. At the end of the century its revenues are two and a half times that of its nearest competitor, Hewlett-Packard, and its net income as a percent of sales is slightly larger than that of HP. Its initial success rests on the virtuous path that it had followed in its punched-card business, that of using the learning and income from the commercializing of a previous project to introduce a new one. The 650, a vacuum tube–based general-purpose stored program computer, is followed by the transistor-based 1400. The resulting learning and revenues leads to the world-dominating Systems 360 and 370; however, their successor, the Future Systems, fails. Here complexity is the fatal flaw. The Greek term is *hubris*. IBM tries to do too much. Learning from their mistake, IBM's managers turn to enhancing their company's capabilities in the industry's other sectors: minicomputers, peripherals, software, and services.

Then the Fates intervened. First, one of IBM's own senior managers is instrumental in making the Japanese industry a viable competitor. Next, the Japanese industry makes a crushing attack on the U.S. memory chip business. But at that same moment IBM unintentionally rescues the U.S. industry by mass-producing and mass-marketing a product first commercialized by youthful hobbyists. It does so almost at the cost of its own life. In the process, again unintentionally, it turns two of its suppliers, selected by middle-level managers, into the industry's path definers in the U.S. PC sector, which quickly dominates the industry worldwide. Nevertheless, IBM survives and in 1996 remains the industry giant.

On the other hand, by 1996 RCA, the protagonist in the U.S. consumer electronics industry, pays the ultimate price for leaving the virtuous path: it dies, and so does the U.S. industry. In the 1960s RCA achieves world dominance comparable to IBM's and does so by following the same virtuous path. But then it turns to a false path where it lives on hope more than on learning. First, it challenges IBM despite having little in the way of learned capabilities—some in product development, but certainly none in production or, particularly, marketing. Second, it turns to acquiring enterprises in which its managers have no learning at all. In terms of the Greek epic, RCA is lured by the Sirens from the business press, the academy, and Wall Street to the rocks of corporate disaster.

As a result, the Japanese, as exemplars of two different virtuous paths of learning, conquer world markets. Sony relies on continuing product development based on technical capabilities, while Matsushita turns to new product lines with its functional capabilities.

Again, the gods set the stage and the Fates alter the course of events. In both industries the gods are government officials—middle-level bureaucrats in the U.S. Justice Department's antitrust division. In the late 1950s, just as the inventing of the Electronic Century begins, the antitrust division signs consent decrees that settle antitrust suits with the two protagonists: with IBM in 1956 and with RCA in 1958. The consent decree with IBM is not on computers, but on punched-card tabulators. By that decree IBM agrees to sell, as well as lease, punched-card tabulators.

But the decree's critical provision is that IBM agrees to license existing and future patents to any person making a written application. As a result, the wide range of peripherals and other hardware devices invented or improved during the commercializing of the System 360 and then the System 370 become available to all. In 1969 the threat of a second antitrust suit leads IBM's senior managers to "unbundle" its software, making IBM software available for IBM-compatible hardware. But this in itself is not enough to build a competitive IBM-compatible system. Then, the Fate's see to it that Gene Amdahl, unable to raise $40 million of venture capital, turns to Fujitsu. With IBM plug-compatible mainframes, the Japanese industry quickly dominates the Japanese and then the European markets. This mainframe success in the 1980s allows for Japan's achievements in servers in the 1990s.

The 1958 consent decree with RCA comes at a critical moment in the consumer electronics industry's history. That decree ends the 1924 packaged license agreement with the Federal Trade Commission that had opened up RCA's patents to all applicants on the condition they buy a full package of all such patents, even if only one was desired. By the 1958 consent decree, domestic customers are to get their licenses without charge. Foreign buyers, however, must continue to pay a full price. Since the RCA Princeton Laboratory's income comes primarily from licensing, their products go to foreign makers before domestic ones. Thus the consent decree force-feeds the maturing of Japan's and Europe's (Philips) color television sectors. For example, on the basis of this technology, Sony commercializes its Trinitron television tube, which replaces the RCA tricolor tube, briefly hailed as a symbol of U.S. mass production (see chapter 3).

The point of closing this epic story of consumer electronics and computers with the role of the gods and the Fates is that the evolution of both industries was profoundly affected by outside factors. In the absence of these forces, RCA would have still self-destructed. But the Japanese industry certainly benefited from the gifts of the gods in the form of the consent decree. And the Fates did profoundly shape the evolution of the computer industry.

If Gene Amdahl had been able to raise $40 million in the United States, the Japanese industry would have had to overcome the same barriers to entry that thwarted the European companies and GE and RCA in their attempts to compete with the IBM 360 and 370. Never has the shaping of a major national industry rested on a comparable transaction, especially one that involved such a relatively small amount of money.

Differences between the Evolution of Consumer Electronics and Computers and that of Chemicals and Pharmaceuticals

The epic and unique nature of these two electronics industries is further demonstrated by comparing them to another set of high-technology industries, chemicals and pharmaceuticals. The story of their evolution was just the reverse of the two electronics industries. The national industries of Europe, particularly those of Germany and Switzerland, led the way before World War I. They were followed by those of the United States, but the Japanese enterprises never became players during the twentieth century. Japan's chemical companies made almost no direct investment in facilities or personnel in the United States and Europe, nor did its pharmaceutical companies. The pharmaceutical companies did have technical agreements with Western firms, but their foreign direct investment was tiny. In 1988 their exports ranked thirteenth, just behind Bulgaria.[1]

So I conclude book one of this two-book series by asking this question: Why were the Japanese chemical and pharmaceutical industries unable to enter the U.S. and European markets, while their compatriots in consumer electronics and computers did so successfully? Clearly these successes and failures cannot be explained by national cultural or institutional reasons. There are two answers to this question. One emphasizes historical timing, the other emphasizes once again the uniqueness of the electronics story and how that story differs from those of leading high-technology industries of the Industrial Century. This comparison of the evolution of the chemical and pharmaceutical industries introduces themes of book two.

DIFFERENCES IN HISTORICAL TIMING OF JAPANESE DEVELOPMENT

One important difference between chemicals and pharmaceuticals on the one hand and consumer electronics and computers on the other concerns the structure of the Japanese economy at the time of each industry's early development of barriers to entry.

The basic infrastructure of the chemical and pharmaceutical industries — and, hence, the barriers to entry — had been completed by the 1920s. For example, forty-eight of the fifty largest chemical companies in the 1990s in the United States were established before the 1930s. The youngest two entered in 1932 and 1940. Much the same was true of pharmaceuticals, though it occurred somewhat later in time.

Moreover, as the chemical and pharmaceutical industries were being built in Europe and the United States, Japan's industrialists and government officials were occupied with the building of a comprehensive industrial infrastructure to transform their feudal society into a modern one. Japanese enterprises were both too far behind technologically and too busy meeting the unprecedented demands of industrializing within the space of a generation to attempt to enter and compete globally in such high-technology industries as chemicals and pharmaceuticals.

Furthermore, a critical instrument in this economic development was the *zaibatsu*, a group of firms in several industries — metals, machinery, transportation equipment, electrical equipment, and others — as well as a bank and trading company under the control of a single headquarters. Membership in a *zaibatsu* had two important effects on these enterprises. First, they remained single-sector enterprises. Product diversification happened at the *zaibatsu* level, not at the level of the individual enterprise. Second, the strategies and structures of these industrial enterprises were defined by the central needs of the *zaibatsu* group. After World War II, as *zaibatsu* members, Japanese chemical companies were hindered in their ability to compete internationally. These constraints continued to hinder their ability to catch up. Each of Japan's five largest chemical companies were members of a *zaibatsu*. Three — Mitsubishi Chemicals, Sumitomo Chemicals, and Mitsui Chemicals — were descendants of the initial transformers of Japan's infrastructure at the beginning of the century. The remaining two — Showa Danko and Ube Industries — had their beginnings only in the 1920s.[2]

By contrast, the first-movers in electronics had begun to build their industries' infrastructure only by the 1950s. And during this period Japan's consumer electronics companies, Sony and Matsushita, had no connections with a *zaibatsu*. Moreover, in computers, only two, Mitsubishi Electric and Fujitsu, had an initial tie with a *zaibatsu*, and Fujitsu quickly loosened its ties. Two other computer makers, NEC and Toshiba, received their technologies and financing from U.S. companies, the former from AT&T and the latter from GE. Even so, because of the barriers that IBM created so quickly, it took the Fates, and especially Gene Amdahl, to make the Japanese computer industry competitive.

A COMPARISON OF THE TWO SETS OF INDUSTRIES

Nevertheless, the contrasting evolution of the two sets of industries stems from more than just differences in the timing and structure of Japanese economic development. More fundamental were the basic differences between the two sets of industries, differences that emphasize once again the uniqueness of electronics. In chemicals and pharmaceuticals there were *many more* multisectored, multi-industry core companies commercializing and enhancing a larger number of products based on *many more* multiple basic technologies. As a result, when one company failed, its national industry did not die; several other companies were in place to carry the industry along. Nor did a single enterprise shape the industry in the manner of IBM and RCA. So there were no epic stories comparable to that of consumer electronics and computers. Here I make no attempt to do more than point out the basic differences in the evolution of these two industries in the briefest manner.

From their very beginnings, the German and Swiss first-movers were exploiting the potentials of organic chemistry to commercialize synthetic dyes, drugs, and film, each having three very different types of markets. At the same time, other German and U.S. firms were using the new electrolytic technologies to commercialize a wide range of products based on inorganic chemistries, including not only basic chemicals, but also metals, such as aluminum; other end products, such as acetylene and liquid oxygen; and even devices that used their chemicals, such as welding and cutting machinery. The polymer-petrochemical revolution set off by World War II led both chemical and petroleum companies to commercialize a wide variety of synthetic products that replaced the existing markets for natural materials— cotton, wool, silk, wood, and stone—and created a new industry, plastics, that offered a wide range of specialized and nonspecialized products for an even greater number of markets.

So too, pharmaceuticals were transformed by a series of new medical technologies commercialized simultaneously by several core companies. Early in the twentieth century, the first chemically made drugs replaced those derived from natural materials, and new scientific knowledge in microbiology and immunology led to the creation of entirely new drugs. Another wave of innovations came in the 1940s with the discovery of penicillin and other antibiotics. One result was that between 1929 and 1969 prescription drugs rose from 29 percent to 83 percent of consumer expenditures on medical drugs. Then in the 1970s and 1980s came molecular modeling, recombinant DNA, and genetic engineering.

An evolving stratification across product lines emerged out of the competition between the core companies in these three major industrial categories—chemicals, petroleum, and pharmaceuticals. The petroleum companies came to dominate the primary feedstocks and basic chemicals markets. Core chemical companies moved into a broader range of higher-value, more specialized chemicals. And several chemical companies, after the 1980s, moved into the pharmaceutical industry, with some spinning off their chemical activities altogether.

I have included two tables, appendices 8.1 and 8.2, to illustrate the point that in chemicals and pharmaceuticals, more companies, using more technologies, produced a larger number of products for a wider range of markets than was the case in the industries of this book.

Appendix 8.1 lists the fifty largest producers of industrial chemicals in the United States in 1993, which altogether accounted for 80 percent of output. In chemicals there were eighteen U.S. core companies. These eighteen core companies competed not only with each other, but with foreign companies, of which ten are listed on appendix 8.1. Another set of twelve competitors were the world's largest producers of petroleum. In addition, three enterprises, whose primary activities were in other manufacturing industries, had built integrated learning bases in chemicals. Aside from the two of the fifty core companies founded after the 1920s, the only new entrants are four spin-offs from existing companies. Finally, three conglomerates had acquired major chemical companies.

Appendix 8.2 lists the thirty largest pharmaceutical enterprises in the world in 1993. Here there are ten U.S. core companies with revenues larger than Sun Microsystems, #20 in *Datamation's* Global 100 list. Among the top thirty pharmaceutical producers are seven chemical companies (one U.S. and six non-U.S., all are listed in appendix 8.1) as well as two U.S. enterprises that are major consumer products producers.

The same firms that pioneered in commercializing these technologies also invented and continued to perfect the multidivisional organizational structure to manage their increasingly diversified product lines. The M-form, as that structure became known, permitted the enterprise to realize the potential of both its technical learning and its functional capabilities. The managers of the operating divisions, with their product development, production, and marketing departments, were responsible for the division's performance. In essence, the M-form created an integrated learning base for each major product line. Central headquarters included senior executives accountable for the performance of the enterprise as a whole and a corporate staff that acted as a liaison and provided services to both the operating divisions and the general executives. These staff units usually included departments for finance, legal affairs, personnel, and, most important of all, advanced research. In this way a corporation gained efficiency from the full use of its resources through scale and diversification and handled the resulting complexity through the operational decentralization of the multidivisional structure.

In meeting these strategic issues, senior executives had to consider the status and the intentions of a sizable number of competitors, not only those in their own industry, but also those in related sectors and industries; and not only those at home, but also those abroad. An evaluation of the success of this strategic planning process provides a central theme for book two of this series. Clearly the assessment of competitors was far less complex for the managers in the consumer electronics and computer industries. In the former, the managers of the leading four Japanese enterprises, three of whom were headquartered in Osaka, had only to evaluate the competitive potential of RCA and Philips, as well as each other. In computers, the managers of the Japanese Big Five, all headquartered in Tokyo, had to appraise the strategies primarily of IBM, H-P, Compaq, Sun, Intel, and Microsoft—just as the strategic concerns of the U.S. enterprises just listed involved examining the activities of each other at home and the Big Five abroad.

The Industrial Century and the Electronic Century Compared

Appendix 8.3, "Founding Dates of the 1994 Fortune 500 Companies," reinforces the messages of appendices 8.1 and 8.2. Business enterprises do not necessarily follow the human cycle of birth, growth, maturity, decline, and death. Once the first-movers and their immediate followers established their integrated learning bases, the barriers to entry became high enough to assure continuing dominance (unless they deserted the virtuous path of growth, as did RCA). As appendix 8.3 illustrates, of the Fortune 500 in 1994 (including financial services, retailing, utilities, transportation, and services, as well as industrial firms), almost half (248, to be exact) had been established during the half-century between the 1880s and the 1920s. Less than 20 percent were established after 1950. The decades from 1880 through 1920 were those in which the core chemical and pharmaceutical companies were established. Eight of the Japanese Big Nine were established in the first three decades of the twentieth century, and Sony in the fifth.

Appendix 8.3 makes a major historical statement. The industries created during the Industrial Century were not replaced by those that laid the foundations for the Electronic Century, as represented by the Fortune 500 companies and the industries in which they were leaders. But their ways of operation were transformed by the revolutionary audio, video, and information technologies whose evolution has been the subject of this book. The combination of these industrial and electronic technologies has produced what was termed at the beginning of the twenty-first century as the "New Economy."

In this New Economy the Japanese have historical advantages. They have had long experience in the operation of established industries and in commercializing the new electronic technologies. In addition, they are doubly advantaged by the mutually reinforcing nature of their nexuses. In the single Tokyo-Osaka industrial district there exists both a computer industry nexus as well as the world's only remaining consumer electronics nexus. The United States, of course, has no such comparable nexus. Even its IT leaders are dispersed throughout the nation.

On the other hand, as the Electronic Century begins, the U.S. IT industry appears to possess the advantage in software and services. Well before the beginning of the new century, the computer had become the transmitter of audio, video, and written information. The resulting New Economy has created two new sets of demands for software and services. For one, the privatizing of the Internet and its opening to commercial use in 1995 created unparalleled opportunities for entrepreneurial start-ups of all varieties, with almost no entry barriers. The number of hosts rose from 2.2 million in 1994 to 5.8 million in 1995 and to 93 million five years later. The resulting entrepreneurial opportunities far exceed those created by the coming of IBM's mass-marketed personal computers. Here the United States has the powerful advantage of a large venture capital industry. The second demand stems from the opportunities, and indeed necessities, for reconfiguring almost every aspect of the operation of industrial age enterprises, as represented by the Fortune 500 companies. This transformation will require a wide range of new software and services.

So as the Electronic Century opens, historical findings indicate that the Japanese will retain the advantage in commercializing new and enhancing existing hardware systems. But the United States will have the advantage in commercializing the software and services needed to exploit fully the new hardware technologies. Europe's computer industry, too, might again become viable in these two sectors. In any case, at the beginning of the new century, the United States and Europe remain Japan's primary market, as they had been during the previous century.

Appendices

[1]Tables and charts essential for understanding the text are placed in the text. Those in the Appendix provide supporting and documenting data.

APPENDIX 2.1. Estimated Number of Radio Sets
Sold by Major U.S. Companies in 1940

Company	Thousands of Sets	Percent of Total
1 RCA	1,700	14
2 Philco	1,675	14
3 Zenith	1,050	9
4 Emerson (mostly midget sets)	1,050	9
5 Galvin (Motorola)	950	8
6 Colonial (for Sears, Roebuck)	650	5
7 Belmont	550	5
8 Noblitt Sparks	400	3
9 GE	350	3
10 Crosley	350	3
Top 10 Total	8,725	74
11 Stewart-Warner	250	2
12 Simplex	250	2
13 Electrical Research Laboratories	250	2
14 Sonora	200	2
15 Wells Gardiner (for Montgomery Ward)	200	2
16 Detrola	175	1
17 Farnsworth	100	1
18 Sparks Worthington	100	1
All others	1,584	13
Grand Total	11,834	100

Source: W. Rupert Maclaurin, *Invention and Innovation in the Radio Industry* (New York: Macmillan Company, 1949), p. 146, with permission. Figures include exports.

APPENDIX 2.2. RCA Revenues, 1971–1975 (figures in millions of dollars)

	1971	1972	1973	1974	1975	Percent Change
Consumer Electronics	968	1,098	1,149	1,130	1,171	21%
Commercial Electronics	476	531	644	671	609	28%
Broadcasting	566	611	684	725	796	41%
Hertz	597	636	677	722	715	20%
Communications	118	137	165	195	234	98%
Government Business	423	396	381	356	355	–16%
Other	397	454	581	828	936	136%
	3,545	3,863	4,281	4,627	4,816	36%

RCA Net Profits, 1971–1975 (figures in millions of dollars)

	1971	1972	1973	1974	1975	Percent Change
Consumer Electronics	53.7	57.7	48.0	11.1	25.2	–53%
Commercial Electronics	0.2	11.7	25.8	(7.4)	(48.3)	–
Broadcasting	26.3	36.0	47.7	48.3	52.1	98%
Hertz	10.1	15.4	19.3	23.2	27.4	171%
Communications	11.7	13.6	18.2	25.7	31.2	167%
Government Business	5.0	3.4	3.3	3.7	3.3	–34%
Other	21.7	20.3	21.4	8.7	19.0	–12%
Extraordinary Charges	(244.5)	–	–	–	–	–
	(115.9)	158.1	183.7	113.3	110.0	–

Source: RCA, 1975 annual report

Note: Consumer Electronics includes radio and television sets, video and audio players, and audio records. Commercial Electronics includes TV tubes and components, electronic equipment for broadcasting, and communications systems. Broadcasting includes NBC network TV and radio services to individual stations. Hertz includes the Hertz vehicle renting and related services. Communications includes businesses of furnishing overseas voice and record communications services. Government Business includes a variety of military-related communications and instrumentation services. Other includes the production of tufted carpet.

APPENDIX 3.1. U.S. Exports and Imports of Major Consumer Electronics Products, 1965–1990 ($1,000)

	Home Radios		Color Television		Videotape Recorders	
	Exports	Imports	Exports	Imports	Exports	Imports
1965	5,274	125,103	a	a		
1970	4,007	305,227	17,755	141,858	16,651	8,779
1975	4,877	374,561	50,012	220,751	44,735	34,931
1980	20,718	486,304	276,983	311,785	76,087	498,333
1985	13,986	609,763	85,806	1,113,770	68,798	4,165,103
1990	35,217	506,777	423,108	1,659,132	a	4,223,254

Source: U.S. Bureau of the Census, Statistical Abstract of the United States, and Electronic Industry Association, for the selected years. Exports include units produced by Japanese- and European-owned plants in the United States.

a Not separately reported.

APPENDIX 4.1. The Two Paths of Computing:
A Chronology of the U.S. Computer Industry

<u>Legend</u>:
▲ Organizational Development (founding, acquisition, etc.)
● Product Introduction
▼ Technological Development
◆ Other (Government action, misc.)

Year	Commercial & Home Computing	Shared Technologies: Semiconductors & Networking	Scientific/Engineering Computing
The Early Years			
1946			▼ Eckert & Mauchly of U. of Penn. deliver ENIAC
1947			▼ Aiken of Harvard delivers Mark1
1950			▼ ERA delivers its Atlas
1951			▼ Forrester of MIT completes Whirlwind simulator
			● Eckert & Mauchly (Sperry Rand) deliver UNIVAC I to U.S. Census Bureau
1952		◆ AT&T licenses transistor technology	
1953			● December 1952, IBM introduces the 701, the Defense Calculator
1954	● IBM introduces "computing's Model T," the 650		
1956	◆ IBM negotiates consent decree with DOJ, hastening shift from punch cards to computers		
1957		▲ Fairchild Semiconductor founded	
1959		▼ TI's Kilby and Fairchild's Noyce patent the integrated circuit	
1960	● IBM introduces 1401, transistor-powered with a range of peripherals		
1961	● IBM begins planning the System 360		● DEC introduces PDP
			▲ SDS founded

APPENDIX 4.1. (*Continued*)

Year	Commercial & Home Computing	Shared Technologies: Semiconductors & Networking	Scientific/Engineering Computing
The Data-Processing Era, 1960s–1970s			
1962			● Control Data announces first supercomputer, 6600
1963			● DEC introduces PDP-5
1964	● IBM announces System 360		
1965	● IBM releases first products in 360 family		● DEC introduces PDP-8, its "initial masterpiece"—the first mass-produced minicomputer ● SDS delivers SDS910
1967	● IBM System 360 reaches full output	▲ National Semiconductor moves to Silicon Valley	
1968		▲ Robert Noyce and Gordon Moore found Intel	▲ Ed de Castro leaves DEC to found Data General
1969	◆ IBM unbundles software and services in response to DOJ suit	▲ AMD founded ▼ ARPANET funded	▼ Bell Labs develops UNIX operating system
1970	● IBM announces System 370 ▲ GE sells computer business to Honeywell ▲ Gene Amdahl leaves IBM to found Amdahl		
1971	▲ RCA sells computer business to Sperry Rand ▲ Amdahl joins with Fujitsu, giving Japan an entry into computers	▼ Intel develops microprocessor—the "computer on a chip"	▲ William Poduska leaves Honeywell to found Prime Computer
1972			● HP enters computers with HP3000 minicomputer ▲ Seymour Cray leaves Control Data to found Cray Research
1974	▲ IBM terminates FS project, the company's "Vietnam"		
1975	● Ed Roberts introduces Altair 8800, the first microcomputer kit		
1976	● Bill Gates and Paul Allen write version of BASIC for the Altair		● Wang introduces Wang Word Processing System ● Tandem introduces its first fault-tolerant computer

APPENDIX 4.1. (*Continued*)

Year	Commercial & Home Computing	Shared Technologies: Semiconductors & Networking	Scientific/Engineering Computing
1977	● Apple Computer, Radio Shack, and Commodore introduce microcomputers (the Apple II, TRS-80, and PET, respectively)	▼ ARPA establishes TCP/IP protocol	● DEC introduces VAX-11/780 to compete with low-end mainframes
1978			
1979	● Dan Bricklin develops VisiCalc, the first spreadsheet application		
1980	● Oracle introduces RDBMS, the relational database system	▲ Robert Metcalfe of 3Com gets funding from Xerox to commercialize Ethernet technology	

The Microcomputer Era, 1980s–1990s

Year	Commercial & Home Computing	Shared Technologies: Semiconductors & Networking	Scientific/Engineering Computing
1981	● IBM introduces its PC, which grew to $5B in sales in four years and revealed a mass market for both business and home computer users		▲ William Poduska leaves Prime to found Apollo ▲ James Clark founds Silicon Graphics
1982	▲ Rod Canion, leaving TI, founds Compaq ▲ Mitch Kapor founds Lotus ▲ John Warnock founds Adobe Systems ● Bastion and Ashton introduce WordPerfect		▲ Scott McNealy, Vinod Khosla, and Andy Bechtolsheim found Sun Microsystems ● HP introduces its first workstation, the HP9000
1983		▲ Ray Noorda acquires Novell and shifts from peripherals to networking software for PCs	
1984	● Apple launches Macintosh, equipped with the first successful graphical user interface ▲ Michael Dell founds Dell Computers	▲ Cisco founded	▲ John Hennessy and other Stanford researchers found MIPS technologies to commercialize RISC chips ● DEC launches its first workstation, VAXstation 1
1985	● Microsoft releases Windows 1.0, following Apple's lead in graphic interfaces ▲ Gateway 2000, AST, and Packard-Bell enter PC market		

APPENDIX 4.1. (*Continued*)

Year	Commercial & Home Computing	Shared Technologies: Semiconductors & Networking	Scientific/Engineering Computing
1986	▲ Honeywell exits the computer business ● Compaq introduces Deskpro 386	● Cisco introduces TCP/IP router	● IBM introduces its first workstation, RT-PC, which fails commercially
1987	● IBM releases OS/2, "receiving a chilly reception"		● Sun introduces work station with SPARC chip ● Silicon Graphics introduces RISC-based workstation
1988	● Microsoft releases Windows 2.0		● IBM introduces AS/400 minicomputer
1989		▼ Tim Berners-Lee develops core elements of World Wide Web	▲ HP acquires Apollo
1990	● Microsoft introduces Windows 3.0 ● DEC introduces VAX 9000 mainframe		
1991		● Motorola, IBM, and Apple announce plans for Power PC, a RISC-based micro-processor for PC, Macintosh, and UNIX systems	● IBM launches RS600 workstation
1993		● Intel releases Pentium chip, trumping the Power PC ▼ Mark Andreeson and Eric Bina develop first browser, Mosaic, at U. of Illinois	● Microsoft releases Windows NT, effectively defeating Novell's cross-platform O/S challenge
1994		▲ Jim Clark and Mark Andreesen found Netscape and release Navigator browser	
1995	● Microsoft releases Windows 95 ▲ IBM acquires Lotus	◆ Internet privatized and opened to commercial use ● Microsoft releases Internet Explorer 2.0 browser bundled into Windows 95 ▼ Sun introduces Java	

APPENDIX 4.2. Data-Processing Industry
Shipments and Revenues by U.S. Firms, 1955–1979,
Selected Years (billions of dollars)

Year	Domestic	Worldwide
1955	less than 1	less than 1
1960	0.5	1
1965	2	3
1970	7	10
1975	15	21
1979	28	37

Source: Cortada, James W., *Historical Dictionary of Data Processing: Organizations*, p. 10, with permission of the author.

APPENDIX 4.3. Annual Exports and Imports of Computer Equipment in the U.S. Market, 1967–1971 (millions of dollars)

Exports-Imports	1967	1968	1969	1970	1971
Exports	475	530	786	1,237	1,262
Imports[1]	20	18	37	60	119
Net Exports	455	152	749	1,177	1,143

Source: Cortada, James W., *Historical Dictionary of Data Processing: Organizations*, p. 21, with permission of the author.
[1]Parts not included.

APPENDIX 4.4. Value of Computer Systems in the United States, 1955–1979, Selected Years (billions of dollars)

Year	General Purpose (Mainframes)	Minicomputers	Small Business
1955	0.5	0	0
1960	1	0	0
1965	5	0	0
1970	18	1	0
1975	30	5	0
1979	50	7	2.5

Source: Cortada, James W., *Historical Dictionary of Data Processing: Organizations*, p. 11, with permission of the author.

APPENDIX 4.5. Estimated Revenues from Service
Sector of Data-Processing Industry, 1955–1979,
Selected Years (billions of dollars)

Year	Total
1955	0.3
1960	0.4–0.5
1965	0.5–0.7
1970	1.1
1975	3.2
1979	5.5

Source: Cortada, James W., *Historical Dictionary of Data Processing: Organizations*, p. 22, with permission of the author.

APPENDIX 4.6. Estimated Software Revenues,
1964–1980, Selected Years (millions of dollars)

Year	Custom Programming	Packages	Total
1964	150–175	50–100	225–275
1968	300	100	400
1970	300	200	500
1972	350	300–350	650–700
1974	400	300–350	700–750
1976	400–425	750	1,150–1,175
1978	500	1,000	1,500
1980	600	1,500	2,100

Source: Cortada, James W., *Historical Dictionary of Data Processing: Organizations*, p. 23, with permission of the author.

APPENDIX 5.1. Financial Performance of Microsoft and the Leading Application Software Companies, 1986–1995

Company	1986	1987	1988	1989	1990	1991	1992	1993	1994	1995
Revenue[1]										
Microsoft	198	346	591	804	1,183	1,843	2,759	3,753	4,649	5,937
Oracle	55	131	282	584	917	1,028	1,179	1,503	2,001	2,967
Computer Assoc.	191	309	709	1,090	1,296	1,348	1,509	1,841	2,148	2,623
Lotus	283	396	469	556	685	829	900	981	971	1,150
Borland	30	38	82	91	113	227	483	464	394	254
Adobe	16	39	83	121	169	230	266	314	598	762
Novell	82	183	281	422	498	640	933	1,123	1,998	2,041
SAP[2]	–	–	101	217	333	465	513	634	1,182	1,875
WordPerfect[3]	52	103	179	281	430	622	579	708	–	–
Net Income										
Microsoft	39	72	124	171	279	463	708	953	1,146	1,453
Oracle	6	16	43	82	117	(12)	62	142	284	442
Computer Assoc.	19	37	102	164	158	159	163	246	401	432
Lotus[4]	48	72	59	68	23	33	80	56	(21)	–
Borland	1	1	2	(3)	12	27	(110)	(49)	(70)	(12)
Adobe	4	9	21	34	40	52	44	57	6	94
Novell	10	20	30	49	94	163	249	(35)	207	338
SAP	–	–	14	41	54	81	78	84	181	282

Percentage Annual Growth in Sales

Microsoft	—	75%	71%	36%	47%	56%	50%	36%	24%	28%
Oracle	—	138%	115%	107%	57%	12%	15%	27%	33%	48%
Computer Assoc.	—	62%	129%	54%	19%	4%	12%	22%	17%	22%
Lotus	—	40%	18%	19%	23%	21%	9%	9%	-1%	18%
Borland	—	27%	116%	11%	24%	101%	113%	-4%	-15%	-36%
Adobe	—	144%	113%	46%	40%	36%	16%	18%	90%	27%
Novell	—	123%	54%	50%	18%	29%	46%	20%	78%	2%
SAP	—		—	115%	53%	40%	10%	24%	86%	59%
WordPerfect	—	98%	74%	57%	53%	45%	-7%	22%	—	—

Net Income as a Percentage of Sales

Microsoft	20%	21%	21%	21%	24%	25%	26%	25%	25%	24%
Oracle	11%	12%	15%	14%	13%	-1%	5%	9%	14%	15%
Computer Assoc.	10%	12%	14%	15%	12%	12%	11%	13%	19%	16%
Lotus	17%	18%	13%	12%	3%	4%	9%	6%	-2%	—
Borland	3%	3%	2%	-3%	11%	12%	-23%	-11%	-18%	-5%
Adobe	25%	23%	25%	28%	24%	23%	17%	18%	1%	12%
Novell	12%	11%	11%	12%	19%	25%	27%	-3%	10%	17%
SAP	—		14%	19%	16%	17%	15%	13%	15%	15%

Source: Hoover's Guide to Computer Companies, 1996; Hoover's Handbook of Emerging Companies 1993–1994; SEC filings; Company annual reports.

[1] Revenue figures are actuals.

[2] SAP was private until 1988.

[3] WordPerfect was acquired by Novell in 1994.

[4] Lotus was acquired by IBM in 1995.

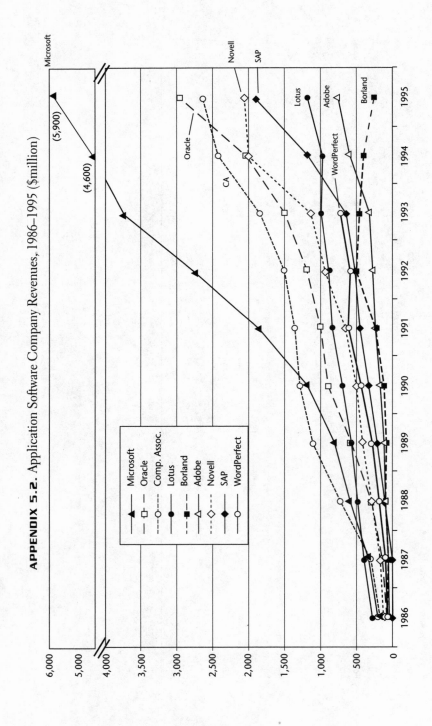

APPENDIX 5.2. Application Software Company Revenues, 1986–1995 ($million)

APPENDIX 5.3. Application Software Company Net Income, 1986–1995 ($million)

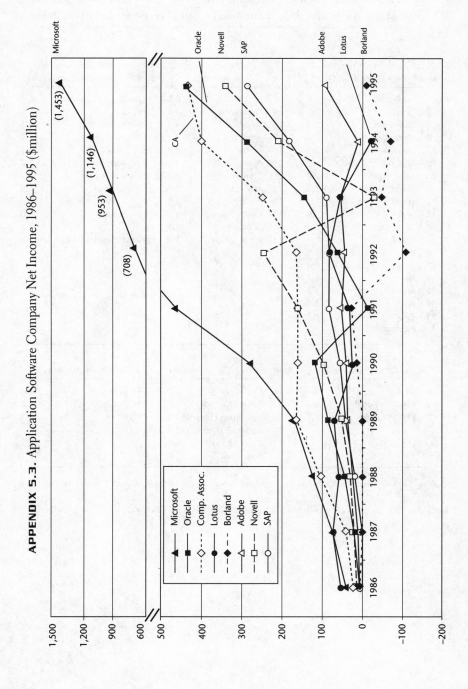

APPENDIX 8.1. The Fifty Largest Industrial Chemical Producers in the United States, 1993 (in terms of chemical-product revenues in billion dollars)

Rank	Industrial Chemical Core Companies (18)		Rank	Petroleum Companies (12)		Rank	U.S. Subsidiaries of Foreign Industrial Chemical Core Companies (10)	
1	Du Pont	15.6	3	Exxon	10.0	4	Hoechst Celanese	6.3
2	Dow	12.5	8	Occidental	4.1	9	BASF	4.0
5	Monsanto	5.6	11	Shell[1]	3.9	13	ICI America	3.5
7	Union Carbide	4.6	12	Amoco	3.7	17	Miles (Bayer)	3.1
15	Rohm & Haas	3.2	14	Mobil	3.5	23	Ciba-Geigy	2.5
18	Air Products (1940)	2.9	16	Arco	3.2	26	Akzo	2.7
20	Allied Signal	2.9	21	Chevron	2.7	27	Rhone-Poulenc	2.2
28	Dow Corning	2.0	22	Ashland	2.6	33	Unilever	1.8
29	Ethyl	1.9	25	Phillips	2.3	42	Solvay—America	1.2
31	Hercules	1.8	35	Elf-Atochem[1]	1.7	49	Henkel	1.0
34	Great Lakes Chemical (1932)	1.7	47	Texaco	1.1		(No Japanese subsidiaries in top 50)	
36	Lubrizol	1.5	48	B.P. America[1]	1.0			
37	American Cyanamid	1.4						
38	Nalco	1.4						
40	Morton International	1.2						
41	Witco	1.2						
43	Cabot	1.2						
44	International Flavors	1.2						

Rank	Core Companies in Other Industries (3)		Rank	Spin-Offs from Existing Companies (4)		Rank	Conglomerates (3)	
6	GE	5.4	24	Praxair	2.4	19	W.R. Grace	2.3
10	Eastman Kodak	3.9		(Union Carbide)		32	FMC Corp.	1.8
45	PPG Industries	1.5	30	Huntsman (Texaco)	1.8	46	Olin	1.1
			39	Lyondell (Arco)	1.3			
			50	Cytec (American Cyanamid)	1.0			

Source: Compiled from William J. Storck, "Top 100 Chemical Producers Post Little Sales Growth," *Chemical and Engineering News,* May 9, 1994, p. 14.

[1]Subsidiary of foreign petroleum company. Elf-Atochem was formed in 1983 by the French government.

APPENDIX 8.2. The World's Thirty Largest Producers of Pharmaceuticals, 1993
(in terms of pharmaceutical and medical devices revenues in billion dollars)

Rank	Company		Estimated Revenues ($ billions)
U.S. Core Companies (10)			
2	Bristol-Myers Squibb		11.1
3	Merck		10.4
5	SmithKline Beecham[2]		9.2
6	Abbott Laboratories		8.4
7	American Home Products		8.3
11	Pfizer		7.4
15	Eli Lilly		6.4
17	Warner-Lambert		5.7
22	Schering-Plough		4.3
23	Upjohn		3.6
Non-U.S. Core Companies (12)			
4	Roche Holding	Switzerland	9.6
9	Glaxo Holdings	U.K.	8.0
13	Takeda Chemical Industry	Japan	6.7
20	Sankyo	Japan	4.7
21	Pharmacia	Sweden	4.5
22	Boeringer-Ingelheim	Germany	3.4
23	Yamanouchi Pharm.	Japan	3.4
24	Schering	Germany	3.2
27	E. Merck	Germany	3.2
28	Shionogi	Japan	3.1
29	Wellcome[3]	U.K.	3.1
30	Astra	Sweden	3.0

Rank	Company		Estimated Revenues ($ billions)
U.S. Companies in Related Industries (2)			
1	Procter & Gamble[1]		16.6 (1995)
19	Johnson & Johnson		5.2 (1995)
[31]	American Cyanamid[4]		2.8] (1991)
Non-U.S. Chemical Companies (6)			
8	Hoechst	Germany	8.1 (1995)
10	Bayer	Germany	7.7 (1995)
12	Ciba-Geigy	Switzerland	7.0 (1991)
14	Rhone-Poulenc	France	6.5 (1995)
16	Sandoz	Switzerland	6.3 (1991)
18	ICI Zeneka	U.K.	5.5 (1994)

Source: Compiled and calculated from *"Fortune Global 500," Fortune,* July 25, 1994, pp. 178 and 180 and other sources.

[1]Figure represents total revenues for personal care products. The breakdown between over-the-counter drugs and consumer chemicals not available.

[2]Formed as a merger of SmithKline Beckman and Beecham in 1989.

[3]Acquired by Glaxo Holdings to form Glaxo Wellcome in 1995.

[4]American Cyanamid spun off its industrial chemicals in 1993.

APPENDIX 8.3. Founding Dates of the 1994 Fortune 500 Companies

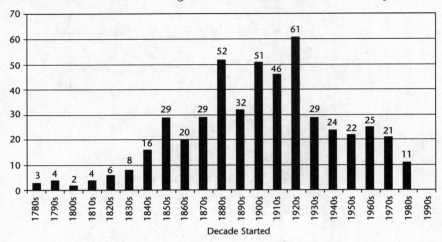

Source: Harris Corporation, "Founding Dates of the 1994 *Fortune* 500 U.S. Companies," *Business History Review,* 70, no. 1 (Spring 1996), p. 89, with permission. To be cited from this source.

Notes

**CHAPTER 2: Consumer Electronics: The United States—
The Creation and Destruction of a National Industry**

1. The most useful studies dealing with the beginning of the electronics industry and the formation of RCA are Hugh G. J. Aitken, *The Continuous Wave: Technology and American Radio, 1900–1932*, Princeton University Press, 1985, particularly chs. 5–10; W. Rupert Maclaurin, *Invention and Innovation in the Radio Industry*, Macmillan Company, New York, 1949, particularly chs. 5–9; Robert Sobel, *RCA*, Stein and Day, New York, 1986, chs. 1–3; Kenneth Bilby, *The General: David Sarnoff and the Rise of the Communications Industry*, Harper & Row, New York, 1986, chs. 2–4; Margaret Graham, *RCA & the VideoDisc: The Business of Research*, Cambridge University Press, Cambridge, U.K., 1986, pp. 30–38. Thomas K. McCraw, *American Business and How It Worked*, Harlan Davidson, Wheeling, Ill., ch. 7, provides an outstanding overview of the RCA experience and its place in the broader development of American business.

2. For the acquisition of American Marconi and the formation of RCA, Aitken, *Continuous Wave*, ch. 8; Bilby, *The General*, ch. 3.

3. For more information on Westinghouse's activities, Aitken, *Continuous Wave*, pp. 432–436, pp. 469–474. Frank Conrad set up KDKA as an offspring of his

amateur radio station, for which he received permission in April 1920 to go back on the air after the required suspension of operations during the wartime emergency.

4. Aitken's *Continuous Wave* provides the most detailed review of the transactions, pp. 476–482. The quotation is from p. 498. See also Bilby, *The General,* pp. 47–51.

5. The information for this and the next two paragraphs is from Sobel, *RCA,* pp. 48–49; U.S. Bureau of the Census, *Historical Statistics of the United States, Colonial Times to 1970,* bicentennial ed., part II, Washington, D.C., 1975, pp. 700, 796; Maclaurin, *Invention and Innovation,* p. 134, for turnover and survival rate of radio manufacturers; also *Fortune,* 2/35, p. 76.

6. These issues are reviewed in Aitken, *Continuous Wave,* ch. 10; Sobel, *RCA,* pp. 49–74. Aitken mentions Harbord only once, in a footnote p. 514. In December 1922 Harbord had replaced Edward J. Natley, who had remained American Marconi's president after its acquisition by General Electric.

7. For this and the next paragraph on antitrust and licensing policies, see Sobel, *RCA,* pp. 67–68; Aitken, *Continuous Wave,* pp. 497–502; Graham, *RCA & the VideoDisc,* pp. 40–42; Maclaurin, *Invention and Innovation,* pp. 133–136, reports that such "packaged licensing was available to all $100,000 customers."

8. Aitken, *Continuous Wave,* pp. 482–486, has the most incisive summary of the negotiations with AT&T and the formation of the networks. Quotation from p. 485. Aitken can be supplemented by Sobel, *RCA,* ch. 3; Bilby, *The General,* ch. 4; and Thomas S. H. Lewis, *Empire of the Air: The Men Who Made Radio,* Burlingame, N.Y., 1991, pp. 182–183.

9. Maclaurin, *Invention and Innovation,* p. 131, for quote; also Aitken, *Continuous Wave,* pp. 511–512.

10. Aitken, *Continuous Wave,* pp. 502–509, has an excellent brief summary of Sarnoff's moves to independence and self-sufficiency that can be supplemented by Sobel, *RCA,* pp. 82–98; and by Bilby, *The General,* pp. 99–101, for the initial acquisition, and pp. 105–109, for the final settlement under the consent decree. From the phonograph industry's beginning at the turn of the century, it had been dominated by two companies, Victor and Columbia Phonograph. The latter had moved its headquarters to London in 1920. See Alfred D. Chandler Jr., *Scale and Scope: The Dynamics of Industrial Capitalism,* Harvard University Press, 1990, pp. 354–355.

11. For RCA's performance and divestments, Sobel, *RCA,* pp. 98–104. For sales and other statistics, Bureau of the Census, *Historical Statistics,* part II, p. 796.

12. Maclaurin, *Invention and Innovation,* ch. 7, has the most complete review of the impact of the Great Depression on the United States radio industry; also *Fortune,* 2/35, pp. 75–79, 164–173.

13. For Philco's and RCA's other competitors, Maclaurin, *Invention and Innova-*

tion, pp. 139–146. Maclaurin estimates that RCA had more exports than Philco, but Philco outsold RCA in the domestic market. Philco's story is well reviewed in *Fortune*, 2/35, pp. 75–79, 164–173; and *Fortune*, 11/44, pp. 115–121, 232–243.

14. For radio components, Maclaurin, *Invention and Innovation*, pp. 149–150; and for Magnavox, Aitken, *Continuous Wave*, p. 125.

15. Bilby, *The General*, pp. 95–96, 105–108, describes RCA's venture into sound equipment for motion pictures, which led the company into the production of Hollywood films when it became a partner with Joseph P. Kennedy in the formation of Radio-Keith-Orpheum (RKO).

16. For the coming of television, Joseph H. Udelson, *The Great Television Race: A History of the American Television Industry, 1925–1941*, University of Alabama Press, University, Ala., 1982, provides a careful detailed study of the coming of television. Chs. 1–3 deal with pre-electronic developments, ch. 4 takes the story to the mid-1930s, ch. 5 to 1939, and ch. 6 to 1941. Maclaurin, *Invention and Innovation*, ch. 10, provides a valuable overview. Sobel, *RCA*, ch. 7; Bilby, *The General*, ch. 6; and Graham, *RCA & the VideoDisc*, pp. 52–55, provide additional information on the RCA story.

17. For this and the next paragraph, Udelson, *The Great Television Race*, pp. 124–131, p. 153 for Zenith; and Bilby, *The General*, pp. 130–131.

18. For this and the following paragraph, Udelson, *The Great Television Race*, pp. 150–158 for early programs, such as films, plays, and sporting events, pp. 135–143 for NTSC; Bilby, *The General*, pp. 134–138, quotation in the next paragraph is from p. 137.

19. RCA's wartime experience described in this and the following paragraphs comes from Sobel, *RCA*, pp. 136–143; Bilby, *The General*, pp. 139–143. For the establishment of the RCA Laboratories, Graham, *RCA & the VideoDisc*, pp. 58–59. The quotation regarding the lab is from p. 58, the two quotations on wartime technological developments from p. 59.

20. For this and the next three paragraphs, the information is from Sobel, *RCA*, pp. 143–154, 165; Bilby, *The General*, pp. 173–175; Bureau of the Census, *Historical Statistics*, part II, p. 796; and Steven Klepper and Kenneth L. Simons, "Technological Extinctions of Industrial Firms: An Inquiry into their Nature and Causes," *Industrial and Corporate Change* 6, no. 417 (March 1997). The article's section on television, pp. 415–430, reinforces the historical story told here. The article points out that television's introduction brought a small boomlet. By 1958 the number of firms peaked at fifty-eight.

21. The color television story covered in this and the next seven paragraphs is based on a brief sketch by Graham in *RCA & the VideoDisc*, pp. 61–67; a more detailed story in Bilby, *The General*, chs. 8 and 9; and briefly in Sobel, *RCA*, pp. 154–167. Also, McCraw, *American Business, 1920–2000*, p. 131 for quotation; S. M. Bensen, "AM vs. FM: The Battle of the Bands," *Indus-*

trial and Corporate Change 1 (1992):375–396, provides a useful review of the impact of television on the definition of the AM and FM radio bands. For the experience of two of RCA's smaller competitors, Zenith and Admiral, see "The Decline of U.S. Consumer Electronics Manufacturing: History, Hypothesis and Remedies," *The Working Papers of the MIT Commission on Industrial Productivity, Vol. I*, MIT Press, Cambridge, Mass., pp. 48–59, 60–69.

22. Quotations in this and following four paragraphs are from Graham, *RCA & the VideoDisc*, pp. 62, 65–66.

23. For color TV market share, *Working Papers of the MIT Commission, Vol. I*, p. 45, appendix C. Market share given in Klepper and Simons, "Technological Extinctions," cited in endnote 20, lists RCA with 30 percent in 1968 and 20 percent in 1978, and Zenith with 20 percent in 1968 and 21.2 percent in 1978.

24. On the consent decree and licensing revenues, see Graham, *RCA & the VideoDisc*, pp. 80–82; and Bilby, *The General*, pp. 215–216, 222–223.

25. The complex role of RCA's research organization described in this and the next two paragraphs is from Graham's outstanding ch. 3 and pp. 76–91 of ch. 4. For the three projects, pp. 66–67 (quotation is from p. 67). Additional information for these paragraphs comes from conversations with Professor Graham and Nathaniel Marshall, a product development manager at RCA during these years. The research for the primarily military communication division was carried on by its own operating unit on Long Island and supported by the Advanced Development Group at Camden.

26. Graham, *RCA & the VideoDisc*, p. 88.

27. *Fortune*, 5/4/81, pp. 140–153. Quotation is from Sobel, *RCA*, p. 196.

28. For RCA's computer story, see Kenneth Flamm, *Creating the Computer: Government, Industry and High Technology*, the Brookings Institution, Washington, D.C., 1988, pp. 36, 52, 57, 96, 111, 122–125; Franklin Fisher, James W. McKie, and Richard B. Manche, *IBM and the U.S. Data Processing Industry: An Economic History*, Praeger Publisher, New York, 1983, pp. 71–75, 124–125, 203–228. Fisher reports, "Apparently only three 501s were delivered to customers outside of RCA prior to 1960" (p. 72). Quotations on Bizmac, p. 72, and on the 3301, p. 202. See also Sobel, *RCA*, pp. 170–182, 199–207.

29. For the Spectra series, Fisher et al., *IBM*, pp. 204–215; Graham, *RCA & the VideoDisc*, pp. 11, 81–82; and Thomas J. Watson Jr. and Peter Petre, *Father, Son & Co.: My Life at IBM and Beyond*, Bantam Books, New York, 1990, pp. 215–219, and for John Burns, pp. 294–295.

30. Sobel, *RCA*, p. 203. *Fortune*, 5/4/81, pp. 142–144, has a useful evaluation of RCA's computer failure. The quotation in this paragraph is from p. 142, that in the next paragraph from p. 179.

31. For General Electric, see Maclaurin, *Invention and Innovation*, pp. 147–148; and *MIT Commission on Industrial Productivity*, p. 45.

32. For Philco, Flamm, *Creating the Computer*, pp. 122–123, 127; Fisher et al., *IBM*, pp. 88–89; also *Business Week*, 9/16/61, p. 34; *Financial World*, 9/27/61.

33. For Ford's acquisition of Philco, *Business Week*, 1/26/75; for Ford's plans to dispose of most of Philco's activities, *Moody's Industrial Manual for 1975*, pp. 366; and for sale to GTE, *Moody's Industrial Manual for 1976*, p. 519.

34. For Sylvania and its acquisition and operation by GTE, *Business Week*, 11/15/82; *Wall Street Journal*, 1/16/81, p. 17:6, 1/23/81, p. 4:6. *Moody's Public Utility Manual for 1975*, p. 1669, lists the businesses and properties of GTE Sylvania Incorporated and the properties acquired from Philco-Ford; *Moody's Public Utility Manual for 1983*, p. 1846, lists the sale of GTE Products Corporation, the successor to GTE Sylvania Inc., to North American Philips, Philips's U.S. subsidiary.

35. For this and the next paragraph on RCA's acquisitions, see Sobel, *RCA*, pp. 188–198; *Moody's Industrial Manual for 1970*, pp. 1537–1541, provides a useful chronology of these acquisitions and later sales of these properties.

36. Sobel, *RCA*, p. 203, lists senior capital (debt) for these years.

37. Revenues and net profits in appendix 2.2 are from Sobel, *RCA*, p. 215, which are taken from RCA's annual reports. Interest expense figures in the next paragraph are from RCA's annual reports.

38. For this and the following paragraph, Sobel, *RCA*, ch. 13, pp. 220–248; *Fortune*, 5/4/81, pp. 140ff. The RCA and Hertz debts are calculated from *Moody's Industrial Manuals*, 1976 and 1982.

39. Sobel, *RCA*, pp. 242, 258, provides revenue and profit tables for 1978–1985; and *Fortune*, 5/4/81.

40. Sobel, *RCA*, ch. 14; Bilby, *General*, p. 299, for Bradshaw quotation; Graham, *RCA & the VideoDisc*, ch. 9.

41. For this and the next paragraph on the GE sale, Robert Slater, *The New GE: How Jack Welch Revived an American Institution*, Business One Irwin, Homewood, Ill., 1993, pp. 117–121, 195–198 (Welch's quotation in this paragraph is from p. 121).

42. Slater, *The New GE*, pp. 194–198 (quotation p. 195).

43. For Zenith's financial record, *Hoover's Handbook of American Companies, 1996*, Reference Press, Austin, Tex., 1995, p. 943.

44. For Philco and Emerson, see endnote 33 and 34. For Emerson, (no author), *A Century of Manufacturing, 1890–1990*, Emerson Electric Co., St. Louis, 1989, pp. 200–201; for Warwick, see ch. 3 and endnote 27. The information on Admiral comes from *MIT Commission on Industrial Productivity*, p. 50. The Japanese acquisitions are described in ch. 3.

45. Gene Gregory, *Japanese Electronics Technology: Enterprise and Innovation*, John Wiley & Sons, New York, 1998, p. 175.

CHAPTER 3: Consumer Electronics: Japan's Paths to Global Conquest

1. For Matsushita, John P. Kotter, *Matsushita Leadership: Lessons from the 20th Century's Most Remarkable Entrepreneurs*, Free Press, New York, 1997, chs. 5–9; for the National brand names, pp. 84–85, 102; Mark W. Fruin, *Japanese Enterprise System: Competitive Strategies and Cooperative Structures*, Clarendon Press, Oxford, U.K., 1992, pp. 148–152; and the *International Directory of Company Histories*, vol. 2, St. James Press, Detroit, 1990, pp. 55–56. At the same time Sanyo was split off, Matsushita set up two legal corporate firms— 1) Matsushita Electric Works, controlled by 2) Matsushita Electric Industrial Company, *International Directory*, vol. 7, 1992, pp. 302–303.

2. Kozo Yamamura, "A Compromise with Culture: The Historical Evolution of Managerial Structure of Large Japanese Firms," in Harold F. Williamson, ed., *Evolution of Managerial Structures*, Temple University Press, Philadelphia, 1975, pp. 169–171.

3. For the war and the immediate postwar experience, Kotter, *Matsushita*, chs. 10–11, and *International Directory*, vol. 2, 1990, p. 55; and for Matsushita Electric Works, p. 102.

4. For the post-1951 moves, including the ones with Philips and JVC and the acquisition of Nakagawa Electric (refrigerators), see Kotter, *Matsushita Leadership*, chs. 12 and 13; Mark Mason, *American Multinationals in Japan: The Political Economy of Japanese Capital Controls*, Harvard University Press, Cambridge, Mass., 1992, pp. 36–41, 93–94. The quotation is from the *International Directory*, vol. 2, 1990, p. 54.

5. Fruin, *Japanese Enterprise System*, pp. 178–182, provides an excellent summary of Matsushita's growth and the development of its internal structure during the 1950s and 1960s. Quotation is from p. 179.

6. *International Directory*, vol. 2, 1990, pp. 56 and 302–303; Marie Anchordoguy, *Computers, Inc.: Japan's Challenge to IBM*, Harvard University Press, Cambridge, Mass., 1989, p. 44.

7. For Sony and the development of its technological learning base, Akio Morita with Edwin Reingold and Mitsuko Shimomura, *Made in Japan: Akio Morita and Sony*, E. P. Dutton, New York, 1986, especially ch. 4; *International Directory*, vol. 12, 1996, p. 453; John Nathan, *Sony, The Private Life*, Houghton-Mifflin Company, Boston, 1999, pp. 31–35, for the acquisition of the transistor license in 1953 and the first mass-produced "pocketable" radio; F. M. Scherer, *International High-Technology Competition*, Harvard University Press, Cambridge, Mass., 1992, p. 54, for sale of micro–television sets in the United States; John E. Tilton, *International Diffusion of Technology: The Case of Semiconductors*, Brookings Institution, Washington, D.C., 1971, pp. 141–145; and Mason, *American Multinationals in Japan*, pp. 36–41.

8. For the development of Sony's marketing organization and its growth in 1960, see Morita, *Made in Japan*, pp. 83–86; Nathan, *Sony*, pp. 58–71; and *International Directory*, vol. 12, 1996, pp. 453–454.

9. For the development of the Trinitron tube, Nathan, *Sony*, pp. 45–48. When the development began, RCA was producing twenty thousand sets a month to Sony's one thousand; for joint venture with CBS, pp. 97–98, 131–134; for Sony's plant in California, p. 103.

10. In addition to Fruin, this development in production processes can be followed in Gene Gregory, *Japanese Electronic Technology: Enterprise and Innovation*, John Wiley & Sons, New York, 1985, pp. 173–178, also pp. 63–70 (quotation is on p. 174). Man-hours per television set, for example, dropped from 3.48 in 1974 to 1.15 in 1978, p. 177.

11. For the beginnings of the industry with Ampex and RCA, see Cusumano et al., pp. 57–62; Graham, p. 68; and Minami et al., pp. 286–288 (full citations in next endnote).

12. The details of the historically complex Beta-VHS contest are admirablly explained in Michael A. Cusumano, Yiorgos Mylonadis, and Richard S. Rosenbloom, "Strategic Maneuvering and Mass-Market Dynamics: The Triumph of VHS over Beta," *Business History Review*, 66 (Spring 1982):51–94. Additional information comes from Margaret Graham, *RCA & the VideoDisc: The Business of Research*, Cambridge University Press, Cambridge, U.K., 1986; and Joung-hae Seo, "Research and Development Competition and Innovation in the Video Cassette Recorder Industry," in Ryoshin Minami et al., eds., *Acquiring, Adopting and Developing Technologies: Lessons from the Japanese Experience*, St. Martin's Press, London, 1995, ch. 11. Anita M. McGahan, Leslie L. Vadez, and David Yoffie, "Creating Values and Setting Standards: The Lessons of Consumer Electronics for Personal Digital Assistants," in David B. Yoffie, ed., *Competing in the Age of Digital Convergence*, Harvard Business School Press, Boston, 1997, pp. 250–252, provides a brief summary.

13. Quotation from Cusumano et al., p. 71.

14. Quotations in this and the next paragraph are from Cusumano et al., "The Triumph of VHS over Beta," p. 78 and p. 80.

15. Quotations are from Graham, *RCA & the VideoDisc*, pp. 188–195.

16. Quotations in this paragraph are, respectively, from Cusumano et al., "The Triumph of VHS over Beta," p. 81; Graham, *RCA & the VideoDisc*, p. 206.

17. Quote from Gregory, *Japanese Electronic Technology*, p. 176. Figures from Cusumano et al., "The Triumph of VHS over Beta," p. 62.

18. Graham, *RCA & the VideoDisc*, p. 213, for RCA's videodisk losses and shutdown, p. 214–216, for videotape rentals; Cusumano et al., "The Triumph of VHS over Beta," pp. 52, 65, for format growth, and p. 86, for Zenith's switch; for Philips's licensing of the VHS in 1983, see Alan Cawson, Kevin Morgan, Douglas Webber, Peter Holmes, Anne Stevens, *Hostile Brothers: Competition*

and Closure in the European Electronic Industry, p. 258. As a holder of 35 percent of Matsushita's equity, Philips's licensing of the VHS rather than obtaining it on OEM basis is understandable.

19. For Matsushita after the VCR, *International Directory,* vol. 2, 1990, p. 56; and vol. 7, 1992, p. 303; *Hoover's Handbook of World Business,* 1993, pp. 322–323; and *Hoover's Global 250: The Story Behind the Most Powerful Companies on the Planet,* Hoover's Business Press, Austin, Tex., 1997, pp. 330–331, reports the sale in 1995 of 80 percent of MCA to Seagram for $5.7 billion and lists the percentages of sales by product line.

20. For a detailed account of Matsushita's Hollywood adventure, see Dennis McDougal, *The Last Mogul: Lew Wasserman, MCA, and the Hidden History of Hollywood,* Crown, New York, 1998, for its entry into Hollywood, pp. 481–487, and on its exit, 494–497, 505–507.

21. *Datamation,* 7/97, pp. 45, 76.

22. For Sony, *International Directory,* vol. 12, 1996, pp. 453–456; *Hoover's Handbook of World Business,* 1993, pp. 404–405, and *Hoover's Global 250,* pp. 482–483. Scattered references in Nathan, *Sony,* pp. 137–174, provide an excellent account of the commercialization of the CD; also Graham, *RCA & the VideoDisc,* pp. 137–147. For the CD-ROM, in addition to *International Directory,* vol. 12, 1996, p. 454, Takashi Shibata, "Sony's Successful Strategy for Compact Disks," *Long Range Planning,* 26, no. 4 (1993):16–21, considers the differences between Sony's CD strategy and that of Matsushita's OEM strategy; and Stephen Manes and Paul Andrew, *Gates,* Simon & Schuster, New York, 1993, pp. 334–339 and pp. 407–410, for Microsoft's interest and connection in the CD-ROM and the CD. As pointed out on p. 339, the CD-ROM became a niche rather than a major line for its producers.

23. For CBS/Sony Records, Nathan, *Sony,* pp. 130–133, 175–176 (quotation p. 175); for the Columbia Pictures experience, Nathan, *Sony,* chs. 8–10.

24. For this paragraph and the next on the commercializing of the DVD in the 1990s, *The Wall Street Journal,* 12/09/99, p. B1 ff; for Toshiba's role, *Wall Street Journal,* 10/13/97, p. 38 ff (which is also the source for the earlier comments on the initial sales of CDs); also http://www.cdpage.com/DVD/dvdhistory.html; http://www.circuitcity.com. Sony's authorizing of Philips to handle the licensing of the DVD to other manufacturing companies is indicated in Mitchell Shiner, *Computer Dictionary,* Macmillan Computer Publishing, Indianapolis, Ind., 1998, p. 206.

25. For Sony's moves into video games, laptops, and desktops, Nathan's, *Sony,* pp. 286, 292, 304–305, 318; and *New York Times,* 1/1/96, p. 47, 5/25/99, p. D5, 3/10/99, C4.

26. For Sanyo, *International Directory,* vol. 2, 1990, pp. 91–92 (quotation from p. 91); Fruin, *Japanese Enterprise System,* pp. 179, 185; Martin Fransman, *Japan's Computer and Communications Industry: The Evolution of Industrial Giants*

and Global Competitiveness, Oxford University Press, Oxford, U.K., 1995, p. 493; *Hoover's Handbook of World Business*, 1993, pp. 428–429.

27. F. M. Scherer, *International High Technology Competition*, Harvard University Press, Cambridge, Mass., 1992, p. 54; (no author), *Emerson Electric Co.: A Century of Manufacturing, 1890–1990*, Emerson Electric Co., St. Louis, 1989, pp. 200–201.

28. *Hoover's Handbook of World Business*, 1993, pp. 428–429; *Hoover's Global 250*, pp. 456–457, includes sources of Sanyo's revenues. For its move into cellular telephones, see Fransman, *Japan's Computer and Communications Industry*, p. 493.

29. For Sharp, *International Directory*, vol. 12, 1996, pp. 447–449. For the shipments of desk calculators to the United States in 1967, Mason, *American Multinationals and Japan*, p. 184. And for later products, Fransman, *Japan's Computer and Communications Industry*, pp. 274–292.

30. *Hoover's Handbook of World Business*, 1993, pp. 436–437, and *Hoover's Global 250*, pp. 476–477.

31. These nexus companies are reviewed in *International Directory*. For Kyocera, see *International Directory*, vol. 2, 1990, pp. 50–51; for Pioneer, vol. 3, 1991, pp. 604–607; for TDK, vol. 2, 1990, pp. 109–111. TDK, by providing high-fidelity tape in 1969, became a major player in audio recording. In addition, Alps Electric, the world's largest manufacturer of floppy disk drives, is described in vol. 2, 1990, pp. 5–6.

32. Gregory, *Japanese Electronics Technology*, p. 117.

33. For Casio, *International Directory*, vol. 16, 1997, pp. 82–84. Scherer, *International High-Technology Competition*, p. 65, credits Casio with marketing the first true minicalculator, built around a single MOS/SI chip of U.S. design. *Hoover's Handbook of World Business*, 1993, pp. 186–187, and *Hoover's Global 250*, pp. 154–155.

34. Tilton, *Semiconductors*, p. 114, and Franco Malerba, *The Semiconductor Industry: The Economies of Rapid Growth and Decline*, University of Wisconsin Press, Madison, Wisc., 1985, p. 61. One other small semiconductor base was established by Italy's Olivetti in 1961 in collaboration with the U.S. company Fairchild Semiconductor—see Malerba, pp.117–118. After General Electric purchased Olivetti's computer division, the Italian firm continued in semiconductors as a small specialized producer. (Full Tilton citation in Chapter 4, endnote 62.)

35. For Philips, Pieter J. Bowman, *Anton Philips of Eindhoven*, Weidenfeld and Nicholson, London, 1958, pp. 88–90, on the expansion after 1919, pp. 131–136, for radio; *International Directory*, vol. 13, 1996, pp. 400–403.

36. For Telefunken, Joseph H. Udelson, *The Great Television Race: A History of the American Television Industry 1925–1941*, University of Alabama Press, University, Ala., 1982, pp. 109–111; Bowman, *Anton Philips*, pp. 150–156, 164–165;

Alfred D. Chandler, Jr., *Scale and Scope: The Dynamics of Industrial Capitalism*, Harvard University Press, Cambridge, Mass., 1990, p. 548.

37. For this and the next four paragraphs on Philips after World War II, *International Directory*, vol. 13, 1996.

38. Quotation from *International Directory*, vol. 13, 1996, pp. 401–402.

39. For Grundig, *Financial Times*, 9/4/81, p. 27; *New York Times*, 9/6/83, D1; *International Directory*, vol. 13, 1996, pp. 402–403.

40. North American Philips, *International Directory*, vol. 13, 1996, pp. 396–399 (for the quotation, p. 397).

41. For the Grundig investments, Cawson et al., *Hostile Brothers*, pp. 297–305.

42. Cawson et al., *Hostile Brothers* (for the quotation, p. 322).

43. For this and the next paragraph, *International Directory*, vol. 13, 1996, pp. 402–403; for quotation, p. 403; *Hoover's Handbook of World Business*, 1993, pp. 380–381; and *Hoover's Global 250*, pp. 398–399. Cawson et al., *Hostile Brothers*, pp. 321–323, provides an overview of Philips's reorganizations in the aftermath of the VCR battle; and pp. 338–342 describes the differences between Philips's CD and Sony's CD-ROM and the complexity of its operations. See Manes and Andrews, *Gates*, pp. 335–338, 408–410 for information on Gates's continuing interest in the 1980s in commercializing the CDI.

44. Philips's continuing operating difficulties and resulting internal reorganizations, and the cast-off and adding-on of new product lines, are reviewed in *Business Week*, 3/01/99, p. 21; the *Economist*, 5/08/99, p. 66; and *Barron's*, 2/21/00, p. 18. *Barron's* defines Philips's product lines as "three high-growth and high-margin businesses," without mentioning how competitive these businesses had become. *Business Week* describes the uncertain fate of the central research laboratories.

45. For Thomson SA, *Hoover's Handbook of World Business*, 1993, pp. 466–467; Cawson et al., *Hostile Brothers*, pp. 264–266, 284–285, 323–324. See also Patrick Friedenson, "France: The Relatively Slow Development of Big Business in the Twentieth Century," in Alfred D. Chandler Jr., Franco Amatori, Takashi Hikino, eds., *Big Business and the Wealth of the Nations*, Cambridge University Press, Cambridge, U.K., 1997, pp. 236–237.

46. Alfred D. Chandler Jr., *Giant Enterprise: Ford, General Motors, and the Automobile Industry*, Harcourt Brace & World, New York, 1964, p. 3.

CHAPTER 4: Mainframes and Minicomputers: The Computer Industry Created in the United States

1. This review of the coming of the computer is taken from two outstanding historically oriented studies by Kenneth Flamm, *Creating the Computer: Government, Industry, and High Technology* and *Targeting the Computer: Government Support and International Competition*, 1988 and 1987, respectively, Brookings

Institution, Washington, D.C.; supplemented by Martin Campbell-Kelly and William Aspray, *Computer: A History of the Information Machine*, Basic Books, New York, 1996; and Paul E. Ceruzzi, *A History of Modern Computing*, MIT Press, Cambridge, Mass., 1998. The book by Campbell-Kelly and Aspray places the digital computer within the broader framework of the evolution of information processing devices. Ceruzzi's book is excellent on the developing technology of the computer industry. The digital computer processes bits of data digitally. Its predecessor, the analogue computer, did so serially.

2. Flamm, *Creating the Computer*, pp. 58–59; Campbell-Kelly and Aspray, *Computer*, pp, 69–76; I. Bernard Cohen, *Howard Aiken: Portrait of a Computer Pioneer*, MIT Press, Cambridge, Mass., 1999, pp. 73–120.

3. Campbell-Kelly and Aspray, *Computer*, has a good review of the creation of Forrester's Whirlwind and of Eckert's and Mauchly's ENIAC, pp. 157–164, 80–97. The most thorough study of Whirlwind is by Kent C. Redmond and Thomas M. Smith, *Project Whirlwind: The History of a Pioneer Computer*, Digital Press, Bedford, Mass., 1980; and for the ENIAC, Scott McCartney, *ENIAC: The Triumphs and Tragedies of the World's First Computers*, Walker, New York, 1999.

4. For ERA, Flamm, *Creating the Computer*, pp. 43–46.

5. For UNIVAC, Campbell-Kelly and Aspray, *Computer*, pp. 105–128; also Ceruzzi, *Modern Computing*, pp. 27–34, 45.

6. Campbell-Kelly and Aspray, *Computer*, pp. 34–36. James Rand's father in 1898 had formed Rand Ledger Company, which commercialized the first "vertical" filing system. The young Rand invented Kardex, a card-based record-keeping system, and set up his own rival business in 1915. For his later career, ibid., pp. 117–130, and 135–136.

7. Flamm, *Creating the Computer*, p. 107.

8. Thomas Watson Jr. described the SSEC as "a weird gigantic hybrid of electronic parts and mechanical parts, half a modern computer and half a punch card machine," Thomas J. Watson Jr. and Peter Petre, *Father, Son and Co.: My Life at IBM and Beyond*, Bantam Books, New York, 1990, p. 190.

9. For a brief review of IBM's 700 series, see Flamm, *Creating the Computer*, pp. 82–84 (quotation on p. 84); also Ceruzzi, *Modern Computing*, pp. 34–36, 70–74.

10. Watson and Petre, *Father, Son & Co.*, p. 244.

11. The Hollerith story and the continuing development of the tabulating computing industry is succinctly told in JoAnne Yates, "Business Use of Information and Technology from the 1880s to 1950s," in Alfred D. Chandler Jr. and James W. Cortada, eds., *A Nation Transformed by Information: How Information Transformed the United States from Colonial Times to the Present*, Oxford University Press, New York, 2000, pp. 107–136.

12. For this and the next two paragraphs, Ceruzzi, *Modern Computing*, has a good

brief review of the transformation of the punched-card tabulator into the 650 computer, pp. 18–20, 43–44. Campbell-Kelly and Aspray, *Computer*, pp. 131–135, indicates the impact of IBM's 1401; also Ceruzzi, *Modern Computing*, pp. 75–77; and James W. Cortada, *Historical Dictionary of Data Processing: Organizations*, Greenwood Press, New York, 1987, pp. 161–162.

13. Watson and Petre, *Father, Son & Co.*, pp. 194–203, 243–248.

14. Flamm, *Creating the Computer*, pp. 83.

15. For COBOL and FORTRAN, James W. Cortada, *Historical Dictionary of Data Processing: Technology*, Greenwood Press, New York, 1987, pp. 71–79, 172–178; Ceruzzi, *Modern Computing*, pp. 90–94.

16. Watson and Petre, *Father, Son and Co.*, pp. 196–203; Flamm, *Creating the Computer*, pp. 84–85; Emerson W. Pugh, *Building IBM: Shaping an Industry and its Technology*, MIT Press, Cambridge, Mass., 1995, pp. 237–242.

17. For IBM's defense work, Flamm, *Creating the Computer*, pp. 86–95; Pugh, *Building IBM*, pp. 232–237 (quotation from p. 237).

18. Pugh, *Building IBM*, pp. 253–256; the quotations in this and the next paragraph are from p. 255.

19. Flamm, *Creating the Computer*, pp. 96–97; Pugh, *Building IBM*, pp. 263–270; and Campbell-Kelly and Aspray, *Computer*, pp. 137–144, particularly on the challenges facing the System 360 planners; and Ceruzzi, *Modern Computing*, pp. 144–153, on the technological innovations in software and hardware.

20. The task group, SPREAD (an acronym for system programming, research, engineering, and development), and its report are covered in Pugh, *Building IBM*, pp. 270–273.

21. This and the following paragraph are based on Cortada, *Technology*, pp. 212–220 (quotation from p. 214); Flamm, *Creating the Computer*, pp. 97–100; Pugh, *Building IBM*, pp. 275–277, 282–291, 301–304.

22. For the continuing manufacturing and software crisis, Watson and Petre, *Father, Son & Co.*, pp. 349–360; and Pugh, *Building IBM*, pp. 291–296. Pugh (p. 294) states that in order to develop the new operating system, "over a thousand persons were employed during the peak year," and Watson (p. 353) writes that "by 1966 we had two thousand people working on" the basic software. Watson adds that the total cost of creating the software operating system came to half a billion dollars. Three types of operating systems were developed—BOS (basic operating system), TOS (tape operating system), and DOS (disk operating system): Pugh (pp. 295–296). For IBM revenue, Flamm, *Creating the Computer*, p. 102.

23. Flamm, *Creating the Computer*, p. 99, for the quotation in this paragraph, and pp. 210, 211, for the quotations in the next paragraph. The parentheses are Flamm's.

24. For IBM's marketing, Robert Sobel, *IBM: Colossus in Transition*, Times Books, 1981, pp. 79–86. Professor James McKenney, a specialist in computer develop-

ment since the 1950s, emphasizes the "prowess and ubiquity of IBM's marketing strategy." Its strength, he stresses, rested on close collaboration during the 1950s with industry leaders—Procter & Gamble in groceries, American Airlines in air transportation, and Union Pacific in railroads—to develop industry-specific systems; its provision of twenty-four-hour assistance; and the creation of an outstanding sales force of industry specialists who maintained close contact with the product designers. See James L. McKenney, *Waves of Change: Business Evolution Through Information Technology*, Harvard Business School Press, Boston, 1995, pp. 106–120. He provides an excellent example of the effectiveness of this strategy in air transportation. JoAnne Yates, "Application Software for Insurance in the 1960s and Early 1970s," *Business and Economic History* 24 (Fall 1995):123–133, does the same for insurance.

25. The information on Sperry Rand comes from Flamm, *Creating the Computer*, pp. 107–111 (quotations from pp. 107–108); Cortada, *Organizations*, pp. 235–240, *Technology*, pp. 366–371; James C. Worthy, *William C. Norris: Portrait of a Maverick*, Balling Publishing House, Cambridge, Mass., 1987, pp. 27–32.

26. For Control Data, see Flamm, *Creating the Computer*, pp. 111–112; Cortada, *Organizations*, pp. 101–107; Franklin M. Fisher, James W. McKie, and Richard B. Manche, *IBM and the U.S. Data-Processing Industry: An Economic History*, Praeger Publishers, New York, 1983, pp. 90–94 (quotation from p. 91); and most detailed of all, Worthy, *Norris*, pp. 26–32, chs. 3 and 4; also Watson and Petre, *Father, Son & Co.*, pp. 283–284. For an instructive summary of the debate within the firm over the move to develop the OEM business, see Worthy, *Norris*, pp. 60–62.

27. For National Cash Register, Flamm, *Creating the Computer*, pp. 118–119; Cortada, *Organizations*, pp. 204–205; and Richard S. Rosenbloom, "From Gears to Chips: The Transformation of NCR and Harris in the Digital Era," Harvard Business History Seminar, 2/18/88, pp. 7–15, and "A Comparison of NCR's and Burroughs's Entry into Computers," Business History Seminar, 10/2/89, pp. 1–6.

28. For Burroughs Corporation, Flamm, *Creating the Computer*, pp. 116–118; Cortada, *Organizations*, pp. 87–89; Fisher, *IBM*, pp. 79–85; Ray W. MacDonald, *Strategy for Growth: The Story of Burroughs Corporation*, Newcomen Society, New York, 1978, pp. 12–18.

29. For Honeywell, Flamm, *Creating the Computer*, pp. 113–114; Cortada, *Organizations*, pp. 147–148; Fisher, *IBM*, pp. 68–71; Campbell-Kelly and Aspray, *Computer*, pp. 142–143, 146.

30. For GE's first years in computers, Flamm, *Creating the Computer*, pp. 125–127, and Fisher, *IBM*, pp. 180–186.

31. Fisher, *IBM*, pp. 186–202. Quotations for this paragraph and the next are from pp. 199–200; also Robert Slater, *The New GE: How Jack Welch Revived an*

American Institution, Irwin, Homewood, Ill., 1993, pp. 20–21, reports that GE's senior management never approached computers with the same degree of commitment that was evident at IBM. For further information see Homer R. Oldfield, *King of the Seven Dwarfs: General Electric's Ambiguous Challenge to the Computer Industry*, IEEE Computer Society Press, Los Alamitos, Calif., 1996, pp. 230–233. As a result, the APL project's initial products were compatible neither with GE's existing computer lines nor with those of IBM. Software development remained a continuing problem.

32. For RCA, see ch. 2, endnotes 28–30.

33. For DEC, Flamm, *Creating the Computer*, pp. 127–129 (quotation from p. 127); Cortada, *Organizations*, pp. 115–120, and *Technology*, pp. 296–299 (quotation from p. 297); Fisher, *IBM*, pp. 271–273; Cerruzzi, *Modern Computing*, pp. 127–136 (quotation from pp. 132–133).

34. For DEC's story after 1965 and through the 1970s, Glenn Rifkin and George Harrar, *The Ultimate Entrepreneur: The Story of Ken Olsen and Digital Equipment Corporation*, Contemporary Books, Chicago, 1988. Chs. 8–9 describe the continuing swift growth of the company. The revenue and profit figures and the OEM sales are given on pp. 71–72. Cortada, *Organizations*, p. 119, has somewhat different but comparable revenue and profit figures, with the revenues rising from $4.1 million in 1961 to $142.6 million in 1970, a growth rate of 44 percent per year. Ceruzzi, *Modern Computing*, pp. 198–200, 243–247, tells of the virtues of the PDP-11 and the VAX series in maintaining DEC's leadership in the 1970s.

35. For SDS, Flamm, *Creating the Computer*, pp. 129–131; Cortada, *Organizations*, pp. 243–245, 276–277; Fisher, *IBM*, pp. 263–271, 395–397; Ceruzzi, *Modern Computing*, pp. 165–167.

36. For Data General, Cortada, *Organizations*, pp. 109–111; Fisher, *IBM*, pp. 409–410; Rifkin and Harrar, *Olsen*, ch. 10.

37. For Prime, Flamm, *Creating the Computer*, p. 131; Fisher, *IBM*, pp. 411–412; Cortada, *Organizations*, pp. 222–223.

38. For Hewlett-Packard, Cortada, *Organizations*, pp. 142–143; "Hewlett-Packard Corporation," Graduate School of Business, Stanford University, S-M-150R, 1973; *Datamation*, 6/81, p. 110. Between 1972 and 1979 its revenues from data-processing products rose to nearly 50 percent of its total revenue.

39. For Wang, Fisher, *IBM*, p. 414; Ceruzzi, *Modern Computing*, pp. 254–256. For Tandem and Stratus, see Flamm, *Creating the Computer*, p. 131 (footnote). Other specialized minicomputer makers included Datapoint, whose 6600 (produced in 1977) specialized in "distributed data processing capabilities." Perkin-Elmer, a maker of complex analytical and avionic instruments, introduced in 1975 its 7132 computer to be used with the types of products it produced. Harris, a maker of printing equipment, did the same for the printing industry with a high-performance 500 series in 1978: Fisher, *IBM*, pp. 412–415.

40. *Datamation*, 6/83, p. 90.

41. Pugh, *Building IBM*, pp. 302–304.

42. Ibid., pp. 304–307. The all-semiconductor main memory introduced in September 1970 made IBM the leader in semiconductor memories.

43. Ibid., p. 312.

44. Ibid., pp. 307–311 (quotation from p. 310). Charles Ferguson and Charles Morris, *Computer Wars*, Times Books, New York, 1993, pp. 31–35, have an excellent perceptive survey of Project FS in which they argue that "FS was absurdly ambitious." Marie Anchordoguy, *Computers Inc.: Japan's Challenge to IBM*, Harvard University Press, Cambridge, Mass., 1989, pp. 135–141, indicates how in 1975 knowledge of IBM's work in VLSI led Japan's MITI and its leading computer companies to form their first VLSI development project, which lasted from 1976 through 1979 at a cost of $360 million (see ch. 6).

45. Ibid., p. 309.

46. For peripherals, Fisher, *IBM*, pp. 124, 286–303; Cortada, *Organizations*, pp. 164–165, 191–194; Pugh, *Building IBM*, pp. 299–300.

47. For Control Data, see Fisher, *IBM*, p. 288; Worthy, *Norris*, pp. 63–64; Cortada, *Organizations*, pp. 48, 104–106. Also see Fisher, *IBM*, pp. 302–303, for the plug-compatible peripherals of specific companies.

48. For Amdahl, Cortada, *Organizations*, 47–49; Flamm, *Creating the Computer*, pp. 131–132, 195–196; and Gene M. Amdahl, "The Early Chapters of the PMC Story," *Datamation*, 2/79, pp. 113–119 (quotation from p. 113).

49. Flamm, *Creating the Computer*, p. 195.

50. For leasing, Fisher, *IBM*, pp. 303–316; Cortada, *Organizations*, p. 165. In the single year of 1969, leasing companies purchased $2.5 billion worth of IBM products.

51. The activities of Control Data and Cray Research are summarized briefly in Flamm, *Creating the Computer*, pp. 111–113; and Cortada, *Organizations*, pp. 105–106. In 1972 Control Data made a joint venture with NCR and in 1975 with Honeywell to produce new lines of peripherals.

52. For Sperry Rand, Flamm, *Creating the Computer*, pp. 108–111; and Cortada, *Organizations*, pp. 251–252.

53. For Honeywell, Flamm, *Creating the Computer*, pp. 114–115; Cortada, *Organizations*, pp. 150–151; *Hoover's Handbook of American Companies 1993*, Reference Press, Austin, Tex., 1992, p. 328, for Honeywell's position in thermostats and other home, building, and industrial control devices. For 1979 revenues, *Datamation*, 6/81, p. 102.

54. For Burroughs, MacDonald, *Burroughs*, pp. 18–25 (quotations from pp. 18–21); Cortada, *Organizations*, pp. 90–91; and Fisher, *IBM*, pp. 242–249, 381–382.

55. For NCR, Rosenbloom, "From Gears to Chips," pp. 19–27; "NCR and Burroughs," pp. 6–12.

56. On table 4.2 I focus on 1984 and 1985 because the figures for 1982 and 1983 are based on different categorization schemes from those for 1984 and 1985. Between these two periods, *Datamation* began reclassifying significant amounts of revenue out of hardware categories and into a separate "Maintenance" category. Thus 1982 and 1983 figures help illustrate changes in relative rankings, but do not necessarily provide a good picture of a given firm's absolute growth. See footnotes 1 and 2 on table 4.2.

57. For ADP and other data-processing services companies (also called "service bureaus"), see Fisher, *IBM*, pp. 316–321; Cortada, *Organizations*, pp. 18–22, 72–73.

58. Welke quotation from Fisher, *IBM*, p. 322; 1980s estimates of software revenues from Cortada, *Organizations*, pp. 22–23.

59. Watson and Petre, *Father, Son & Co.*, p. 381. Watson adds, "But to me the bundle was simply another tradition that had to go, just as we had agreed in 1956 to sell our machines as well as rent them, and to license our patents to other companies" (p. 381). Martin Campbell-Kelly, "Development and Structure of the International Software Industry, 1950–1990," *Business and Economic History* 24 (Winter 1995): pp. 73–92, provides an excellent review of the evolution of the packaged software industry.

60. For Computer Sciences and other software companies, Fisher, *IBM*, pp. 322–326; For software statistics, Cortada, *Organizations*, pp. 19–24.

61. End-use percentages are from Richard N. Langlois and W. Edward Steinmueller, "The Evolution of Competitive Advantage in the Worldwide Semiconductor Industry, 1947–1996," in David C. Mowery and Richard R. Nelson, eds., *Sources of Industrial Leadership: Studies of Seven Industries*, Cambridge University Press, Cambridge, U.K., 1999, p. 37.

62. This and the previous paragraph are about AT&T's 1952 licensing conference. See John E. Tilton, *International Diffusion of Technology: The Case of Semiconductors*, Brookings Institution, Washington, D.C., 1971, pp. 66–67, 74–76; Cortada, *Technology*, pp. 59–60, and *Organizations*, pp. 54–55.

63. For Texas Instruments, Cortada, *Organizations*, pp. 261–265, and *Technology*, p. 60; Pugh, *IBM*, p. 280; Tilton, *Semiconductors*, p. 26. In the early 1960s the Justice Department was carrying on suits against large firms for price fixing.

64. For market share data, Tilton, *Semiconductors*, p. 115; Franco Malerba, *The Semiconductor Business: The Economics of Rapid Growth and Decline*, University of Wisconsin Press, Madison, Wis., 1985, p. 159 for market shares, pp. 100–122 for the role of U.S. firms in Europe; and P. R. Morris, *A History of the World Semiconductor Industry*, Peter Petegrinus, London, 1990, pp. 91–94.

65. The negotiations are described in detail in Mark Mason, *American Multinationals and Japan: The Political Economy of Japanese Capital Controls, 1899–1980*, Harvard University Press, Cambridge, Mass., pp. 174–187; also Anchordoguy, *Computers, Inc.*, pp. 28–29.

66. Mason, *American Multinationals and Japan*, pp. 218–231, discusses Motorola's

extended negotiation with the Japanese government; also Malerba, *The Semiconductor Business*, cited in note 64.

67. The U.S. market share information comes from Mariann Jelinek and Claudia Bird Schoonhoven, *The Innovation Marathon: Lessons from High Technology Firms*, Basil Blackwell, Oxford, England, 1990, p. 126. As the authors note: "These figures are difficult to obtain, and more difficult to substantiate. Estimates vary substantially by product and by market, and figures from different sources are seldom truly comparable." However approximate, they do indicate the market strength of TI and Motorola.

68. For Fairchild, see Tilton, *Semiconductors*, pp. 66–67; Cortada, *Organizations*, pp. 123–128, *Biographies*, pp. 193, 237–238; also Michael R. Leibowitz, "Founding Father: Robert Noyce," *P/C Computing*, 5/89, pp. 95–100.

69. Morris, *World Semiconductor Industry*, pp. 98–100, 125; Malerba, *The Semiconductor Business*, pp. 109, 117–119, 168–169.

70. AnnaLee Saxenian, *Regional Advantage: Culture and Competition in Silicon Valley and Route 128*, Harvard University Press, Cambridge, Mass., 1994, pp. 85–88, reviews the shift to mass production. For capital cost, Malerba, *The Semiconductor Business*, p. 18. The cost of Intel's projected plant was given to me by David Yoffie. The quotation from *Dataquest*, 6/15/80, is given in Morris, *World Semiconductor Industry*, p. 85.

71. For National Semiconductor, Cortada, *Organizations*, pp. 126–127; Jelinek and Schoonhoven, *Innovation Marathon*, pp. 99–103, 106, and quotation from pp. 123–124. *Hoover's Guide to Computer Companies*, Hoover's Business Press, Austin, Tex., 1996, p. 156. For Advanced Micro Devices, *Hoover's Guide to Computer Companies*, 1996, p. 32.

72. For Intel, Gordon E. Moore, "Intel—Memories and Microprocessors," in Elkan Blout, ed., *Power of Boldness: Ten Master Builders of American Industry Tell Their Success Stories*, Joseph Henry Press, Washington, D.C., 1996, pp. 77–101, quotation on p. 81.

73. For the development of the microprocessor at Intel, see Ceruzzi, *Modern Computing*, pp. 219–221, quotations from pp. 218, 220; Moore, "Memories and Microprocessors," pp. 97–98; Jelinek and Schoonhoven, *Innovation Marathon*, pp. 112–114, 145–156; and Saxenian, *Regional Advantage*, pp. 85–86, which includes the dropping prices for microprocessors.

74. For global market shares, see Malerba, *Semiconductor Business*, p. 159; for TI's early efforts toward large-scale production, Morris, *World Semiconductor Industry*, pp. 93–94. Two smaller start-ups located outside of Silicon Valley began to produce standardized chips in the 1970s. MOSTEK was established in 1969 in Colorado Springs by a TI engineer, R. Petritz. In the late 1970s it had a market share of 1.3 percent. Another 1 percent market share was held by Analog Devices, established in 1965 in Norwood, Mass., to produce a chip that transformed pressure, temperature, and sound into electronic signals: Morris, *World*

Semiconductor Business, pp. 85, 117. Scattered references in Jelinek and Schoonhoven, *Innovation Marathon,* ch. 4, on Advanced Micro Devices. (The U.S. market share figures are from p. 126.)

75. Saxenian, *Regional Advantage,* pp. 1–5.

76. James C. Williams, "The Rise of Silicon Valley," *Innovation and Technology* (Spring/Summer 1990): 24; Saxenian, *Regional Advantage,* ch. 2, has an excellent review of the extensive literature on the growth of the Valley and its culture; quotation on Fairchild is from p. 31.

77. For the market shares in this and the following two paragraphs, see Langlois and Steinmueller, "Worldwide Semiconductor Industry," pp. 41–55. For additional information on the Japanese invasion of memory chips, see Ferguson and Morris, *Computer Wars,* pp. 108–109; Anchordoguy, *Computers Inc.,* pp. 137–147 for the development of the VLSI chip; Saxenian, *Regional Advantage,* pp. 88–95 (the Hewlett-Packard quotation from p. 90). The consequences were so drastic that Andrew Grove, speaking at a Semiconductor Association dinner in 1990, recalled his belief that Silicon Valley was to be Japan's new techno-colony, in Andrew S. Grove, "Silicon Valley: The Next Techno-Colony?" Semiconductor Industry Association Forecast Dinner, September 26, 1990.

CHAPTER 5: The Microprocessor Revolution: The Computer Industry Recast in the United States

1. Paul E. Ceruzzi, *A History of Modern Computing,* MIT Press, Cambridge, Mass., 1998, ch. 7, describes the coming of the personal computer. Martin Campbell-Kelly and William Aspray, *Computer: A History of the Information Machine,* Basic Books, New York, 1996, pp. 240–244, briefly reviews the Altair story. For the founding of Microsoft, Stephen Manes and Paul Andrews, *Gates,* Simon & Schuster, New York, 1993, pp. 67–76.

2. The following paragraphs on Apple, Commodore, and Tandy are based on Richard M. Langlois, "External Economies and Economic Progress," *Business History Review* 66 (Spring 1992):13–19, under the subheading "The industry begins in 1977"; the quotations in the next paragraph are from pp. 15–16. James W. Cortada, *Historical Dictionary of Data Processing: Organizations,* Greenwood Press, New York, 1987, pp. 60–64, 94–95, 255–258, provides brief sketches of their histories. For Tandy, Milton Moskowitz, Michael Katz, and Robert Levering, *Everybody's Business: An Almanac (The Irreverent Guide to Corporate America),* Harper & Row, San Francisco, 1980, pp. 331–333. The market share statistics are from John Friar and Mel Horwitch, "The Emergence of Technology Strategy: A New Dimension of Strategic Management," *Technology and Society* 7 (1985):152. For more additional detailed information, Campbell-Kelly and Aspray, *Computer,* pp. 244–253, and Ceruzzi, *Modern Computing,* pp. 264–268.

3. The following account is based on James Chposky and Ted Leonsis, *Blue Magic: The People, Power, and Politics Behind the IBM Personal Computer*, Facts on File Publications, New York, 1988, chs. 3–8; supplemented by Langlois, *External Economies*, pp. 20–23 (quotation in next paragraph from Langlois is on p. 20). *Blue Magic* was written by members of the Project Development Group that commercialized the PC, based on lengthy interviews with other participants and documentary data. The authors point out that the story would have been far less complete if several of the group leaders had not left the company. A brief review of the development of the PC is in Charles Ferguson and Charles Morris, *Computer Wars*, Times Books, New York, 1993, pp. 23–27.

4. For Intel, Chposky and Leonsis, *Blue Magic*, pp. 26–27; Ferguson and Morris *Computer Wars*, pp. 24–25. The first quotation is from Michael Leibowitz, "Founding Father: Robert Noyce," *P/C Computing*, 5/89, p. 100. The Moore quotation is from Gordon Moore, "Intel—Memories and the Microprocessor," in Elkan Blout, ed., *The Power of Boldness: Ten Master Builders of American Industry Tell Their Success Stories*, Joseph Henry Press, Washington, D.C., 1996, p. 98.

5. For this and the next two paragraphs on Gates, see Chposky and Leonsis, *Blue Magic*, chs. 9–10; and Manes and Andrews, *Gates*, chs. 11–12, especially pp. 157–158, for Paterson's operating system, and p. 175, for the $75,000 purchase of QDOS; and Ceruzzi, *A History of Modern Computing*, pp. 269–271.

6. For suppliers, see Chposky and Leonsis, *Blue Magic*, p. 66; for marketing and advertising, ch. 13, pp. 75–77, 98, for the quotation on strategic goals, p. 120; also Campbell-Kelly and Aspray, *Computer*, pp. 256–257.

7. Chposky and Leonsis, *Blue Magic*, p. 145.

8. Ibid., pp. 106–107.

9. Langlois, in *External Economies*, pp. 23–28, has an excellent review of the rise of the clones worldwide. A good contemporary account of that rise, including the quotation in this paragraph, is *Business Week*, "The PC Wars: IBM vs. the Clones," 7/28/86, pp. 62–68. Number of PCs shipped were provided by James Cortada.

10. For market share in 1989 (22.3 percent), see *Datamation*, 6/15/90, p. 184; and for 1985, *Datamation*, 6/15/86, p. 45.

11. The information for this and the two following paragraphs on Compaq is based on *Management Today*, "Compaq's Compact," 5/85, pp. 92–98 (as noted there, "Whatever TI's recent troubles, it is a wonderful training ground for hardheaded, rather conservative managers, very different from the West Coast, Silicon Valley types," p. 92); also *Business Week*, "The PC Wars: IBM vs. the Clones," 7/28/86, and *Business Week*, "How Compaq Gets There Firstest with the Mostest," 6/26/89, pp. 146–150; also Chposky and Leonsis, *Blue Magic*, p. 162, and Moore, "Intel," pp. 100–101.

12. The information for this and the next paragraph is from *Business Month*, "Take That Goliath," 12/87, p. 25; *Fortune*, "Compaq Bids for Leadership," 9/29/86, pp. 30–32 (includes quotation on Gates's contribution); *Forbes*, "Soft Dollars, Hard Choices," 9/4/89, pp. 106–109: Compaq had no service force. Like automobiles, machines were serviced by franchise dealers, p. 109. The relation between Compaq and Microsoft is described by Manes and Andrews, *Gates*, pp. 203, 324, 348. See also *New York Times*, 1/10/88, F-14; *New York Times*, 7/9/89, F 4. Ferguson and Morris, *Computer Wars*, pp. 52–53, indicates how Compaq reverse-engineered the PC/2 proprietary bios, a program IBM hoped would give its PC a competitive advantage.

13. For Apple, Langlois, "External Economies," pp. 31–33, 45–46, briefly summarizes the Apple experience (quotation from p. 46); also Cortada, *Organizations*, pp. 60–63. John Sculley with John A. Bryne, *Odyssey: Pepsi to Apple . . . A Journey of Adventure, Ideas, and the Future*, Harper & Row, New York, 1987, chs. 8–12 and accompanying subchapters, reviews in detail Apple's 1985 crisis and the resulting changes in command. The strengths and weaknesses of its operating systems are reviewed in Ceruzzi, *Modern Computing*, pp. 273–276, including the quotation in the next paragraph; and Campbell-Kelly and Aspray, *Computers*, pp. 271–276.

14. For this paragraph and the previous on IBM's PC development, Ferguson and Morris, *Computer Wars*, pp. 56–58; Langlois, "External Economies," p. 25, for the AT, and p. 29, for the PS/2.

15. For comparative revenues in 1988, *Datamation*, 6/15/89, p. 154.

16. The growth of Dell and its rivals is reviewed in *The New York Times*, 7/21/91, F-4-5; 3/13/93, D-1; 5/28/93, D-3; 7/15/93, D-4; 8/2/93, D-2; 8/22/93; and *Business Week*, 3/22/93, pp. 83–86. For Gateway 2000 (which moved to North Sioux City, South Dakota, in 1990), see *New York Times*, 5/27/93, D-1, D-6; 9/27/95, D-10. For Packard Bell, *New York Times*, 10/12/94; 7/6/95; 9/12/95, D-1, D-3. For AST Research, *Hoover's Guide to Computer Companies*, Hoover's Business Press, Austin, Tex., 1996, p. 50; and *New York Times*, 9/13/95, D-1, D-2.

17. For a useful overview of the development of workstations, see "Note on Microprocessors: Overview of PCs and Workstations," Harvard Business School Case N9-389-136, pp. 7–10. Ferguson and Morris, *Computer Wars*, pp. 37–50, has an excellent brief review of the development of the RISC chip; also Ceruzzi, *Modern Computing*, pp. 287–290. For the development of UNIX, see Ferguson and Morris, *Computer Wars*, pp. 103–105; Cortada, *Technology*, pp. 289–290; Ceruzzi, *Modern Computing*, pp. 282–285; and Campbell-Kelly and Aspray, *Computer*, pp. 219–222.

18. For Sun and Apollo, Carliss Y. Baldwin and Kim B. Clark, "Sun Wars: Competition within a Modular Cluster, 1985–1990," in David Yoffie, ed., *Competing in the Age of Digital Convergence*, Harvard Business School Press, Boston,

1997, ch. 3. For Apollo, also see AnnaLee Saxenian, *Regional Advantage, Culture and Competition in Silicon Valley and Route 128*, Harvard University Press, Cambridge, Mass., 1994, pp. 126–128; quotation from Carliss Baldwin and Jack Soll, "Sun Microsystems, Inc., 1987, (A)," Harvard Business School, Case N9-290-051 (1990), p. 3.

19. For Sun, in addition to the citations in the previous note, Mark Hall and John Barry, *Sunburst: The Ascent of Sun Microsystems*, Contemporary Books, Chicago, 1990. Also valuable is Jonathan Khazam and David Mowery, "The Commercializing of RISC: Strategies for the Creation of Dominant Designs," *Research Policy* 23 (1994):89–102; and Raghu Garud and Arun Kumaraswamy, "Changing Competitive Dynamics in Network Industries: An Exploration of Sun Microsystems' Open Systems Strategy," *Strategic Management*, 14 (1993):351–369. See Ceruzzi, *Modern Computing*, pp. 282–283, for Joy's technical capabilities, and pp. 263, 291–292, 297, for the significance of Metcalfe's Ethernet.

20. Hall and Barry, *Sunburst*, p. 26.

21. *Datamation*, 6/15/88, p. 154; 6/15/91, p. 222; also 4/1/92, pp. 3–6.

22. Baldwin and Clark, "Sun Wars," p. 148–150, and an excellent article in *The New York Times*, 12/31/89, D-5.

23. For Hewlett-Packard, *Datamation*, 6/15/83, p. 106; also 6/15/93, pp. 22, 28; *Business Week*, 9/11/89, pp. 106–112; 8/15/90, pp. 22–26; 4/1/91, pp. 76–79; 3/22/92; *New York Times*, 3/21/91, D-1.

24. For IBM, Ferguson and Morris, *Computer Wars*, pp. 45–50; *New York Times*, 4/23/89, F-1; 2/9/90, D-1. For the AS/400 minicomputer, Ceruzzi, *Modern Computing*, p. 250. For revenues and market share, *Datamation*, 6/15/93, p. 22.

25. For DEC, Ceruzzi, *Modern Computing*, pp. 243–247, 285–287; *Datamation*, 4/1/92, pp. 34–36; Ferguson and Morris, *Computer Wars*, pp. 103–105.

26. Information on Silicon Graphics and Intergraph comes from *Hoover's Guide to Computer Companies*, 1996; for Motorola, *International Directory of Company Histories*, vol. 11, St. James Press, Detroit, 1995, pp. 327–328; also for Intergraph, *Datamation*, 6/1/89, p. 38, and 6/15/86, p. 118; and for Silicon Graphics, *Business Week*, 7/18/94, pp. 56–63. As its products became used for the making of motion pictures, Silicon Graphics began to produce large systems (table 5:1).

27. *Business Week*, 10/1/90, pp. 103–104, and 10/6/91, pp. 79–80; Ferguson and Morris, *Computer Wars*, p. 157; also David Packard, *The H-P Way*, HarperBusiness, New York, pp. 113–121.

28. For Seagate, Pugh, *Building IBM*, pp. 299–300; Fisher, *IBM*, p. 397; *Hoover's Guide to Computer Companies*, 1996, p. 194. As a major supplier for IBM's PC, Seagate reported that it quickly acquired one-half of the microcomputer disk drive market.

29. For Quantum, *Business Week*, 7/8/91, pp. 84–85. For Conner Peripherals, *Hoover's Handbook of American Business 1993*, Reference Press, Austin, Tex., 1992, p. 213; and *New York Times*, 5/27/90, B-1, 3. For Western Digital, *Hoover's Guide to Computer Companies*, 1996, pp. 236–237. In 1988 Conner acquired 49 percent of Olivetti's disk drive business, and in 1991, 51 percent. By 1990, 29 percent of its income came from Compaq, 12 percent from Olivetti, and 10 percent from Toshiba.

30. *Hoover's Guide to Computer Companies*, 1996, p. 134, for Lexmark; p. 208, for Storage Technology.

31. Ferguson and Morris, *Computer Wars*, pp. 60–61; Paul Carroll, *Big Blues: The Unmaking of IBM*, Crown, New York, 1993, p. 129, for IBM's investments and Intel's losses in 1983. See Robert A. Burgleman, "Fading Memories: A Process Study of Strategic Business Exit in Dynamic Environments," Working Paper, Stanford University, June 1993, for shutting down the DRAM plants.

32. Mariann Jelinek and Claudia Bird Schoonhoven, *The Innovation Marathon: Lessons from High Technology Firms*, Basil Blackwell, Oxford, U.K., 1990, p. 97.

33. On AMD's market share, *Hoover's Handbook 1993*, p. 93; also Ferguson and Morris, *Computer Wars*, pp. 142–143. I am indebted to David Yoffie for the information on Intel's second sources.

34. Burgleman, "Fading Memories," pp. 22–24 (quotation from p. 24).

35. Ferguson and Morris, *Computer Wars*, pp. 60–61; Harvard Business School (HBSA Case 1-389-063), "Intel Corporation, 1988," pp. 13–14, for income figures; Carroll, *Big Blues*, p. 131, for sale of Intel stock.

36. This and the preceding paragraph from *New York Times*, 4/9/92, A-1, D-4, which has the quotation; HBS, "Intel Corporation, 1988," pp. 1–14; also *New York Times*, 2/14/90, D-1, for income figures. Intel also sold DRAMs made by Samsung over its own label and PCs, add-on boards, and platforms on a similar OEM basis. In 1989 these lines accounted for 26 percent of its revenues.

37. For this and the next paragraph, *New York Times*, 4/8/91, D-1; 7/14/91, F-1; 10/3/91, D-1; 5/11/93 (no page); 1/1/96; and Carroll, *Big Blues*, pp. 293–298; also Ferguson and Morris, *Computer Wars*, pp. 213–214.

38. Ferguson and Morris, *Computer Wars* dates the Intel-IBM "Friendly Divorce" in mid-1992: "IBM would henceforth diversify the base of microprocessor vendors and supply more of its needs internally," they write on p. 60, "Intel has always sold its chips to all comers." On pp. 61–65 they review the relationship during the PC years. Also, *New York Times*, 4/4/93, F-11; 5/11/93 (no page); 11/14/93, F-10. For market share data, *New York Times*, 2/20/94, F-13. National Semiconductor was especially hard hit between 1989 and 1992: *Hoover's Computer Companies*, 1996, p. 157.

39. The information for the service sector comes from *Hoover's Computer Companies*, 1996; and Hoover's Online (http://www.hoovers.com).

40. Quotation from Michael A. Cusumano and Richard W. Selby, *Microsoft Secrets: How the World's Most Powerful Software Company Creates Technology, Shapes Markets, and Manages People*, Free Press, New York, 1995, pp. 157–158, 401–402.

41. W. Edward Steinmueller, "The U.S. Software Industry: An Analysis and Interpretive History," in David C. Mowery, ed., *The International Computer Software Industry, A Comparative Study of Industry Evolution and Structure*, p. 31.

42. *Datamation*, 6/15/88, p. 162, and 6/15/93, p. 22.

43. Carroll, *Big Blues*, pp. 88–91 (quotations from pp. 89, 91); Ferguson and Morris, *Computer Wars*, pp. 69–71; Manes and Andrews, *Gates*, pp. 285–288.

44. The continuing story of the relationship between Gates and IBM is told in Ferguson and Morris, ch. 5 (quotation p. 75); and Carroll, *Big Blues*, ch. 8., especially pp. 182–185, and ch. 10, especially pp. 233–234. Their brief versions need to be checked against the many details of this complicated story presented in Manes and Andrews, *Gates*, chs. 19–30. Carroll, *Big Blues*, p. 119, indicates that Gates offered to sell 10 percent of Microsoft's shares to IBM. He notes that Gates talked with one senior IBM manager who "never got very specific." Since no offer was made, no offer was discussed and then rejected by IBM's top management.

45. Ferguson and Morris, *Computer Wars*, pp. 78–81 (quotation is from p. 79).

46. Carroll, *Big Blues*, pp. 182–185, 233–235 (quotations from pp. 183–185); Manes and Andrews, *Gates*, pp. 369, 375–377. After unsuccessfully developing an "elegant" PC, NeXt successfully produced an effective UNIX operating system.

47. Ferguson and Morris, *Computer Wars*, pp. 80–83 (quotation on p. 81); Carroll, *Big Blues*, chs. 12–13. A reworked OS/2.2 did make a modest comeback: *New York Times*, 7/31/94, D-1. For Microsoft's revenue and income, *Hoover's Guide to Computer Companies*, 1996, p. 152. Cusumano and Selby, *Microsoft Secrets*, p. 137, for Microsoft's achievements in these fields.

48. *Hoover's Handbook of American Business*, 1993, p. 406, for Microsoft's percentages of revenues in these product groups.

49. Campbell-Kelly and Aspray, *Computer*, pp. 278–279; Cusumano and Selby, *Microsoft's Secrets*, pp. 137–141, 147–153; and Manes and Andrews, *Gates*, pp. 288–295 (1994 edition), provide details of this critically significant deal.

50. Cusumano and Selby, *Microsoft Secrets*, pp. 168–170.

51. G. Pascal Zachary, *Show-Stopper! The Breakneck Race to Create Windows NT and the Next Generation at Microsoft*, Free Press, New York, 1994, pp. 28–35.

52. Quotation is from Zachary, *Show-Stopper*, p. 279.

53. For Novell's Netware 386, *Hoover's Guide to Computer Companies*, 1996, p. 164.

54. For Oracle, *International Directory*, vol. 6, 1992, pp. 272–274; and *Hoover's Guide to Computer Companies*, 1996, pp. 170–171.

55. For Computer Associates, *International Directory*, vol. 6, 1992, pp. 224–226 quotation.

56. For Lotus, *International Directory*, vol. 6, 1992, pp. 254–256; and *Hoover's Guide to Computer Companies*, 1996, pp. 138–139.

57. For WordPerfect, *International Directory*, vol. 10, 1995, pp. 556–559.

58. For Borland, *International Directory*, vol. 9, 1994, pp. 80–82 (quotation from p. 81); and *Hoover's Guide to Computer Companies*, 1996, pp. 56–57. Kahn's initial lines included simplified PC language for computers and a desktop organizer.

59. For Adobe, *International Directory*, vol. 10, 1995, pp. 22–24; and *Hoover's Guide to Computer Companies*, 1996, pp. 30–31.

60. For SAP, *International Directory*, vol. 16, 1997, pp. 441–444; and *Hoover's Guide to Computer Companies*, 1996, pp. 184–185.

61. For Novell, *International Directory*, vol. 6, 1992, pp. 269–271 (quotation from p. 270); also *International Directory*, vol. 23, 1998, pp. 359–362 (quotation from p. 361); and *Hoover's Guide to Computer Companies*, 1996, pp. 164–165. The decline in income in 1993 reflected this strategy of growth.

62. Cusumano and Selby, *Microsoft Secrets*, p. 145.

63. For the next four paragraphs on the founding of the Internet, Janet Abbate, *Inventing the Internet*, MIT Press, Cambridge, Mass., 1999, chs. 2, 4, 6; Campbell-Kelly and Aspray, *Computer*, pp. 282–300; Ceruzzi, *Modern Computing*, pp. 295–304; Katie Hafner and Matthew Lyon, *Where Wizards Stay Up Late: The Origins of the Internet*, Simon & Schuster, New York, 1996, ch. 8.

64. Abbate, *Internet*, p. 52–53, for IMP/host description.

65. Ibid., pp. 200–205, first quotation from p. 201; Campbell-Kelly and Aspray, *Computer*, p. 295, for second quotation; Ceruzzi,*Modern Computing*, pp. 296–299.

66. Abbate, *Internet*, p. 186, for number of hosts; pp. 204–205, for adoption of TCP/IP.

67. For Cisco, *International Directory*, vol. 11, 1995, pp. 58–60; and *Hoover's Guide to Computer Companies*, 1996, pp. 66–67.

68. For the development of the World Wide Web and the browser, Ceruzzi, *Modern Computing*, pp. 299–304, quotations from pp. 302 and 299.

69. For the browser and Mosaic, Abbate, *Internet*, p. 217. For Netscape, *International Directory*, vol. 15, 1996, pp. 320–322; and *Hoover's Guide to Computer Companies*, 1996, p. 330.

70. For privatization of the Internet, Abbate, *Internet*, pp. 191–205 (quotation on p. 199).

CHAPTER 6: The National Competitors: Europe's Computer Industries Die, Japan's Industry Challenges

1. The British story is told in a careful, detailed manner in Martin Campbell-Kelly, *ICL: A Business and Technical History*, Clarendon Press, Oxford, U.K.,

1989. It also provides essential insights on the response of other European and Japanese competitors to IBM's System 360. It is summarized and supplemented by Kenneth Flamm, *Creating the Computer: Government, Industry and High Technology*, Brookings Institution, Washington, D.C., 1988, pp. 142–150. Flamm, p. 150, also points out that in 1968 the Labour government merged Plessey, Britain's largest defense electronics contractor, into ICL. For more on ICL, *International Directory of Company Histories*, vol. 6, St. James Press, Detroit, 1992, pp. 240–242; for Ferranti, James W. Cortada, *Historical Dictionary of Data Processing: Organizations*, Greenwood Press, New York, 1987, pp. 128–129. Campbell-Kelly, *ICL*, pp. 45, 86–87, 129–130, for the cutting off of U.S. company ties with BTM and Powers-Samas; ch. 10, for the ICT merger and its subsequent mergers; and pp. 213–214, for arrangements with RCA.

2. For the quotation, Flamm, *Creating the Computer*, p. 150; also see Campbell-Kelly, *ICL*, chs. 11–12, for the ties of ICL with Honeywell and English Electric with RCA (p. 221); also valuable is Ross Hamilton, "Despite Best Intentions: The Evolution of the British Minicomputer Industry," *Business History* 38(1995):81–104. "Western Europe's Computer Industry," *Datamation*, 9/76, pp. 63 ff, provides a more detailed overview of ICL and its three other European competitors in 1975.

3. Campbell-Kelly, *ICL*, pp. 283, 322, 329, for R&D expenses, pp. 337, 339. For losses in 1981, Flamm, *Creating the Computer*, p. 150.

4. Campbell-Kelly, *ICL*, pp. 337–345, for the Fujitsu agreement. Also *International Directory*, vol. 6, 1992, p. 242; and *Hoover's Handbook of World Business 1993*, Reference Press, Austin, Tex., 1993, p. 230, for Fujitsu's further acquisition of ICL's shares and, in the same year, the purchase of 50 percent of the European computer maintenance division of Bell Atlantic. For the acquisition of Nokia Data Holding, *Hoover's Global 250: The Story Behind the Most Powerful Companies on the Planet*, Hoover's Business Press, Austin, Tex., 1997, p. 218; and for its move out of marketing PCs and servers into software and services, *Hoover's Guide to Computer Companies*, Hoover's Business Press, Austin, Tex., 1996, pp. 112–113.

5. For France, Flamm, *Creating the Computer*, pp. 150–159; *International Directory*, vol. 3, 1991, pp. 122–123, 563–565; Campbell-Kelly, *ICL*, p. 223.

6. For this and the following paragraph on Unidata and Cii-HB, Flamm, *Creating the Computer*, pp. 157–158; for ICL's negotiations with Cii, p. 277.

7. This and the next paragraph, *International Directory*, vol. 3, 1991, p. 123, pp. 563–567; *Datamation*, 6/15/86, p. 78, 6/15/93, pp. 22–23. *Hoover's Guide to Computer Companies*, pp. 142–143.

8. For Italy, *International Directory*, vol. 3, 1991, pp. 144–146; *Hoover's Handbook of World Business*, 1993, pp. 366–367; Franco Malerba, *The Semiconductor Industry: The Economics of Rapid Growth and Decline*, University of Wisconsin,

Madison, Wisc., 1985, pp. 117–118, 127, 144–145. The U.S. company Fairchild Semiconductor was Olivetti's major chip supplier. I am indebted to Chiara Falasa, a research associate at ICSIM, for a draft of an excellent paper, "The Rise and the Fall of Olivetti Computers," unpublished, September 1997.

9. For Olivetti in the 1990s, *International Directory*, vol. 3, 1991; and *Hoover's Guide to Computer Companies*, 1996, pp. 168–169; and *Datamation*, 6/15/86, p. 73, and 6/15/93, pp. 22–23. The 1996 sale to the foreign consortium is in *Business Week*, 2/3/97, p. 22. In this chapter I cite *Datamation*'s 1991 and 1992 lists, and then the 1996 list, for *Datamation* did not list revenues worldwide for each company for 1993, 1994, and 1995.

10. For Germany, Flamm, *Creating the Computer*, pp. 159–165 (quotation p. 163), pp. 163–165, for the government's role; *International Directory*, vol. 14, 1996, pp. 444–447; and Malerba, *The Semiconductor Industry*, pp. 79, 126. Others with market share in Germany included ITT, AEG-Telefunken, Britain's BMT, and France's Machines Bull.

11. *Datamation*, 6/15/86, p. 72; Malerba, *Semiconductor Industry*, pp. 166–167. Of the two other German companies marginally involved in computers, BASF got its mainframes from Hitachi and its minicomputers from Nixdorf; Mannesman produced printers and software.

12. For Nixdorf, Flamm, *Creating the Computer*, pp. 163–164; Campbell-Kelly, *ICL*, pp. 304–307; and *International Directory* vol. 3, 1991, pp. 154–155. The one other computer start-up in Europe was Norway's Norsk Data, which produced specialties for local markets: Flamm, *Creating the Computer*, p. 168.

13. For Siemens-Nixdorf's market share worldwide in 1992, *Datamation*, 6/15/93, p. 22; and for sources of revenue, *Hoover's Handbook of World Business*, 1993, pp. 440–441. For Siemens-Nixdorf's 1996 revenues and income, *Datamation*, 7/97, p. 46, and for rankings, p. 80. For its percent of Siemens AG's total sales, *Hoover's Global 250*, 1997, p. 48, and for its percentage of revenue across the several sectors, *Datamation*, 7/97, p. 80, also p. 45.

14. For the proposed sale of Siemens-Nixdorf's PC operations to Acer, see *Wall Street Journal Europe*, 4/24/98, p. 3, and 5/11/98, p. 21; for its cancellation, *Dow Jones Online News*, 9/08/98; also *Wall Street Journal Europe*, 9/29/98, p. 14. For Fujitsu Siemens Computers, see their Web site: http://www.fujitsu-siemens.com.

15. For the rankings, Mark W. Fruin, *Japanese Enterprise System: Competitive Strategies and Cooperative Structures*, Clarendon Press, Oxford, U.K., 1992, p. 359, table 5.

16. For IBM Japan before 1960, Mark Mason, *American Multinationals in Japan: The Political Economy of Japanese Capital Controls 1899–1980*, Harvard University Press, Cambridge, Mass., 1992, pp. 114–130, to the Occupation, and pp. 187–191, for after it. Before the war IBM Japan had been Japan Watson.

17. Marie Anchordoguy, *Computers, Inc.: Japan's Challenge to IBM*, Harvard Uni-

versity Press, Cambridge, Mass., 1989, chs. 2 and 3; Flamm, *Creating the Computer*, pp. 179–185.

18. Flamm, *Creating the Computer*, pp. 185–187; Martin Fransman, *Japan's Computer and Communications Industries: The Evolution of Industrial Giants and Global Competitiveness*, Oxford University Press, 1995, Oxford, U.K., pp. 137–138. For TRW's military computers, Davis Dyer, *TRW: Pioneering Technology and Innovations Since 1900*, Harvard Business School Press, Boston, Mass., 1998, pp. 242–243.

19. For the FONTAC program, Anchordoguy, *Computers, Inc.*, pp. 44–45.

20. Market shares are from Anchordoguy, *Computers, Inc.*, p. 34.

21. For the Ogata program, Anchordoguy, *Computers Inc.*, pp. 44–54. Quotations in this and the previous paragraph are from Flamm, *Creating the Computer*, pp. 187, 188.

22. Anchordoguy, *Computers Inc.*, p. 34, for market share.

23. The information for this and the next four paragraphs comes from a detailed review of the New Series Project, Anchordoguy, *Computers Inc.*, pp. 106–121. The table on p. 116 lists when the M-series came onstream, indicating how soon they were able to be shipped to the European manufacturers on an OEM basis. The quotation from Fujitsu's president is on p. 111. Also, James Cortada notes that between 1973 and 1979 the Heizer Corporation, a venture capital firm, had 31 percent of Amdahl's equity, James W. Cortada, *Historical Dictionary of Data Processing: Organizations*, Greenwood Press, New York, 1987, pp. 47–49, which provides a useful review of the Amdahl story in general. Also see *International Directory*, vol. 3, 1991, pp. 109–111. In continuing the development of the System 370, IBM's major problem was debugging the software. Thus, when learning of Hitachi's "sting," Fujitsu's president commented that his company "did not have to steal IBM information; it received it through Amdahl," p. 113. For the "Sting" case in 1982, see Anchordoguy, pp. 145–150; also *International Directory*, vol. 12, 1996, p. 238.

24. Anchordoguy's comment on the crucial significance of the New Series Project is on p. 120. Gene Gregory, *Japanese Electronic Technology: Enterprise and Innovation*, John Wiley and Sons, New York, 1985, does not discuss MITI's New Series Project but in chs. 15–17 has an excellent review of the competitive computer battles between IBM and its Japanese competitors after 1976.

25. NTT's support and the MITI-sponsored VLSI project are summarized in Flamm, *Creating the Computer*, pp. 198–200. Flamm stresses NTT's role in developing Japan's semiconductor technology. Also see Anchordoguy, *Computer's Inc.*, pp. 53–57, 121–122, for NTT funding for the New Series Project, and pp. 137–141, for VSLI; and Fransman, *Japan's Computer and Communications Industry*, pp. 141–158, for both.

26. For Fujitsu, Seiichiro Yonekura and Hans-Jurgen Clahsen, "Innovation by Externalization: A New Organizational Strategy for High-Tech Industries—Fuji

Denki, Fujitsu, and FANUC," in Takeshi Yuzawa, ed., *Japanese Business Success: The Evolution of a Strategy*, Rutledge, London, 1994, ch. 3, has an excellent detailed account of the evolution of Fujitsu's learning experience; also *International Directory*, vol. 2, 1990, pp. 22–23, 224–227; vol. 3, 1991, pp. 139–141. For Fujitsu's relation with NTT, Fransman, *Japan's Computer and Communication Industry*, pp. 134–136.

27. For this and the five following paragraphs, *International Directory*, vol. 16, 1997, pp. 224–227; *Hoover's Handbook of World Business*, 1993, pp. 234–235; *Hoover's Global 250*, 1997, pp. 218–219; and *Datamation*, 6/15/93, p. 22.

28. For NEC's origin and evolution through World War II, Mason, *American Multinationals in Japan*, pp. 28–34, 95–96, 142–144; Fransman, *Japan's Computer and Communication Industry*, pp. 27–34, for radio equipment, pp. 262–263; *International Directory*, vol. 2, 1990, pp. 67–68. NEC was #6 on *Datamation's* 1996 list (#4 in 1995).

29. For this and the next two paragraphs on NEC's post–World War II developments, Fransman, *Japan's Computer and Communications Industry*, pp. 259–287, provides an excellent review of the evolution of NEC's competence; also *International Directory*, vol. 2, 1990, pp. 67–68. Fransman, pp. 80–81, 259, 284–285, for relations between ITT and NEC; and p. 286, for the development of its own operating system.

30. Fransman, *Japan's Computer and Communications Industry*, pp. 270–278, p. 259, for product lines as a percent of sales based on NEC's annual reports. For financial figures in the next paragraph, see *Hoover's Global 250*, 1997, pp. 390–391, and *Datamation*, 7/97, p. 76.

31. For this and the following eight paragraphs on Toshiba up to the beginnings of its participation in the New Series Project, see Fruin, *Japanese Enterprise System*, pp. 90, 96, 138, 217, 232–239 (quotation on GE's mentorship on p. 233); Mason, *American Multinational in Japan*, pp. 41, 52–58; *International Directory*, vol. 12, 1996, p. 484; Hidemasa Morikawa, *Zaibatsu, The Rise and Fall of Family Enterprise Groups in Japan*, University of Tokyo Press, Tokyo, 1992, pp. 64–65; Mira Wilkins, *The Emergence of Multinational Enterprise: American Business Abroad from Colonial Times to the Present*, Harvard University Press, Cambridge, Mass., 1970, pp. 94. As Fransman notes, in the 1930s production of vacuum tubes in Japan was dominated by Tokyo Electric, Fransman, *Japan's Computer and Communications Industry*, p. 262. Quotation on GE's 1965 capital infusion is from *International Directory*, vol. 12, 1996, p. 48.

32. For the NEC/Toshiba partnership, Anchordoguy, *Computers, Inc.*, pp. 117–119. For their role in the VLSI semiconductor project, pp. 143–144.

33. For Toshiba in the 1980s and 1990s, Fruin, *Japanese Enterprise System*, pp. 232–255, has an excellent detailed review of the evolution of Toshiba's product lines, management (multidivisional) structure, and strategic planning. It can be supplemented by *International Directory*, vol. 12, 1996, p. 484.

34. For the alliances in this paragraph and the financial figures in the next two paragraphs, *International Directory*, vol. 12, 1996, p. 485; *Hoover's Handbook of World Business*, 1993, pp. 478–479; *Hoover's Global 250*, 1997, pp. 526–527.

35. For Hitachi, Fruin, *Japanese Enterprise System*, pp. 151–153, 337; Fransman, *Japan's Computer and Communications Industry*, pp. 30–31, 38–39; Mason, *American Multinationals in Japan*, p. 132; and *International Directory*, vol. 12, 1996, p. 237.

36. For postwar Hitachi, Fruin, *Japanese Enterprise System*, pp. 178, 182–185; *International Directory*, vol. 12, 1996, pp. 237–238.

37. For this and the next two paragraphs on Hitachi from the New Series Project and beyond, see *International Directory*, vol. 12, 1996, pp. 237–238; *Datamation*, 6/15/90, p. 189; *Hoover's Handbook of World Business*, 1993, pp. 254–255; and *Hoover's Global 250*, 1997, pp. 238–239; also *Datamation*, 6/15/93, p. 22.

38. For Hitachi's performance in the 1990s in this and the next two paragraphs, *Hoover's Global 250*, 1997, pp. 238–239. For Hitachi's 1996 global position, *Datamation*, 7/97, pp. 45, 75, for its success in combining ECL and CMOS chip and memory technologies in its central processing unit and the resulting "impressive gains," p. 49.

39. For Oki, *International Directory*, vol. 2, 1990, pp. 72–73; *Hoover's Handbook of World Business*, 1993, pp. 364–365.

40. For Mitsubishi Electric, Mason, *American Multinationals in Japan*, pp. 132, 196; Fruin, *Japanese Enterprise Systems*, pp. 138, 142, 180; *International Directory*, vol. 2, 1990, pp. 57–59; Yasuo Mishima, *The Mitsubishi: Its Challenges and Strategy*, JAI Press, Inc., Greenwich, Conn., 1989, pp. 212–216. For worldwide ranking in 1996, *Datamation*, 7/97, pp. 45, 76.

41. For the Japanese PC industry, Jason Dedrick and Kenneth L. Kraemer, *Asia's Competitive Challenge: Threat or Opportunity to the United States and the World*, Oxford University Press, New York, 1998, pp. 78–86 (quotation p. 79); also, for NEC, Fransman, *Japan's Computer and Communications Industry*, pp. 273–277. For NEC's U.S. market share in personal computers in 1980, Alfred D. Chandler Jr., *Scale and Scope: The Dynamics of Industrial Capitalism*, Harvard University Press, Cambridge, Mass., 1990, p. 612.

42. Dedrick and Kraemer, *Asia's Competitive Challenge*, pp. 84–86; also, Michael Hobday, *Innovation in East Asia: The Challenger to Japan*, Edward Elgar, Aldershot, 1995.

43. For Taiwan, Dedrick and Kraemer, *Asia's Competitive Challenge*, pp. 146–173.

44. Alice H. Amsden, *The Rise of the Rest: Challenges to the West from Late-Industrializing Economies*, Oxford University Press, New York, 2001, pp. 172–173, for relations with U.S. companies; and pp. 197–201, for ODM and OBM contracts and hardware manufacturing. I am in debt to Professor Alice Amsden for information on Taiwan, particularly Acer's shift to Latin American and other developing markets.

45. For Acer, Dedrick and Kraemer, *Asia's Competitive Challenge*, pp. 152–157; also *International Directory*, vol. 16, 1997; *Hoover's Guide to Computer Companies*, 1996, pp. 28–29; *Datamation*, 7/97, p. 45, for Acer's distribution of sales across product sectors. For the Acer contract with Siemens-Nixdorf, see endnote 14.

46. For Singapore, Dedrick and Kraemer, *Asia's Competitive Challenge*, pp. 175–184.

47. For Korea, Dedrick and Kraemer, *Asia's Competitive Challenge*, pp. 122–134, (quotation p. 131;) also, Youngil Lim, *Technology and Productivity: The Korean Way of Learning and Catching Up*, MIT Press, Cambridge, Mass., 1999; *Datamation*,7/97, for Samsung's worldwide ranking in 1996. For Hong Kong's role, Dedrick and Kraemer, *Asia's Competitive Challenge*, pp. 71, 196–197.

CHAPTER 7: The Consumer Electronics and Computer Industries as the Electronic Century Begins

1. Financial and product line data are from *Hoover's Global 250: The Stories Behind the Most Powerful Companies on the Planet*, Austin, Tex., 1997. For Matsushita, pp. 330–332; for Sony, pp. 490–491; Sharp, pp. 476–477; Sanyo, pp. 446–457.

2. For Bull and Olivetti, *Hoover's Guide to Computer Companies*, Hoover's Business Press, Austin, Tex., 1996, pp. 142–143, 168–169.

3. *Datamation*, 7/97, pp. 48, 59.

4. *Datamation*, 6/15/96, p. 36. *Datamation*'s 7/97 issue for 1996, besides its annual listing of *Datamation*'s Global 100 on pp. 45–46, also includes a "breakout" of each of the hundred companies' total IT sales into the percentages of its products sold in seven different sectors, pp. 74–82.

5. Martin Fransman, *Japan's Computer and Communications Industry: The Evolution of Industrial Giants and Global Competitiveness*, Oxford University Press, New York, 1995, pp. 181–182, 347 (also a reference to Spectrum in ch. 5).

6. Paul E. Cerruzzi, *A History of Modern Computing*, MIT Press, Cambridge, Mass., 1998, p. 287.

7. For Sun, *International Directory of Company Histories* vol. 7, St. James Press, Detroit, 1993, p. 500; quotation from *Hoover's Guide to Computer Companies*, p. 210.

8. For Compaq, see *Hoover's Guide to Computer Companies*, p. 72.

9. For Packard Bell and AST Research, see *Hoover's Guide to Computer Companies*, pp. 174–175 and pp. 50–51.

10. For Dell, Gateway, and Apple, see *Hoover's Guide to Computer Companies*, pp. 92–93, 106–107, and 44–45.

11. Gene Gregory, *Japanese Electronic Technology: Enterprise and Innovation*,

John Wiley & Sons, New York, 1985–1986, ch. 6, "The Great Engineering Gap," provides useful reviews of technical training of Japanese managers and engineers.

12. Ibid., ch. 14. The references to Canon are on pp. 215–216.

13. Masahisa Fujita and Ryoichi Ishii, "Global Location Behavior and Organizational Dynamics of Japanese Electronics Firms and Their Impact on Regional Economies," in Alfred D. Chandler Jr., Peter Hagström, and Orjön Sölvell, eds., *The Dynamic Firm: The Role of Technology, Strategy, Organization, and Regions*, Oxford University Press, New York, 1998, pp. 361–372. For the nexus firms and the quotation in the next paragraph, ibid., p. 375. For nexus firms, see also Alan Cawson, Kevin Morgan, Douglas Webber, Peter Holmes, and Anne Stevens, *Hostile Brothers, Competition and Closure in the European Electronics Industry*, Clarendon Press, Oxford, U.K., 1990, p. 268, for Pioneer; p. 327, for Alps Electric; and pp. 337, 342, for Kyocera.

14. Martin Kenney and Urs von Burg, "Institutions and Economies: Creating Silicon Valley," in Martin Kenney, ed., *Understanding Silicon Valley: The Anatomy of an Entrepreneurial Region*, Stanford University Press, Stanford, Calif., 2000, pp. 223–224.

CHAPTER 8: The Significance of the Epic Story

1. Alfred D. Chandler Jr., Takashi Hikino, and David C. Mowery, "The Evolution of Corporate Capabilities and Corporate Strategy and Structure within the World's Largest Chemical Firms: The Twentieth Century in Perspective," in Ashish Arora, Ralph Landau, and Nathan Rosenberg, eds., *Chemicals and Long-Term Economic Growth: Insights from the Chemical Industry*, New York: John Wiley & Sons, 1998, pp. 446–448.

2. Basil Achilladelis, "Innovation in the Pharmaceutical Industry," in Ralph Landau, Basil Achilladelis, and Alexander Scriabine, eds., *Pharmaceutical Innovation*, Chemical Heritage Press, Philadelphia, 1999, p. 25.

PERMISSIONS

The author gratefully acknowledges permission from the following sources to reprint material in their control:

Business History Review for table 5 from *Strategic Maneuvering and Mass-Market Dynamics: The Triumph of VHS over Beta*, by Michael A. Cusumano, Viorgos Mylonadis, and Richard S. Rosenbloom, *Business History Review*, vol. 66, no.1 (Spring 1992), p. 73, which appears as tables 3.1 and 7.1 in *Inventing the Electronic Century*. Copyright © 1992 *Business History Review*.

Business History Review for a table titled "Founding Dates of the 1994 Fortune 500 Companies," by Harris Corp., *Business History Review*, vol. 70, no. 1 (Spring

1996), p. 89, which appears as appendix 8.3 in *Inventing the Electronic Century*. Copyright © 1996 *Business History Review*.

James W. Cortada for five tables from *Historical Dictionary of Data Processing: Organizations*, pp. 10, 21, 11, 22, and 23, which appear as appendices 4.2, 4.3, 4.4, 4.5, and 4.6 respectively in *Inventing the Electronic Century*. Copyright © James W. Cortada.

Datamation for a table compiled from *Datamation*, June 15, 1986, pp. 44–46; June 1, 1985, pp. 38–39; and June 1, 1984, pp. 55–56, which appears as table 4.2 in *Inventing the Electronic Century*. Figures for U.S. companies are drawn solely from the 1984 and 1986 *Datamation* reports; the 1985 report was used solely for foreign company revenues in 1983. Copyright © 1984, 1985, 1986 Cahners Publishing Company.

Datamation for a table from "*Datamation* 100, 1995," *Datamation*, June 1, 1995, pp. 47, 48, 57, 61, 62, and 66, which appears as table 5.1 in *Inventing the Electronic Century*. Copyright © 1996 Cahners Publishing Company.

Datamation for a table from *Datamation*, July 1997, pp. 49, 50, 55, 57, 62, 71, and 73, which appears as table 7.2 in *Inventing the Electronic Century*. Copyright © 1997 Cahners Publishing Company.

Datamation for a table from *Datamation*, July 1997, p. 45, which appears as table 7.3 in *Inventing the Electronic Century*. Copyright © 1997 Cahners Publishing Company.

Greenwood Publishing Group, Inc., for a table from *IBM and the U.S. Data Processing Industry: An Economic History*, by Franklin M. Fisher (Praeger Publishers, 1983), p. 65, which appears as Table 4.1 in *Inventing the Electronic Century*. Copyright © 1983 Greenwood Publishing Group, Inc., Westport, Connecticut.

Macmillan Company for a table from page 146 of *Invention and Innovation in the Radio Industry* by W. Rupert Maclaurin, which appears as appendix 2.1 in *Inventing the Electronic Century*. Copyright © 1949 Macmillan Company.

MIT Press for a figure from "Decline of U.S. Consumer Electronics" in *Working Papers of the MIT Commission on Industrial Productivity*, by the MIT Commission on Industrial Productivity, vol. 2, p. 45, which appears as table 2.1 in *Inventing the Electronic Century*. Copyright © MIT Press.

Index

About the Author

Alfred D. Chandler Jr. is the Straus Professor of Business History Emeritus at the Harvard Business School. After graduating from Harvard in 1940 and spending five years in the United States Navy, he returned to Harvard for his Ph.D. He taught history at MIT from 1951 to 1963 (there he was the assistant editor of *The Letters of Theodore Roosevelt*), at Johns Hopkins from 1963 to 1970 (there he was the editor of *The Papers of Dwight David Eisenhower*), and at Harvard Business School from 1970 until his retirement in 1989.

His major books—*Strategy and Structure* (1962), *The Visible Hand* (1977), and *Scale and Scope* (1990)—all received the Newcomen Book Award in Business History. In addition, *The Visible Hand* was awarded the Pulitzer and Bancroft prizes and *Scale and Scope* received two awards. With coauthor Steve Salsbury he wrote *Pierre S. du Pont and the Making of the Modern Corporation* (1970). With coeditors he published other works including *Managerial Hierarchies* (1980), *The Coming of Managerial Capitalism* (1985), *Big Business and the Wealth of Nations* (1997), and *A Nation Transformed by Information* (2000).

These historical writings led to awards from professional associations including the American Academy of Management Award for Scholarly Contributions to Management (1985), the American Academy of International Business Eminent Scholar Award (2000), and the American Historical Association 1997 Award for Scholarly Distinction.

Date Due

APR 0 6 2002			